CULTIVATING
A LANDSCAPE
OF PEACE

Matthew Dennis

CULTIVATING
A LANDSCAPE
OF PEACE

Cornell University Press

New York State Historical Association

Iroquois-European Encounters in Seventeenth-Century America

Ithaca and London

Cooperstown, New York

First published 1993 by Cornell University Press.
First printing, Cornell Paperbacks, 1995.

International Standard Book Number 0-8014-2171-3 (cloth)
International Standard Book Number 0-8014-8301-8 (paper)
Library of Congress Catalog Card Number 92-56771

Printed in the United States of America

*Librarians: Library of Congress cataloging information
appears on the last page of the book.*

⊛ The paper in this book meets the minimum requirements
of the American National Standard for Information Sciences—
Permanence of Paper for Printed Library Materials, ANSI Z39.48-1984.

FOR LIZZIE, SAM, AND LEAH

Contents

List of Maps and Illustrations   ix

Acknowledgments   xi

Introduction   1

PART I   LANDSCAPE, HISTORY, AND REPRESENTATION:
          THE CONSTRUCTION OF THE IROQUOIS

1. Iroquoia: Land, World View, and Landscape   13

2. Owasco into Iroquois: War, Peace, and the Social
   Construction of the Five Nations   43

3. Deganawidah and the Cultivation of Peace:
   Iroquois Ideology, Political Culture, and
   Representation   76

PART II   NEW WORLDS

4. Settlement and Unsettlement: New Netherland,
   Beverwyck, and the Dutch Frontier   119

5. Commerce, Kinship, and the Transaction of
   Peace   154

6. False Starts and Failed Promises: New France
   and the French Frontier   180

7. Kinship, Conversion, Conquest, and the
   French-Iroquois Discourse of Frustration   213

Epilogue: Iroquois Reconstruction   257

Index   273

Maps and Illustrations

MAPS

Iroquoia and its frontiers, ca. 1670s   *16*
Iroquoia, ca. 1670s   *19*
Visscher's New Netherland in 1655   *122–23*
Du Creux's New France, 1660   *210–11*
Iroquois country and plan of forts on River Richelieu   *216*
Bressani's New France, 1657   *242–43*

ILLUSTRATIONS

The First Woman cast through a hole in the Sky-world   *23*
Iroquoian women's work   *29*
Huron deer hunt   *39*
Palisaded Iroquoian town under siege   *51*
Howlett Hill archaeological site   *55*
Aerial view of excavations at the Howlett Hill site   *56*
An Iroquois longhouse   *57*
The Mohawk village of Caughnawaga   *61*
Mohawk elm bark feast bowl   *66*

Woven reed armor of the Iroquois   *70*

Iroquois defeat in encounter with Champlain in 1609   *73*

Reciting the laws of the Confederacy   *99*

The Baker, by Job Adriaensz Berckheyde   *151*

Sychnecta   *173*

Marie de l'Incarnation   *184*

Acknowledgments

So many have done so much to contribute to the success of this project that I would like to take this opportunity to thank them. I deeply appreciate the guidance provided by Gunther Barth, James Kettner, and William Simmons at the University of California at Berkeley. In an earlier version, the present work was co-winner of the New York State Historical Association Manuscript Award for 1987, an honor for which I thank the Association. The Huntington Library in San Marino, California, offered an Exxon Visiting Fellowship and beautiful surroundings, which assisted me as I began to revise. In particular, I thank its former director, Robert Middlekauff, for making the Huntington a congenial place for scholars, for his interest, and for his support of my work.

From August 1987 to July 1988, I had the extraordinary privilege of working at the Newberry Library in Chicago as a Rockefeller Foundation Fellow, in the D'Arcy McNickle Center for the History of the American Indian. The collections, the community of scholars, and the ambiance fostered by its staff make the Newberry one of the foremost research libraries in the world. I thank the Rockefeller Foundation, the Newberry Library, its staff, and all the participants in the 1987–88 Fellows' Seminar. I am also grateful to the participants in the Early American History Colloquium and to the participants in various seminars and colloquia on American Indian culture and history. James Axtell, Denys Délage, Gregory Dowd, Christian Feest, William N. Fenton, Donald Parman, Daniel Richter, George Sabo,

Robert St. George, and Melburn Thurmon deserve individual acknowledgment for their helpful comments and criticisms. My greatest debt is to Frederick E. Hoxie, director of the McNickle Center, a man of warmth, intellect, humanity, and energy, who comes closest to my ideal image of the scholar of American Indian history.

At various stages, Christine Leigh Heyrman, Stephen Nissenbaum, Neal Salisbury, and Richard White discussed the project and provided useful suggestions. The work of George R. Hamell has also been suggestive, and I thank him for his generosity in providing me with offprints and copies of his published and unpublished papers on the Iroquois. Stephen Aron read the entire manuscript, and I benefited greatly from his insight and assessment. Let me also acknowledge, collectively, my colleagues in the history department at the University of Oregon, especially John Thiebault, as well as miscellaneous captive student audiences, for their interest and support. I am especially grateful to Ray Birn, who read the manuscript during a busy period in his own schedule and offered a thoughtful critique. I also thank the Office of Research and Sponsored Programs at the University of Oregon, which provided important financial support in the form of a summer research award, and the University of Oregon Humanities Center.

I am grateful to Peter Agree at Cornell University Press for his support throughout this project and for the assistance of copy editor Valerie Haskins and production editor Elizabeth Holmes.

My dearest debt, which I happily incur and try to repay every day, is to Elizabeth Reis, woman of the nineties—both the 1690s and 1990s. Critic, confidant, nurturer, both to me and to our children, Samuel and Leah, she more than anyone else enabled me to complete this project. No, she did not do my research or type the manuscript—she writes her own books—but this is surely her book as well.

MATTHEW DENNIS

Eugene, Oregon

CULTIVATING
A LANDSCAPE
OF PEACE

Introduction

A mid-seventeenth-century Jesuit chronicler, writing about the
American Indians, tells us that "we cannot go very far back in our
researches in their history, as they have no Libraries other than the
memory of their old men; and perhaps we should find nothing worthy
of publication."[1]

I hope that my book will be read as a lengthy refutation of this
Jesuit chronicler's view of history in general and of the history of the
Five Nations of the Iroquois in particular. Not only can we push our
researches back into an ancient past, using archaeology, ethnography,
and folklore, in addition to conventional historical sources, but in
doing so we will find much that is "worthy" and that forces us to
reexamine the cultural history of early America. My goal, however,
is not simply to write a history of the Iroquois in the seventeenth
century but rather to construct a complex, multicultural portrait of
the strange and fascinating people who jostled each other in and
around what is now called New York, but which has been alternatively
conceived of as Iroquoia, New Netherland, and New France. If ethnohistorical methods can help us understand native thought and practice, then they can also help illuminate for us the almost equally
foreign ideas and actions of seventeenth-century Dutch and French

[1] Reuben Gold Thwaites, ed., *The Jesuit Relations and Allied Documents: Travels and Explorations of the Missionaries of New France, 1610–1791; the Original French, Latin, and Italian Texts, with English Translations and Notes*, 73 vols. (Cleveland, 1896–1901), 45:205.

people.[2] Each group demands sensitive treatment, on its own terms, even while we consider them together as a collection of actors on a larger historical stage.

For this reason, I have attempted to integrate the historical analysis of seventeenth-century native and European peoples in a way that some might find unusual but that I believe is essential for understanding the complex assemblage of cultures, ethnicities, nationalities, religions, and races of early America. My study of the Iroquois, Dutch, and French takes the different and discrete worlds of these peoples seriously, at the same time that it attempts to analyze the conjunctions of societies and individuals in particular landscapes and to examine the sense of reason that explained the larger colonial world—in contrasting ways—to those who actually lived in it. This approach has the advantage of confronting the unique pieces of early America while also providing the possibility of a new synthesis, and thus addressing the concerns of some scholars that the exciting percolations of colonial American historiography in recent decades have left the field muddy.[3]

My book participates in a new cultural history on two levels. In it I seek to elucidate the nature and meaning of life (and the transformation of life) predominantly among three groups—the Five Nations of the Iroquois, the Dutch, and the French—who shared cultural frontiers. And second, and more important, I analyze the nature and significance of the intercultural conversations, or cultural interactions, among them from different perspectives. I argue that each group

---

[2] Like James H. Merrell, I wonder about the usefulness of the term "ethnohistory," which, despite the contributions of the enterprise it labels, may contribute to a segregated approach to the study of Native Americans. See Merrell, review of *Handbook of North American Indians*, vol. 4, *History of Indian-White Relations*, ed. Wilcomb E. Washburn, in *Ethnohistory*, 38 (Winter 1991), 79–80. See also Merrell, "Some Thoughts on Colonial Historians and American Indians," *William and Mary Quarterly*, 3d ser., 46 (January 1989), 94–119; and see Bruce G. Trigger, "Ethnohistory: The Unfinished Edifice," *Ethnohistory*, 33 (Summer 1986), 253–67.

[3] On the recent historiography of early America, and the challenges that its renaissance poses to synthesis, see Jack P. Greene and J. R. Pole, "Reconstructing British-American Colonial History: An Introduction," in Greene and Pole, eds., *Colonial British North America: Essays in the New History of the Early Modern Era* (Baltimore, 1984), 1–17. See also the preface to David Hackett Fischer, *Albion's Seed* (New York, 1989) for a somewhat different sense of recent developments and strategies for synthesis. Of course, the call for synthesis goes beyond the colonial field; see especially Thomas Bender, "Wholes and Parts: The Need for Synthesis in American History," *Journal of American History*, 73 (June 1986), 120–36, and David Thelen et al., "A Round Table: Synthesis in American History," in ibid., 74 (June 1987), 107–30. In early American history itself, a number of grand new synthetic projects have been launched recently; in addition to Fischer, *Albion's Seed*, see Bernard Bailyn, *The Peopling of British North America*, several volumes projected (New York, 1986–); Jack P. Greene, *Pursuits of Happiness: The Social Development of Early Modern British Colonies and the Formation of American Culture* (Chapel Hill, N.C., 1988).

experienced a peculiar new world and fashioned its own particular history, at the same time that they all commingled and constructed the complex New World they were forced to share.

The Five Nations, for example, remained distinctly Iroquois in thought and action, even as they adjusted to Europeans. The new French Canadians too were distinctive, not only in relation to the Iroquois, but also compared to the French who remained in Europe. When the two worlds of French Canada and Iroquoia came together in the seventeenth century, they did not produce a single history. Yes, their conjuncture produced exchanges of people, some trade, diplomacy, and a great deal of violence, but the meaning of these interactions and events to those involved and to historians is not simple and uniform. My book attempts to demonstrate that these two societies (as well as the Dutch) understood themselves and the other in unique ways, based on their particular world views, material circumstances, and experiences. Different interpretive worlds—not just different individuals confronted each other along cultural frontiers.

Given the common assumption and conventional practice of treating the history of early America as the story of English colonization, some readers may be surprised that the English play so limited a role in this book. Aware, like many other historians, of the diversity of early America and the anachronisms that result from confining exploration of its history to the current political boundaries of the United States, I have been concerned with a region that is now partly in Canada and with the historical experiences of non-English peoples. My story centers on Iroquoia, the land of the Five Nations, and its European margins in the seventeenth century. Until late in that century, after the 1664 conquest of New Netherland and its transformation into Anglo–New York, the English shared no direct border with the Five Nations and played only an indirect, or once-removed, part in shaping the cultural interactions between the Iroquois and the new European worlds they encountered. The Covenant Chain that would unite English and Iroquois was the product of a later time; although the epilogue attempts to join my story to the history of that hybrid diplomatic structure, I am chiefly concerned with an earlier time and discourse, when it seemed that other possibilities existed for constructing a New World.

My book speaks in specific ways to the larger problem of cultural interaction in colonial America. I attempt to replace the crude "clash of cultures" model, assigned especially to Indian-White relations, with one more appropriate for all early Americans, which permits appreciation of the fascinating and complex process of cultural accommodation and conflict. War and peace were only extremes on the continuum of relationships possible among and between various groups. More important was that vast middle range of interactions characterized by neither absolute harmony nor total warfare, neither full understanding nor complete ignorance, neither unmarred cooperation nor utter contention. By restoring a sense of the particular cultural experiences and meanings of diverse people, and by focusing on the social conversations they shared, we can begin to advance beyond the fragmentation that has been a byproduct of the renaissance in American colonial history.

Perhaps we should call this "Cubist" history, for Cubism strikes me as an apt metaphor for the historical approach I have adopted. The essence of Cubist painting was the depiction of various points of view, or perspectives, simultaneously on one canvas. Picasso, Georges Bracque, and others suggested that multiple perspectives—described and ordered by the artist and confined to a single painting, but not dissolved into a single angle of vision—permitted a truer depiction, or interpretation, of the artist's subject than did a single viewpoint. My own work on the Iroquois, Dutch, and French in seventeenth-century America draws on the postmodern possibilities within the modernism of Cubism, while it is also subject to the same constraints that the Surrealist painter René Magritte would point out in *The Treason of Images* (1928–29) with his inscription "Ceci n'est pas une pipe" [this is not a pipe]. As one art critic observed, "no painter had ever made the point that 'A painting is not what it represents' with such epigrammatic clarity before."[4]

At the same time, I must admit that I cannot really tell my story from the Iroquois point of view (or the Dutch or the French, for that matter), nor can I really recreate the past. And my attempt to present multiple perspectives without collapsing them into a single point of view (my own) is as limited as Picasso's; after all, I control the discourse as he controlled the canvas. Nonetheless, after we admit the limitations, the new possibilities of an approach that some might term "decentered" are considerable. Representation of multiple perspectives in a sensitive translation allows us to see how and why people in that

[4]See Robert Hughes, *The Shock of the New* (New York, 1981), 243–44; the painting is pictured on p. 245.

early American place and time acted, in their own societies and with others, in conflict, cooperation, and often in confusion. Iroquois, Dutch, and French people lived simultaneously together and separately; they made separate histories even as they made a common one that I strive to write.

The book is divided into two parts. Part I examines the Iroquois world in its physical, cultural, and ideological dimensions. It traces the historical experience that transformed various autonomous bands into the Five Nations, constructing in the process a single socially and politically integrated people. And it analyzes Iroquois political culture and representation, based on an expansive vision of peace bequeathed by the prophet Deganawidah, which emerged from Iroquois experience and guided action throughout the seventeenth century and beyond, even as it adjusted to the changing circumstances of a New World.

Part II assesses the New World created by the dynamic interplay of natives and Europeans, in Iroquoia and along its cultural frontiers. My "Cubist" approach is designed to accommodate the multiple realities which coexisted in that complex physical and social landscape, as well as to acknowledge the asymmetry of the Iroquois-European encounters in which the very core of an established Iroquois world confronted peculiar new societies peripheral to the French and Dutch nations. Substantial sketches of the origins and nature of these two colonial enterprises and the new societies they produced in the American wilderness are included as essential background for the analysis of Iroquois-Dutch and Iroquois-French relations. The worlds of Beverwyck and Quebec profoundly affected the Five Nations, even if the Iroquois did not know or experience them in the same way as Dutch burghers or French *habitants*.

Two chapters are devoted to the Dutch, their commercial colonialism, and the uniquely successful relationship they forged with the Five Nations, which grew out of their quest for profit, their tolerance, and, ironically, their lack of curiosity about and understanding of Iroquois culture. Two chapters address New France, its state- and church-directed colonial enterprise and its covert and overt invasions of Iroquoia. The French remained persistently hostile to the Five Nations, despite—or because of—Iroquois attempts to enlarge their universe of peace, extending it to the priests, *habitants,* and native people of Canada. The unfulfillment and frustration of this discourse of peace led ultimately, in the last quarter of the seventeenth century, to a modification of Iroquois methods of diplomacy. But the Five Nations remained largely consistent in their vision and found new means to realize it and to flourish in the late seventeenth century and beyond.

The Iroquois were a blood-thirsty, aggressive people, or so many histories, novels, and movies have informed us. Even their white admirers, in the course of well-meaning attempts to transform the Iroquois from ignoble into noble savages or from barbarians into latter-day Romans, gloried in their military might and the empire that they supposedly amassed. Beginning with the chroniclers of New France and continuing in the writings of New York colonial politician and scholar Cadwallader Colden, romantic novelist James Fenimore Cooper, pioneer anthropologist Lewis Henry Morgan, and eminent nineteenth-century historian Francis Parkman, a myth of the imperial Iroquois took shape that only now is being challenged by historians.[5] In fact, the Iroquois were considered "savage" by those who feared them and fought them; that is, their enemies, on the basis of their own experience and world view, had every reason to view the Iroquois with trepidation and disgust. Nonetheless, without denying such a perspective, historians should attempt to shift the angle of vision and examine the view from Iroquoia in order to understand Iroquois culture and its deep appreciation of peace.

The Five Nations of the Iroquois—the Mohawk, Oneida, Onon-

---

[5]See Thwaites, ed., *Jesuit Relations;* Cadwallader Colden, *The History of the Five Nations Depending on the Province of New-York in America* (London, 1727–47); James Fenimore Cooper, *The Leatherstocking Tales,* New American Library edition, ed. Blake Nevius, 2 vols. (New York, 1985 [orig. pub. as separate works, 1823–41]), especially *The Last of the Mohicans: A Narrative of 1757* (1826); Lewis Henry Morgan, *The League of the Ho-de-no-sau-nee, Iroquois* (Rochester, N.Y., 1851); Francis Parkman, *France and England in North America,* New American Library edition, ed. David Levin, 2 vols. (New York, 1983 [orig. pub. as separate works, 1865–92]). Even the acclaimed recent feature film *Black Robe,* released in 1991 and based on the novel of the same name by Brian Moore (New York, 1985), casts the Iroquois in their traditional role as cannibalistic savages, notwithstanding the claims of its producers and critics who believe the film shatters stereotypes. It should be acknowledged that some of these writers did see another side of the Iroquois; Morgan, for example, recognized the Iroquois love of peace and the ways in which this regard for harmony was institutionalized among the Five Nations. Nonetheless, without any sense of contradiction, Morgan's work contributed substantially to the martial image of the Iroquois, picturing even their efforts toward peace in aggressive, military terms, as in a "Pax Iroquoia." The most important recent challenge to such a characterization is Daniel K. Richter and James H. Merrell, eds., *Beyond the Covenant Chain: The Iroquois and Their Neighbors in Indian North America* (Syracuse, N.Y., 1987), which denies the Iroquois an empire but acknowledges that the Five Nations did "win the respect, even fear, of natives and European peoples near and far" (7–8). In essence, this work challenges interpretations of the results rather than the motives of Iroquois expansionist policy.

daga, Cayuga, and Seneca—united politically and socially in a Great League of Peace some time in the fifteenth century. In present-day New York State, between the Mohawk River in the east and the Genesee River in the west, they constructed a cultural landscape—a human geography and ecology—that provided them relative peace, security, and prosperity. Kinship ties, reckoned primarily through women, organized the Iroquois' lives and particularly the multifamily dwellings in which they lived. These longhouses symbolized the Five Nations' kinship state; with the Mohawks watching the eastern door, and the Senecas standing guard in the west, the people of the longhouse enjoyed a unique safety and strength in Iroquoia.[6]

The Iroquois ideal of peace appears most clearly in the great chartering myth embodied in the Deganawidah Epic.[7] Cosmogonical and cosmological in a political sense, the epic provided the Iroquois an explanation of their past and a practical guide for their present and future. It tells of the coming of a great prophet, Deganawidah, who ended the bloodshed between nation and nation, between brother and brother, and provided a charter of peace known as the Great Law. Peace for the Iroquois was not an abstract concept; rather, it was concrete, integral, something grounded firmly in the social, economic, and political organization of their everyday lives. Fundamentally, they conceived of peace and lived it in terms of a domestic harmony—which they institutionalized within households, lineages, clans, and villages. Peace was possible only within a group cemented by consanguinity and a common sense of moral order. More than the

---

[6]William N. Fenton, "Northern Iroquoian Culture Patterns," in Bruce G. Trigger, ed., *Handbook of North American Indians: Northeast* (Washington, D.C., 1978), 15:296–321, provides a brief, authoritative overview of the culture and history of the Five Nations.

[7]The Deganawidah Epic was first published by Horatio Hale, *The Iroquois Book of Rites*, ed. William N. Fenton (Toronto, 1962 [orig. pub. Philadelphia, 1883]), but portions of the narrative, its motifs, symbols, and metaphors appear often in the writings of seventeenth-century European missionaries, traders, soldiers, and colonial officials. For a description and analysis of the various versions see Fenton's introduction to Arthur C. Parker, *Parker on the Iroquois*, ed. William N. Fenton (Syracuse, N.Y., 1968), 38–46; see also William N. Fenton, "Structure, Continuity, and Change in the Process of Iroquois Treaty Making," in Francis Jennings et al., eds., *The History and Culture of Iroquois Diplomacy: An Interdisciplinary Guide* (Syracuse, N.Y., 1985), 3–36. Paul A. W. Wallace, *The White Roots of Peace* (Philadelphia, 1946) provides a convenient shorthand version of the epic and law. The Deganawidah Epic continues to inform and inspire people of the Five Nations, as became clear during the events surrounding the bicentennial of the United States Constitution; Iroquois historians, leaders, and activists, for example, claim the work of Deganawidah and the political structure he created as the original inspiration for the frame of government constructed by the founders of the United States; one example was an address by Dr. John Mohawk, "Great Law of Peace/U.S. Constitution," delivered 19 September 1987 at "Iroquoian Influences on the U.S. Constitution," a conference sponsored by the Wisconsin Oneida Nation and others.

absence of war, peace meant a practical way of life lived face-to-face
with other people—kinspeople—who found shelter, security, and
strength under the branches of the Great Tree of Peace.

But the Dutch and French encountered by the Five Nations came
from vastly different worlds. Along the Iroquois-Dutch cultural frontier, trade, more than anything else, most historians have argued,
brought the two peoples together, organized their interaction, and
provided a motive for mutual toleration. Despite the success of their
partnership, the peoples of Iroquoia and New Netherland had little
in common, possessed limited understanding of the other's world,
and did little to address intercultural ignorance. In a way that strikes
us today as familiar and not extraordinary, the relationship between
Iroquois and Dutch was all business. Or was it? Reexamination of the
history and ethnography of the Five Nations suggests that emphasis
on the economic aspects of Iroquois interaction with the Dutch in
particular and Europeans in general may be misplaced. The Iroquois
understood their relationship with the settlers of New Netherland in
ways that challenged and confounded the Dutch. Whereas Europeans
increasingly organized their lives in terms of commerce and the forces
of the market, the Iroquois conceived of human interaction fundamentally in kinship terms.

In general, the Five Nations lacked a means to achieve peaceful
relations with those not tied to them by consanguinity or affinity. The
archaeological record suggests that, from an ancient time, their response to the dangers posed by the proximity of hostile outsiders was
to transform them symbolically and physically into kinspeople. Unpredictable raiding activity that raged back and forth, even if spo-
radically, created a cycle of violence and chaos, which left no one
secure. Small lineages or bands, then tribes or nations, arranged nonaggression pacts, reconceived themselves as kinspeople and consum-
mated such bonds, redefined earlier forms of violence as internecine
and banned them, constructing institutions to limit their occurrence
and mitigate their effects. By continually expanding their domestic
world and by insisting that domestic violence had no place in Iroquois
society, the Five Nations enlarged their world of peace. Foreign affairs, then, as an Iroquois conceptual category, hardly existed for
much of the seventeenth century. Instead of constructing alliances in
which negotiating parties remained fully discrete entities, the Five
Nations sought complete mergers with others—the many became one.
As a single people—represented by the Iroquois Longhouse or Ex-

tended Lodge—they possessed one mind and lived under one law. As the Longhouse lengthened, it encompassed new people—even Europeans, the Iroquois hoped—and the domestic world of peace became appropriate and effective in maintaining harmony and prosperity throughout a larger universe.

Ultimately, the demands of sustained interaction with Europeans in the seventeenth and eighteenth centuries required that the Iroquois adjust their traditional practice of constructing fictive and eventually actual kinship links. Although the Iroquois sought to forge bonds of kinship and reciprocity, the Dutch hoped to maintain social and cultural distance, interposing an impersonal market between themselves and the Indians. New France, on the other hand, at least as embodied by its Jesuit missionaries, proved willing to participate in the amalgamation process, but not on Iroquois terms. The French themselves, of course, sought the conversion and Frenchification of the Five Nations. They could never contemplate their own absorption into the Iroquois Longhouse, and New France's Jesuit fathers could never provide a satisfactory response to such an Iroquois entreaty as "if you love, as you say you do, our souls, love our bodies also, and let us be henceforth but one nation."[8]

Whereas the Dutch reluctantly became the Five Nations' "brothers" in order to trade, the Iroquois traded in order to cultivate the Dutch settlers as kinspeople. And whereas the French insidiously became their "fathers" in order to dominate the Iroquois spiritually, politically, and socially, the Five Nations accepted Jesuit missionaries because they hoped the Black Robes represented a vanguard entering the Iroquois Longhouse, anticipating Iroquois naturalization of the French and the creation of a new world of peace.

These peoples—Iroquois, Dutch, French, and others—faced each other along cultural frontiers that simultaneously separated them and joined their worlds together. Borrowing techniques of analysis and interpretation from anthropology and literary criticism, one may hope to discover and translate the discourses—of words and deeds—within and between these societies and to write a historical account that presents multiple visions yet begins to explain the coherence, not simply the tumult, of early America. The "clash of cultures" idea and the simplistic victimization model ascribed to Native American experience can be refined to permit understanding of the creative means

---

[8]Quoted in Wallace, *The White Roots of Peace*, 45.

that native peoples employed to accommodate and resist colonialism. And historians should be able to accomplish such a revision without losing touch with the immediate pain and confusion endured by native peoples in the process. Conflict and cooperation were firmly grounded in real worlds, landscapes that different societies shaped in diverse, culturally specific ways. A focus on landscape and discourse, then, permits us to see the early colonial world in a fresh way—set in real places, understood differently by people facing each other across cultural divides, and cast in terms neither heroic nor tragic.

Finally, sensitivity to such particular realities helps to account for the ethnocentrism present in contemporary accounts, while assisting our attempts to avoid perpetuating it in our own histories. The Five Nations and the colonists of New Netherland and New France, despite considerable contrasts, had enough in common to allow interaction and perhaps to delude each of them that they had amassed a greater understanding of the other than they in fact ever possessed. Conducted through the illusion of cultural knowledge about the other, ironically, the Iroquois-Dutch relationship flourished, and driven by a strangely similar vision of transformation and incorporation, paradoxically, the Iroquois-French relationship failed.

PART I

Landscape, History, and Representation: The Construction of the Iroquois

1

Iroquoia: Land, World View, and Landscape

The world the twins made was a balanced and orderly world, and this was good. The plant-eating animals created by the right-handed twin would eat up all the vegetation if their number was not kept down by the meat-eating animals which the left-handed twin created. But if these carnivorous animals ate too many animals, then they would starve, for they would run out of meat. So the right- and left-handed twins built balance into the world.

—Iroquois Creation Myth

Iroquoia did not yet exist as the second millennium dawned in that area of America north of the Allegheny Mountains, west of the Hudson River Valley, and extending to the Great Lakes Erie and Ontario. Yet A.D. 1000 roughly marked an important shift in the region's history. Local bands of people called "Owasco," gradually reshaping themselves and their traditional lives, began to devise a way of life that would characterize the historic Iroquois by the time of their encounter with European explorers, traders, and settlers.

How can we know those people and that place, separated from us by a chasm of time and difference? With humility, we must admit ultimately that we will never truly see through seventeenth-century Iroquois eyes, let alone eleventh-century ones, nor can we ever really speak for them. We can, however, examine Iroquois history as we examine the histories of other peoples: by studying their inscriptions in what is often called the "historical record."[1] The seventeenth-

---

[1]Historians are increasingly viewing this record more broadly to include nonliterary

century Five Nations seem only slightly more exotic to us today than
the seventeenth-century Dutch, French, or English; and to assume a
proprietary right to study, and a natural ability to understand, these
distant European men and women is only marginally less arrogant
than to assert such claims over the historic Iroquois.[2] In each case,
we must study the discourses of words and actions—inscribed in documents, in archaeological remains, in folklore, in landscapes—and
construct a history that interprets and translates people's experiences,
events, and processes for modern readers.[3]

Even without written documents, Iroquois men and women created
a historical record as they lived and interpreted their lives. And in
their encounter with outsiders—Native American and European—
they played their part in shaping the larger historical collage.[4] In a
nonliterary fashion, the ancient "pencilings upon the surface of the

---

sources. In addition, some have questioned the very possibility of "setting the record straight"
or "filling gaps" in our knowledge. See, for example, James Clifford, "Introduction: Partial
Truths," in Clifford and George E. Marcus, eds., *Writing Culture: The Poetics and Politics of
Ethnography* (Berkeley, Calif. 1986), 1–26. See also Dominick LaCapra, *History and Criticism*
(Ithaca, N.Y., 1985), especially 15–44.

[2]Renato Rosaldo, "From the Door of His Tent: The Fieldworker and the Inquisitor," in
Clifford and Marcus, eds., *Writing Culture*, 77–97, for example, criticizes the *Annales* school
paradigm of the *longue durée* for tempting historians into committing the discipline's cardinal
sin: anachronism.

[3]I am advocating, of course, an ethnographic approach to the past here. For the best
statement of this method for historians, see Rhys Isaac, "Discourse on the Method: Action,
Structure, and Meaning," an appendix in *The Transformation of Virginia, 1740–1790* (Chapel
Hill, N.C., 1982), 323–57. On the act of translation in ethnography—with important implications for historians—see Vincent Crapanzano, "Hermes' Dilemma: The Making of Subversion in Ethnographic Description," in Clifford and Marcus, eds., *Writing Culture*, 51–76.
Paraphrasing Walter Benjamin, Crapanzano writes: "Like translation, ethnography is also a
somewhat provisional way of coming to terms with the foreignness of language—of cultures
and societies. The ethnographer does not, however, translate texts the way the translator
does. He must first produce them. Text metaphors for culture and society notwithstanding,
the ethnographer has no primary and independent text that can be read and translated by
others. . . . Despite its frequent ahistorical—if synchronic—pretense, ethnography is historically determined by the moment of the ethnographer's encounter with whomever he is
studying" (51). In a similar way, history is historically determined as historians produce—
rather than merely recover and record—historical texts. Historians, like ethnographers and
Hermes, render the foreign familiar through interpretation while simultaneously preserving
its very strangeness (see Crapanzano, 52). See also Talal Asad, "The Concept of Cultural
Translation in British Social Anthropology," in ibid., 141–64. On the ways that one might
"inscribe" the historical record without recourse to writing, see Paul Ricoeur, "The Model
of the Text: Meaningful Action Considered as a Text," in Paul Rabinow and William Sullivan,
eds., *Interpretive Social Science: A Reader* (Berkeley, Calif., 1979), 73–101. For an expansion
of the concept of writing—of inscription and textualization—with implications for the history
of "nonliterate" people, see Jacques Derrida, *Of Grammatology*, trans. Gayatri Chakravorty
Spivak (Baltimore, 1976).

[4]For a fascinating critique of an American history that neglects Native Americans, see
James Axtell, "Colonial America without the Indians: A Counterfactual Scenario," in Frederick E. Hoxie, ed., *Indians in American History* (Arlington Heights, Ill., 1988), 47–65.

earth which neither rain, nor floods, nor the ravages of time have erased . . . [have] left us . . . a record far more satisfactory, enduring and truthful," Arthur C. Parker, the Seneca ethnologist and archaeologist, wrote rather romantically early in this century.[5] Archaeology alone will not tell all that we want to know, however, and its findings should not be granted the privileged status of reality or "base" compared to "mere" representation or "superstructure" reflected in other kinds of sources. Pot shards, post molds, and refuse pits excavated in the present, of course, do not interpret themselves; other pieces of evidence— literary and oral—should, and inevitably must, affect our historical interpretation. A sense of developing Iroquois circumstances, action, world view, and ideology can be assembled out of the evidence differently preserved in these sources.

What will emerge is a narrative of a historical process, of a people who in the first six hundred years of the present millennium formed themselves into Iroquois and their landscape into Iroquoia, on the foundation of their social, political, spiritual, and ecological experiments with peace. This dynamic process would continue into the seventeenth century and beyond, influenced as much by Iroquois history as by the exigencies of European colonization.

When Europeans first set eyes on the New World, they saw wilderness, virgin land untamed by humanity.[6] Even those like Pilgrim William Bradford, who was excited about its possibilities, often understood the land before them as little more than "a hidious & desolate wildernes, full of wild beasts & willd men."[7] Worse, if the landscape disclosed any pattern at all to Puritans such as Michael Wigglesworth, it was the order of Satan:

> A Waste and howling wildcrness,
> Where none inhabited

[5]Arthur C. Parker, *An Erie Village and Burial Site at Ripley, Chautauqua, N.Y.*, *New York State Museum Bulletin*, no. 117 (Albany, 1907), 467–68.

[6]For a brilliant critique of the Virgin Land myth, with especial reference to the demographic catastrophe of European colonization, see Francis Jennings, *The Invasion of America: Indians, Colonialism, and the Cant of Conquest* (Chapel Hill, N.C., 1975), 15–31. The classic treatment of wilderness in America is Roderick Nash, *Wilderness and the American Mind* (New Haven, Conn., rev. ed., 1982); see especially chap. 2. See also Henry Nash Smith, *Virgin Land: The American West as Symbol and Myth* (Cambridge, Mass., 1950). Michael Williams, *Americans and Their Forests: A Historical Geography* (Cambridge, Mass., 1989) offers the definitive account of his subject.

[7]Harvey Wish, ed., [William Bradford's] *Of Plymouth Plantation* [1620–47] (New York, 1962), 60.

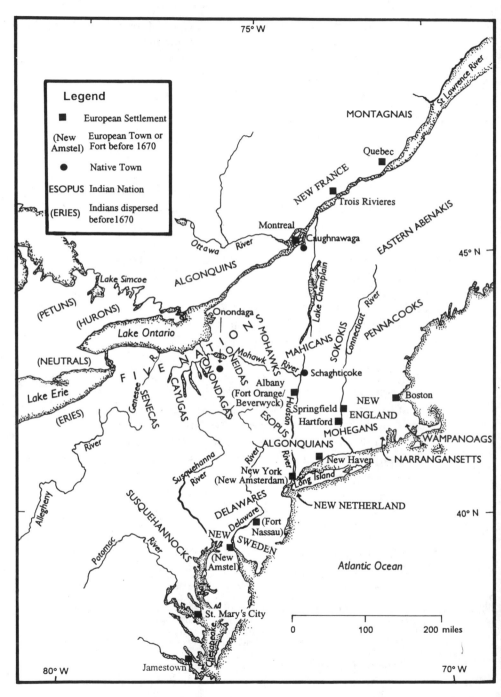

Iroquoia and its frontiers, ca. 1670s.

> But hellish fiends, and brutish men
> That devils worshipped.[8]

Many Europeans similarly failed to recognize or acknowledge America as the product of centuries of cultural modification, as a "landscape"[9] shaped by the desires of its denizens to provide themselves a prosperous, secure, and fulfilling existence. Yet, ironically, the fact of Native American transformation of the land was noted in Bradford's history itself. Within days of landing, Bradford reported, Captain Miles Standish and a shore party found native houses, fields, and caches of Indian corn and beans, which they happily appropriated and which helped them survive a difficult winter.[10]

Iroquoia, like other Native American landscapes, was neither the "Devil's den" of Wigglesworth nor the terrestrial paradise of some English promoters.[11] The seventeenth-century Dutch chronicler Johan de Laet described it as "excellent and agreeable, full of noble forest trees and grape vines, and nothing is wanting but the labor and industry of man to render it one of the finest and most fruitful lands in that part of the world."[12] Like many English explorers and publicists, de Laet failed to notice how the hand of man—or woman—had molded and cultivated nature. Though he disparaged the inhabitants as indolent savages, others who settled New Netherland under Dutch auspices would report substantial alterations, if not "improve-

[8]Michael Wigglesworth, "God's Controversy with New England," in *Proceedings of the Massachusetts Historical Society, 1871–1873,* [vol. 12] (Boston, 1873), 83.

[9]Landscape here does not refer to a fully "natural" (in the sense of undisturbed by people) feature of environment but to constructed space. It is a human-made system superimposed on the face of the land. Landscape functions and evolves not from natural laws alone but through conscious and unconscious human action to serve particular communities. See John Brinkerhoff Jackson, *Discovering the Vernacular Landscape* (New Haven, Conn., 1984), especially 3–10, 12. Jackson calls landscape "a composition of man-made or man-modified spaces to serve as infrastructure or background for our collective existence." This landscape "underscores not only our identity and presence, but also our history" (8). Often their constructed quality appears invisible, and landscapes are misinterpreted as natural or "wild"—on the one hand, by those within a society who take them for granted or, on the other hand, by outsiders who attribute the shape of the land to nonhuman agencies. See also John R. Stilgoe, *Common Landscape in America, 1580–1845* (New Haven, Conn., 1982), 3–29.

[10]Bradford, *Plymouth Plantation,* 63–64.

[11]Arthur Barlowe, for example, reporting on the Roanoake reconnaissances, cast "Virginia" as a new Eden: "The earth bringeth foorth all things in aboundance, as in the first creation, without toile or labour." The soil was "the most plentifull, sweete, fruitfull, and wholsome of all the world." And its people were "most gentle, loving, and faithfull, void of all guile, and treason, and such as lived after the manner of the golden age"; quoted in Edmund S. Morgan, *American Slavery, American Freedom: The Ordeal of Colonial Virginia* (New York, 1975), 27, 26.

[12]Johan de Laet's "New World" (1626), in J. Franklin Jameson, ed., *Narratives of New Netherland, 1609–1664* (New York, 1909), 48.

ments," of the landscape by its native peoples, especially through burning and agriculture. Complaining about the openness and un-ruliness of Indian gardens, the seventeenth-century Dutch colonist Adriaen van der Donck nonetheless noted that the natives "raise an abundance of corn and beans, of which we obtain whole cargoes in sloops and galleys in trade." Without any apparent sense of irony, van der Donck reflected upon Indian horticulture, which kept so many Europeans alive in the early years of settlement: "Although little can be said in favour of their husbandry, still they prefer their practices to ours."[13] Indeed, the landscape of Iroquoia offered its inhabitants and creators a good life, a history, and an identify as a people. The Iroquois sought to make it a place of peace.[14]

Northward-flowing streams cut through Iroquoia, on their way to Lake Ontario. These watercourses drained the glaciated valleys, gouged out of sedimentary formations, in present-day north-central New York. Where they were blocked, these valleys filled with water, forming the Finger Lakes. In the southern reaches of Iroquoia, high hills rose up, near the border of modern Pennsylvania, and from those high places streams flowed south into the Allegheny, Sus-quehanna, and Delaware drainages. In the west, the Niagara es-carpment—with its uplifted sedimentary formations—extended into southwestern Ontario toward the land of the Hurons. In the east, southeast of Lake Ontario, the Mohawk River originated in the uplifted plateau south of the Adirondack Mountains.[15]

[13]Thomas F. O'Donnell, ed., [Adriaen van der Donck's] *A Description of New Netherlands* (Syr-acuse, N.Y., 1968 [orig. pub. Amsterdam, 1655]), 96. On burning, see, for example, 20–21.
[14]Scholars have long recognized the impact of Native Americans on their environments. See especially the pioneering work of geographer Carl O. Sauer. See also Williams, *Americans and Their Forests*, 32–49. Richard White, "Native Americans and the Environment," in W. R. Swagerty, ed., *Scholars and the Indian Experience: Critical Reviews of Recent Writing in the Social Sciences* (Bloomington, Ind., 1984), 179–204, reviews the growing body of work in the field. See also William Cronon and White, "Ecological Change and Indian-White Relations," in Wilcolm E. Washburn, ed., *Handbook of North American Indians: History of Indian-White Relations* (Washington, D.C., 1988), 4:417–29, gen. ed. William C. Sturtevant, 20 vols. projected (Wash-ington, D.C., 1978–). As exemplars, see Cronon, *Changes in the Land: Indians, Colonists, and the Ecology of New England* (New York, 1983) and White, *The Roots of Dependency: Subsistence, Environment, and Social Change among the Choctaws, Pawnees, and Navajos* (Lincoln, Neb., 1983). For a lively introduction to the "new" environmental history, see Donald Worster et al., "A Round Table: Environmental History," *Journal of American History*, 76 (March 1990), 1087–1147.
[15]William N. Fenton, "Northern Iroquoian Culture Patterns," in Bruce G. Trigger, ed., *Handbook of North American Indians: Northeast* (Washington, D.C., 1978), 15:296–97; James W. Bradley, *Evolution of the Onondaga Iroquois: Accommodating Change, 1500–1655* (Syracuse, N.Y., 1987), 11–14; Ulysses Printiss Hedrick, *A History of Agriculture in the State of New York* (New York, 1966 [orig. pub. 1933]), 1–19; John H. Thompson, ed., *Geography of New York State* (Syracuse, N.Y., 1966). See also Arthur C. Parker, "The Natural Forces That Molded

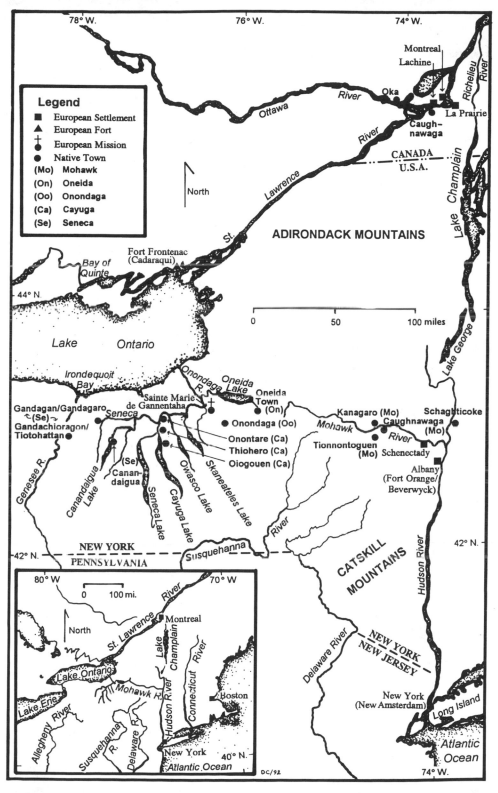

Iroquoia, ca. 1670s. Placement of native towns is approximate; habitations shifted location periodically, and in some cases communities were renamed.

Deciduous forests of birch, beech, maple, and elm trees, with a coniferous admixture of pine and hemlock, spread throughout Iroquoia. In the northern reaches, fir and spruce flourished, and in the east, oaks, chestnuts, and poplars grew around the Hudson River and its tributaries. Trees more characteristic of the Ohio River drainage— sycamore, walnut, butternut, and hickory—predominated in parts of western Iroquoia inhabited by the Senecas. In the Seneca-Genesee River country meadows and large savannas alternated with forested tracts. These lands supported an abundance of wild game. Deer, bear, small mammals, game birds, and fresh water fishes found Iroquoia a hospitable place to live. And in a similar way, the many wild plants gathered by the Iroquois prospered in this landscape.[16]

Yet, despite the work of ice and wind, rain and sun, and the biological imperatives of plants and animals, Iroquoia was a cultural as well as a natural place. As the environmental historian Donald Worster has suggested, in the process of transforming the earth, "people have also restructured themselves and their social relations."[17] Surely the opposite is true as well. The people of the Five Nations shaped and interpreted their environment as they lived within it, and it in turn constrained and helped to reshape them. In ways both conscious and unconscious, the Iroquois engaged in a dialogue with nature, and they understood that conversation in culturally specific ways.[18]

Iroquoia was also a supernatural, spiritual place, a complex, interlinked world of strange animation.[19] It was a fluid, variable world in

---

the Genesee Country," *Rochester Historical Society Publication Fund Series*, vol. 4 (Rochester, N.Y., 1925), 103–19. A number of European travelers have left accounts of the region, including Charles T. Gehring and William A. Starna, trans. and eds., *A Journey into the Mohawk and Oneida Country, 1634–1635: The Journal of Harmen Meyndertz van den Bogaert* (Syracuse, N.Y., 1988); van der Donck, *Description of New Netherlands;* John Bartram, *Travels in Pensilvania and Canada* (Ann Arbor, Mich., 1966 [orig. pub. 1751]); Adolph B. Benson, ed. and trans., *The America of 1750; Peter Kalm's Travels in North America*, 2 vols. (New York, 1937).

[16]In addition to the above sources, see also F. W. Waugh, "Iroquis [*sic*] Foods and Food Preparation," *Anthropological Series*, 12, *Memoirs of the Canadian Geological Survey*, 86 (Ottawa, 1916).

[17]Donald Worster, "Transformations of the Earth: Toward an Agroecological Perspective in History," in Worster et al., "A Round Table," 1090.

[18]Ibid., 1106.

[19]The characteristics of this world emerge for us most clearly in Iroquois folk narratives, which should not be dismissed lightly. See J. N. B. Hewitt, *Iroquoian Cosmology*, in *Annual Reports of the Bureau of American Ethnology*, 21 (1903), 127–339, and 43 (1928), 449–819; Jeremiah Curtin and Hewitt, *Seneca Fiction, Legends, and Myths*, in ibid., 32 (1918), 37–813; Harriet Maxwell Converse, *Myths and Legends of the New York Iroquois*, ed. Arthur C. Parker, *New York State Museum Bulletin*, no. 125 (1908), 5–195; Parker, *Fundamental Factors in Seneca Folklore, New York State Museum Bulletin*, no. 253 (1924), 49–66; various works by William M. Beauchamp, for example, *Iroquois Folk Lore Gathered from the Six Nations of New York* (Syracuse, N.Y., 1922); various works by William N. Fenton, especially "This Island, the World on the

which virtually every element possessed the potential to live and act. The Iroquoian word *ongwe'* contained such a conception; more than "human being," it denoted "all beings that assumed human shapes or attributes, and in the primitive world of thought," wrote the native Iroquoian enthnologist J. N. B. Hewitt, "all beings could upon occasion assume the human form and characteristics, and man shared with them these attributes." Hewitt continued, *"Ongwe'* signifies 'man-being,' that is to say, the being which is of the substance of which all beings are formed."[20] Animals and plants; water, earth, and sky; fire, wind, rain, sun, and snow; thunder, lightening, shooting stars, and eclipses; stone giants, dwarfs, horned serpents, flying heads, often arrayed in families and societies, interacting with each other and with humans: all of these beings "peopled" Iroquoia.[21]

Changeability rather than stasis characterized the Iroquois universe. Of course, seasons came and went in cycles, subsistence tasks followed familiar patterns, and children grew into men and women and ultimately passed into the Land of Souls. But the world was not always so predictable or idyllic. Its varied inhabitants possessed powers of metamorphosis, and the superficial world was not always what it might seem to be. An unsuspecting husband could learn that his wife was, in fact, *Ka-tar-hwat,* a fabulous reptile; friends or foes might turn out to be secret witches; trees might talk, and during sleep people's disembodied spirits might roam the landscape.[22] Relationships were reciprocal and often mutually beneficial, but in Iroquoia conflict mixed with cooperation, anxieties and fears simmered below the surface, and health, prosperity, and security came only at a high price. Good and evil coexisted naturally if uneasily, symbolized by the cosmic twins of Iroquois creation myth: while Sapling—representing life—shaped

Turtle's Back," *Journal of American Folklore,* 75, no. 298 (1962), 283–300; Martha Champion Randle, "The Waugh Collection of Iroquois Folktales," *Proceedings of the American Philosophical Society,* 97, no. 5 (1953), 611–33; Randle, "Psychological Types from Iroquois Folktales," *Journal of American Folklore,* 65 (1952), 13–21; Elisabeth Tooker, *Native American Spirituality of the Eastern Woodlands* (New York, 1979). Peter L. Boice, "The Iroquois Sense of Place: Legends as a Source of Environmental Imagery," *New York Folklore,* 5 (Winter 1979), 179–88, provides a useful summary.

[20]J. N. B. Hewitt, "Cosmology Notes [1902]," Hewitt Papers, unpublished manuscript, no. 3693, National Anthropological Archives (henceforth NAA), Smithsonian Institution, Washington, D.C.

[21]See Matthew Dennis, "Cultivating a Landscape of Peace: The Iroquois New World," Ph.D. diss., University of California, Berkeley, 1986, 14–58.

[22]See, for example, "The Story of Ka-tar-hwat, a Fabulous Reptile...," Hewitt Papers, NAA ms. 445; "Bull-frog," and "Miscellaneous note from Peter White," in ibid., ms. 3860, box 1; "A Visit to the Land of the Disembodied Spirits," in ibid., ms. 2211.

the world into a rich habitable place, his evil brother Flint toiled to spoil that creation. Flint embodied the destructive powers of the universe, as the close identification of the words for "flint arrow tip" and for "ice" in some Iroquoian tongues suggests. Arrows and ice both froze life. Yet both necessarily contributed as well to Iroquois existence.[23]

The contrasts between this world and that of seventeenth-century European colonists, not to mention our own, are sufficiently striking to disguise the important similarities. The Iroquois universe may have been somewhat less hierarchical and more reciprocal, perhaps more dynamic and differently gendered, than early modern Europe's Great Chain of Being. And though the Iroquois, according to hopeful missionaries and curious travelers, seemed to worship a paramount deity,[24] alas, he was not Jesus Christ. As historian James Axtell has demonstrated, Europeans—whether Catholic or Protestant—in their "invasion within" confronted native people with an exclusive cosmology that rejected native belief as (at best) superstition and native life as savage.[25] Yet colonists came to America with an ordered world picture not completely at odds with the Iroquois universe.

Like the Iroquois, the people of early modern Europe understood that they occupied a niche in an interconnected, spiritual world. With God at the top and the basest of inanimate elements, liquids, and metals at the bottom, a great chain joined and ordered the parts of the universe. As Sir John Fortescue, the fifteenth-century jurist, wrote on the law of nature:

> In this order hot things are in harmony with cold, dry with moist, heavy with light, great with little, high with low. In this order angel is set over angel, rank upon rank in the kingdom of heaven; man is set over man, beast over beast, bird over bird, and fish over fish,

---

[23]See, for example, Hewitt, *Iroquoian Cosmology;* Hewitt, "Note on Genesis Story—Native," Hewitt Papers, NAA ms. 2588.

[24]Bartram, *Travels in Pensilvania,* wrote in 1743, for example, that Onondaga religion was "very confused and mixed with superstition. Yet they seem not only to acknowledge a deity, but even to worship him in unity and spirit" (79); Jesuit Joseph-François Lafitau, summarizing a number of earlier French writers on the subject, concluded in 1724: "Generally all the people of America, whether nomadic or sedentary, have strong and forceful expressions which can only be designated a God. They call him the Great Spirit, sometimes the Master and Author of Life" (William N. Fenton and Elizabeth L. Moore, eds. and trans., [Joseph-François Lafitau's] *Customs of the American Indians Compared with the Customs of Primitive Times, Publications of the Champlain Society,* 48, 2 vols. [Toronto, 1974 (orig. pub. Paris, 1724)], 1:101).

[25]James Axtell, *The Invasion Within: The Contest of Cultures in Colonial North America* (New York, 1985), especially 7–19.

The First Woman cast through a hole in the Sky-world by the Master of Life, or Sky-holder, in the Iroquois creation myth. Below the Turtle awaits; on his back the world will be created. Despite its Westernized representation of these mythic figures, this early eighteenth-century engraving accurately expresses a central motif in Iroquois cosmology. Detail of engraving, from Joseph-François Lafitau, *Moeurs des sauvages amériquains, comparées aux moeurs des premiers temps* (Paris, 1724), courtesy of Special Collections, Knight Library, University of Oregon.

on the earth in the air and in the sea: so that there is no worm that crawls upon the ground, no bird that flies on high, no fish that swims in the depths, which the chain of this order does not bind in most harmonious concord. Hell alone, inhabited by none but sinners, asserts its claim to escape the embraces of this order.[26]

Human beings occupied the middle of the chain, balanced below by classes of inanimate substances and sensitive creatures who lacked

[26]Quoted in E. M. W. Tillyard, *The Elizabethan World Picture* (London, 1943), 39.

understanding, and above by purely rational or spiritual classes freed from attachment to lower faculties.

In ways the Iroquois might have appreciated and that suggest modern ideas of ecology, the chain was also a ladder. As the Shakespeare scholar E. M. W. Tillyard explained, "The elements are alimental. There is a progression in the way the elements nourish plants, the fruits of plants beasts, and the flesh of beasts men. And this is all one with the tendency of man upward towards God."[27] Each class of being excelled in some particular, and within each class existed a primate, the noblest expression of its group. The elephant or lion was to beasts as the dolphin or whale was to fish, and the eagle was to birds as the emperor was to men. Within classes and between them inhered a hierarchy that maintained universal order. In Shakespeare's *Coriolanus*, Aufidius speculated about Coriolanus's place in Rome:

> I think he'll be to Rome
> As is the aspray to the fish, who takes it
> By sovereignty of nature.

The passage has meaning only through a recognition that the eaglelike osprey was a king of birds, and the fish—as Rome was to Coriolanus—should voluntarily offer itself up to him.[28]

The Iroquois and other Native Americans similarly recognized masters among classes of life and hierarchies that linked them together. Northern bear ceremonialism implied, for example, special regard for this animal, and within species "bosses," or "keepers of the game," held special sway. Like the osprey's fish and Coriolanus's Rome, bears and other creatures were required to submit to Native American hunters, though reciprocally men were obliged to observe taboos and propitiate their quarry ritually.[29]

The people of early modern Europe, though they sought balance and order through their Great Chain of Being, also appreciated the flux in their world. The four elements—earth, water, air, and fire—

---

[27]Ibid., 40.
[28]Ibid., 41–42, 48–49.
[29]A. Irving Hallowell, "Bear Ceremonialism in the Northern Hemisphere," *American Anthropologist*, n.s., 28, no. 1 (1926), 1–175; see also Waugh, *Iroquois Foods*, especially 130–35; Boice, "Iroquois Sense of Place," 181; van den Bogaert, *Journey into Mohawk Country*, 6, 35–36n45; Bartram, *Travels in Pensilvania*, 24–25. Calvin Martin, *Keepers of the Game: Indian-Animal Relationships and the Fur Trade* (Berkeley, Calif., 1978) provides a provocative discussion of a Native American cosmology.

were the basis of all matter and resided in their own hierarchy. Yet they were "mixed," as Tillyard commented, "in infinitely varied proportion and they were at perpetual war with each other." When properly balanced, the elements produced a better, higher compound, but when imperfectly combined they gave birth to inferior things. Health resulted when the elements were perfectly balanced in the body, and the king of metals existed through an alchemically supreme mixture of elements. Everyone knew that sick men and women could get well and that base substances could be transformed into gold.[30]

The European and early American colonial worlds, like that of the Iroquois, could be radically altered when strange and troubling or wonderful occurrences upset the normal order of things. The historian David D. Hall has reminded us that seventeenth-century New England was "an enchanted universe." The people of New Netherland and New France similarly lived in "worlds of wonder." New Netherlanders interested themselves in the supernatural, watched the skies for comets or eclipses—likely to be signs of God's displeasure—and hoped that He might be merciful. Whether through the interventions of God or Satan, extraordinary events punctuated the patterned experience of people throughout the old and New World. Ghosts visited at night, women were delivered of monstrous births, balladeers reported a rainstorm of blood, earthquakes shook, comets blazed, and multiple suns dazzled amazed onlookers. Monsters, werewolves, and witches stalked New England and New France, and perhaps New Netherland as well, just as they wandered through the Iroquois landscape.[31]

In that landscape—at once natural, cultural, and spiritual—the Iroquois sowed, but did not always reap, peace and prosperity. How did they proceed, cultivating that landscape, and what impact did they

---

[30]Tillyard, *Elizabethan World Picture*, 79–82; quotation from 79.

[31]David D. Hall, *Worlds of Wonder, Days of Judgment: Popular Religious Belief in Early New England* (New York, 1989), especially 71–116; Keith Thomas, *Religion and the Decline of Magic* (London, 1971). See also Carlo Ginsburg, *The Cheese and the Worms: The Cosmos of a Sixteenth-Century Miller*, trans. John and Anne Tedeschi (Baltimore, 1980), and Ginsburg, *The Night Battles: Witchcraft and Agrarian Cults in the Sixteenth and Seventeenth Centuries*, trans. John and Anne Tedeschi (Baltimore, 1983) for a fascinating treatment of early modern European cosmology and exceptional individuals who challenged and confirmed it. On popular belief in New France, see Daniel A. Scalberg, "Religious Life in New France under the Laval and Saint-Vallier Bishoprics, 1659–1727," Ph.D. diss., University of Oregon, 1990, especially 70–81. That New Netherlanders too lived in an enchanted world and, in their own way, sought to divine the meaning of providence is suggested in Donna Merwick, *Possessing Albany, 1630–1710: The Dutch and English Experiences* (New York, 1990), 191.

have on the natural and human ecology? Iroquois men and women sought a good life through a varied, complementary subsistence, and they changed the land to that purpose.

Shaping landscape as they lived in it, Iroquois people most transformed those spaces closest to their villages. The Five Nations occupied town sites for a half century or longer, though they began to limit their stay in particular locations to about twenty-five years or so as population increased in the period just prior to contact with Europeans.[32] The Iroquois cleared the land around these habitations, girdling or felling trees with fire and chisel, in order to plant vast fields of corn, beans, squashes, sunflowers, and tobacco. When the supplies of firewood dwindled, when the ground became compacted and the soil exhausted or infested with weeds, when insect pests and rodents invaded fields and houses, and refuse dumps filled, the Iroquois removed their villages to new scenes. Relocation allowed abandoned sites to recover, as hunting or gathering places, or even as horticultural land after a considerable number of years. An Indian told Adriaen van der Donck in the 1640s, for example, "I see that you are clearing that piece of land to cultivate it. It is very good soil and bears corn abundantly—which I well know because it is only 25 or 26 years ago that we planted corn there and now it has become wooded again."[33]

[32]James A. Tuck, *Onondaga Iroquois Prehistory: A Study in Settlement Archaeology* (Syracuse, N.Y., 1971), 213–14; Bradley, *Evolution of the Onondaga,* generally supports Tuck's conclusion while acknowledging the difficulty of determining lengths of occupation; see, for example, 27, 116–18. See also William Starna, "Mohawk Iroquois Populations: A Revision," *Ethnohistory,* 27 (1980), 371–82; Dean R. Snow, "People in Contact: Indians and Europeans in the Seventeenth Century," symposium paper presented at Haffenreffer Museum of Anthropology, Brown University, Bristol, Rhode Island, September 26–27, 1986; Mary Ann Palmer Niemczycki, *The Origins and Development of the Seneca and Cayuga Tribes of New York State, Rochester Museum and Science Center Research Records,* no. 17 (Rochester, N.Y., 1984). Cf. Conrad Heidenreich, *Huronia: A History and Geography of the Huron Indians, 1600–1650* ([Toronto], 1971), 213–16.

[33]Ada van Gastel, "Van der Donck's Description of the Indians: Additions and Corrections," *William and Mary Quarterly,* 3d ser., 47 (July 1990), 414, provides a correction of the translation in van der Donck's *Description of New Netherlands,* 20. Heidenreich, *Huronia,* 113, speculated that Hurons may have sought areas of secondary growth timber because construction of houses and other structures required great quantities of logs under ten inches in diameter; at best, a period of 35–40 years (and perhaps over 50), he estimated, would be required to allow a forest to regenerate to this state (*ibid.,* 187–88). On the reasons for village relocation, see ibid., 213–16; George M. Wrong, ed., H. H. Langton, trans., *Sagard's Long Journey to the Country of the Hurons, Publications of the Champlain Society,* 25 (Toronto, 1939 [orig. pub. 1632]), 92–93; Lafitau, *Customs of the American Indians,* 2:69–72; William A. Starna, George R. Hamell, and William L. Butts, "Northern Iroquoian Horticulture and Insect Infestation: A Cause for Village Removal," *Ethnohistory,* 31, no. 3 (1984), 197–207; on the factors influencing the selection of village sites among the Hurons, see 109–14. The Five Nations Iroquois differed from the Hurons in some important ways, especially in emphasizing

Iroquois fields varied from ten or twenty to several hundred acres, according to the size of the community. In Huronia, where corn was cultivated even more intensely than in Iroquoia, fields grew so large, according to Recollet lay missionary Gabriel Sagard, that one stood a greater chance of getting lost in them than in the outlying meadows and forests.[34] Corn fields seemed to be all paths meandering through an endless forest of stalks growing as high as or higher than a man. Following a military expedition against the Onondagas in 1666, soldiers in New France reported that cornfields extended for two miles on each side of the Iroquois town. In 1669 a French visitor among the Senecas observed a village standing in a clearing six miles in circumference. And in 1687, the expedition of Jacques-René de Brisay, marquis de Denonville, against the Senecas took over a week "getting the grain cut." Denonville himself pitched in along with his lieutenants, who "bore themselves with great credit, and were busy at it from morning to night." Altogether, they claimed to have destroyed 400,000 minots (1,200,000 bushels) of standing and cached corn in four Seneca villages.[35]

Iroquois women planted these vast tracts by placing corn, bean, and squash or pumpkin seeds together in single mounds. Observing planting taboos, they disturbed the earth as little as possible, often planting in the same mounds each spring, in hollows left from the removal of the previous year's corn stalks, and hoeing and weeding only minimally. As the beans grew, they wound their way around corn stalks for support and helped to shelter lower plants and collect rain. Such horticulture proved remarkably efficient and conservative at high levels of yield. In the Iroquoian system of organic agriculture, farmers benefited from the natural nitrogen fixation that occurs as bacteria develop at the roots of leguminous plants. Beans planted in corn hills

---

security in their town sites, see, for example, the description of a Seneca town sacked by the French in 1678 in Nathaniel Shurtleff Olds, ed. and trans., "Journal of the Expedition of Marquis de Denonville against the Iroquois: 1687, by Chevalier de Baugy," in *Rochester Historical Society, Publication Fund Series,* 9 (Rochester, N.Y., 1930), 38.

[34]Sagard, *Long Journey,* 104.

[35]Waugh, *Iroquois Foods,* 6–7; Elisabeth Tooker, "Subsistence of the Huron Indians," in Bruce Cox, ed., *Cultural Ecology: Readings on Canadian Indians and Eskimos* (Toronto, 1973), 27; Gordon M. Day, "The Indian as an Ecological Factor in the Northeastern Forest," *Ecology,* 34 (April 1953), 333; de Baugy, "Journal of Denonville's Expedition," 38–44; Denonville to the Minister of the Marine Jean-Baptiste, marquis de Seignelay, August 25, 1687, in E. B. O'Callaghan ed., *The Documentary History of the State of New-York,* 4 vols. (Albany, 1849–51), 1:147. A minot is a French measure of volume (now obsolete), varying according to locality and the nature of the commodity measured; its value was approximately three (French) bushels, or 39.36 liters (*Oxford English Dictionary*).

enriched the soil and slowed nitrogen exhaustion. And by planting in the same mounds over a period of seasons, Iroquois women reduced the erosion and soil leaching associated with systems of agriculture that rely on plowing in deep furrows.[36]

The Iroquois horticultural landscape emerged through a process that was at once natural, cultural, spiritual, and gendered. The roles of men and women were complementary and reciprocal, but the core of Iroquois habitations was decidedly feminine. Women's lives centered in lodges, villages, and the surrounding cleared spaces used for cultivation and gathering. While Iroquois men helped to construct houses and cleared fields, they worked on behalf of women who "owned" these structures and places; men's identity and status stemmed from their relationship to those women or to their actions in masculine zones beyond the clearings, where they achieved note through hunting, diplomacy, or warfare. In the localized, feminine sphere, women farmers produced the major portion of Iroquois subsistence. They planted, tended, harvested, processed, stored, and cooked the community's vegetable foods. Working communally, often in women's societies, they carried out these tasks in religiously prescribed ways, giving thanks to Mother Earth and "Our Great Three Sisters"—corn, beans, and squashes, united spiritually as they were physically in Iroquoian fields—and conducting the rituals that would sanctify the practice and promote a fruitful harvest. Women soaked seeds in magical decoctions before planting to protect them, to aid in germination, and preserve crops from insect infestation or bird predators. The Iroquois recognized the extraordinary power inherent in women as the bearers of life, and with respectful caution women observed the taboo prohibiting their participation in planting and other activities during the perceived volatile and potent periods of menstruation.[37]

[36]Sagard, *Long Journey*, 103–4; Lafitau, *Customs of the American Indians*, II, 54–55, 69; van der Donck, *Description of New Netherlands*, 68–71, 96. On Iroquoian horticulture, its practicality and efficiency, see Heidenreich, *Huronia*, especially 184–85; R. Douglas Hurt, *Indian Agriculture in America: Prehistory to the Present* (Lawrence, Kans., 1987), 34–35; Daniel K. Onion, "Corn in the Culture of the Mohawk Iroquois," *Economic Botany*, 18 (March 1964), 60–66.

[37]Nancy Bonvillain, "Gender Relations in Native North America," *American Indian Culture and Research Journal*, 13, no. 2 (1989), 1–28, provides a useful overview; see especially 14–17 on the Iroquois. See also Elisabeth Tooker, "Women in Iroquois Society," in Michael K. Foster, Jack Campisi, and Marianne Mithun, eds., *Extending the Rafters: Interdisciplinary Approaches to Iroquoian Studies* (Albany, 1984), 109–23; Judith K. Brown, "Economic Organization and the Position of Women among the Iroquois," *Ethnohistory*, 17 (1970), 151–67; Hurt, *Indian Agriculture*, 67; Lafitau, *Customs of the American Indians*, especially, 2:47, 54–56 (on menstrual separation see 1:178); Waugh, *Iroquois Foods*, 7, 12–13, 17–21. In addition, see W.

Iroquoian women's work, from Joseph-François Lafitau, *Moeurs des sauvages amériquains,
comparées aux moeurs des premiers temps* (Paris, 1724) courtesy of Special Collections, Knight
Library, University of Oregon. Women's lives centered on their matrilocally organized
longhouses and towns, though women's tasks took them beyond village clearings, into the
fields and forests of Iroquoia, to farm and gather wild products, like the maple sap shown
here.

In general, contemporary European observers saw the disordered fields and the absence of livestock among Indians as signs of their backwardness,[38] and especially they condemned native people for agricultural regimes that made women the producers rather than men. Typically, Europeans saw cultural difference as inferiority when observing Native American societies. Contrasting gender arrangements represented for colonists, then, one emblem of Indian savagery, and the persistence of such notions makes it difficult to see the balance that the Iroquois and other native peoples sought to cultivate in their lives.

The portrayal of Native American women as drudges allowed European men to criticize Indian men in particular and native cultures in general. William Wood, in his *New England Prospect* (1634), for example, contrasted the apparently laborious, unending toil of women with the lazy "gurmandizing" of their husbands. He wrote of these women with pity: "Commendable is their milde carriage and obedience to their husbands, notwithstanding all this their customarie churlishnesse and salvage inhumanitie, not seeming to delight in frownes or offering to word it with their lords, not presuming to proclaime their female superiority to the usurping of the least title of their husband's charter, but rest themselves content under their helpless condition, counting it the womans portion." Sketching the contrast between societies, men could show dissatisfied colonial women how comparatively privileged was their position, and so defend their colonial societies from old world criticisms. Women's positions in the Algonquian societies of southern New England differed from those occupied by women in Iroquoian societies. Nonetheless, even the sympathetic eighteenth-century observer John Bartram could write, Iroquois "men [are] lazy and indolent at home, the women continual slaves, modest, very loving, and obedient to their husbands." And the

---

L. Grant, ed., *Voyages of Samuel de Champlain, 1604–1618, Original Narratives of Early American History*, gen. ed., J. Franklin Jameson (New York, 1907), 327. Lewis Henry Morgan, *Houses and House-Life of the American Aborigines* (Chicago, 1965 [orig. pub. as *Contribution to North American Ethnology*, vol. 4 (Washington, D.C., 1881)]), 65–66, 127–28, argued that the descriptions of the Five Nations as a "gyneocracy" were not overdrawn.

[38]In a similar way, eighteenth-century English writers would criticize the farms and agricultural habits of colonists, especially non-English settlers. In the Middle Colonies, for example, Swedish, German, Dutch, and French farmers were taken to task for disorderly fields, inadequate plowing and weeding, and the failure to employ fertilizers. See Anonymous, *Animal Husbandry: Containing an Account of the Soil, Climate, Production and Agriculture of the British Colonies in North America and the West Indies with Observations on the Advantages and Disadvantages of Settling in Them, Compared with Great Britain and Ireland*, 2 vols. (London, 1775), 1:104–7.

economic (and political) roles of Iroquois women were sufficiently unnatural to Europeans and Americans that transforming men into farmers would become a major objective of missionaries, philanthropists, and policy makers in the early republic.[39]

Modern geographers, anthropologists, and historians have better recognized the sophistication of Native American agriculture. Hardly primitive, these horticultural systems "do not deserve the invidious terms ["primitive," "slash and burn," "shifting"] given them," commented the historical geographer Carl O. Sauer.[40] In the development of agriculture over the centuries, people have increasingly widened the gap between wild and domestic forms. The result in the modern world has been the advent of "agroecosystems" that have radically simplified the natural ecological order, limiting both the number of species found in an area and the intricacies of their interconnections.[41] Although ancient agriculturalists sometimes inflicted great damage on their environments, those who practiced digging in shifting garden plots—like the Five Nations—found a way to shape their landscape to their advantage without destroying it. After European colonization, even as they incorporated fruit trees and new domestic animals into their subsistence, the Iroquois continued to cultivate fields in traditional ways, not because they lacked a spirit of innovation but because they had found a practical and efficient long-term solution to their subsistence needs, one that made sense to them intellectually, morally, and religiously.

Anthropologists and ecologists have most closely studied small-scale or tribal societies practicing "shifting agriculture" in rain forest environments.[42] Many of their conclusions may be applied to the Iroquois and their neighbors. The Iroquois "swidden" plots and their surrounding environments share certain features with the tribal agricultural systems of the tropics. Both are at least partially "closed

[39]See Wood, "Squaw Drudges and Lazy Gourmands in New England," in James Axtell, ed., *The Indian Peoples of Eastern America: A Documentary History of the Sexes* (New York, 1981), 118–22; Bartram, *Travels in Pensilvania*, 77.

[40]On the nature and efficiency of so-called primitive agriculture, see Carl O. Sauer, "The Agency of Man on Earth," in William L. Thomas ed., *Man's Role in Changing the Face of the Earth*, 2 vols. (Chicago, 1956), 2:56–58, quotation on 57.

[41]See Worster, "Transformation of the Earth," 1096–1101.

[42]Though tainted by the myth of the "wandering" or "roaming" savage, "shifting" agriculture is nonetheless a reasonably inoffensive term, as is "swidden," from the Old Norse "swithe" meaning "to singe," "to smart from burning" (*Oxford English Dictionary*, "swithe," "swithen"), which evokes a sense of pain inflicted on the earth appropriate to Iroquois understanding of the animate landscape. On swidden farming see Andrew Goudie, *The Human Impact: Man's Role in Environmental Change* (Cambridge, Mass., 1981), 39–40.

cover systems" because not all trees are removed from crop fields and because crops are planted, not in rows aligned in open fields, but rather in a tightly woven, seemingly haphazard way that maintains a dense biological fabric. Shifting cultivation patterns imitate their natural context by combining many cultivated plants in the same fields, just as outlying areas support diverse combinations of wild plants.

Unlike the soil found in tropical rain forests, which is often poor in comparison to the lushness of its plant life, the soil in many parts of Iroquoia proved especially fertile. Burning plots released nutrients locked in their plant communities and transferred those nutrients to the soil, where they could sustain the growth of plants more directly useful to the human inhabitants. In the tropics, swidden agriculturalists could maintain the productivity of their landscape only by shifting their fields often, allowing impoverished soil to recover. In Iroquoia, better soil allowed the Five Nations to plant for longer periods in one place without significant deterioration. Eventually fields declined in fertility, but Iroquois lands remained productive longer than did fields subjected to exhaustive plowing practices, and by shifting their cultivation and habitation the Iroquois maintained a prosperous, balanced landscape, a landscape of ecological peace.

The Iroquois employed fire widely, not only as the most efficient tool in creating their horticultural lands, but also to shape their greater landscape in ways that would render it more safe, congenial, and productive. Early visitors to Iroquoia frequently mentioned unusually open country, "beautiful, broad meadows," amid otherwise forested land. Often Europeans believed these meadows and prairies to be natural features of the environment, and they found them especially appealing in contrast to more dense and seemingly sinister woods. On the other hand, Denonville commented on the inconvenience of building a fort at Niagara, where the Niagara River emptied into Lake Ontario, because timber was available only at a distance. The large tracts of open land in Iroquoia, though sometimes natural, were often the result of ancient and contemporary burning, a cultural artifact rather than simply a natural feature.[43]

[43]Waugh, Iroquois Foods, 7–8; Day, "Indian as an Ecological Factor," 338; Williams, Americans and Their Forests, 43–48; [Harman Meyndertsz van den Bogaert], "Narrative of a Journey into the Mohawk and Oneida Country," in J. Franklin Jameson, ed., Narratives of New Netherland, 1609–1664 (New York, 1909), 145; van der Donck, Description of New Netherlands, 18; Father Simon le Moyne, "Papers to the First Settlement at Onondaga," in O'Callaghan, ed., Documentary History of New-York, 1:34; Denonville to Minister of the Marine de Seignelay, August 25, 1687, in ibid., 146–48.

Indeed, the eighteenth-century observer George H. Loskiel criticized the Iroquois use of fire. "They never think of sparing the forest trees," he wrote. "The greatest havoc...is made by fires, which happen either accidentally, or are kindled by the Indians, who in spring, and sometimes in autumn, burn the withered grass, that a fresh crop may grow for the deer. These fires run on for many miles, burning the bark at the roots of the trees in such a manner, that they die. A forest of fir trees is in general destroyed by these fires."[44] Loskiel's condemnation betrayed the traditional fear of fire characteristic of modern Western civilization. Although the fire contained in a family hearth, sending out chimney smoke as a symbol of safety, domesticity, and modest prosperity, warmed the souls of Europeans and Americans, unrestrained wild fire struck terror in their hearts as it evoked the torments of Hell. Theologian and physician Henry Cornelius Agrippa described the infernal fire in 1533 as a "parching heat, consuming all things," and as "darkness, making all things barren." And Puritan ministers horrified their congregations with images of the eternal fire awaiting the unregenerate, who would soon join, in the words of Samuel Willard, "the piercing groans of creatures lying upon a terrible rack, and scorched with the flames of a seven times heated furnace!"[45]

Those who settled in New Netherland emigrated from societies with long-standing fears of fires, not only in the netherworld but in their daily lives as well. Often town people, they had lived tightly clustered in urban landscapes built of wood, which made them vulnerable to accidental fires ignited by careless neighbors. More frightening, though, was the genuine threat of arson, a well-known weapon used regularly during the Middle Ages and the early modern period by the unruly lower nobility as well as by petty criminals, vagrants, demobilized soldiers, refractory peasants, and the like. More than the English or the French, the Dutch who settled in the New World carried these fears to America and constructed an urban life—in Beverwyck and New Amsterdam—that would make those fears legitimate.[46]

---

[44] Quoted in Waugh, *Iroquois Foods,* 53n.

[45] Samuel Willard, *The Compleat Body of Divinity* (Boston, 1726), 241; Stilgoe, *Common Landscape of America,* 299. On European and American attitudes toward fire see 298–300; see also Stephen J. Pyne, *Fire in America: A Cultural History of Wildland and Rural Fire* (Princeton, N.J., 1982).

[46] Bob Scribner, "The *Mordbrenner* Fear in Sixteenth-Century Germany: Political Paranoia or the Revenge of Outcasts," in Richard J. Evans, ed., *The German Underworld: Deviants and*

Yet for North American Indians in general, and the Iroquois in particular, fire represented not destruction and degradation, but rather creation and benign transformation. Smoke carried Iroquois thanks and supplications aloft to their gods, while smoking calmed their minds; glowing embers and ashes, blown on the afflicted by masked members of medicine societies, made sick people well; fire ritually consumed the bones of animals who had allowed themselves to be killed; flames and firebrands even tortured captives as they were symbolically transformed into kinsmen.[47] In confronting the idea of Hell, presented to them by the Jesuit missionary Joseph Jouvency, a group of Montagnais Indians conveyed their understanding of fire and their deep appreciation of it as a tool. "When they first heard of the eternal fire and the burning decreed as a punishment for sin," Father Jouvency reported, "they were marvelously impressed; still, they obstinately withheld their belief because, as they said, there could be no fire where there was no wood; then, what forest could sustain so many fires through such a long space of time?"[48] That strange and horrible place—Hell—less frightened than intrigued the Montagnais, even as they doubted its existence. They understood the various forms and properties of fire, and Hell defied their empirical knowledge and native logic. Even when they employed fire on a strictly controlled basis—to prepare food, provide warmth, and illuminate lodges—eventually local supplies of firewood were exhausted. On the other hand, the holocausts of wildfire—which better corresponded to the fires of Hades, perhaps—occurred infrequently under native management,

---

Outcasts in German History (London, 1988), 29–56. My thanks to John Thiebault for bringing this work to my attention.

[47]On the meaning of smoke and the act of smoking, see for example, Waugh, *Iroquois Foods*, 25–26; Michael K. Foster, "Another Look at the Function of Wampum in Iroquois-White Councils," 107 and 114n27, and "Glossary of Figures of Speech in Iroquois Political Rhetoric," 118 ("Fire") and 121 ("Smoking"), in Francis Jennings et al., eds., *The History and Culture of Iroquois Diplomacy: An Interdisciplinary Guide to the Treaties of the Six Nations and Their League* (Syracuse, N.Y., 1985). On smoke, ashes, curing, and the Iroquois False Faces, see William N. Fenton, *The False Faces of the Iroquois* (Norman, Okla., 1987), especially 27, 74, 102–3. On the use of fire in ritual, see Bartram, *Travels in Pensilvania*, 24; Lafitau, *Customs of the American Indians*, 1:149; Nathaniel Knowles, "The Torture of Captives by the Indians of Eastern North America," *Proceedings of the American Philosophical Society*, 82, no. 2 (Philadelphia, 1940), 151–225; Thomas S. Abler, "Iroquois Cannibalism: Fact not Fiction," *Ethnohistory*, 27 (Fall 1980), 309–16. Of course, victims of torture may have had other ideas about the benign nature of burning, though many Indians seemed to accept the logic of the painful exercise.

[48]Thwaites, ed., *The Jesuit Relations and Allied Documents*, 73 vols. (Cleveland, 1896–1901), 1:289; on Indian burning in Canada, and the increasing imitation of such activity by modern foresters, see Henry T. Lewis, "Indian Fires of Spring," *Natural History*, January 1980, 76–83.

and even these blazes burned themselves out. No landscape could fuel such an inferno indefinitely.

Like the Montagnais, the Iroquois understood the properties of fire and employed it consistently to shape and maintain their landscape. They burned over fields to clear them of trees, to promote fertility, and to rid them of insects and reptiles. They set fires to drive game and to enrich pastures upon which deer depended. And they used fire to improve berry harvests and to remove forest litter that covered acorns and nuts.[49]

Ecologists now recognize the benefits fire can offer.[50] Burning releases mineral elements to the soil, directly as ash from living and dead organic matter, and indirectly through intensified decomposition. Fire can reduce cover, and thereby increase insolation and soil temperature, stimulating growth. Burning often releases seeds, stimulates flowering and fruiting of shrubs and herbs, and encourages plant reproduction. Fires selectively eliminate parts of plant communities, reducing the competition for moisture, nutrients, heat, and light. Yields from shrubs producing berries often increase after burning. The greater abundance of berries and forage plants, which follow fire, favors the herbivores who eat such foods. In turn such conditions favor the carnivores (including humans) occupying the next position on the food chain.[51]

Fires prevent forests from achieving too great a uniformity of species, which can make them vulnerable to sudden, catastrophic events; they maintain a diversity in the plant mosaic and create "ecotones"— edge communities between different kinds of habitats—in which animal life flourishes. Frequent burning militates against large-scale fires that might prove truly destructive. Smaller-scale burning reduces or-

[49]Van der Donck, *Description of New Netherlands*, 20–21; Day, "The Indian as an Ecological Factor," 334–39; Omer C. Stewart, "Fire as the First Great Force Employed by Man," in Thomas, ed., *Man's Role in Changing the Face of the Earth*, 1:120; H. J. Lutz, "The Vegetation of Heart's Content, A Virgin Forest in Northwestern Pennsylvania," *Ecology*, 11 (January 1930), 18, 20. Cf. Emily W. B. Russell, "Indian-Set Fires in the Forests of the Northeastern United States," *Ecology*, 64, no. 1 (1983), 78–88, who argues that Native American landscape burning has been overstated as a frequent and intentional practice.

[50]See H. E. Wright, Jr. and M. L. Heiselman, "The Ecological Role of Fire in Natural Conifer Forests of Western and Northern America," *Quaternary Research*, 3 (October 1973), 319–28; see also Stewart, "Fire as the First Great Force Employed by Man," 115–29; Sauer, "Agency of Man on Earth," 54–56; Day, "The Indian as an Ecological Factor," 334–39; Williams, *Americans and Their Forests*, 43–48.

[51]In addition to references above, see Pyne, *Fire in America*, especially 34–44, for a convenient summary of the principles of fire ecology; 45–59, summary treatment of fire in the Northeast through the colonial period; and 71–83, on fire and the American Indian.

ganic forest litter before it can accumulate as kindling for massive wild fire, and it helps reduce the susceptibility of forests to blowdowns of larger trees that also can fuel devastating blazes. Regular fires, finally, help regulate insect and parasite populations that easily attack homogeneous forests and in the process create massive fuel concentrations for high-intensity holocausts.

In the context of modern ecology, Iroquois use of fire seems remarkably sophisticated. Adriaen van der Donck observed native fires in New Netherland in the 1640s: "The Indians have a yearly custom ... of burning the woods, plains and meadows in the fall of the year, when the leaves have fallen, and when the grass and vegetable substances are dry. Those places which are then passed over are fired in the spring in April." Van der Donck was impressed that "notwithstanding the apparent danger of the entire destruction of the woodlands by the burning, still the green trees do not suffer. The outside bark is scorched three or four feet high, which does them no injury, for the trees are not killed."[52] Employing fire ecologically and symbolically, the Five Nations helped forge the landscape of Iroquoia that offered a rich, meaningful existence.

In other, less dramatic ways the Iroquois also attempted to cultivate a landscape of balance and peace. Working with natural processes, they organized their subsistence tasks on seasonal rounds. Taking what nature provided, and stimulating nature to offer more of that which they wanted most, the Iroquois sought to construct and maintain a stable and satisfying way of life.

Beyond the village clearings and fields of Iroquoia was a less domesticated, more dangerous, masculine zone, where men hunted and fished and women cautiously gathered the foods that completed their subsistence. In the way that men complemented women, and that war coexisted with peace, these forested places were essentially related to the core horticultural landscape. Although maize provided the basis of Five Nations' subsistence, fish, meat, maple sap, and wild fruits and plants contributed fundamentally to a mixed hunting-horticultural system. The adoption of agricultural life by the Iroquois did not represent a linear advance along a continuum of progress, a continuum in which agriculture is deemed more civilized than the "barbaric"

[52]Van der Donck, *Description of New Netherlands*, 20–21. Van der Donck noted that fires did at times escape the control of those who set them, especially in thick pine woods: "Frequently great injuries are done by such fires, but the burning down of entire woods never happens" (21).

hunter state. Instead, the combination of hunting, fishing, and gathering by the Five Nations and other horticultural peoples constituted a viable, stable system in its own right. By maintaining the complexity of nature and spreading the risks in their subsistence system, the Iroquois lived well during times of agricultural abundance, and they survived during periods of failure.[53]

"They regulate the seasons of the year by the wild beasts, the fish, the birds and the vegetation," observed a Jesuit missionary among the Hurons.[54] He could have been referring to the Five Nations as well. The Iroquois calendar itself described seasonal changes in terms of Iroquois subsistence needs. Even during months in early summer called "berries begin to ripen" or "it (the plants or vegetation) stands up again,"[55] Iroquois men searched for food beyond the clearings. In the 1650s, Adriaen van der Donck wrote,

> To hunting and fishing the Indians are all extravagantly inclined, and they have their particular seasons for these engagements. In the spring and part of the summer, they practice fishing. When the wild herbage begins to grow up in the woods, the first hunting season begins, and then many of their young men leave the fisheries for the purpose of hunting; but the old and thoughtful men remain at the fisheries until the second and principal hunting season, which they also attend, but with snares only.[56]

The Iroquois ate a wide variety of animal foods, from large and small mammals to birds, amphibians and reptiles, fish, molluscs and crustaceans, and insects, and during times of scarcity the list was expanded.[57] Without their *sapaen*, or corn mush, van der Donck observed, "they do not eat a satisfactory meal," but "when they have an opportunity, they frequently boil fish or meat with it." The Indians, he continued, "use for their subsistence every kind of fish and flesh

[53]I am indebted to Richard White, *The Roots of Dependency: Subsistence, Environment, and Social Change among the Choctaws, Pawnees, and Navajos* (Lincoln, Neb., 1983), especially 1–33, whose discussion of Choctaw landscape and subsistence has influenced my understanding of the Iroquois; the demarcation of the boundary between the village clearing—women's, domestic space—and the outlying, forested places of greater danger—men's space—is clearly suggested in the concept of the "Wood's Edge" in Iroquois Condolence Ceremonies and in diplomatic missions; see, for example, Jennings et al., *History and Culture of Iroquois Diplomacy*, 18–20, 124 and Bogaert, *Journey into Mohawk Country*, 12, 43n88.

[54]Thwaites, ed., *Jesuit Relations*, 15: 157.

[55]Waugh, *Iroquois Foods*, 35.

[56]Van der Donck, *Description of New Netherlands*, 96–97.

[57]See Waugh, *Iroquois Foods*, especially 131–40.

that is fit for food, which the country and the places of their settlements affords, and that they can obtain."[58]

When Harmen Meyndertsz van den Bogaert entered a Mohawk village in December 1634 he found most of the people away hunting deer and bear. Deer provided the most important source of meat in the Iroquoian diet, and they lived in abundance in the second growth forests, edges, and openings that village removal and native fires promoted. Iroquois men hunted throughout the year, but there was a seasonal and communal emphasis in hunting deer and certain other game. In addition to arrows, bullets, and snares, Iroquois men made "extensive fikes and palisades, which narrow at their terminating angles, wherein they drive multitudes of animals and take great numbers," according to van der Donck. The fire used to drive and enclose their game would have contributed further to the maintenance of rich game lands.[59]

Significantly, the Mohawk word *dequoquoha* (*tewakoha*), to go hunting, meant literally "let's go and get it!" The term seems to imply the retrieval of something owned, like the fruit of crops sown. In a sense, the Iroquois harvested the animal food that they cultivated out beyond their village clearings, where they managed game resources in a systematic way that was simultaneously practical and religious. Detailed knowledge of animal habits and an effective system of spiritual beliefs and practices made Iroquois hunting—and fishing and gathering—efficient and productive. Their knowledge of the animals that shared their world came from their Creator, who had placed them together in a contractual relationship. Success in hunting depended on the careful fulfillment of rituals, the respectful observance of taboos, and sometimes the direct intervention of magic supernatural beings. As

[58]Ibid., 75–76. On Iroquois subsistence and ecological time, see Fenton, "Northern Iroquoian Cultural Patterns," 297–302; Lewis Henry Morgan, *League of the Ho-de-no-sau-nee, Iroquois,* ed. William N. Fenton (Secaucus, N.J., 1962 [orig. pub. 1851]). Autumn hunts are described ibid., 345. Father Isaac Jogues to Provincial of the Jesuits at Paris, 5 August 1643, "The Jogues Papers," ed. John D.G. Shea, *New-York Historical Society Collections,* 2d ser. (New York, 1857), 3:194; Johannes Megapolensis, Jr., "A Short Account of the Mohawk Indians," ed. John Romeyn Brodhead, ibid., 151. On Iroquois fishing, see van der Donck, *Description of New Netherlands,* 96–97; Bartram, *Travels in Pensilvania,* 48; William M. Beauchamp, *Aboriginal Use of Wood in New York, New York State Museum Bulletin,* no. 89 (June, 1905), 146–49. Heidenreich, *Huronia,* 208–12, analyzes fishing and subsistence among the Hurons, who probably resembled the Five Nations but whose diet was more dependent on fish.

[59]Bogaert, *Journey into Mohawk Country,* 4 and 31n21; William Engelbrecht, "Factors Maintaining Low Population Density among the Prehistoric New York Iroquois," *American Antiquity,* 52 (January 1987), 16; Heidenreich, *Huronia,* 204–7; van der Donck, *Description of New Netherlands,* 97, 21, 64. See also Champlain, *Voyages,* 298–99.

Huron deer hunt, an etching from Samuel de Champlain, *Les voyages de la Nouvelle France occidentale, d cte Canada . . .* (Paris: Pierre Le-Mur, 1632), courtesy National Archives of Canada, Ottawa (C 113066). Like the Hurons depicted here, the Iroquois employed "fikes" and palisades in their hunts, driving and funneling large game into enclosures where they could be harvested systematically.

numerous European observers have recorded, Iroquois men hunted at times and in ways religiously prescribed; they offered tobacco to the "little people" who aided them in the chase or to the "keepers of the game"; they disposed of animal remains respectfully, in the branches of trees or in fires; they employed hunting magic prescribed by shamans; they avoided the consumption of animals understood to be evil or unclean; they asked permission of the animals that yielded themselves as game, and they ritually thanked those who allowed themselves to be killed. Failure to fulfill their obligations or violation of this world's harmony could result in dire consequences. John Bartram heard from his Iroquois guides, for example, that deer and elk had completely abandoned a favorite salt lick for a period of years because the place had been spoiled by a quarrel among Indians.[60]

When a Mohawk orator proclaimed to the French in 1645 that "all the country that lies between us is full of Bears, of Deer, of Elk, of Beaver and of numerous other animals," he was acknowledging the landscape patterns described above: nucleated villages and gardens, surrounded by zones uninhabited by humans but maintained by the Iroquois both as security buffers and as game lands. Like the Choctaws examined by the historian Richard White, the Five Nations sought secure upland locations for their habitations, leaving rich bottom lands for deer and other game and the wilder places as protective shields against invasion. During Samuel de Champlain's first penetration of Iroquoia in 1609, as a member of an Algonquin and Huron war party, he passed through vast tracts of "very fine woods and meadows," teeming with deer, bears, beavers, and fowl, and he commented that "although they are pleasant, [these lands] are not inhabited by any savages, on account of their wars; but they withdraw as far as possible from the rivers into the interior, in order not to be suddenly surprised." In 1687 the "particularly wild and inaccessible" country that

[60]"[Mohawk] Wordlist," ed. and trans. Gunther Michelson, in Bogaert, *Journey into Mohawk Country*, 61. On the creation and instruction of game animals in the Iroquois creation myth, see Hewitt, *Iroquoian Cosmology, Part Two*, 536. On the "little people" see, for example, Boice, "Iroquois Sense of Place," 180; Beauchamp, *Iroquois Folk Lore*, 41. On rituals and taboos connected with game animals, see Waugh, *Iroquois Foods*, 131–33, 135n; Thwaites, ed., *Jesuit Relations*, 31:73, 44:301–3; Bartram, *Travels in Pensilvania*, 24–25, 27; Shea, ed., "Jogues Papers," 194–96. William Christie MacLeod, "Conservation Among Primitive Hunting Peoples," *Scientific Monthly*, 43 (December 1936), 565, saw the origins of the mid-seventeenth-century war between the Five Nations and the Eries in the latter's violation of Iroquois conservation practices; Christie cited Baron Lehontan's *Voyages* (1682–1703), arguing that the Five Nations attacked the Eries because they had trespassed and "had acted contrary to the customs of all Indians, for they had left none of the beavers alive; they killed both males and females."

separated Seneca from Onondaga villages prevented invading French troops from pursuing retreating Iroquois men, women, and children. And John Bartram in the eighteenth century and Harmen Meyndertsz van den Bogaert in the seventeenth century gave similar testimony to the vast, rich, and protective zone of landscape that surrounded the core settlements of the Five Nations.[61]

Did the people of the Five Nations know what they were doing when they created these hunting lands and marches? Did they act self-consciously as "ecologists," cultivating game resources as they sought protection from enemies? It is tempting to separate the Iroquois view of their constructed environment from our own scientific understanding of Iroquoia. Charting energy flows and food chain relations between organisms within the Iroquois biosphere, and making determinations on the conservation and dissipation of energy, the nature of adaptation, and the maintenance of homeostasis within the ecosystem, we might conclude that the Iroquois functioned in an environmentally sound manner. Such a conclusion might be important in making a historical judgment about the viability of Iroquois society in its particular historical and ecological context. But in placing undue emphasis on imposed "operational" models—descriptions of "actual" environments "in accordance with the assumptions and methods of the science of ecology"[62]—we risk losing sight of the reason motivating Iroquois action. And it is becoming increasingly clear that

[61]Thwaites, ed., *Jesuit Relations*, 27:289–91; see also ibid., 40:185, in which an Iroquois orator urged "that there might be no war except on the Elks, Beavers, Bears, and Deer,— in order that all might enjoy together the dainty dishes that are obtained from these good animals"; Champlain, *Voyages*, 160; de Baugy, *Journal of Denonville's Expedition*, 39; Bartram, *Travels in Pensilvania*; Bogaert, *Journey into Mohawk Country*; White, *Roots of Dependency*, 7–15. Mary Ann Palmer Niemczycki, "The Genesee Connection: The Origins of Iroquois Culture in West-Central New York," *North American Archaeologist*, 7, no. 1 (1986), 41, argues that by 1450 Iroquoian settlements in the Genesee Valley were abandoned "in spite of the rich agricultural land it offered." Warfare and concerns for defense thus transformed this land into hunting and buffer zones. Snow, "Peoples in Contact," characterized the Mohawks and other northern Iroquoians as practicing an "upland subtype" of swidden agriculture, rather than the "intensive riverine subtype" typical of the American midcontinent; this represented an adaptation to human as well as the natural ecology.

[62]On the assumptions, concepts, and methodology of ecological anthropology, see Roy A. Rappaport, "Nature, Culture, and Ecological Anthropology," in Harry L. Shapiro, ed., *Man, Culture, and Society* (Oxford, rev. ed., 1971), 237–67; on "operational" and "cognized" environmental models, see 247–48. Operational models may overstate the certainty of our own ecological knowledge, and their construction certainly reflects our own biases. Complicating the picture further, ecological theory itself is caught in a revisionist swing, leaving historians unsure of what, precisely, an ecosystem is and how it works (see Worster, "Transformation of the Earth," in "Round Table," 1092–93). As Richard White put it, "Historians thought ecology was the rock upon which they could build environmental history; it turned out to be a swamp" ("Environmental History, Ecology, and Meaning," in ibid., 1115).

native societies have often behaved in ways more environmentally sound than those with a scientific world view. Attempts to understand why people acted in a particular fashion are at least as important as functional explanations. To interpret history simply in terms of our own construction can leave the motivation of historical actors unexplained and lead to anachronism and irrelevance. As William Cronon insists, the production of subsistence is more than "a system of bundled calories and nutrients that sustains the life of a human community by concentrating the trophic energy flows of an ecosystem; it is also an elaborate cultural construct."[63]

While the Iroquois behaved in a prudent fashion within their habitat, their behavior was not merely the product of a utilitarian adaptation to natural forces, and it did not result in a total transformation of nature. Within a natural, cultural, and spiritual setting, they produced and reproduced a dynamic way of life that was uniquely their own. Neither were Iroquois actions conservationist or ecological in a modern sense.[64] The Five Nations and their world emerged as the result of a complex historical development over a period of centuries. We begin to trace Iroquoia's historical construction by turning to the Five Nations' ancestors, the Owasco people, who in the second millennium began an experimental process, gradually assembling a culture and landscape that seventeenth-century observers would recognize as Iroquois.

[63]Cronon, "Modes of Prophecy and Production: Placing Nature in History," in "Round Table," 1124.

[64]Calvin Martin, *Keepers of the Game*, 157–88, is correct in suggesting that Native Americans had their own reasons for creating their particular relationships with nature, and that the different contexts of their lives makes it unrealistic to expect that twentieth-century Americans can simply imitate them.

2

Owasco into Iroquois:
War, Peace, and the Social
Construction of the Five Nations

Then in later times they made additions
To the great house.
> —Condolence Ceremony,
> Roll Call of the Chiefs (1907)

Thou upholdest our Cabins, when thou comest among
us.
> —concluding song in Iroquois peace council with
> French Jesuits in Onondaga (1655)

The history of the Iroquois and their lengthy experiment with peace begins not in the seventeenth century, when they first encountered Europeans face to face, but in a more ancient time. We must push our search back to A.D. 1000 or so, when the ancestors of the people who would become the Five Nations had not yet constituted themselves into a League of Peace, or even into the constituent nations that would form this confederation. A thousand years ago, Owasco people—so named because the first reported archaeological site was found near Owasco Lake, at Auburn, New York—lived in autonomous villages, hamlets, and camps, without any overarching structure or even any sense of political unity, throughout what is today western and central New York and northern Pennsylvania.[1] Their lives were

---

[1]Although most now believe that Algonquian-speaking people also shared in Owasco culture, the Owasco are generally considered the direct precursors of the Iroquois. See, for example, James W. Bradley, *Evolution of the Onondaga Iroquois: Accommodating Change, 1500–1655* (Syracuse, N.Y., 1987), 10, 11; Dean R. Snow, *The Archaeology of New England* (New York, 1980), 310. Owasco culture predominated, roughly, from A.D. 1000 to A.D. 1300, in

hardly idyllic. Chronic, deadly feuding made life uncertain and dangerous and as population increased throughout the region the prospects for heightened violence must have seemed great. Yet this chapter tells a different story.

Breaking the cycle of violence by putting an end to the bloody feuds that plagued their world, Owasco men and women initiated a pattern of peaceful amalgamation and integration among themselves, cultivating the idea that they were—or could become—kin. As villages merged and consolidated and then affiliated with even larger groups undergoing the same process, the Iroquois who had emerged out of this development sought—and sometimes found—social peace to complement the ecological balance, which they also consciously strove to construct. The historical experience of consolidation in the interest of peace—understood in terms of balance and harmony among kinspeople within a single domestic world—became central to Iroquois identity and culture and guided Iroquois actions in the seventeenth century.

Owasco people were farmers. Tending gardens and following nature's seasonal rounds, they procured a diversified subsistence of fish, game, and wild plants, which supplemented their vegetable diet. Sometime before 1000 B.C., horticultural products had found their way into northeastern North America; gradually and at a varying rate they were integrated into the subsistence patterns of its people. Archaeologists have not yet determined when, precisely, the ancestors of the historic Iroquoians first began to farm. Although many suspect

---

what archaeologists designate the Late Woodland Period. See various chapters on the general "prehistory" of the region by James E. Fitting, Robert E. Funk, and James A. Tuck, as well as Tuck, "Northern Iroquoian Prehistory," in Bruce G. Trigger, ed., *Handbook of North American Indians: Northeast*, in William C. Sturtevant, gen. ed., *Handbook of North American Indians*, 20 vols. projected (Washington, D.C., 1978–), 15:14–57, 322–33. The following discussion draws also from these works: William A. Ritchie, *The Archaeology of New York State* (Garden City, N.Y., 1965); James A. Tuck, *Onondaga Iroquois Prehistory: A Study in Settlement Archaeology* (Syracuse, N.Y., 1971); Dean R. Snow, "Iroquois Prehistory," in Michael K. Foster et al., eds., *Extending the Rafters: Interdisciplinary Approaches to Iroquoian Studies* (Albany, 1984), 241–57; Mary Ann Palmer Niemczycki, *The Origins and Development of the Seneca and Cayuga Tribes of New York State*, Rochester Museum and Science Center Research Records, no. 17 (Rochester, N.Y., 1984); Charles F. Wray et al., *The Adams and Culbertson Site, Charles F. Wray Series in Seneca Archaeology*, 1 Rochester Museum and Science Center Research Records, no. 19 (Rochester, N.Y., 1987). For an insightful critique of the concept, "prehistory," see Neal Salisbury, "American Indians and American History," in Calvin Martin, ed., *The American Indian and the Problem of History* (New York, 1987), 46–54; see also Bruce G. Trigger, "American Archaeology as Native History: A Review Essay," *William and Mary Quarterly*, 3d ser., 40 (July 1983), 413–52.

that cultivation began earlier, perhaps as early as A.D. 200, it is in the Owasco period (1000–1300) that agricultural life can be seen with certainty in the archaeological record.[2]

The practice of horticulture implied a commitment to some form of sedentary life among the Owasco. Indeed, they lived in villages, hamlets, and satellite camps throughout the region, ranging in size from perhaps a few dozen to a few hundred people. At the largest reported site, in west-central New York near Canandaigua Lake, no more than 350 people made their home. While it seems logical that Owasco people began to live in permanent villages as a result of the introduction of horticulture, it is more likely that the Owasco and their ancestors began to farm because they preferred a settled way of life.[3]

As early as A.D. 500, Middle Woodland people in what became the Owasco region began to adopt more localized settlement patterns in contrast to the seasonally mobile way of life characteristic of their Late Archaic and Early Woodland forebears. These ancestors constructed their villages at productive fishing stations along rivers or at the edges of marshes and shallow lakes. Although their subsistence activities emphasized fishing, they continued to hunt and gather wild plants. More important, they developed a semi-sedentary way of life that kept them settled in their villages on a year-round basis, or at least during the spring, summer, and fall, which, not so coincidentally, corresponded to the growing season. The acquisition of semidomesticated plants, such as goosefoot (*chenopodium*), and efficient strategies of hunting, fishing, and collection, and preservation and storage, made a more geographically centralized life possible.[4]

At the beginning of the Owasco period, people built their villages in the fertile sites of their fishing grounds, on flood plains or just above on slightly higher terrain. The numerous cache pits and remains of large vessels found in these habitations suggest a stable and prosperous communal life. Yet by the end of the period, Owasco people seldom lived in these low-lying, indefensible locations. By the mid-twelfth century, the Owasco typically located their villages on more secure hilltops, above steep approaches, away from waterways, and surrounded them with palisades and ditchworks. These village loca-

---

[2]See Tuck, "Northern Iroquoian Prehistory," 324–26.
[3]Ritchie, *Archaeology of New York*, 286; Tuck, "Northern Iroquoian Prehistory," 325.
[4]Tuck, "Northern Iroquoian Prehistory," 325–26; Snow, "Iroquoian Prehistory," 249, 252–53.

tions, removed from other natural resources, and the increasing evidence of cultivated plants in archaeological remains, attest to the predominance of horticulture in Owasco life.[5] But the stockaded hilltops of the Owasco should caution us to avoid viewing this life in idyllic terms. The rejection of semisedentary life, and a return to center-based wandering by some Owasco people during this time—perhaps for the same reasons that motivated others to fortify their communities—should remind us that the development from Owasco into Iroquois was neither natural nor unilinear but historically contingent. The breakup of some Owasco villages and the defensive posture of others dramatically suggest the dangers and fears that increasingly crept into Owasco daily life.[6]

The Maxon-Derby archaeological site (occupied ca. A.D. 1100) lies in Onondaga County, New York, on a gentle slope of a low ridge that lacks any natural defensive features. This early Owasco village covered about two acres, was unpalisaded, and housed a maximum of 200 to 250 people. It was inhabited over a number of years, during which time the Owasco dwellers shifted the locations and modified the forms of their lodges on the site. During the early history of the village, the inhabitants seem to have lived in small, oblong houses with rounded ends. In the spring, when the ground was moist, they screwed bluntly pointed saplings into the earth and bent them over, making arborlike structures that could then be covered with bark. In addition to these small lodges, Owasco people built two dwellings at Maxon-Derby that more closely resembled Iroquois longhouses, both of which measured approximately sixty feet in length.

Archaeologists cannot determine whether these houses were constructed simultaneously with the smaller types or represented a replacement form. Nonetheless, the extended lodges were the result of gradual additions made to the structures over time. And the appearance of these proto-Iroquoian dwellings may suggest that the town experienced an increase in population, not merely through natural increase but by means of amalgamation of outsiders, as Owasco people drew together into fewer, larger villages. While the existence of multiple hearths in smaller Owasco lodges indicates that more than one

[5]Owasco reliance on horticulture is also suggested by the dental disorders, principally tooth decay, that archaeologists have observed in nearly every skeleton recovered at Owasco sites. Tooth decay was probably the by-product of a high starch diet associated with agriculture. See Ritchie, *Archaeology of New York*, 274–75.
[6]Niemczycki, *Origins of the Seneca and Cayuga*, 87.

family occupied a single house, many more families—probably related to each other—could live together in an extended lodge. This housing pattern represented a departure from tradition: an Owasco decision to concentrate and integrate a number of families within a single dwelling. And it may well have anticipated the extended family-clan social structure characteristic of the Five Nations in the seventeenth century, which cemented Iroquois communities together.[7]

Although the early Owasco community at Maxon-Derby apparently experienced peace and prosperity, conflict and a growing fear for safety may well have convinced later Owasco people to relocate their villages on higher, less accessible ground and to protect them with elaborate palisades, if those factors did not force them to abandon their sedentary ways altogether. The Sackett archaeological site on Arsenal Hill, near present-day Canandaigua, New York, represents a middle or late Owasco settlement. The village covered more than three acres, enclosed by an ellipsoidal ditch measuring 343 feet by 202 feet. The inhabitants dug the trench to a depth of two to three feet and to a width of seven to eleven feet, heaping up dirt to support a row of interior posts. Outlying ditchworks suggest that the settlement expanded over a number of years as population increased, most likely due as much to the incorporation of other Owasco individuals or small communities as to the fertility of Owasco people. At Sackett, people lived in small, oval, wigwamlike houses similar to those at Maxon-Derby. Although archaeologists failed to locate any proto-longhouses at the site, some features of the smaller lodges—narrow shelves or benches around the interior, for example—were standard in later Iroquois dwellings.

All these changes—the increase and nucleation of village populations, settlement in secure locations, erection of palisades and other defensive structures, and construction of proto-longhouses at late Owasco sites—suggest that the Owasco were moving toward the characteristic Iroquois settlement patterns and social and political organization. In the late Owasco period, we see the beginning of a process that would create the seventeenth-century Five Nations.[8]

[7]Ritchie, *Archaeology of New York*, 281–84; Snow, "Iroquoian Prehistory," 255; James A. Tuck, "The Iroquoian Confederacy," *Scientific American*, Feb. 1971, 35.

[8]Ritchie, *Archaeology of New York*, 286. Ritchie dated the Sackett site A.D. 1140 ± 150 years and favored a later rather than an earlier date (274). Tuck, "Northern Iroquoian Prehistory," 326–27, placed the site in the Late, or Castle Creek, Phase of Owasco culture. Ritchie uncovered an Owasco hamlet at the Bates site in Chenango County, New York, where a single large dwelling, elongated in four expansions, grew in length from thirty-eight to seventy-

What emerges from the archaeological reconstruction of later Owasco life is a picture of an increasingly localized, complexly organized, isolated, defensive, and parochial people. At the same time that Owasco villages grew in size and decreased in number, they became more completely self-sufficient, because of a greater emphasis on horticulture and a declining dependence on hunting and fishing, though these subsistence activities remained important. Trade declined; in pre-Owasco times exchange networks had connected Woodland bands with the elaborate cultures of the Ohio Valley, and perhaps beyond to Cahokia in mid-America. The nature and frequency of travel changed as Owasco people settled further from waterways and developed forest routes that kept them closer to home. Diffused cultural patterns that ancestors of the Owasco shared with people throughout northeastern North America—complex mortuary ceremonialism, featuring numerous and exotic burial goods, for example—faded in the isolated Owasco communities as they developed their own, simpler "microtraditions."[9]

As localized Owasco groups withdrew into themselves, they constructed new means of cultural and social integration. The incipient Iroquois longhouse, the dominant architectural form by late Owasco times, was such an integration. Among the Iroquois, extended lodges housed people of a common matrilineal family and clan, and among the Owasco ancestors of the Iroquois the gradual emergence of the longhouse may reflect and express physically the formation of matrilineal family and clan structures.[10] Iroquoianists believe that clans

three feet. This small village, dated A.D. 1190, was palisaded (284). The Chamberlin archaeological site, approximately three miles southeast of Maxon-Derby, represents a later Owasco settlement (ca. A.D. 1290). A ring of earth, suggesting a palisade, surrounded the town, and houses more than eighty feet long were identified. As in other Owasco longhouses, hearths were located along one wall, rather than down the center of the dwelling in Iroquois fashion. These extended lodges constituted the characteristic Owasco type by the end of the Owasco era. On the Chamberlin site see Tuck, *Onondaga Prehistory*, 29–31; Tuck, "Iroquois Confederacy," 35; Bradley, *Evolution of the Onondaga,* 14–21.

[9]Ritchie, *Archaeology of New York,* 293, 295–96; Tuck, "Northern Iroquoian Prehistory," 326; Tuck, "Iroquois Confederacy," 35; Snow, "Iroquoian Prehistory," 255–56. Microtraditions were particularly pronounced in the development of divergent styles of pottery decoration. Dena F. Dincauze and Robert J. Hasenstab, "Explaining the Iroquois: Tribalization or a Prehistoric Periphery," *Comparative Studies in the Development of Complex Societies,* vol. 3, session 4, World Archaeological Congress (September 1986), especially 9–10, have proposed an explanation of Iroquois tribalization based on their fourteenth-century response on the periphery to encroachment by an expansive secondary core (related to a primary core in Cahokia) centered in the Ohio Valley. It is by no means inconceivable that these pressures contributed to the developments under discussion here, which Dincauze and Hasenstab summarize.

[10]On the nature and meaning of longhouses in Iroquois life, see Lewis Henry Morgan,

originally formed about 1000 B.C. as a consequence of widespread Early and Middle Woodland patterns of trade and ritualism, not simply as an outgrowth of kinship groups. During the Owasco period clans probably developed further and assumed some of the new integrative functions characteristic of the Iroquois.[11]

Religious concepts issue only equivocally from archaeological excavation. Nonetheless, artifacts unearthed at Owasco sites, such as images of the human face formed in clay and on smoking pipes, and an antler pendant carved into a mask, suggest some affinity between Owasco and Iroquois belief systems. These artifacts may anticipate, according to some archaeologists, motifs made popular in False Face Society curing rituals, especially since turtle shell rattles later associated with these rites have also been recovered from Owasco sites. Current research questions such an interpretation, but the faces may nonetheless indicate the advent of curing and social societies not unlike those common among later Iroquois communities.[12]

Miniature pots and pipes similarly suggested later Iroquois belief and ritual to James A. Tuck, the archaeologist who found them on Owasco sites. In these objects, Tuck saw the paraphernalia of "dream-guessing," a practice among the Iroquois that sought to discover and satisfy the hidden wishes of the soul as a means to health and vitality. The absence of such ceremonial and ritual material in the pre-Owasco

---

League of the Ho-de-no-sau-nee, Iroquois, ed., William N. Fenton (Secaucus, N.J., 1962 [orig. pub. Rochester, N.Y., 1851]), 315–19; Lewis Henry Morgan, *Houses and House-Life of the American Aborigines* (Chicago, 1965 [orig. pub. in *Contributions to North American Ethnology,* 4 (Washington, D.C., 1881)]), 34, 64–67, 125–28; Peter Nabokov and Robert Easton, *Native American Architecture* (New York, 1989), 76–91, especially 85–87. New research on the nature of life within these Iroquois houses, with implications for understanding the proposed transition from patrilinear to matrilinear social organization among prehistoric Iroquois is reported in Mima Kapches, "The Spatial Dynamics of Ontario Iroquoian Longhouses," *American Antiquity,* 55, no. 1 (1990), 49–67.

[11]Snow, "Iroquoian Prehistory," 251–53, 255–56; Tuck, "Northern Iroquoian Prehistory," 326–27; Elisabeth Tooker, "Women in Iroquois Society," in Foster et al., eds., *Extending the Rafters,* 109–23, which provides a useful summary of Iroquois clan and political systems (see especially 110–11). Clans emerging during this period would not necessarily have been the same ones observed in the colonial era, though their function—to provide hospitality, reciprocity, and social integration—may well have been similar.

[12]Ritchie, *Archaeology of New York,* 299; Snow, *Archaeology of New England,* 316; cf. Zena Pearlstone Mathews, "Of Man and Beast: The Chronology of Effigy Pipes among Ontario Iroquoians," *Ethnohistory,* 27 (Fall 1980), 295–307. See also William N. Fenton, *The False Faces of the Iroquois* (Norman, Okla., 1987), 66–71. Fenton was reluctant to see these human face effigies as early examples of False Faces; nonetheless, he reported their increasing appearance in the archaeological record in the fifteenth century, "a period when the Iroquois began to concentrate in large towns, form political alliances leading to the league, and celebrate the rites of medicine societies such as the False Faces." "Such activities became possible under the new conditions," he continued, "but we have no solid evidence of what was really going on" (70).

archaeological record may suggest that Iroquoian religious beliefs and practices took shape in the Owasco period. The appearance of these early forms of curing or dream-guessing rites may have served to bind the developing Owasco communities together and to help them address the new problems they faced as they entered a new era.[13] We may see in these artifacts, then, a foreshadowing of the integrative institutions that united the people of the Five Nations and upheld their law of peace.

But why did Owasco people, dramatically if gradually, transform the nature of their lives? The concentration of inhabitants and their construction of great earthworks and palisades attest to an increasing concern for defense. And the discovery at Sackett of arrow-riddled skeletons, some with as many as eleven arrow points embedded in bone, offers striking "mute testimony" to the danger of violent death that Owasco people faced in their daily lives. Taken together, this material evidence suggests that, beginning some time toward the middle of the Owasco period—roughly, in the mid-twelfth century—endemic internecine warfare developed, because the arrows that killed the Owasco men at the Sackett site were of Owasco manufacture. Why did Owasco people begin to slay each other, initiating a pattern of warfare and blood revenge that would continue into the Iroquoian era?[14]

Some scholars have argued that the shift in emphasis from hunting activities, dominated by men, to horticulture, dominated by women, allowed men to change the object of their hunts from animals to men. Released from many subsistence tasks, and finding power in their larger numbers, they took to the warpath more frequently, engaging in what one historian has described as an "insane, unending, continuously attritional" warfare. The increase of their population and the development of a system of subsistence based on more intensive farm-

[13]Tuck, *Onondaga Prehistory*, 40–41; on dream-guessing, see J. N. B. Hewitt, "The Iroquoian Concept of the Soul," *Journal of American Folk-Lore*, 8 (1895), 107–16; Anthony F. C. Wallace, "Dreams and the Wishes of the Soul: A Type of Psychoanalytic Theory among the Seventeenth-Century Iroquois," *American Anthropologist*, n.s. 60 (1958), 234–48, which in slightly revised form appears in Wallace, *The Death and Rebirth of the Seneca* (New York, 1970), 59–75.
[14]Tuck, *Onondaga Prehistory*, 293. Cultural similarity—as among the Owasco bands, or among seventeenth-century Iroquoians for that matter—does not preclude such warfare, and we should not necessarily expect peoples sharing common languages and customs to share a single polity or society. Nonetheless, the warfare described below has been termed (perhaps inappropriately) "internecine" or fratricidal by scholars. And, significantly, the Iroquois themselves would retroactively represent it as a cycle of violence pitting brother against brother.

Palisaded Iroquoian town under siege, from Joseph-François Lafitau, *Moeurs des sauvages amériquains,*
comparées aux moeurs des premiers temps (Paris, 1724), courtesy of Special Collections, Knight Library,
University of Oregon. As an initial response to internecine violence, the Iroquois sought more
isolated, defensible locations for their towns and surrounded them with elaborate palisades and
earthworks. Later, through consolidation and amalgamation of formerly hostile communities, they
attempted to construct a landscape of peace.

ing might well have led to an accelerating demographic demand upon land and game resources; game was important not merely as a supplement to a vegetable diet, but also as a source of hides, furs, and bones needed in the manufacture of tools. Together, these factors seem to provide both opportunity and motive for increased warfare,[15] but recent research suggests alternative hypotheses.

The advent of agriculture and changing gender arrangements may have made such internecine fighting possible, but they did not make it inevitable, nor in fact do they seem to explain what happened historically. Increased population and more concentrated settlement may have placed greater stress on local ecosystems, but Owasco communities—or later Iroquoian ones—did not exceed the carrying capacity of their common environment. The ancestors of the Owasco had begun to live a more sedentary life *before* they participated in a fully developed agricultural complex. And as farming was not a prerequisite to settled life, internecine warfare was not its necessary result. Like their descendants, Owasco people enjoyed abundance and prosperity in the diversity of their subsistence, and there was plenty to go around.[16] Nonetheless, they increasingly found themselves living in a landscape of violence, a world of fear that humans, not impersonal environmental forces, had created. And they chose to live in isolated, palisaded villages and to raid those around them—their cultural if not their social or political brethren. We are thus faced with the puzzling fact of this violent landscape as the Owasco era gave way to the Iroquoian.

Archaeologists have discerned four regional variants of Owasco culture: ancestral Mohawk in the easternmost part of Iroquoia,

[15]See John Whitthoft, "Ancestry of the Susquehannocks," in Whitthoft and W. Fred Kinsey III, eds., *Susquehannock Miscellany*, Pennsylvania Historical and Museum Commission (Harrisburg, Pa., 1959), 32–34; Ritchie, *Archaeology of New York*, 281; see also Tuck, "Northern Iroquoian Prehistory," 326; quotation from Alfred L. Kroeber, "Cultural and Natural Areas of Native North America," *University of California Publications in American Archaeology and Ethnology*, 38 (Berkeley, Calif., 1939), 148–49.

[16]On the relationship between environment, agriculture, and warfare in the region, see Bruce G. Trigger, "Settlement as an Aspect of Iroquoian Adaptation at the Time of Contact," in Bruce Cox, ed., *Cultural Ecology: Readings on Canadian Indians and Eskimos* (Toronto, 1973), 35–53, especially 49–50; William Engelbrecht, "Factors Maintaining Low Population Density among the Prehistoric New York Iroquois," *American Antiquity*, 52 (January 1987), 13–27, especially 14–16, 22; Snow, "Peoples in Contact: Indians and Europeans in the Seventeenth Century," unpublished symposium paper, delivered at the Haffenreffer Museum of Anthropology, Bristol, Rhode Island, September 26–27, 1986; and Snow, *Archaeology of New England*, 314, which even suggests that intervillage warfare may have hampered hunting and fishing and thus encouraged rather than hindered horticulture and its intensification.

Onondaga-Oneida in north-central New York, Cayuga-Seneca in the west, and Neutral-Erie on the Ontario peninsula. But the Owasco people and outsiders who joined them were more alike than different at the dawn of the Iroquois period. The trends begun in Owasco times continued, and in the increasing consolidation of divided Owasco people into ever larger, isolated communities, individual tribes emerged that would later form the Iroquois League of Peace (and, for that matter, the rival confederations in northeastern North America—Huron-Petun, Neutral, Erie, and Susquehannock). Archaeologists have learned more about the formation of the Onondaga tribe than about that of the other constituent Iroquois groups, though recent and continuing research on the Mohawks and Senecas particularly elaborates our understanding of tribal construction and confederation. On the basis of this work, we can begin to describe and interpret these developments throughout Iroquoia in late aboriginal times and place in a wider context the unique response of the Five Nations to the common problem of internecine warfare.[17]

Continuing the trends begun in the Owasco era, one group of Owasco people living in north-central New York bound themselves together into a new tribal group, the Onondagas. In many ways they continued to live like their Owasco ancestors, but the Onondaga way of life nonetheless signaled an evolutionary shift with profound implications for Iroquoia. The process of village fusion continued until only two major palisaded communities existed in Onondaga. Within their territory, the Onondagas effected a pacification that assured their internal safety and provided them strength when they faced

[17]Tuck, *Onondaga Iroquois Prehistory*, 16. The following reconstruction of Onondaga "prehistorical" development draws heavily on this work and on Bradley, *Evolution of the Onondaga*. On Mohawk "prehistory," see especially the work of Dean R. Snow, and the findings of the Mohawk Valley Project, which are beginning to appear; see also Snow, "Peoples in Contact; and Snow, *Archaeology of New England*, 90–94, 308–19. On Seneca and Cayuga developments, see Charles F. Wray and Harry Schoff, "A Preliminary Report on the Seneca Sequence in Western New York, 1550–1687," *Pennsylvania Archaeologist*, 8, no. 2 (1953), 53–63; Wray, *Manual for Seneca Iroquois Archaeology* (Rochester, N.Y., 1973). Important revisions appear in Niemczycki, *Origins and Development of the Seneca and Cayuga* and Niemczycki, "The Genesee Connection," 15–44; Wray et al., *The Adams and Culbertson Sites*. Iroquoian archaeologists divide Iroquois "prehistory" into a number of phases, corresponding somewhat loosely to important cultural developments, especially changes in political organization and material culture. The following approximate dates are Tuck's (see *Onondaga Prehistory*, 19): Oak Hill Phase (1300–1400); Chance Phase (1400–1500), when, he suggests, the newly established five Iroquois nations came together in their confederation; Garoga Phase (1500–1575); Onondaga Proto-Historical Phase (1575–1654). Though recently subjected to some modification—especially in western New York—these phases have been generally endorsed; see Niemczycki, "The Genesee Connection."

outside aggression. Social and cultural integration achieved in relative separation from other Iroquois people made internal peace possible, and it set the stage for continued fusion and alliance with other Iroquois people, who were undergoing a similar process of tribal development in other parts of Iroquoia.

In the period between the mid-thirteenth and the mid-fifteenth centuries, three or four proto-Onondaga communities coexisted uneasily in Onondaga. Living in mutual fear, they located their villages on hilltops at safe distances from one another and surrounded them with defensive structures. They continued to farm, hunt, fish, and gather wild foods in the pattern their Owasco forebears had passed on to them. At the archaeological sites of these communities, investigators have observed population increases and considerable expansion and shifting within villages. Some smaller Owascoid lodges still existed among these people, but more striking was the discovery of extremely long houses at many of the sites. Longhouses, with internal arrangements much like historic Iroquois structures (storage areas at the end of the house, benches or beds built along internal walls, and interior hearths arranged along a center aisle), measured as long as 210 feet at one early village, and as long as 334 and 400 feet at two other late fourteenth–early fifteenth-century sites.[18]

The palisades and earthworks built by the Onondagas' immediate ancestors were even more impressive than those constructed at Owasco villages and must have required great toil. At the Kelso archaeological site, near Elbridge, New York, early Onondagas dug trenches, pushed poles into the damp earth, and interwove smaller brush between them, making a double or triple wall of defense that stood at least fifteen feet high around their village. An early Mohawk site in Montgomery County, New York, which was occupied in the fourteenth century, exhibited a similar powerful emphasis on defense. An oval, double-walled stockade enclosed the village. Some archaeologists have even speculated that the two palisades may have been bridged at the top with a platform upon which defenders could stand and fight, shielded by a higher outer wall.[19] These elaborate structures testify to the ongoing fears that early Iroquois people faced as a result of endemic internecine warfare.

Concern for safety, archaeologists believe, caused the smaller bands

[18]Tuck, *Onondaga Prehistory*, 59–60, 79–85, 96–97; Tuck, "Northern Iroquois Prehistory," 327–28; Tuck, "Iroquois Confederacy," 35.
[19]Tuck, *Onondaga Prehistory*, 72; Ritchie, *Archaeology of New York*, 306, 313–14.

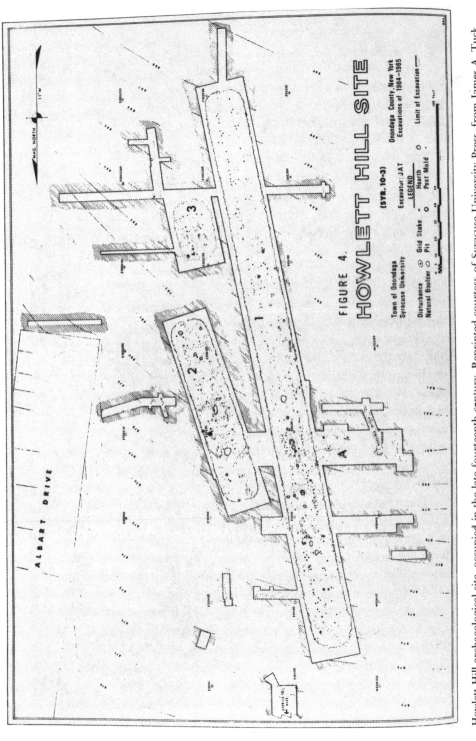

Howlett Hill archaeological site, occupied in the late fourteenth century. Reprinted courtesy of Syracuse University Press, from James A. Tuck, *Onondaga Iroquois Prehistory: A Study in Settlement Archaeology* (Syracuse, 1971). House 1, excavated 1964–65, measured some 334 feet in length, making it the largest house then known in Iroquoia.

Aerial view (looking south) of excavations at the Howlett Hill site, occupied late in the fourteenth century, showing the post-mold patterns of longhouses, which had been repeatedly expanded. Reprinted courtesy of Syracuse University Press, from James A. Tuck, *Onondaga Iroquois Prehistory: A Study in Settlement Archaeology* (Syracuse, 1971).

GÄ-NO-SOTE
or
BARK HOUSE.

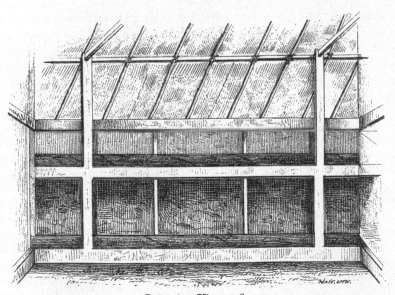

Interior View of
BARK HOUSE.

An Iroquois longhouse, from Lewis Henry Morgan, *League of the Ho-de-no-sau-nee, Iroquois* (Rochester, N.Y., 1851). This nineteenth-century replica varies from typical longhouses of an earlier time, both in its gable construction and its relatively short length. Seventeenth-century longhouses could extend for a hundred feet or more and typically had rounded, arborlike roofs. Courtesy of Special Collections, Knight Library, University of Oregon.

of late Owasco and early Onondaga people remaining in Onondaga
to amalgamate with the larger communities that were taking shape.
In this fashion, communities grew more than they would otherwise
have grown simply through natural increase. And through this process of amalgamation, a pattern of dispersed settlement gave way fully
to a nucleated one, characterized by dense concentration in villages,
which were surrounded by vast tracts of unsettled territory. In these
villages and concentric unoccupied zones, the early Onondagas sought
isolation and security; they began to remake Onondaga into a landscape of peace.[20]

Applying recently developed techniques in settlement archaeology
and ceramic analysis to the Onondagas, James A. Tuck was able to
trace single Onondaga communities over hundreds of years and
through numerous village removals and relocations.[21] Tuck concluded from his site excavations that the Onondaga tribe formed, not
only by the incorporation of outlying bands, but also by the construction of nonaggression agreements, leading ultimately to a full ethnic
amalgamation of the few major proto-Onondaga communities. Community patterning over time reflected this striking development. The
sudden disappearance of a large community in the archaeological
record and the simultaneous appearance of a new village, ten miles
away, dangerously close to another well-established community, Tuck
interpreted as the relocation of a single community. In that move, we
can see the formation of the Onondaga Nation. Without a formal
agreement of consolidation into a single tribal unit, such a provocative
relocation would have represented a fundamental violation of village
space and spelled disaster for one or both of the communities.[22]

This village merger and tribal formation—and the two-village settlement pattern it inaugurated—occurred some time in the mid-
fifteenth century, and the Onondagas continued to live in this fashion

[20]Tuck, *Onondaga Prehistory*, 212; Tuck, "Northern Iroquoian Prehistory," 327.

[21]On larger shifts within American archaeology, especially new concern, in the 1950s,
about "context" and settlement patterns (148–53), and new techniques in the 1960s, for
deriving insights into social and political organization from ceramic evidence (199–201), see
Gordon R. Willey and Jeremy A. Sabloff, *A History of American Archaeology* (London, 1974).
Richard S. MacNeish, *Iroquois Pottery Types: A Technique for the Study of Iroquois Prehistory*,
National Museum of Canada, Bulletin no. 124 (Ottawa, 1952), reoriented recent Iroquoian
archaeology with its analysis of ceramics and its hypothesis that the Iroquois were the product
of an extended chronological, *in situ* development.

[22]Tuck, *Onondaga Prehistory*, 92, 139–41; see also Tuck, "Iroquois Confederacy," 35–39;
Tuck, "Northern Iroquoian Prehistory," 326–27. Tuck identified the new village with the
older, vanished community by means of the distinct continuity he observed in pottery decoration at the two sites. Together they formed a single microtradition.

into the colonial period. This fusion was part of a much larger process; the host village, identified as the Christopher archaeological site near Pompey, New York, had itself formed from the amalgamation of two smaller proto-Onondaga towns. And in the larger Iroquois confederation we observe a continuation of that process. It came to be constructed, perhaps some time in the following century, from the Onondaga and the four other nations—Mohawk, Oneida, Cayuga, and Seneca—each of which underwent a similar formation. And as it took shape, the Iroquois League of Peace was not viewed as a closed political entity once it had united the Five Nations. The Iroquois saw their confederation as part of a peace-making process that would continue as it embraced more people under the Great Tree of Peace, until their entire universe was pacified. Archaeological data cannot, of course, offer a definitive explanation of how the Onondaga and the other Iroquois nations formed; but a weariness of warfare and a deep desire to be free of fear probably motivated the Five Nations as they molded their social, political, and physical landscape.[23]

Common tribal names and ethnic identities must have followed quickly from the village consolidations throughout Iroquoia. Marriage within the new tribal groups solidified each nation's sense of common identity and transformed the political amalgamation into a full social unity based on kinship. The clan system, which had assumed new responsibilities in the Owasco period, probably acquired its historic functions in this period. Clans bound communities and nations together in a form of kinship even when real blood ties were lacking. Exogamous clan marriage rules—prohibiting marriage between members of the same clan—further served to integrate people within particular nations and, after the formation of the Iroquois confederation, throughout Iroquoia.[24]

[23]On the Christopher site and the achievement of consolidation, see Tuck, *Onondaga Prehistory*, 122–25, 212–14, and Tuck, "Iroquois Confederacy," 37; Bradley, *Evolution of the Onondaga*, 26–34. See also Niemczycki, *Origins and Development of the Seneca and Cayuga*, 87–88, 91–94, which argues that the Senecas and Cayugas followed a similar developmental process. On the Mohawks, see Snow, *Archaeology of New England*, 308–9, 316–19. Tuck, "Northern Iroquoian Prehistory," 327, noticed that the prophet Deganawidah was said to have blotted out the sun in the traditional account of his founding of the League; a solar eclipse was visible in central New York in 1451. Of course, speculation on the League's date of origin varies widely, from the fifteenth century, or earlier, to the colonial era; most scholars agree, however, that it preceded direct contact with Europeans.

[24]Niemczycki, *Origins and Development of the Seneca and Cayuga*, 45–68, 84–85. Niemczycki emphasizes the importance of the tribe among the emergent Iroquois, defined as "a confederation of multilineage communities linked through the cross-cutting clans and nonlineal sodalities to which their members belong" (84); this "may be accompanied by the territorial

The process of amalgamation and integration is also objectified in Iroquois dwellings. The long houses at early Onondaga sites indicate the existence of large and growing social groups, and they reflect the early stages of a bold social and political experiment in peace. The four-hundred-foot longhouse at the early fifteenth-century Schoff site at Onondaga, New York, probably housed a single matrilineal extended family or clan.[25] Such a massive structure concretely represented, in architectural terms, the social solidarity of these early communities. But as villages continued to grow and the Onondaga Nation took shape, increases in population and in the size of social units could no longer be accommodated in their architectural structures. Lodges of four hundred feet, with only two doors, posed substantial problems to those who lived within them, to say nothing of how impractical it would be to extend them further.

Growing confidence in the deeper solidarity developing among the Onondagas (and other Iroquois people) allowed them to adjust their living arrangements, while retaining the longhouse, and its extendability, as a symbol of unity and peace through incorporation. As tribal identity was achieved among the Onondagas, then, house size decreased and became standardized. The typical Iroquois extended lodge of the colonial period measured from fifty to eighty feet in length and seventeen to eighteen feet in width. This shift seems to reflect the social reorganization that necessarily occurred following tribal formation. Patterns of marriage limited to a single community were no doubt extended to encompass the two villages of the Onondaga Nation. And with a more effective clan structure binding communities together, the Onondaga and the other nations did not need to establish physically what they had now firmly constituted socially and symbolically. The clans, constructed of adopted as well as real kin, and composed of multiple lineages even if identified vaguely with

---

consolidation of a large population in a compromise between dispersal and nucleation in which the population remains distributed within several villages" (85). Such was the case with the people of the Five Nations, who maintained very close intratribal and intertribal ties while settling in several separate, often distant, communities spread throughout Iroquoia. On clans and their integrating effect on Iroquois society, see Morgan, *League of the Iroquois*, 78–87; Fenton, "Northern Iroquoian Culture Patterns," 309–12; A. A. Goldenweiser, "On Iroquois Work, 1912 and 1913–1914," in *Summary Report of the Geological Survey Branch of the Canadian Department of Mines for the Calendar Years 1912 and 1913* (Ottawa, 1914), 464–75, 365–72; Annemarie Anrod Shimony, *Conservatism among the Iroquois at the Six Nations Reserve, Yale University Publications in Anthropology*, 65 (New Haven, 1961), 27; Tooker, "Women in Iroquois Society," 110–18.

[25] Tuck, "Northern Iroquoian Prehistory," 328; Tuck, *Onondaga Prehistory*, 95, 96.

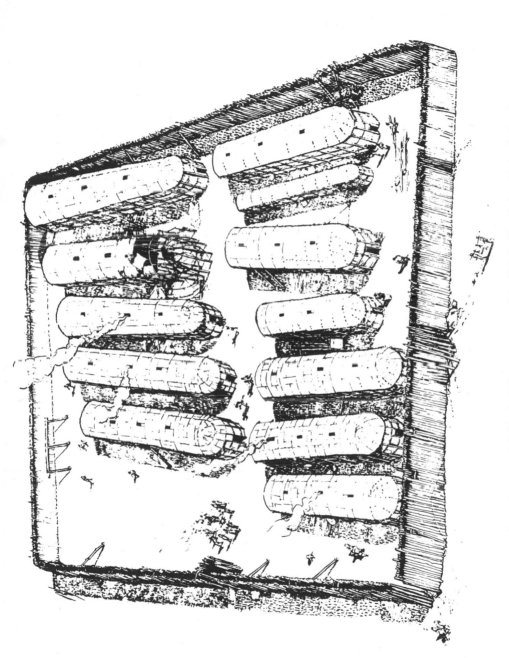

The Mohawk village of Caughnawaga, inhabited 1666–93, courtesy of the Tekakwitha Shrine, Mohawk-Caughnawaga Museum, Fonda, New York.

a single extended family, could now be housed in separate, smaller dwellings, each occupied by fewer people genuinely related through kinship or affinity, that is, through marriage.[26]

The archaeological record reflects the constitution of the Onondaga Nation—and later, the Great League of Peace—in other suggestive ways. The Iroquois institutions taking shape in earlier periods seem to have emerged more clearly as community convergence led to the formation of the five Iroquois nations. In addition to clans, the existence of medicine societies resembling those among the seventeenth- and eighteenth-century Iroquois is indicated in the human face motifs that abound at Onondaga sites dating from the late fifteenth century to the colonial period. Archaeologists contend that the institutions these artifacts suggest assumed a crucial socially integrative function in the newly formed communities. Like Iroquois clans, ritual and ceremonial groups such as the False Face, Eagle, Bear, Buffalo, and Little Water Societies cut across traditional kin lines and established new patterns of interaction which equally involved members from older communities.[27]

At the same time, the archaeological record reflects a new trend away from the localism that had characterized the immediate ancestors of the Iroquois, as well as a subtle shift in settlement location and fortification, and perhaps suggests a growing sense of security among the peoples of the new tribes and the larger confederacy. Among the Onondagas, for example, internal distinctiveness in their ceramics all but disappeared; styles and motifs were increasingly standardized among them, so that pots produced by different women in different villages were virtually indistinguishable. This seems also to have been true among the Senecas and Cayugas, who in addition to establishing

[26]Tuck, "Northern Iroquoian Prehistory," 328; Tuck, *Onondaga Prehistory*, 167, 170, 182; William Engelbrecht, "New York Iroquois Political Development," in William W. Fitzhugh, ed., *Cultures in Contact: The Impact of European Contacts on Native American Cultural Institutions, A.D. 1000–1800* (Washington, D.C., 1985), 173–74. On Iroquois longhouses in the colonial period see descriptions in George M. Wrong, ed., H. H. Langton, trans., [Father Gabriel Sagard's] *Long Journey to the Country of the Hurons, Publications of the Champlain Society*, 25 (Toronto, 1939 [orig. pub. Paris, 1632]), 93–95; William N. Fenton and Elizabeth Moore, eds. and trans., [Father Joseph-François de Lafitau's] *Customs of the American Indians Compared with the Customs of Primitive Times, Publications of the Champlain Society*, 48, 2 vols. (Toronto, 1974 [orig. pub. Paris, 1724]), 2:19–23; W. L. Grant, ed., *Voyages of Samuel de Champlain, 1604–1618, Original Narratives of Early American History*, gen. ed., J. Franklin Jameson (New York, 1907), 313–14; John Bartram, *Travels in Pensilvania and Canada* (Ann Arbor, Mich., 1966 [orig. pub. 1751]), frontispiece, 20–21, 40. See also Morgan, *Houses and House-Life*, 125–30; Nabokov and Easton, *Native American Architecture*, 76–86.
[27]Tuck, *Onondaga Prehistory*, 213; see also Tuck, "Iroquois Confederacy," 42; Bradley, *Evolution of the Onondaga*, 64, 217n24.

greater uniformity within their tribes—as measured by ceramic analysis—increasingly exhibited a marked similarity and unity with each other during the sixteenth century. Indeed, this process of convergence spread throughout Iroquoia. Increased communication, migration, alliance, and consolidation produced—at least by the end of the sixteenth century—a pan-Iroquois material culture related to the Five Nations' emerging identity and society, expressed eventually in their League of Peace. In Iroquois material culture, archaeologists have also discovered an increase in nonlocal materials, like marine shell, native copper, and, beginning in the second quarter of the sixteenth century, European materials, copper, iron, and glass. The marked increase of these substances, and the uniformity of their initial appearance and occurrence among the constituent nations, imply both a new, nonlocal vision and cooperation among the emergent Five Nations.[28]

Perhaps as a result of this new expansiveness and sense of unity, the Iroquois began to exhibit subtle changes in the sites they chose for villages and the fortifications they constructed to protect them. While continuities in settlement patterns remained more important than innovations, nonetheless the Onondagas and others now occasionally placed their villages on secondary elevations, above river valleys rather than on hilltops, and tentatively they replaced massive fortifications with simpler palisades.[29]

The Iroquois League of Peace represented a culmination of an experimental process. This cultural creation, beginning at the band level, continuing with the consolidation of tribes, and then extending throughout Iroquoia, strongly favored pacification, amalgamation, and integration. For the people who found themselves arrayed throughout Iroquoia in a grand confederation, there was no reason to expect that the process of peace would end. Instead, experience

---

[28]Tuck, *Onondaga Prehistory*, 219–20; Tuck, "Iroquois Confederacy," 42; Tuck, "Northern Iroquoian Prehistory," 331–32. See also Ritchie, *Archaeology of New York*, 316; Bradley, *Evolution of the Onondaga*, 37–38, 41–43, 212–13n36, 69–78, 104; Niemczycki, *Origins of the Seneca and Cayuga*, especially summaries on 68, 75–77.

[29]See Bradley, *Evolution of the Onondaga*, 34–35; the Burke site, which gives rise to these speculations about changing village location and fortification, may be exceptional. Less complex fortifications may have been an adaptation to larger populations, which would have taxed local environments more heavily, necessitating more frequent village relocations. By the eighteenth century, Iroquois settlements assumed dispersed patterns, and longhouses gave way to smaller, nuclear family dwellings. See, for example, Niemczycki, *Origins of the Seneca and Cayuga*, 77, and Thomas S. Abler and Elisabeth Tooker, "Seneca," in Trigger, ed., *Handbook of North American Indians: Northeast*, 15:507.

was to serve as an ongoing formula for stability, security, prosperity, and peace, both within and beyond the boundaries of Iroquoia. Their achievement in the fifteenth and sixteenth centuries suggested to the Iroquois that other peoples, individually and in larger political groups, could be peacefully incorporated into their human and natural landscape and transformed symbolically, and quite literally, into Iroquois.[30]

Greater prosperity, in addition to security, was a by-product of tribal consolidation and confederation. Expanded, nucleated settlements effected a larger-scale and more intensive horticulture among the Iroquois, even as they maintained a diversified subsistence. Beyond their villages and fields, the unoccupied land that they created provided zones of safety and reciprocity as well as rich gathering and hunting grounds. These large spaces between Iroquois towns, and extending to the borders of Iroquoia, bound the Five Nations together into a common landscape of peace and prosperity. Deganawidah, the ancient Iroquois prophet, and the original sachems of the confederation had represented these margins as "one dish, in which shall be placed one beaver's tail, and we shall all have co-equal right to it." The bowl signified that "they will make their hunting grounds one common tract and all have a coequal right to hunt within it." And in the Condolence Ceremony they bequeathed to the Five Nations, the founders enjoined the Iroquois to "clear the forest paths" between their villages, remove the thorns that embedded themselves in travelers' feet, eliminate the "border of bushes" that separated communities, and make the intervening landscape "lie flat."[31]

The increased sizes of the Iroquois communities in the colonial period placed greater strains on the land in the vicinity of villages.

---

[30]Bradley, *Evolution of the Onondaga,* 83–87, sees the incorporation of some remnants of the St. Lawrence Iroquois by the Onondagas as another example or extension of this process.

[31]Paul A. W. Wallace, *The White Roots of Peace* (Philadelphia, 1946), 31–32; Arthur C. Parker, "The Traditional Narrative of the Origins of the Confederation of the Five Nations, Commonly Known as the Iroquois," in *The Constitution of the Five Nations, or the Iroquois Book of the Great Law,* in William N. Fenton, ed., *Parker on the Iroquois* (Syracuse, N.Y., 1968 [orig. pub. as *New York State Museum Bulletin,* no. 184 (Albany, 1916), 7–158]), 103; William M. Beauchamp, *Civil, Religious and Mourning Councils and Ceremonies of Adoption of the New York Indians, New York State Museum Bulletin,* no. 113 (Albany, 1907), 393; J. N. B. Hewitt, "Constitution of the Iroquois League, Or that for which the Fire was Kindled which Established the Long Lodge," NAA ms. 3599 and Hewitt, "The Laws of Adoption," NAA ms. 496; William N. Fenton, "Structure, Continuity, and Change in the Process of Iroquois Treaty Making," in Francis Jennings et al., eds., *History and Culture of Iroquois Diplomacy: An Interdisciplinary Guide to the Treaties of the Six Nations and Their League* (Syracuse, N.Y., 1985), 21. For a seventeenth-century example of this rhetoric and symbolic action, see Reuben Gold Thwaites, ed., *The Jesuit Relations and Allied Documents,* 73 vols. (Cleveland, 1896–1901), 41:73.

Villagers exhausted soil and depleted firewood sources more quickly than they had in the past. But the vast territory available in Iroquoia allowed land to recover easily under the traditional Iroquois pattern of village relocation. Such moves began to take place more frequently in the late sixteenth and early seventeenth centuries, every twenty-five years or so, as opposed to the seventy or more years of occupation typical in the fourteenth century.[32] More frequent village removals and concentrated settlement patterns, which provided safety and efficient subsistence without overburdening the landscape, allowed the Iroquois a more secure, prosperous life. Like a vast sea, Iroquoia served simultaneously to separate, join, and support Iroquois communities.

We should be careful not to romanticize our view of the Iroquois world on the eve of their direct encounter with Europeans. Hardship, want, and war continued and could never be permanently banished. At the Adams and Culbertson sites (ca. 1560–75) in west-central New York, which have been identified as the initial paired settlements of the newly formed Seneca Nation, archaeologists have unearthed evidence of at least two severe food shortages, perhaps associated with epidemic disease, and the assimilation of a large number of foreign women, most likely refugees or captives of war. At a site some thirty miles away (ca. 1440–1510), excavation indicated burned dwellings and slaughter of numerous men. It is not clear who destroyed this community, nor is the origin of the women who joined the emergent nation certain. One hypothetical reconstruction linked these sites tentatively by suggesting aggression, conquest, and assimilation by the Seneca people at Adams and Culbertson. Another likely reconstruction envisions attack by outsiders, then aid, sanctuary, and incorporation by the people forming themselves into Senecas. Despite our uncertainty, it is clear that war remained a threat, as did drought and famine; together they functioned as environmental factors that forced a creative response by Seneca and other Iroquois people.[33]

Such ongoing struggles with the natural and human environment notwithstanding, the establishment of the Great League of Peace did

---

[32]Tuck, *Onondaga Prehistory*, 213–14. See also Trigger, "Settlement as an Aspect of Iroquoian Adaptation," especially 47–49.

[33]Wray et al., *The Adams and Culbertson Sites;* for summary and interpretation see 239–56; on famine and death indicated by osteological and mortuary evidence, see 241–42, 255; on the assimilation of outside women and the possible relationship to violence, see 247–48. The authors note that explorers of the eastern seaboard observed drought and famine during the years 1564–70 (242).

Mohawk elm bark feast bowl, a facsimile of an old bowl taken to Canada by Mohawks led by Joseph Brant in the eighteenth century, decorated by a Seneca artist on the Cattaraugus Reserve in 1899. The bowl's interior is divided into five sections by painted beavers' tails, symbolizing peace and plenty. Above each section is the name of one of the Five Nations. According to Harriet Converse, "the dipping of the spoon into each portion allotted to its fire [each nation] signified union and fidelity." Photograph courtesy of the New York State Museum.

bring to a close a chapter of internecine warfare, chaos, and terror. Pan-Iroquois cultural and political organization effectively militated against internal violence, and it provided the basis for a lasting peace. But the continued existence of fortified villages throughout Iroquoia reflected the recognition that not everyone had joined in the great experiment. The Five Nations remained at odds with those Iroquoian and Algonquian peoples on their margins who had not joined the confederation. Some scholars have suggested that the League itself was primarily designed to enable the Iroquois to direct aggression outward, toward the tribes and rival confederations that surrounded them. Indeed, some contend that the Great Peace actually encouraged a pattern of more intensive long-range raiding. In a classic formulation of such a view, Lewis Henry Morgan asserted: "After the formation of the League, the Iroquois rose rapidly in power and influence. ... One of the first results of their federal system was a universal spirit of aggression; a thirst for military glory and political aggrandizement, which made the forests of America resound with human conflicts from New England to the Mississippi."[34]

In a variation on this theme, Anthony F. C. Wallace proposed seeing the confederation as a body motivated by two purposes: one internal and limited—maintaining unity, strength, good will; the other external and unlimited converting all humankind, by force if necessary.[35] In the context of continuing threats and rivalry, characterized by small-scale raiding and blood feud throughout northeastern North America, the Five Nations would both protect their own communities and attack those beyond Iroquoia considered hostile. Their historical experience and its representation in oral traditions suggest that the Iroquois believed they were destined to create an ever-larger domain of peace through a continuation of their process of alliance and amalgamation. But before the advent of Europeans, there is little evidence that the Iroquois believed their vision would be promoted by warfare, and certainly not by the new, larger scale, and more deadly kinds of war produced by European colonization.

Native warfare changed substantially after colonization, distorted by the changing geopolitical organization of the continent and the introduction of more deadly weapons. Continuing, intensified hostilities between the Five Nations and various groups—the Hurons, for example—during the period of these groups' decline makes it easy to blame the Iroquois for causing their demise. Thus, historians such as George T. Hunt have seen native hostilities in the region during the mid-seventeenth century as the "Wars of the Iroquois." Nonetheless, it now seems likely that it was European disease and the population loss and social dislocation it engendered, more than any other

---

[34]Tuck, *Onondaga Prehistory*, 222; Tuck, "Northern Iroquoian Prehistory," 330–31; Morgan, *League of the Iroquois*, 8.

[35]Anthony F. C. Wallace, "The Dekanawidah Myth Analyzed as the Record of a Revitalization Movement," *Ethnohistory*, 5 (1958), 118–30, especially 124–25; Wallace, *Death and Rebirth of the Seneca*, 42–43.

factor, that caused the destruction of the Hurons and other rivals of the Iroquois.[36]

Conquest had not created the Iroquois League; internecine fighting, which caused chaos in the Owasco and early Iroquois worlds, did not annihilate communities or create empires but instead provided the incentive to invent peaceful solutions. And the intermittent if chronic, ritualized skirmishes, which pitted the individual nations of the Iroquois against outside foes, continued in this period in frustration and in spite of the larger Iroquois goal of peace; these raids were not instruments intended to effect an imperial vision.

Early seventeenth-century Jesuit observers, in fact, belittled Iroquoian warfare, characterizing it as "consisting of a few broken heads along the highways, or of some captives brought into the country to be burned and eaten there."[37] Finally, if the Iroquois confederation had internal and external aspects, as Wallace contends, these must have been inextricably linked, for, as history had proven, it was precisely through a transformation of outsiders into insiders, foreigners into nationals, and a replacement of external threats with a security based on unity, that the Iroquois tribes and the League of Peace had been created.[38]

Because war and peace were thus historically intertwined in Iroquois life, and because the nature of each and their linkage have been so misunderstood, we must briefly examine aboriginal warfare among the Five Nations in the context of their great experiment with peace. The Iroquois rejected warfare on too great or too costly a scale, for practical as well as philosophical reasons. Although the conflicts of the

---

[36]George T. Hunt, *The Wars of the Iroquois: A Study in Intertribal Trade Relations* (Madison, Wisc., 1940). Hunt is challenged by K. H. Schlesier, "Epidemics and Indian Middlemen: Rethinking the Wars of the Iroquois, 1609–1653," *Ethnohistory*, 23 (1976), 129–46. A major debate rages between scholars who argue dramatic population collapse before direct contact with Europeans in the sixteenth century and those who argue that population decline followed sustained interaction with Europeans in the seventeenth century. Both agree that disease was the major cause of devastation. For recent discussion of these issues, see Dean R. Snow and Kim M. Lamphear, "European Contact and Indian Depopulation in the Northeast: The Timing of the First Epidemics, *Ethnohistory*, 35 (Winter 1988), 15–33, who hold the latter position. They have criticized Henry F. Dobyns, *"Their Number Become Thinned": Native American Population Dynamics in Eastern North America* (Knoxville, Tenn., 1983), who represents the former position. For Dobyns's reply, see "More Methodological Perspectives on Historical Demography," *Ethnohistory*, 36 (Summer 1989), 285–99; see also Snow and Lamphear, " 'More Methodological Perspectives': A Rejoinder to Dobyns," ibid., 299–304. For a treatment of the problem that generally supports Dobyns but does not settle the debate regarding the Iroquois, see Ann F. Ramenofsky, *Vectors of Death: The Archaeology of European Contact* (Albuquerque, N.M., 1987), especially 71–102.
[37]Thwaites, ed., *Jesuit Relations*, 19:81.
[38]On the representation of this process in Iroquois ideology, see chap. 3 below.

Five Nations later expanded and took on new, unprecedented dimensions, we should see such a development not as a logical, inevitable result of Iroquois culture but rather as an aberration forced on the Five Nations by the deforming effects of European colonialism.

Aboriginal warfare sometimes occurred in the shape of ritual confrontations between groups, in which few men were hurt. The Dutch surgeon and commercial emissary van den Bogaert witnessed one of these ceremonial combats on a rare journey into Mohawk and Oneida country in the winter of 1634–35. The contest pitted nine Iroquois men against eleven others, some of whom wore "armor and helmets which they made themselves from thin reeds and cords woven together so that no arrow or axe could penetrate to cause serious injury."[39] This traditional armor reflected the relative safety and ceremonial quality of much native fighting, which would change forever with the introduction of European technology. As the Jesuit missionary and scholar Joseph-François Lafitau observed, "Since the Europeans have traded with the Indians giving them guns, powder and balls, those who can obtain them have almost abandoned their other arms, especially the defensive ones, which, as they are not strong enough to give protection from a musket ball, do nothing except weight them down."[40] But early observations of intertribal war suggest that Iroquois battles with external opponents often were not fundamentally different in character from the staged, mock contest van den Bogaert watched.

The French explorer Samuel de Champlain found himself in the middle of one such engagement in July 1609, when he and two French companions accompanied a band of Montagnais, Algonquins, and Hurons near the lake that later bore his name. We can see this battle—the first encounter between Frenchman and Iroquois—as a performance of traditional, aboriginal blood feud. But it was also a failure, for not all of the actors knew their roles. As the party of sixty men, with Champlain in tow, approached the land of the Iroquois, the Frenchman became increasingly concerned about defense and the possibility of ambush. The Indians built barricades around their nightly camps and drew their canoes up close along the unfortified water's edge to facilitate a quick escape, but they refused to post any

---

[39]Charles T. Gehring and William A. Starna, trans. and eds., *A Journey into Mohawk and Oneida Country, 1634–1635: The Journal of Harmen Meyndertz van den Bogaert* (Syracuse, N.Y., 1988), 9, 39n67.
[40]See Lafitau, *Customs of the American Indians*, 2:115–16 and plate VIII.

Woven reed armor of the Iroquois (figure in lower right, marked E), from Samuel de Champlain, *Les voyages de la nouvelle France occidentale, dicte le Canada* . . . (Paris: Chez Claude Collet, 1632). Though effective in warding off arrows and blows in the context of traditional, ritualized warfare, such armor provided little protection from bullets, as the Iroquois discovered during the battle with Champlain in 1609. Illustration courtesy of the National Archives of Canada, Ottawa (C 113065).

sentries; they completely ignored Champlain's martial expertise and his criticism of their "soothsayers" and war magic. The Indians, for now, better understood the play. The scale of battle would be small, risks would be limited, and an ambush was less likely than an orchestrated, open confrontation, which would take place in the light of day.[41]

As the journey continued, his Indian hosts constantly asked Champlain about his dreams. He had none to report until one morning, when he confided a vision of their Iroquois enemies drowning in a lake, which the group received with great enthusiasm. Because of the particular meaning of dreams in the lives of these Montagnais, Algonquins, and Hurons, Champlain's excellent performance in native terms suggested to them that he was a qualified actor in the developing play. Despite Champlain's expressed criticisms, his dream revelation further confirmed the native understanding of events and enhanced their power. Finally, the climax drew near as the approaching opponents—Champlain's mixed band and a group of Mohawks—sighted each other in their canoes. Each side withdrew from the water, uttering loud cries, and barricaded itself as darkness set in. In a conference that night, the opponents agreed to fight the next morning, in daylight, "so as to be able to recognize each other." To be anonymous and to miss the meaningful gestures and verbal discourse of battle would be to undermine the encounter's significance for each party. As Champlain recalled, "The entire night was spent in dancing and singing, on both sides, with endless insults and other talk." Clearly, in this customary practice each actor had his prescribed lines and actions, and the two sides had carefully arranged themselves on a single stage.[42]

When morning arrived, Champlain saw the enemy leave their cover and mass for battle. "They came at a slow pace toward us, with a dignity and assurance which greatly amused [impressed] me," he remembered. At their head were three chiefs, designated by large plumes, and Champlain's allies directed him to kill them with his arquebus. Once again, Champlain regretted that he was not permitted

[41]Champlain, *Voyages*, 157–60; Lafitau, *Customs of the American Indians*, 2:98–172, provides an extended discussion of Indian warfare; see Marian W. Smith, "American Indian Warfare," *Transactions of the New York Academy of Sciences*, 2d ser., 13 (June 1951), 348–65; Daniel K. Richter, "War and Culture: The Iroquois Experience," *William and Mary Quarterly*, 3d ser., 40 (October 1983), 528–59, provides a useful analysis of Iroquois warfare and its distortions in the colonial period.

[42]Champlain, *Voyages*, 162–64; Lafitau, *Customs of the American Indians*, 2:142.

to take command "that I might give order and shape to their mode of attacking their enemies." Champlain thus missed the point about the encounter; the attack had its own native order, shape, and meaning, which he unwittingly revealed in his chronicle when he recounted details about their approach, temporary fortifications, dream interpretations, war magic, tactical planning, negotiations with their foes, and orchestration of the battle itself. Nonetheless, this contest would assume a new shape because Champlain's Indian companions proved willing to change its script unilaterally in disturbing ways.[43]

Champlain's party countered the Iroquois with its own formation, so that each side stood firmly facing the other. With the Frenchmen out of sight, the Mohawks clung to expectations of a thoroughly conventional and favorable encounter, given their numerical advantage. "On occasions of this sort," Lafitau explained, "their small number permits them to draw together, so to speak, body to body, and fight as in a duel, as the heroes of the Iliad and Aeneid did. Quite often they know each other and do not beat each other up without first paying each other compliments, as Virgil and Aeneas do."[44] But on this July morning in 1609, instead of such ritualized action, featuring the exchange of arrows and insults—neither of which could be expected to inflict mortal damage—Champlain marched to the front of the massed line through a passageway opened by his Indian allies. The Mohawks were surprised to see him and were shocked by the discharge of his arquebus, which killed two chiefs with a single shot, "although they were equipped with armor woven from cotton thread and with wood which was proof against their arrows."[45] Thus ended the conventional play—a scene or two prematurely, and a failure in the final act.

Historians have seen this battle and one that followed in 1610 as crucial in determining the long-term hostility between New France and the Five Nations. In fact, Champlain had engaged in only a minor skirmish, one that in no way made the later bloody conflict between the French and the Iroquois inevitable. The battle is significant, however, as evidence of the nature of traditional aboriginal feud and

---

[43]Champlain, *Voyages*, 164–65. The order and shape of the Indian military maneuvers can be seen in ibid., 157–66; Champlain even described the modeling of the impending battle by the native leaders, using sticks to represent the deployment of men (160). See also Lafitau, *Customs of the American Indians*, 2:143.

[44]Lafitau, *Customs of the American Indians*, 2:143.

[45]Champlain, *Voyages*, 165.

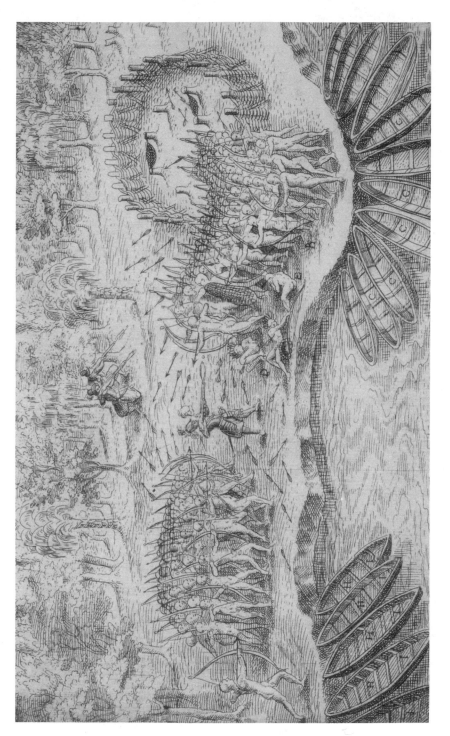

Iroquois defeat in encounter with Champlain in 1609, from Samuel de Champlain, *Les voyages du sieur de Champlain Xaintongeois, capitaine ordinaire pour le roy, en la marine, divisez en deux livres . . .* (Paris: Chez Jean Berjon, 1613), courtesy of the National Library of Canada, Rare Books and Manuscripts Division, Ottawa.

warfare, which became increasingly obsolete in the seventeenth-century New World.

Traditional warfare was not intentionally punitive and destructive, nor was it organized to gain plunder, acquire territory, or conquer people. It operated as a reciprocal though aggressive and even bloody exchange, in which neither side attempted to annihilate its opponent. The stealth of ambush and the generally harmless pomp of massed contests were designed to minimize loss of life. The Iroquois and other native groups refused to risk significant casualties. As Father Lafitau observed, "They feel very much the loss of a single person because of their small number and any loss has such great consequences for the chief of a party that his reputation depends on it. The Indians expect a chief to be not only skilful but also lucky. They are so peculiar in this respect that, if he does not bring back his people and if someone even dies a natural death, he is almost entirely discredited."[46] The Iroquois especially feared the everlasting consequences of death in war, for people slain in battle could not rest in peace; they were interred separately, wandered the landscape ceaselessly as spirits, and never joined their families in the Land of Souls. Ironically, the innovation in fighting that Champlain was soon to introduce signaled the end of an era and encouraged the "cunning," "skulking" tactics of ambush that Europeans would label as "savage."[47]

In the centuries preceeding the arrival of Europeans, the Iroquois transformed themselves into the Five Nations and constructed a landscape of peace. They devised a way of life well suited to their physical surroundings and shaped the land in ways that increased their security and prosperity, adapting themselves to it and molding it into a cultural space in which they sought harmony in their natural, human, and supernatural worlds. They achieved considerable success, but the peace they sought was purchased at a price and was never completely

[46]Lafitau, *Customs of the American Indians*, 2:141.

[47]See Smith, "American Indian Warfare," especially 349–50, 359–61. See also Nathaniel Knowles, "The Torture of Captives by the Indians of Eastern North America," *Proceedings of the American Philosophical Society*, 82, no. 2 (1940), 151–225, especially 152, on the goals and motivations of warfare, and the grisly implication for the few who did become captives or casualties. See J. N. B. Hewitt, "The Iroquois Concept of the Soul," *Journal of American Folk-Lore*, 8, no. 29 (1895), 109, on the grim implications for the afterlife of those killed in war. For extended treatments of Iroquoian warfare, especially in the colonial period, see Cornelius J. Jaenen, *Friend and Foe: Aspects of French-Amerindian Cultural Contact in the Sixteenth and Seventeenth Centuries* (New York, 1976), 127–32, 135, 137–38; Richter, "War and Culture," especially 529n, 535–36.

established. Their world was never free from danger: good coexisted with evil; the spirit of Deganawidah never fully banished the "fire dragon of discord"; internal peace was invariably threatened by external war. Nonetheless, historical experience justified a measure of optimism about the future and provided a model for constructing the peace they sought. The Five Nations and their confederation had emerged from an experimental process of peace based on nonaggression, alliance, consolidation, and integration. The construction of an Iroquois political system thus accompanied the creation of an Iroquois landscape and people, and so we must turn to Iroquois political culture and ideology.

3

Deganawidah and the Cultivation of Peace: Iroquois Ideology, Political Culture, and Representation

"We, the five Iroquois Nations, compose but one
cabin; we maintain but one fire; and we have, from
time immemorial, dwelt under one and the same
roof."... From the earliest times, these five Iroquois
Nations have been called in their language... "the
completed Cabin," as if to express that they constituted but one family.
                    —Jesuit François le Mercier reporting
                      on a meeting with Mohawk envoy,
                    "the Flemish Bastard" (1654)

"God be praised in time and in Eternity; the blood shed for Jesus
Christ in the country of the Iroquois—mingled with the prayers and
vows of so many holy souls, who are interested in the spread of his
Kingdom in the new World—has brought us Peace with those Barbarians."[1] So wrote the Jesuit Superior Barthelemy Vimont, opening
his account of the mission in New France for the years 1644–45. What
was the nature of this peace that God had delivered? Was it real?
Would it last? It would not endure, even though the French Jesuits
and many others in Canada desired it and the Five Nations were
themselves sincere in their hopes for peace. One reason it did not
endure was that the parties that encountered each other at the cultural
frontier held different interpretations of reality; each side understood
"peace" in culturally specific—and ultimately incompatible—ways.

[1] Reuben Gold Thwaites, trans. and ed., *The Jesuit Relations and Allied Documents*, 73 vols.
(Cleveland, 1896–1901), 27:137.

And so we must examine the distinctive concept and practice of Iroquois peace in the context of Iroquois experience, ideology, political culture, and self-representation.

In this chapter I relate and interpret the great chartering myth of the Five Nations, the Deganawidah Epic, which reflected and shaped Iroquois consciousness and action. Initiating new rituals and practices, and inventing new social and political institutions, the prophet Deganawidah and those who followed his teachings found ways to assure domestic concord, to extend the harmony within longhouses, lineages, and clans to wider domains, and to confront the ever-present threats to stability, reason, and peace. In this Chapter I analyze these and other structural arrangements and cultural practices in order to understand the Five Nations' conception of peace and their commitment to it. But I also consider the underside of Iroquois life—the rage and madness produced by the death of kinspeople, the ritual practice of torture and cannibalism, and witchcraft—and try to locate such dangerous behavior within the context of Iroquois culture while promoting an appreciation of the challenges that Iroquois men and women faced in making Deganawidah's vision manifest in their real world.

Father Vimont's optimism sprang from a peculiar event that had inaugurated negotiations between the French and their Iroquois foes on July 5, 1645. On that day at Trois Rivières, a small French settlement on the St. Lawrence above Quebec, one Guillaume Cousture suddenly appeared, "as a man risen from the dead," for he had been a captive among the Five Nations. Accompanying the young Cousture were three Iroquois men, who greeted the surprised *habitants* gathered along the river bank. It was a strange spectacle. They remained offshore, and their leader, Kiotsaeton, stood up in the bow of their boat. As Vimont reported,

He was almost completely covered with Porcelain beads [strings of wampum]. Motioning with his hand for silence, he called out: "My Brothers, I left my country to come and see you. At last I have reached your land. I was told, on my departure, that I was going to seek death, and that I would never again see my country. But I have willingly exposed myself for the good of peace. I come therefore to enter into the designs of the French, of the Hurons, and of the Alguonquins. I come to make known to you the thoughts of all my country."[2]

Shots signifying rejoicing, rather than hostility, were exchanged. The Mohawk ambassadors were received on land and escorted to the house of the sieur de Chanflour, and there they ate and smoked. Trois Rivières honored its guests over the next few days, and by July 12 the French governor, Charles Huault, chevalier de Montmagny, had arrived and real discussions could begin. The Iroquois envoys carefully arranged the space in the courtyard of the fort; at the center of an open area in the middle, "the Iroquois caused two poles to be planted, and a cord to be stretched from one to the other on which to hang and tie the words that they were to bring us,—that is to say, the presents they wished to make us, which consisted of seventeen collars of porcelain beads, a portion of which were on their bodies."[3]

Kiotsaeton rose and began what everyone regarded as a virtuoso performance. The Jesuit remarked that "he walked about the great space as if on the stage of a theatre." He made "a thousand gestures," he spoke in remarkable ways, he sang, he acted out the saga of his journey, and he danced for joy. "Every one admitted that this man was impassioned and eloquent," Vimont wrote. The seventeen matters—represented by that number of collars or strings of wampum—formed the heart of Kiotsaeton's program. Each strand of wampum functioned as a present for his hosts, a gift with a clear message. In turn, these "porcelain beads" thanked the French for saving the lives of Iroquois prisoners and returning them to their own people; they heralded the safe return of captives from Iroquoia to New France; they signified the burial of weapons and Iroquois intentions to control their anger, overcome their grief, and turn their back on vengeance; they metaphorically calmed the waters and cleared the paths along the way between the two countries, and they offered hospitality to those who would join them in Iroquoia; they symbolically joined together the Iroquois, the French, and New France's native allies; they

---

[2]Ibid., 247–49; these events are analyzed in Francis Jennings et al., eds., *The History and Culture of Iroquois Diplomacy: An Interdisciplinary Guide to the Treaties of the Six Nations and Their League* (Syracuse, N.Y., 1985), 127–53. The editors have included an excerpt from the *Jesuit Relations*, which describes the encounter, 137–53. Though I have found their analysis stimulating, my own interpretation differs somewhat from those of the editors; nonetheless, see William N. Fenton's discussion "Rituals of Peace Making," ibid., 127–30, as well as his authoritative "Structure, Continuity, and Change in the Process of Iroquois Treaty Making," ibid., 3–36.

[3]Thwaites, ed., *Jesuit Relations*, 27:251–53.

urged the Hurons to commit themselves to peace; and they explained or apologized for earlier incidents that seemed to stand in the way of peace.[4]

The embassy ended three days later with the departure of the Iroquois, leaving Father Vimont hopeful if puzzled. Vimont's chronicle of these strange occurrences tells us more of the history and culture of the Five Nations than the Jesuit Superior himself knew. The appropriate response by Governor Montmagny, called Onontio ("Big Mountain") by the Iroquois, suggests that he had learned something of the protocol from New France's Huron allies. Yet it is not clear that Montmagny or any other European colonist in New France or New Netherland had developed a firm sense of Iroquois political world view and practical ideology. The 1645 relation appears to be the first recorded example of the Five Nations' Condolence ceremony, which stood at the center of Iroquois political culture and practice.

In its grandest, most important form, the Condolence was (and still is) the great Iroquois convocation for condoling with relatives of deceased chiefs of the League, raising up their successors, and restoring the minds of those in mourning.[5] More broadly, ordinary Iroquois men and women condoled with each other following the deaths of loved ones and used the occasion ritually to recite their history, rehearse social and political principles, and renew their commitment to order and reason. The Condolence served to restore the mystic power, or *orenda,* of the group, which was diminished by the death of even one person; the Iroquois believed that the ceremony would thus "thwart the vicious assaults of death on the power of the people to live in health and peace."[6] The clear intention expressed here—to preserve order and harmony during periods of stress caused by death in the community, or to create the basis for peaceful intercourse in the context of chronic death in blood feud—made the rite an ideal model for Iroquois diplomacy.[7]

---

[4]Ibid., 253–65.

[5]On the Iroquois Condolence ceremony, see J. N. B. Hewitt and William N. Fenton, "Some Mnemonic Pictographs Relating to the Iroquois Condolence Council," *Journal of the Washington Academy of Sciences,* 35 (October 15, 1945), 301–15; Hewitt and Fenton, "The Requickening Address of the Iroquois Condolence Council," in ibid., 34 (March 15, 1944), 65–85; Elisabeth Tooker, "The League of the Iroquois: Its History, Politics, and Ritual," in Bruce G. Trigger, ed., *Handbook of North American Indians: Northeast,* in William C. Sturtevant, gen. ed., *Handbook of North American Indians,* 20 vols. projected (Washington, D.C., 1978–), 15:437–40; Fenton, "Structure, Continuity, and Change," especially 14–21, 27–30.

[6]Hewitt and Fenton, "Requickening Address," 66–68.

[7]See Fenton, "Structure, Continuity, and Change," especially 27–31; see this chap. below.

The Condolence ceremony consisted of five connected rituals. It began with "Journeying on the Trail" or the "Eulogy of Roll Call of the Chiefs," as the condolers traveled to their destination. In 1645, this action would have taken place off stage, and if it occurred we have no record of it. Nonetheless, in the course of his oration, Kiotsaeton suggested something of this ritual in his dramatic reenactment of the entire journey between his own village and Trois Rivières. Kiotsaeton's strange appearance at the margin of the French settlement, standing in the bow of his boat, adorned with wampum, clearly approximated the second ritual of the Condolence, "Welcome at the Wood's Edge." The seventeen collars enumerated by Vimont, in turn, corresponded roughly to the "Fifteen Matters" of the Iroquois "Requickening Address," the third part and core of the Condolence ceremony. Finally, the "Six Songs of Farewell" and "Over the Great Forest," terminated the traditional Condolence, and in 1645 these conventions seem to have been realized in the utterances and feasts that concluded the encounter between the French and Iroquois, and with the latter's departure. With these words, Kiotsaeton and his companions took their leave: "Adieu my brothers; I am one of your relatives. I am going to carry back good news to our country."[8]

Was this talk of kinship merely idle rhetoric? In fact, the Condolence functioned only through a particular sort of reciprocity; it was performed by kinsmen for each other. For the purposes of condolence and requickening, the Iroquois made use of the division of their clans into one of two sides, or moieties. The side that remained "unscathed" or "clear-minded," because it had not suffered a death among its lineages and clans, condoled with the other, the mourning or "bereaved" side. Thus, the Condolence took shape as an internal institution, in which the celebrants gathered together the torn and scattered remains of their cousins, fended off their great adversary Death—"the Great-faceless," mended his destruction, dried their kinsmen's tears, assuaged their grief, and restored them to the ranks of rational men and women. Finally, they installed a new leader, designated by the mourning clan mothers, and crowned him with the name of the deceased chief, thus giving the people new life through

---

[8]On the journey's ritual narration, see Thwaites, ed., *Jesuit Relations*, 27:253–55, 259–61; on the seventeen strings of wampum and their systematic recitation, see ibid., 253–65; on the traditional terminal feast, see ibid., 267, 271–73, 303.

this symbolic resurrection. Having passed through the ordeal together, the cousins forged even firmer bonds.[9]

The procedure of the confederate Condoling Council represented a projection of similar practices at the tribal and community levels. And in this projection—from bands, to tribes, to the League itself—we can see the logic in extending the Condolence to those who were not kin. By the beginning of the seventeenth century, the Iroquois had painstakingly constructed a fragile balance of peace out of the chaos which ruled their lives in an earlier, darker time. They had survived and flourished precisely through their projection of localized, domestic structures onto a wider range of people and landscape. The warfare between autonomous Owasco bands was defined in Iroquois representation as internecine, intrafamilial, thus making it illegitimate, inappropriate, and self-destructive for the Iroquois "family." As they halted the cycle of blood feud, the Five Nations then reified their consanguinity and affinity, intermarrying throughout the villages and tribes of Iroquoia. Finally, in this new context of real and assumed kinship, the Iroquois developed institutions to prevent the actions that now, in fact, would constitute a kind of civil, familial war.[10]

Their use of Condolence rituals in their peace conferences with the French in 1645 foreshadowed attempts by the Five Nations to render the ceremony truly relevant and meaningful by transforming the French, in a sense, into kinsmen. The Condolence expressed principles of union and reciprocity; by performing it the Iroquois institutionalized the procedures prescribed by the prophet Deganawidah; the ceremony included the direct recitation of the Epic of Deganawidah—the creation myth of the Iroquois as a social and political entity. In short, it represented Iroquois history and reality, explaining to themselves their achievement of peace through domestication and naturalization and providing them with a practical means of conserving and expanding that peace.

The Condolence was repeatedly inscribed in the historical record of seventeenth-century America, and it is the best evidence we have

---

[9]Hewitt and Fenton, "Requickening Address," 66–67; see also ibid., 80–84; Hewitt and Fenton, "Mnemonic Pictographs," 301, 303; Tooker, "League of the Iroquois," 439–40.
[10]See chap. 2 above; on the projection of condolence practices from the band to confederate level, see Hewitt and Fenton, "Mnemonic Pictographs," 303, and Hewitt and Fenton, "Requickening Address," 67.

of the existence of the Deganawidah Epic among the Five Nations at that time. Such inscription makes it safe to assume that the sixteenth- and early seventeenth-century Five Nations already possessed a mythic explanation for the origin of their confederacy, which archaeological evidence suggests was formed before direct contact with Europeans, in the mid-sixteenth century or earlier (see Chapter 2). At least as early as the 1630s, the Iroquois League's existence is clear from the accounts of a Dutch expedition among the Mohawks and Oneidas and from the surviving records of various encounters between informed Indians and French Jesuit missionaries. The fact of the League, metaphorically represented by the "extended house" or "completed cabin" in the 1630s (and no doubt earlier) implies the existence of a native explanation of its origins, a history or myth of creation that most likely centered on Deganawidah, Hiawatha, and their heroic exploits.[11] The Epic provided the context and meaning for the rituals performed in the ceremony, and thus the two are inextricably linked in the way that the Roman Catholic Eucharistic Feast is linked with the myth of Christ and the sacred events of the Last Supper and Crucifixion. To miss these connections is to deprive ourselves of a deeper sense of the Condolence and the larger Iroquois culture, ideology, and practice that it expressed.[12]

The Reverend Christopher Pyrlaeus, a Moravian missionary among the Mohawks, was apparently the first European to refer specifically (in 1743) to the political creation myth of Deganawidah and his associate Hiawatha. Pyrlaeus's successor, John Heckewelder, quoted from Pyrlaeus's manuscript in 1819: "The alliance or confederacy of the Five Nations was established, as near as can be conjectured, one age (or the length of a man's life) before the white people (the Dutch) came into the country. Thannawage [Hiawatha?] was the name of the aged Indian, a Mohawk, who first proposed such an alliance."[13]

---

[11]See Charles T. Gehring and William A. Starna, trans. and eds., *A Journey into Mohawk and Oneida Country, 1634–35: The Journal of Harmen Meyndertz van den Bogaert* (Syracuse, N.Y., 1988), 16–17, 46–48; Thwaites, ed., *Jesuit Relations*, 8:115–17; 17:77; 21:21, 201; 33:65, 71.

[12]See Hewitt and Fenton, "Requickening Address," 65, 80–81, on the connection between the myth and the ritual practice of condolence; Horatio Hale, *The Iroquois Book of Rites*, ed. William N. Fenton (Toronto, 1963 [orig. pub. 1883]), constitutes an extended treatment of this connection.

[13]John G.E. Heckewelder, *An Account of the History, Manners, and Customs of the Indian Nations, Who Once Inhabited Pennsylvania and the Neighboring States* (Philadelphia, 1819), 38. See also Tooker, "League of the Iroquois," 420, 422, 424. Hiawatha, apparently, was an Onondaga who was adopted by the Mohawks and became one of the original League chiefs; a place among the League chiefs was never designated, nor was a successor ever appointed, for Deganawidah.

Causing untold confusion, Henry Wadsworth Longfellow later appropriated the name "Hiawatha" and identified him with the Algonquian mythic hero Nanabozho in order to write a poem modeled on the Finnish epic *Kalevala*. The result was the enormously successful *Song of Hiawatha* (1855). Horatio Hale commented, "If a Chinese traveler, during the middle ages, inquiring into the history and religion of the western nations, had confounded King Alfred with King Arthur, and both with Odin, he would not have made a more preposterous confusion of names and characters than that which has hitherto disguised the genuine personality of the great Onondaga reformer."[14]

In the same year as Pyrlaeus's record (1743), Conrad Weiser journeyed to Onondaga as an emissary of peace representing colonial Pennsylvania, and in his account of the proceedings we also see preserved the founding myth of the Five Nations, woven tightly into their Condolence, their discourse of peace.[15] Following Heckewelder's publication and Weiser's report, William Dunlap published his own account of the mythic beginnings of the Iroquois confederacy, which he collected from Ephraim Webster, trader and interpreter among the Onondagas, in 1815.[16] By then, another well-informed observer, Major John Norton (Teyoninhokarawen) the half-Cherokee, half-Scot deputy of Mohawk leader Joseph Brant, had written at greater length about these epic events. His journal testified to the importance and pervasiveness of the myth, though it was not published until its rediscovery in 1970.[17] Since these early accounts, and continuing into our own times, the Deganawidah Epic has been recorded repeatedly and more elaborately by a wide range of scholars and native people.

The first relatively complete scholarly version of the Epic appeared

[14]Hale, *Iroquois Book of Rites*, 36. See also Tooker, "League of the Iroquois," 422.

[15]"Conrad Weiser's Report of his Journey to Onondaga on the affairs of Virginia, in Obedience to the Orders of the Governor [of Pennsylvania] in Council, 13 June, 1743, delivered to the Governor the 1st of September," in Samuel Hazard, ed., *Minutes of the Provincial Council of Pennsylvania, 1682–1790*, 16 vols. (Harrisburg, Pa., 1838–1853), 4:660–69. The major council began on July 30 as follows: "first the Onondagoes rehearsed the beginning of the Union of the five Nations, Praised their Grandfathers' Wisdom in establishing the Union or Alliance, by which they became a formidable Body; that they (now living) were fools to their wise fathers, Yet protected and accompanied by their fathers' Spirit; and then the discourse was directed to the Deputies of the several Nations, ..." (ibid., 663).

[16]William Dunlap, *History of the New Netherlands, Province of New York, and State of New York, to the Adoption of the Federal Constitution*, 2 vols. (New York, 1839), 1:29–30.

[17]Carl F. Klinck and James J. Talman, eds., *The Journal of Major John Norton, 1816*, Publications of the Champlain Society, 46 (Toronto, 1970), 98–105.

as Horatio Hale's *Iroquois Book of Rites* in 1883. Yet fragments of the narrative—its motifs, symbols, and metaphors—which have accumulated in the historical record continue to inform us, linking us to an earlier time and world view. Such fossils, embedded in the writings of seventeenth-century European missionaries, traders, soldiers, and colonial officials, remain important because no single, authoritative version of the Epic exists. Despite this absence, we seem to be dealing with a single myth. The Five Nations, according to the anthropologist William N. Fenton, "recognize the several versions as belonging to the one myth" or, collectively, as constituting "one genre." As Major John Norton wrote in 1816, "in this tradition, there is also some variety in the manner it is related by the different Nations; but all concur in substance."[18]

Taken together, Iroquois myth and ritual can be interpreted as a text constituted by the words and actions of Iroquois people. Although mediated by collectors and translators, Iroquois narratives provide us with a unique means of decoding and reinterpreting Iroquois experience, meaning, and reason.[19] While our Western positivist epistemology might beg us to ask if the events described in the Deganawidah Epic "actually happened," such a question is largely irrelevant for our analysis here. The importance of the Epic resides in the meaning it provided for the Iroquois in the seventeenth century and since. Though we might find satisfaction in the way that the archaeological evidence of Chapter 2 seems to corroborate the general sense of development revealed in the myth, it is the interaction of material circumstances and ideas, rather than the determinism of either, that is important. Experience and material conditions set certain interpretive limits for the Iroquois, but within such malleable bounds the Five

---

[18]For a description and analysis of the various versions of the Epic, see Fenton's introduction to Arthur C. Parker, *Parker on the Iroquois*, ed. William N. Fenton (Syracuse, N.Y., 1968), 38–46. See also Fenton, "Structure, Continuity, and Change," 3–36 (quotation from 14); Fenton, "The Lore of the Longhouse: Myth, Ritual, and Red Power," *Anthropological Quarterly*, 48, no. 3 (1975), 131–47, especially 133. Major John Norton, or "Teyoninhokarawen," is quoted in his *Journal*, 105. Paul A. W. Wallace, *The White Roots of Peace* (Philadelphia, 1946) provided a convenient shorthand version of the Epic and Law. See also Matthew Dennis, "Cultivating a Landscape of Peace: The Iroquois New World," Ph.D. diss., University of California, Berkeley (1986), 112–17.

[19]While the problems of mediation should not be understated, the Iroquois ethnicity and native linguistic skills of a number of nineteenth- and twentieth-century collectors and translators among the Iroquois—Ely S. Parker, J. N. B. Hewitt, and Arthur C. Parker, for example—allow us an unusual degree of confidence in cultural reconstruction and translation based on their texts.

Nations, like other peoples, understood, organized, and represented their lives symbolically.[20]

The Iroquois representation of peace and political order, then, appears most clearly in the great chartering myth embodied in the Deganawidah Epic. Cosmogonical and cosmological in a political sense, the Epic provided the Iroquois an explanation of their past and a practical guide for their present and future.[21] The political mythology of the Iroquois tells of the coming of a great prophet, Deganawidah, who ended the bloodshed and provided a charter of peace known as the Great Law.

Deganawidah appeared in Iroquoia, perhaps as early as the mid fifteenth century, carried by a white stone canoe, to bring the Five Nations the Good News of Peace and Power.[22] With the help of Hiawatha, whom he socialized and converted from cannibalism, Deganawidah put an end to internecine killing, turned warriors into men of peace, introduced a new political structure based on traditional Iroquois kinship and domestic organization, and initiated a set of rituals designed to maintain the harmony and prosperity he had worked to create.

Among the most important episodes in the Epic is Deganawidah's encounter with the woman Jikonsahseh.[23] The prophet praised her

[20]The work of Marshall Sahlins has influenced my ideas on these matters; see *Historical Metaphors and Mythical Realities. Structure in the Early History of the Sandwich Islands Kingdom* (Ann Arbor, Mich., 1981), *Islands of History* (Chicago, 1985), and *Culture and Practical Reason* (Chicago, 1976).

[21]For a useful discussion of myth, see the various essays in Alan Dundes, ed., *Sacred Narratives. Readings in the Theory of Myth* (Berkeley, Calif., 1984).

[22]My reconstruction of the Epic is based on the following sources: Hale, *Iroquois Book of Rites;* Arthur C. Parker, *The Constitution of the Five Nations,* "Book Three," in William N. Fenton, ed., *Parker on the Iroquois* (Syracuse, N.Y., 1968 [orig. pub. as *New York State Museum Bulletin,* no. 184 (Albany, 1916)]); Duncan Campbell Scott, *Traditional History of the Confederacy of the Six Nations Prepared by a Committee of the Chiefs, Royal Society of Canada Transactions,* 3d ser., 5, no. 2 (Ottawa, 1912), 195–246; J. N. B. Hewitt, "A Constitutional League of Peace in the Stone Age of America: The League of the Iroquois and its Constitution," in *Annual Report of the Smithsonian Institution for 1918* (Washington, D.C., 1920), 527–45; Hewitt, "Deganawidah Legend," partially translated by Hewitt and W. N. Fenton, from Chief John Arthur Gibson, Six Nations Reserve (1899), unpublished ms. no. 3528, National Anthropological Archives (henceforth NAA), Smithsonian Institution, Washington, D.C.; Hewitt, "Founding of the League," from J. A. Gibson (1899), NAA ms. 3569; Hewitt, "Dekanawidah's Government of the Iroquois Confederacy by . . . Seth Newhouse" (1885), NAA ms. 3524; see also William N. Fenton, "Seth Newhouse's Traditional History and Constitution of the Iroquois Confederacy," *Proceedings of the American Philosophical Society,* 93, no. 2 (1949), 141–58.

[23]See, for example, Parker, *Constitution* (Chiefs' version), 70–71; Hewitt, "Deganawidah Legend," NAA ms. 3528; Wallace, *White Roots of Peace,* 13–14.

for her willingness to provide sanctuary within her village but convinced her to refuse refuge to murderers; as the first person to commit to the Peace, she became the "mother of nations," and in commemoration Deganawidah ordained that women would have the authority to chose the sachems of the League of Peace.

Much of the narrative concerns the trials, tribulations, and ultimate triumphs of Hiawatha. It was by recounting the wandering of Hiawatha, and his irresolution and relapse along the road to peace, that the Iroquois represented time, history, the ebb and flow of fortune, and the importance of perseverence. Hiawatha, in his journeys, embodied pacification, illustrated the dangers of anger and grief, and discovered the means to control and defeat them, including wampum. Those shell or "porcelaine" beads were more important as a medium of symbolic than of economic exchange; they "propped up one's words" or consoled and restored reason to those overwhelmed by grief.[24]

A final, important narrative thread follows the diabolical career of the hideous Onondaga sachem and sorcerer Thadodaho (meaning "Entangled" in Onondaga). A grotesque, crooked, misshapen man, twisted in mind and body, Thadadaho reveled in the misery he caused others—including Hiawatha—by his witchcraft, and he was the last to submit to the Great Peace. Deganawidah combed the writhing snakes from his hair, made him straight physically and spiritually, and installed him as the Firekeeper, the first League chief among equals. The Epic concludes with the unification of the Five Nations into a great League of Peace and with a series of prescriptions for preserving it.[25]

Deganawidah the prophet represented efficacy, the ability of the Iroquois to shape their social and political landscape. As we have seen in Chapter 2, the Five Nations were hardly passive agents reacting mechanically to the forces of their environment; they promoted and pursued an active program of ecological, social, and political change,

[24]See, for example, Parker, *Constitution* (Chiefs' version), 74–79; Hewitt, "Deganawidah Legend," NAA ms. 3528, and "Dekanawidah's Government by Seth Newhouse," NAA ms. 3524; Wallace, *White Roots of Peace*, 15–22; Norton, *Journal*, 100–102.

[25]See, for example, Hewitt, "Dekanawidah's Government by Seth Newhouse," NAA ms. 3524; Parker, *Constitution*, 27; Wallace, *White Roots of Peace*, 23–24; William M. Beauchamp, *Iroquois Folk Lore Gathered from the Six Nations of New York, Empire State Historical Publication*, 31 (Port Washington, N.Y., 1922), 66–68; the entangled story of Deganawidah, Hiawatha, and Ot-to-tar-ho (Thadodaho) continued in ibid., 69–76 and 76–79; Norton, *Journal*, 103–5.

and Deganawidah personified, expressed, and sanctified that process. From the beginning, Deganawidah had been marked as a man of peace. His chief mission was to halt the terror and chaos of internal warfare and murder, "to stop the business of mutual slaughter," in which Iroquois people figuratively and literally "devoured" each other. Deganawidah arrived in Iroquoia as the "custodian of the Good Tidings of Peace and Power, so that the human race may live in peace in the future."[26]

Nothing more symbolized the self-destructive violence and disorder of the world Deganawidah found than the practice of cannibalism. When the prophet and reformer first encountered Hiawatha, Deganawidah observed him as "the one who eats human flesh." Through trickery and supernatural power, Deganawidah transformed Hiawatha into a civil man of peace. While the cannibal was away on a hunt, Deganawidah concealed himself on the roof of Hiawatha's lodge. From that vantage point, the prophet watched the cannibal return with a human body, which he butchered and set boiling in a noxious stew. As Hiawatha looked into the clay pot, preparing to ladle its contents into a bowl, Deganawidah himself peered down from above. The cannibal was amazed to see the beautiful reflection; he saw a man of wisdom, righteousness, and strength. It was "not the face of a man who eats humans."[27]

The pot or kettle symbolized family, society, and hospitality, and to fill it with the flesh of one's brothers or sisters was an abomination. Hiawatha suddenly realized all of this, and as he sank into remorse, misery, and dejection his observer, Deganawidah, performed another service. He went to Hiawatha, calmed him, assisted in consigning the vile stew to the pit of an uprooted tree (removing it from sight and thought), and provided an appropriate meal. The venison they cooked together symbolized men's legitimate contribution to subsistence; men were to venture into the forest properly, not in pursuit of other men but to hunt deer and other animals. And the antlers they borrowed to crown Iroquois sachems symbolized legitimate authority granted to designated men who would dedicate themselves to righteousness, justice, and peace. When Deganawidah and Hiawatha again gazed into the stew, they saw two identical faces, a reflection of the new calm, safe, and prosperous world that the prophet, and now Hiawatha,

[26]See, for example, Hewitt, "Deganawidah Legend," NAA ms. 3528; Wallace, *White Roots of Peace*, 71.
[27]Wallace, *White Roots of Peace*, 15.

toiled to create. The burial of the sinister human stew represented the end of mutual slaughter and cannibalism, foreshadowing the successful pacification and unification that would mark the climax of the Epic.[28]

Did the Five Nations in fact comply with Deganawidah's prescription? Archaeological remains and eye-witness accounts seem to indicate that they did not. Ritual cannibalism remained important in Iroquois life; its persistence simultaneously suggests the importance of Deganawidah's principles and the difficulty of realizing them fully in the profane world. Evidence of cannibalism in Iroquoian sites began to appear in the fourteenth century, just as feuding activity made the Owasco world more dangerous and encouraged the Owasco communities to seclude themselves on hilltops, behind earthworks and palisades. Cannibalism continued into the colonial period, but it seemed to reach its peak in the mid-sixteenth century. Its decline at the very moment when, most scholars believe, the Iroquois League of Peace emerged should encourage us to distinguish between two sorts of cannibalism: "auto-" or "endo-cannibalism," that is, the consumption of humans within one's own group; and "exo-cannibalism," eating outsiders.[29]

Iroquois myth presents Hiawatha's anthropophagy as endo-cannibalism, and as such it was a bloody emblem of the internecine warfare that the Iroquois sought to control. As Deganawidah and the reformed Hiawatha achieved greater success, and as bands of Owasco people formed themselves into Iroquois nations and then into a larger confederacy, the incidence of cannibalism, and certainly endo-cannibalism, plummeted. Here we can see the peculiar way that the Five Nations interpreted their historical experience and the circumstances they faced, while using that mythic interpretation to chart

---

[28] Ibid.,; Hewitt, "Deganawidah Legend," NAA ms. 3528.

[29] On Iroquoian cannibalism, see Thomas S. Abler, "Iroquois Cannibalism: Fact not Fiction," *Ethnohistory*, 27 (Fall 1980), 309–16; cf. W. Arens, *The Man-Eating Myth: Anthropology and Anthropophagy* (New York, 1979). For an interesting discussion of cannibalism that varies in some important ways from my understanding of the practice among the Iroquois, see Peggy Reeves Sanday, *Divine Hunger: Cannibalism as a Cultural System* (Cambridge and New York, 1986), especially 125–50. For a powerful critique of the term "cannibalism" (as a substitute for "anthropophagy") and its ideological construction, beginning with Columbus, see Peter Hulme, *Colonial Encounters: Europe and the Native Caribbean, 1492–1797* (London and New York, 1986), chaps. 2 and 3, especially 70, 78–87. Hulme convincingly challenges the notion that Caribs made a practice of consuming human flesh, though the term "*canibales*" is derived from the name Carib, which Columbus attached to these people. Later, through a pattern of circular reasoning, the association of Carib with the word "cannibal" was used as proof that these people were "man-eaters."

their future. Perhaps we should not consider the ritual consumption of Owasco people by one another as *endo*-cannibalism, since they shared no common political or social institutions. Iroquois representation and Deganawidah's statesmanship seemed to project kinship onto these autonomous groups, thus defining warfare and cannibalism as endogamous. In the Epic, the reformation of the cannibal Hiawatha suggested that the Five Nations distinguished sharply between endo- and exo-cannibalism—just as they differentiated between intrafamilial and external warfare—accepting the latter perhaps as a fact of life, but defining the former as inappropriate and barbaric. Iroquois myth and history seemed to contain its own momentum. Just as the Five Nations sought to abolish war by expanding their domestic, kin-based universe, the process of transformation expressed in the myth suggested that even exo-cannibalism could become obsolete as warfare ended and outsiders became Iroquois. Deganawidah prescribed that the Five Nations eat neither themselves nor other, potential kinspeople. In a sense, with apologies to the nineteenth-century French lawyer and gourmet, Jean Anthelme Brillat-Savarin, the Iroquois were who they did not eat, and as Deganawidah's mission progressed all the world would be Iroquois.[30]

On the other hand, the Five Nations could never control their world fully; they could never enjoy perfect security within Iroquoia, nor were they able to banish death. As a result, ritual torture and cannibalism—both by the Iroquois and their enemies—continued throughout the seventeenth century. Indeed, the persistence of hostilities proved so frustrating to the Iroquois will to incorporate outsiders that the Five Nations resorted to the symbolic and actual consumption of enemies who consistently defied their expansive vision of peace.

For the Iroquois, adoption was an important means of assuaging grief, replacing those who died, and maintaining population, especially in the face of epidemic disease. Men brought to the villages of Iroquoia as captives in warfare were candidates for such adoption, but they could also suffer a less happy fate: a kind of ritual adoption through torture, death, and cannibalism. In this practice, the Iroquois expressed a rage of bereavement, one that Deganawidah and Iroquois political culture sought to repress internally. The torturer thus found

[30]For more on Iroquois expansion of their domestic sphere in the interest of peace, see below. Brillat-Savarin published his famous, often-quoted aphorism in *The Physiology of Taste* (1825): "Tell me what you eat, and I'll tell you what you are."

a release in subjecting the prisoner—an outsider—to treatment that strikes us today as extraordinarily cruel. While indulging in this violence, Iroquois men and women achieved psychic relief; they defeated their rage by devouring the source of it. And simultaneously, as they consumed their victims, they symbolically transformed them into kinsmen. Jesuit observers thought the Hurons and Iroquois savage and cruel when they caressed captives with fire brands, commenting, "Ah, it is not right that my uncle should be cold; I must warm thee," or when they applied a red-hot axe head to a victim's feet, saying, "Now as my uncle has kindly deigned to come and live among the Huron, I must make him a present, I must give him a hatchet."[31] In essence, Iroquoian people in this manner transformed the raw (foreign, hostile men) into the cooked (kinsmen), and then they ate them in the ultimate exercise of assimilation.[32]

Witchcraft, like cannibalism, was another blight on the terrible landscape that Deganawidah entered. A troubling and dangerous presence, witchcraft attacked people covertly, devastating their lives and contributing to the uncertainty and terror of their existence. Worst of all, witchcraft was an internal problem—like the cannibalism of Hiawatha—in which Iroquois people preyed on each other. And because attackers could not be identified easily, witchcraft bred suspicion throughout the community, undermining even the bonds of family. Even in the absence of war, true peace could not reign in a world afflicted with the surreptitious violence of witches. Thadodaho embodied these dangers. The frightening wizard was notorious, and people were justifiably cautious, but they could not tell who or what worked as the sorcerer's agent. The reformed Hiawatha himself became the tragic victim of Thadodaho's magic. After the deaths of his children and wife through malevolence, Hiawatha strayed from the path of peace and wandered aimlessly in inconsolable grief. Degan-

[31]Thwaites, ed., *Jesuit Relations*, 13: 69.

[32]See Sanday, *Divine Hunger*, 148–49; Nathaniel Knowles, "The Torture of Captives by the Indians of Eastern North America," *Proceedings of the American Philosophical Society*, 82, no. 2 (1940), especially 181–90. The "raw" and "cooked" metaphor comes from Claude Lévi-Strauss and has been employed to good effect by Marshall Sahlins in "Raw Women, Cooked Men, and Other 'Great Things' of the Fiji Islands," in Paula Brown and Donald Tuzin, eds., *The Ethnography of Cannibalism, Special Publication of the Society for Psychological Anthropology* (Washington, D.C., 1983), 72–93. For the intricately related practices of Iroquois warfare, adoption, torture, and cannibalism see William N. Fenton and Elizabeth Moore, eds. and trans., Father Joseph-François Lafitau's *Customs of the American Indians Compared with the Customs of Primitive Times, Publications of the Champlain Society*, no. 49, 2 vols. (Toronto, 1977 [orig. pub. Paris, 1724]), 2:149–63; see also 98–102.

awidah ultimately devised a means of condoling with Hiawatha. But it was also incumbent upon the founders to address the source of Hiawatha's trouble, and in Thadodaho's rehabilitation the Epic suggested the possibility of the reform or control, if not the banishment or destruction, of witchcraft.[33]

The sorcerer Thadadaho epitomized the dualism of good and evil, as did the cannibal Hiawatha. Deganawidah transformed each man, through magic and reason, bringing out the good and banishing the bad. The Iroquois similarly saw a dualism in power and in the effects of medicine and ritual. *Orenda,* benevolent and protecting power, opposed *utgon,* the essence of evil, expressed by witches, disease, or storms. Shamans or healers mobilized *orenda* against *utgon,* but the line between the beneficent and the malignant, between medicine and witchcraft, was easily crossed. Shamans might turn their abilities to evil, or normally benign rituals might become witchcraft if improperly performed. In the peace negotiations of 1645 at Trois Rivières, which began this chapter, the Iroquois orator himself seemed the embodiment of dualism; in reply to an "ill-disposed Huron," he said, "My face is painted and daubed on one side, while the other is quite clean. I do not see very clearly on the side that is daubed over; on the other side my sight is good. The painted side is toward the Hurons, and I see nothing; the clean side is turned toward the French, and I see clearly, as in broad daylight." Thus we observe the Iroquois opposition of clarity/obscurity, light/darkness, peace/war, which they saw within people and which they sought to balance and control. The Deganawidah Epic did not justify such beliefs, but it did clearly reflect them.[34]

Jesuit missionaries, similar purveyors of metaphysical power, could

---

[33]On Iroquois witchcraft, see especially Annemarie Anrod Shimony, *Conservatism Among the Iroquois at the Six Nations Reserve, Yale University Publications in Anthropology,* no. 65 (New Haven, 1961), especially 261–88; Anthony F. C. Wallace, *The Death and Rebirth of the Seneca* (New York, 1970), especially 84–93; Lewis Henry Morgan, *The League of the Ho-de-no-saunee, Iroquois,* ed., William N. Fenton (Secaucus, N.J., 1962 [orig. pub. Rochester, N.Y., 1851]), 164–66.

[34]Wallace, *Death and Rebirth of the Seneca,* 84–85; Shimony, *Conservatism among the Iroquois,* 262–63, 285–88. For seventeenth- and early eighteenth-century observations on Iroquois magic, sorcery, and witchcraft, see Lafitau, *Customs of American Indians,* 1:238, 240, 243–48; 2:209–15. *Otkon,* a Seneca and Cayuga term still in use, corresponds to Wallace's *utgon:* see ibid., 1:236; see also James B. Conacher, ed., and Percy J. Robinson, trans., *The History of Canada or New France by Father François du Creux, S.J., Publications of the Champlain Society,* no. 30, 2 vols. (Toronto, 1951 [orig. pub. Paris, 1664]) (hereafter cited as *Historia Canadensis*), 1:85–88, 113–18, 194–98. On the dualism (especially male/female) reflected in the Condolence, in Iroquois social organization, and in other aspects of Iroquois culture, see Hewitt and Fenton, "Iroquois Requickening Address," 81–83. The Iroquois orator at Trois Rivières in 1645 is quoted in Thwaites, ed., *Jesuit Relations,* 27:269.

be understood in terms of this dualism and the narrow divide between good and evil. Like Iroquois shamans, they purposefully employed their own "magic" to persuade and convert Iroquois people. On January 21, 1674, for example, Father Pierre Milet used his knowledge of an eclipse of the moon to awe Oneida men and women in a contest with their "jugglers," the disparaging term Jesuits often assigned to native shamans.[35] Were these missionaries beneficent curers or maleficent witches? Was their magic employed to benefit or destroy the Five Nations? The Iroquois heard from the disillusioned Hurons that the Jesuits "carried Demons"; we learn this from a Jesuit priest who goes on to report the Indian belief "that we and our doctrine tended only to their ruin." In 1646, Father Isaac Jogues's perceived sorcery ultimately cost him his life. According to another Jesuit chronicler, Jogues's Mohawk hosts came to regard him as an "abomination," who "contaminated" all that he touched: "Sickness having fallen upon their bodies, ... and worms having perhaps damaged their corn, ... these poor blind creatures have believed that the Father had left the Demon among them, and that all our discourses and all our instructions aimed only to exterminate them."[36] Yet the possibility that the Jesuits' power might be domesticated and made benign, that missionaries could be transformed—like Thadodaho—into men promoting health, reason, and security, allowed the Five Nations to invite Jogues and others, to endure their "invasion within," as historian James Axtell has characterized the missionary program for a time. But ultimately their hopes for transformation were disappointed, and they came to understand the Jesuits as witches, that is, men more evil than good, sorcerers committed more to malevolence than benevolence.[37]

Witchcraft, like cannibalism, would persist in the world, and driving out Jesuits would not remove the native forces of subversion. The next great Iroquois prophet would devote considerable energy to the battle against it.[38] Nonetheless, well after the appearance of Handsome Lake and his new Longhouse religion at the turn of the nine-

[35]Thwaites, ed., *Jesuit Relations*, 58:181–85; James Axtell, *The Invasion Within: The Contest of Cultures in Colonial North America* (New York, 1985), especially 99–104.

[36]Thwaites, ed., *Jesuit Relations*, 30:229; 31:73–75.

[37]The understanding of Jesuits missionaries among the Five Nations was contested in the later seventeenth century, especially as the incorporation of outsiders escalated and made their assimilation difficult, and as factionalism increased; see especially Daniel K. Richter, "Iroquois Versus Iroquois: Jesuit Missions and Christianity in Village Politics, 1642–1686," *Ethnohistory*, 32 (January 1985), 1–16.

[38]Wallace, *Death and Rebirth of the Seneca*, 201–2; Wallace, "Origins of the Longhouse Religion," in Trigger, ed., *Handbook of North American Indians: Northeast*, 446–47.

teenth century, belief in and fear of witches continued. Lewis Henry Morgan wrote in 1851 that

> a belief in witches is to this day, and always has been, one of the most deeply-seated notions in the minds of the Iroquois.... Any person, whether old or young, male or female, might become possessed of an evil spirit, and be transformed into a witch.... They were endued with the power of doing evil, and were wholly bent upon deeds of wickedness.... According to the current belief, he [a witch] was not only willing to take the life of his nearest friend, but such an one was the preferred object of his vengeance.... Such was the universal terror of witches, that their lives were forfeited by the laws of the Iroquois.[39]

Witches like Thadodaho were twisted in mind and body and assaulted their victims in a way that fundamentally challenged Deganawidah's mission. As ethnologist Annemarie Anrod Shimony observed, "Iroquois witchcraft is supposed to cause derangement, physical sickness, maiming, and ultimately death ... [;] witching is never far removed from the area of health."[40] The prophet's message of peace contained three parts, one of which concerned physical and mental well-being. He proclaimed, "Health means soundness of mind and body; it also means peace, for that is what comes when minds are sane and bodies cared for."[41] Concern for people's health and vitality paralleled concern for the safety and peace of the Five Nations and thus required that Deganawidah and his followers confront the problem of witchcraft.

But, ironically, prohibition of the practice seemed only to acknowledge the pervasiveness of the problem without effectively controlling it. Witchcraft among the Iroquois was in part a product of the repression of overt hostility and violence within the communities of Iroquoia; it afforded, a secret, threatening way to deal with rivalry, hatred, and jealousy. All the while, Iroquois people struggled to discern whether the physical and mental afflictions that periodically beset them were the result of natural processes or sinister magic. This was a troubled universe, one that even the great prophet could not fully heal. Iroquoia in the seventeenth century may have had some of the charac-

---

[39]Morgan, *League of the Iroquois*, 164–65.
[40]Shimony, *Conservatism Among the Iroquois*, 288.
[41]Wallace, *White Roots of Peace*, 13–14.

teristics of the modern Iroquois communities observed by Shimony, where she noticed "an almost paranoid undercurrent of suspicion, in which each person sees his health and good fortune and even his life threatened by someone or something."[42] In witchcraft, we see perhaps the emotional, social, and psychological costs of effecting the Iroquois peace, as well as a potential seed of its destruction.

With the conversion and enlistment of Thadodaho, Deganawidah accomplished his mission's initial task, and he turned his attention to the consolidation and codification of his diplomatic and political victory. Hiawatha had raised up a string of wampum and declared to the wizard, Thadodaho, "These are the Words of the Great Law. On these Words we shall build the House of Peace, the Longhouse with the five fires that is yet one household. These are the Words of Righteousness and Health and Power."[43]

The Mohawks, Oneidas, Cayugas, then the Senecas, and finally the remainder of the Onondagas were joined together in a confederation, metaphorically housed in one extended lodge that united them, while allowing each the continuing autonomy of its own fire. The contemporary Condolence ceremony's ritual, the Roll Call of the Chiefs, still commemorates and reenacts the installation of the fifty original founders of the League of Peace. As the deer horns of authority were placed on their heads, they became men of peace, committed to the maintenance of harmony in their families, clans, villages, and the greater Longhouse. Deganawidah and the civil chiefs planted a great Tree of Peace at Onondaga, the settlement of Thadodaho, now designated as the Firekeeper. The evergreen "Tree of the Great Long Leaves" (great white pine) sheltered the League, and beneath it the founders spread the soft, white, feathery down of the globe thistle— the Great White Mat of the Law—upon which the lords of the League sat. The Tree's roots spread out in four directions, signifying the extension of the Peace and Law to all humanity. People of good will could see the roots, follow them to their source, and join in the Great Peace.[44] Deganawidah and the chiefs then uprooted a great and lofty pine, exposed a chasm, and discarded their weapons of war. A swift

[42]Shimony, *Conservatism Among the Iroquois*, 261–62.
[43]Wallace, *White Roots of Peace*, 24.
[44]Ibid., 30, 7–8; W. M. Beauchamp, *Civil, Religious and Mourning Councils and Ceremonies of Adoption of New York Indians*, New York State Museum Bulletin, no. 113 (Albany, 1907), 363, 365–77.

current of water swept them away, they replanted the tree, and they proclaimed, "Thus we bury all the weapons of war out of sight, and establish the 'Great Peace.' Hostilities shall not be seen nor heard of any more among you, but 'Peace' shall be preserved among the Confederated Nations."[45]

At the highest, most abstract level, the confederate chiefs formed themselves into a grand council, which considered matters involving the entire League. Chiefs represented particular matrilineal lineages, or *owachiras*, within clans, which in turn resided within individual nations. Their titles and positions were distributed unevenly throughout Iroquoia, reflecting the complexity and dynamism of Iroquois social and political structure. League chiefs commanded great prestige, even if they—like ordinary men and women—possessed little coercive power. They owed their titles to the *owachira* matrons who appointed them and maintained their positions only as long as they exemplified and fulfilled Deganawidah's mission and retained their people's confidence.[46]

The grand council met around the fire at Onondaga. On one side sat the Mohawks and Senecas (the fathers, uncles, or elder brothers), and across from them sat the Oneidas and Cayugas (the sons, nephews, or younger brothers), with the Firekeeper—Thadodaho—and the Onondagas presiding and mediating between the two. The Iroquois prohibited prolonged debate after nightfall in order to avoid the dangers of frayed tempers and hasty judgments. Important propositions were not discussed on the same day they were received by the councils. Deganwidah called for decision making by consensus, which the Five Nations achieved by referring matters first to one side and then to the other. The host Onondagas ratified agreements between the sides or referred matters back to them when disagreement arose. Unanimity was essential, and debate was to proceed in a measured, respectful, courteous manner that suppressed open expression of disagreement or hostility.

---

[45]Hewitt, "Constitution of the Confederacy by Dekanawidah, collected and translated from the Mohawk text by Chief Seth Newhouse," NAA ms. 1343; see also Wallace, *White Roots of Peace*, 7–8, 30–31; Hale, *Iroquois Book of Rites*, 127.

[46]Lafitau, *Customs of American Indians*, 1:287, 290–300. According to Lafitau, the grand Iroquois council conducted itself "with so much zeal for the common welfare that there results from it a harmony and an admirable unanimity which works for the safety of the tribe [confederacy] and which, for that reason, nothing can break asunder" (ibid., 287). See also Norton, *Journal*, 112: "Their Chiefs are called Beloved Men, and come to that station from the general approbation which their conduct thro' life may have merited or received from their Tribe."

Serious differences were aired in private, not publicly in council. Nations and sides strove to speak with one voice, or they did not speak at all; they sought compromise and accommodation. Deganawidah had cautioned the chiefs not to quarrel, for during such episodes, "the white panther (the fire dragon of discord) will come and take your rights and privileges away," precipitating suffering, poverty, and disgrace.[47] Deganawidah warned: "If you chiefs by the council fire should be continually throwing ashes at one another, your people will go astray, their heads will roll, authority will be gone; your enemies then may see that your minds are scattered, the League will be at a standstill, and the Good Peace and Power will be unable to proceed."[48]

The power of the grand council, however, is easily overstated. Local Iroquois communities enjoyed considerable autonomy. The decisions, or nondecisions, of the confederacy were the product of discussions in households, villages, and tribes throughout Iroquoia. These were the deliberations of ordinary men and women rather than specialized elites; the discourse of the League council was, then, only a reflection of the considered debates that characterized *owachira*, clan, town, and nation. The Five Nations diligently, and sometimes in frustrated futility, sought to attain "one voice, one mind, and one heart."[49]

Nonetheless, the great council and the civil chiefs exercised important leadership as they embodied and promoted the fundamental social and political values of the Iroquois. Chiefs "shall be Spiritual advisors of the people for all time to come. The thickness of their skin shall be . . . seven spans of the hand[,] that is to say, they shall be genuine proof against angry passions," the Great Law maintained. Chiefs were cautioned to take no offense at anything said against them, or for any wrongdoing that they might suffer. "Their hearts shall be full of peace and goodwill, their spirits yearning for the good of their people. [L]ongsuffering in carrying out their duties, [their]

---

[47]See Wallace, *White Roots of Peace*, 32–33, 37; Parker, *Constitution*, 103–4; Fenton, "Iroquois Treaty Making," 12–14. For a seventeenth-century analysis of the Five Nations' "very wise" practice of convening annual council meetings at Onondaga, designed to mend ruptures, preserve their union, maintain "a good understanding with one another," see Thwaites, ed., *Jesuit Relations*, 51:237.

[48]Wallace, *White Roots of Peace*, 35.

[49]Beauchamp, *Mourning Councils*, 424–26; Fenton, "Structure, Continuity, and Change," 13. Conrad Weiser's account of negotiations at Onondaga in 1743 provides a good illustration of the workings of consensual politics among the Five Nations; see Hazard, ed., *Minutes of the Provincial Council of Pennsylvania*, IV, 660–69. Weiser, for example, met "in the Bushes," that is informally, before formal, public talks were held; in this way, difficult matters were settled in private, and public discourse could follow in harmony and decorum (661–62). All indications are that this political process was an ancient one.

firmness shall be tempered with tenderness. The spirit of anger and fury shall find no lodgement in them, and in all they say and do [they] shall exercise calmness."[50] Members of the grand council, the *Iroquois Book of Rites* proclaimed, "must have regard for their people... that all may be in peace, even the whole nation.... If there is anything to be done for the good of the people, it is their duty to do it." The league chiefs epitomized the Iroquois ideal of peace and harmony and provided examples of how every Iroquois should live. Like their exemplary leaders, Iroquois men and women were enjoined to eschew rash, passionate decisions and actions, to show respect and regard for others, to repress anger and hostility, to provide hospitality to their kinsmen, and to work for the welfare of the whole.[51]

As men of peace, civil chiefs had no official role in war. Similarly, war leaders had no institutionalized place in League, tribal, or village deliberation, beyond that which they earned as respected members of the group. War parties organized themselves in temporary, improvisational ways. If league chiefs themselves participated, they were required to remove their antlers of authority temporarily, just as the emblems of their office would be shed during illness, at death, or for malfeasance, that is, at times when they lost their ability to reason or function. William M. Beauchamp wrote that "in some cases a sachem was supposed to be barred by his office from taking part in war at all." He concluded such a practice "showed that this people recognized in peace something far better than war. One of their own names for the confederacy was that of the *Great Peace*, and though they fought fiercely they always hailed peace as one of the greatest blessings."[52]

The designation of two Seneca sachems as "war chiefs" poses an apparent contradiction. Yet their role had little to do with war; Deganawidah had appointed them as keepers of the western door of the Iroquois Longhouse and mandated that they screen the messengers to the council, protecting it against "crawling creatures," that is, ruinous, evil propositions. The two Seneca doorkeepers represented security; they existed because Deganawidah and his followers realized that beyond Iroquoia lived people who might threaten their particular vision of peace. This possibility—that some would refuse to join their

[50]Hewitt, "Newhouse Constitution," NAA ms. 1343; see also Parker, *Constitution*, 104.

[51]Hale, *Iroquois Book of Rites*, 164 (quotation), 170. See also Beauchamp, *Mourning Councils*, 388.

[52]Beauchamp, *Mourning Councils*, 342–43. See also Fenton, "Structure, Continuity, and Change," 17.

Great Peace—underscores the fact that the Five Nations were never pacifists. They would defend their League and their dream vigorously, attacking those who persistently endangered them, reducing their enemies, if necessary, to a "heap of bones." While their foes, understandably, could interpret such warfare as aggressive, the Five Nations themselves had no program of military conquest; for the Iroquois these conflicts represented the frustration or failure of their vision, not its realization.[53]

Together the confederate chiefs of the Five Nations facilitated and personified the Iroquois ideal of peace and security. The Iroquois saw them as trees, some of which might occasionally topple; but, grasping each other's hands firmly, the fifty chiefs formed a circle "so strong that if a tree shall fall prostrate upon it, it could neither shake nor break it, and thus our people and our grandchildren shall remain in the circle in security, peace and happiness." The circle of the trees and of the council fire, which represented security; the smoke of the council fire, which brought Iroquois words to the Creator and signaled the existence of peaceful social life; the antlers of authority, which declared that the chiefs, like the deer, provided sustenance to their people and that the Iroquois lived on the flesh of animals not humans: these and other symbols associated with the confederate chiefs, and emanating from the Deganawidah Epic, expressed the importance of peace in Iroquois culture.[54]

As mentors and moral guides, the confederate chiefs worked to construct and maintain peace by reminding their people of Deganawidah's words and the Creator's will:

[53]See Parker, *Constitution*, 97; Hewitt, "Dekanawidah's Government . . . by Seth Newhouse," NAA ms. 3524; Hewitt, "The Iroquois Law of Atonement," NAA ms. 663–b; Hale, *Iroquois Book of Rites*, 164. See also Lafitau, *Customs of the American Indians*, 2:101, 103, on the unofficial status of warfare and attempts in council by "peace partisans" to prevent war; on the careful deliberations that preceded the decision to embark on war, see ibid., 98–104. See the comments of Adriaen van der Donck (1655) on the subordinate place of martial figures among the Iroquois, in Ada van Gastel, "Van der Donck's Description of the Indians: Additions and Corrections," *William and Mary Quarterly*, 3d ser., 43 (July 1990), 420; see ibid., 420–21, on the process of consensual politics among the Iroquois.
[54]These symbols are common in the historical record; for an early example, see the 1645 peace embassies to Three Rivers described above, from Thwaites, ed., *Jesuit Relations*, 27:247–65, 281–91, 303. At one point the Mohawk orator "took hold of a Frenchman, placed his arm within his, and with his other arm he clasped that of an Alguonquin. Having thus joined himself to them, 'Here,' he said, 'is the knot that binds us inseparably; nothing can part us" (261). This ancient metaphor of the human circle or chain would express itself later as a "Covenant Chain," a term that represented a nominal rather than a conceptual shift.

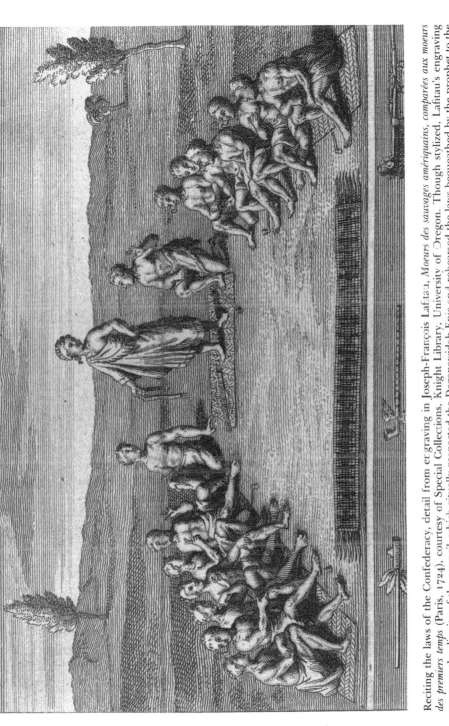

Reciting the laws of the Confederacy, detail from engraving in Joseph-François Lafitau, *Moeurs des sauvages amériquains, comparées aux moeurs des premiers temps* (Paris, 1724), courtesy of Special Collections, Knight Library, University of Oregon. Though stylized, Lafitau's engraving captures the dignity of the council, which ritually reenacted the Deganawidah Epic and rehearsed the laws bequeathed by the prophet to the Iroquois. The standing orator holds a wampum belt, which is shown also at the bottom of the plate. Wampum gave legitimacy to diplomatic speech, according to the Iroquois ritual of "propping up" one's words.

Harken, that peace may continue unto future days! Always listen to the words of the Great Creator, for he has spoken. United people, let no evil find lodging in your minds. For the Great Creator has spoken and the cause of peace shall not become old. The cause of peace shall not die if you remember the Great Creator.[55]

The Deganawidah Epic thus provided a method of government, politics, and diplomacy, one that the Five Nations in fact employed in the real world of seventeenth-century America.

That real world was no less real by virtue of its symbolic construction. Indeed the symbols and metaphors that took as their basic referent the Deganawidah Epic and that proved to be so pervasive in Iroquois discourse suggest that even the concrete entity of the confederacy and its grand council were less important as governmental bodies than as expressions of a larger Iroquois political culture.[56] We have already encountered a number of symbols from the Epic which helped define peace and underscore its fundamental importance. These symbols reflected and helped to frame the Iroquois world view, while they provided a vocabulary for Iroquois social and political discourse: the great tree and four white roots of peace; the chasm in which the hatchet and other weapons of war were confined; the wampum discovered by Hiawatha and used by Deganawidah for Condolence; the council fire or the circle of unity and safety; and the longhouse itself.[57] To these could be added the river or lake with no waves, the path that was straight and contained no obstacles, the eagle that sat atop the Tree of Peace to warn of approaching danger, the great, common dish and kettle of sharing and hospitality, the clouds that covered the sun and implied the absense of clarity and reason, which needed to be restored, the flowing or staining of blood that Deganawidah halted or covered up to end violence and vengeance. All of these images were ubiquitous in Iroquois thought and speech.[58]

[55]Wallace, *White Roots of Peace,* 40.

[56]It is worth emphasizing again the importance of localism in Iroquois society and polity, a point that William N. Fenton made clearly in "The Concept of Locality and the Program of Iroquois Research," in Fenton, ed., *Symposium on Local Diversity in Iroquois Culture, Bureau of American Ethnology Bulletin,* no. 149 (Washington, D.C., 1951).

[57]As Paul A. W. Wallace noted, "the power of symbols is profound,...for symbols are a means by which practical persons, shy of metaphysics and impatient of theory, are enabled to apprehend great ideas, take them to heart, and put them to work" (*White Roots of Peace,* 7).

[58]"Official Symbolism" is discussed in Parker, *Constitution,* 44–49, 98, 101–3; see also Fenton, "Structure, Continuity, and Change," 16–17, and "Glossary of Figures of Speech in Iroquois Political Rhetoric," also in Jennings et al., eds., *History and Culture of Iroquois Diplomacy,* 115–24; Fenton, "Lore of the Longhouse," 140–43; Wallace, *White Roots of Peace,* 31–32, 35.

The Five Nations invoked them especially in the rituals that organized their lives, celebrated and reenacted their political myth, and promoted peace. Ritual practices allowed the Iroquois to represent themselves, their polity and moral order. That representation made sense and persisted because it well described Iroquois reality and experience. Such ceremonies and laws as the Condolence, Atonement, and Adoption helped to meet the psychic and social needs of the people living in Iroquoia under the Great Peace, while maintaining and expanding it. In them, the Iroquois faced the "fire dragon of discord" squarely.

Death as a result of murder posed the greatest threat to the harmony of Iroquois society, because the avenging of it could quickly escalate into blood feud. But even a single death that visited the longhouse through natural causes, rather than through warfare or murder, weakened the *orenda* of the people and imperiled Iroquois society. The Iroquois believed that grief rendered one irrational, anti-social, and dangerous.[59] Normal public life could not continue while one remained in a state of unconsoled mourning. As one seventeenth-century observer, the acting Superior of the Jesuit mission in New France, Jean de Quen, explained: "These people believe that sadness, anger, and all violent passions expel the rational soul from the body, which meanwhile, is animated only by the sensitive soul which we have in common with animals. That is why, on such occasions, they usually make a present to restore the rational soul to the seat of reason."[60]

The death of his daughters and wife made Hiawatha temporarily abandon his people and his mission of peace and become a woodland wanderer in the Epic of Deganawidah. In his aimless journey, Hiawatha discovered the shells that Deganawidah eventually used to assuage his grief and restore him as a sensible, social being. Wiping away Hiawatha's tears, removing obstructions in his ears and throat, Deganawidah proclaimed, "Now shalt thou do thy thinking in peace. ... Now, reason has returned; thy judgement is firm again. Thou art ready to advance the New Mind. Let us together make the laws of the Great Peace, which shall abolish war."[61] Deganawidah thus ended

[59] J. N. B. Hewitt, "The Requickening or Fifteen Matters," NAA ms. 3588; Hewitt and Fenton, "Requickening Address, 66–67; Hewitt and Fenton, "Mnemonic Pictographs," 303; Wallace, *Death and Rebirth of the Seneca*, 76–77, 93–97. Lafitau dealt at length with "Death, Burial and Mourning," in *Customs of the American Indians*, 2:154–55, 216–52.

[60] Thwaites, ed., *Jesuit Relations*, 42:51.

[61] Wallace, *White Roots of Peace*, 21–22; see also A. F. C. Wallace, *Death and Rebirth of the Seneca*, 97–98.

the horror of chronic blood feud and provided an instrument to maintain peace in the face of the crisis of death.

That instrument was the Rite of Condolence and Requickening, a form of symbolic discourse in which the Five Nations would console and rehabilitate the bereaved. The ceremony would puzzle and fascinate European observers like Father Vimont throughout the seventeenth and eighteenth centuries. A later observer recorded the poignancy and compassion with which the "Unscathed Ones" or "Clearminded" spoke to the grieving "Downminded":

> Now then, we say, we wipe away
> The Falling tears, so that peacefully
> You might look around. And then we think
> Something stops up your ears. Now then
> With care have we removed this hindrance
> To your hearing; easily then, it may be,
> You will hear the words to be said.
> And also we think there is a stoppage
> In your throat. Now therefore, we also say
> We remove the obstruction, so that freely
> You may speak in our mutual greetings.
> . . . .
> You are losing your great men. Into the earth
> They are borne; also the warriors;
> Also your women, and your grandchildren as well;
> So that in the midst of blood
> You are sitting. Now therefore, we say,
> We wash the blood stains from your seat,
> So that it may be for a time
> That happily the place may be clean
> For a few days, where pleasantly
> You rest and are looking all around.[62]

These moving words were delivered by condolers toward the middle of the ceremony. At the completion of the rites, grieving Iroquois men and women had recovered their reason and order. The Five Nations had symbolically cleared the forest paths between their own villages—and later between their own and European settlements—removed the thorns from their feet, wiped away their tears and cleared their ears and throats, restored their hearts and rational souls, and pushed away the clouds that covered the sun. They had washed the

[62]Beauchamp, *Mourning Councils*, 357–59.

blood from their corn husk mats, leveled and covered old graves, gathered the unburied bones of people recently killed and hidden them beneath the roots of a great tree, so "that nothing might ever issue from their tombs that could sadden their relatives, and arouse any feelings of revenge in their bosoms." Whether the deceased was a major leader or a less conspicuous member of the *owachira*, the grieving survivors could continue their lives only after condolers had "lifted up their minds."[63]

Numerous examples of such ceremonies and sentiments pepper the historical record. An inscription in the *Jesuit Relations* from the 1650s is typical. Recording the words attached by the Iroquois to each string of wampum, a Jesuit chronicler wrote, "The first one [string or gift] was given to wipe away the tears that are commonly shed upon hearing of the brave warriors killed in battle. The second was intended to serve as a pleasant draught to counteract whatever of bitterness might remain in the hearts of the French.... The third was to furnish a piece of bark, or blanket, to put over the dead, for fear the sight of them might renew the old-time dissensions.... The sixth [was]... to make clear the river, stained with so much blood."[64] Another *Relation* from the same decade quoted an Onondaga envoy referring to "a May-tree [Iroquois Tree of Peace],... which should rear its summit above the clouds, in order that all the Nations of the earth might be able to see it, and that it might mark a rendezvous where all the world could rest in Peace under the shade of its leaves." The envoy continued, proposing "to make a deep pit, extending down into hell, into which should be thrown all slander and suspicion, and everything that might disturb good feeling, and embitter the sweetness of a Peace which heaven had given us."[65]

<hr />

[63]Ibid., 393. On the use of the Condolence in diplomacy, in addition to Fenton, "Structure, Continuity, and Change," see Mary A. Druke, "Iroquois Treaties: Common Forms, Varying Interpretations, also in Jennings et al., eds., *History and Culture of Iroquois Diplomacy*, 85–98.

[64]See Thwaites, ed., *Jesuit Relations*, 50:165–69, 185–91; quotation on 167.

[65]*Ibid.*, 41:51–53. The Jesuit observer also recorded the Iroquois attempt to transform exo-cannibalism into endo-cannibalism and thus necessitate and accomplish its abolition: "to bury so far under ground their war-kettle,—in which they were accustomed to boil human flesh and the dismembered bodies of the captives, whom they cruelly devoured,—that that abominable kettle should never be seen on earth again, because all their hatred was changed into love" (53). For a sampling of other exemplars of the Condolence, from the seventeenth to the early nineteenth centuries, see the following: "Propositions made by certain sachems (sachimas) of the Mohawks...," November 19, 1655, in Jonathan Pearson, trans. and ed., *Early Records of the City and County of Albany and the Colony of Rensselaerswyck*, rev., ed., by A. J. F. van Laer, 4 vols. (Albany, N.Y., 1869–1919), 1: 237; Lawrence H. Leder, ed., *The Livingston Indian Records, 1666–1723* (Gettysburg, Pa., 1956), 46, 88–89, 91; Cadwallader

As previously mentioned, death through murder presented the gravest danger to the peace; the Law of Atonement was designed to prevent the social crisis murder could precipitate. When someone suffered the murder of a kinsman, the Iroquois said that "the sky is torn away—dissolved, and that person will be overwhelmed in the darkness of the night of sorrow." The rage and grief that followed murder might easily degenerate into violence, for relatives inevitably avenged the murder of their kin, and such retaliatory slaughter could quickly escalate into pervasive, devastating blood feud. Fratricidal conflict and indiscriminate killing created a climate of terror in which no one could feel safe. To confront the "amazing conduct" of the "Great Destroyer, the Great Darkness" in their midst, Deganawidah and the founding chiefs provided the Law of Atonement, a system of symbolic and material compensation, by which social harmony could be restored.[66]

Convening the interested parties, the chiefs urged offenders to "withdraw this stone-hatchet from the wound," to "remove the spetters of blood . . . where it has splattered among the people," and to compensate the mourners to "the value of twenty"—twenty strings of wampum, ten for the life of the victim and ten for the life of the murderer, which was symbolically forfeited in the act. "It is with these that their bones shall be wrapt" and the death put behind them. The offender then picked up the wampum, thereby admitting guilt, symbolically withdrew the hatchet, and wiped away the blood. "So then," the arbitrators proclaimed, "now one has restored all things again, now then, immediately, the suffering minds . . . will be fully restored to normal well-being." As the elder woman of the *owachira* accepted the tokens, and as the offender absorbed the community's shame and humiliation, evil was "put away." And with the burial of the deceased

Colden, *The History of the Five Nations Depending on the Province of New-York in America* (Ithaca, N.Y., 1958 [orig. pub. 1727]), 103–8; Norton, *Journal*, 111.

[66]J. N. B. Hewitt, "Means Used in the Settlement of Murder," NAA ms. 3563 (all quotations from this manuscript); Hewitt, "Some Laws of the Ancient Iroquois League," NAA ms. 663-b. Aspects of the Condolence, the Laws of Atonement, and Iroquois handling of "criminal" matters were described early in the eighteenth century in Lafitau, *Customs of the American Indians*, I, 300–308. In addition to his own firsthand experience, Lafitau drew from the observations of earlier Jesuit writers, published in Thwaites, ed., *Jesuit Relations*, 38:281–87. See also Thomas F. O'Donnell, ed., [*Adriaen van der Donck's] Description of New Netherlands* (Syracuse, N.Y., 1968 [orig. pub. Amsterdam, 1655]), 101. According to Major John Norton, *Journal*, 111, "The Laws and Regulations of the Confederacy were few and simple. A man that should spill the blood of another, it was required of him, or of his relations, to appease the kindred of the deceased, with wampum, to a considerable amount, which they were at liberty either to receive or to reject, and remain free to take vengeance."

by those "whose minds are unaffected" the entire community confirmed the atonement process.[67]

In the ritual practice of adoption, the Iroquois also revivified themselves, maintaining or enlarging their Great Peace. When they raised up a new chief to assume the title and responsibilities of the deceased leader, when they gave an old lineage or clan name to one of its young constituents, when they adopted a captive into a family and crowned him or her with the name of the lost member, or when they absorbed refugees or entire nations into their villages, tribes, or confederacy, they assuaged their grief and gave themselves new life. The process by which the Iroquois replaced or augmented their population was one with the historical construction of the League, their "extended lodge." In both cases, the Iroquois embraced new people, ritually transformed them into kinspeople, and made a place for them in the longhouse, extending its rafters if necessary. After uniting the fifth nation to the confederacy, Deganawidah had declared, "Now then we have completed it . . . , we have removed from the border this belt of bushes, we have caused all to lie flat." The Iroquois gave thanks, and Deganawidah responded with a charge to subsequent generations: "This is your work. Thus shall it continue to be as it endures into the future."[68]

---

[67]Quotations from Hewitt, "Means Used in the Settlement of Murder," NAA ms. 3563. See also Hewitt, "Some Laws of the Ancient Iroquois League," NAA ms. 663-b, in which he explained that the murder of women required thirty to forty gifts, for women, it was said, could not so easily defend themselves, and it was only through women that they populated the country. And see Tooker, "League of the Iroquois," 423–24. The Law of Atonement was designed to address internal crisis and as a result was not often witnessed by outsiders. Nonetheless, we can see it in operation in 1657, when an Iroquois envoy sought to atone for the murder of a Jesuit priest, Leonard Garreau, with "two wretched little presents, according to their custom . . . to show their regret at the accident . . . and to dry our tears and assuage our grief" (Thwaites, ed., *Jesuit Relations*, 42:237); see also 43:43, 61. The French seemed unimpressed in these instances, though Lafitau showed more respect for such practices; see *Customs of the American Indians* 1:303–5, 308. See also Leder, ed., *Livingston Indian Records*, 46, 88.

[68]J. N. B. Hewitt, "The Laws of Adoption,—of Persons, Families, Clans and Tribes," NAA ms. 496 (quotations from 5–7). See also Parker, *Constitution*, 49–52; Beauchamp, *Mourning Councils*, 344, 404–10; Lafitau, *Customs of the American Indians*, 171–72; Wallace, *Death and Rebirth of the Seneca*, 102–7; Daniel Richter, "War and Culture: The Iroquois Experience," *William and Mary Quarterly*, 3d ser., 40 (October 1983), 528–59. James Axtell, "The White Indians of Colonial America," in Axtell, *The European and the Indian: Essays in the Ethnohistory of Colonial North America* (New York, 1981), 168–206, discusses the strikingly effective transformation of Europeans into Indians. See also James Lynch, "The Iroquois Confederacy, and the Adoption and Administration of Non-Iroquoian Individuals and Groups Prior to 1756," *Man in the Northeast*, no. 30, 83–99, for some useful suggestions about the Iroquois conception and process of adoption, which he brilliantly sets into the context of Iroquois cosmology. Lynch distinguished between two types of adoption, "assimilative" and "associative." He argued that the latter mode represented an "historical adaptation to a new set of political realities, in which as-

Following warfare the Iroquois incorporated individual refugees and captives in three ways: as trophies of war, as the objects of torture and cannibalism, and as persons given a new birth as living members of the group. We have already noted the gruesome process of assimilation by ingestion. The scalps of war victims also could be adopted ritually to calm rage and grief, and to avenge the deaths of kinspeople. The most common form of naturalization, however, seems to have been the adoption of living outsiders to assume the places of deceased Iroquois people. Despite long-standing perceptions of Iroquois cruelty, some early observers commented on the relative gentleness of the captors; and Iroquois representation of their amalgamating process, not surprisingly, concurred. As Lafitau wrote, "To hear the Iroquois speak, . . . they claim to be less cruel than the others and treat the captives thus [with torture] only by reprisal." And Mary Jemison, the famous captive among the Senecas, asked of European societies, "Do they ever adopt an enemy and salute him by the tender name of brother?"[69]

In fact, captives did not remain so for long; after being presented to mourning families, "often still weeping for the dead whom these captives replace," captives were untied, stripped of their clothes, bathed, and redressed. An adopted man or woman then received visits from newly acquired relatives, and shortly thereafter, Lafitau tells us, "a feast is made for all the village to give him the name of the person whom he is resurrecting." Following other banquets to honor the naturalized Iroquois man or woman, each instantly "enters upon all his rights." "All the hope of the family is placed," Lafitau wrote, in the woman captive, "who becomes the mistress of this family and the branches dependent on it." Or, "if the captive is a man who requickens an Ancient, a man of consequence, he becomes important himself and has authority in the village if he can sustain by his own personal merit the name which he takes."[70]

---

similative adoptions were not necessary nor even desired by either party, but where symbolic identity was still ritually required" (89). In contrast, I argue that the two forms distinguished by Lynch were not so distinctive in fact, and that hope for some degree of assimilation within the context of association was not necessarily discarded; indeed, the original foundation of the Iroquois League of Peace seems to call for an adoptive process based on association.

[69]Wallace, *Death and Rebirth of the Seneca*, 102–3. On the symbolic replacement of dead kinsmen by ritually adopted scalps, see Norton, *Journal*, 111; Lafitau, *Customs of the American Indians*, 2:153–54, 161. Lafitau wrote further: "The condition of a captive to whom life is granted is hard enough among the Algonquin but among the Huron and Iroquois it is gentler in proportion as that of those thrown into the fire is more cruel (ibid., 171); see also Mary Jemison quoted in Axtell, "White Indians," 190.

[70]Lafitau, *Customs of the American Indians*, 2:154, 171–72; see also Reverend Henry Barclay, Missionary of the Society for the Propogation of the Gospel, to Cadwallader Colden, De-

Adopted and naturalized captives were thus symbolically reborn, becoming so fixed in their acquired Iroquois identity that, according to Lafitau, they could discern "almost no difference between the real Iroquois and themselves."[71] As James Axtell has shown, this transformation was often so thorough, even among European men and women, that some refused to return to the lives they left behind, to the great dismay of colonial officials.[72] Refugees seldom had a life to which they could return. The people dislocated by native or colonial warfare, or by the new epidemic diseases that swept through seventeenth-century America, were also gathered in and accepted fully by the Five Nations. They entered the Longhouse as individuals or as entire bands or tribes.

Indeed, as early as the 1650s, Jesuit missionaries reported, some Iroquois villages found themselves with "more strangers among them than pure Iroquois." The priest concluded in 1657 that some communities "now contain more Foreigners than natives of the country. Onnotaghe [Onondaga] counts seven different nations, who have come to settle in it; and there are as many as eleven in Sonnontouan [among the Senecas]."[73] And through much of the seventeenth century, until it became increasingly difficult to assimilate growing numbers of refugees, the Iroquois proved remarkably able to transform foreigners into Iroquois. Father Jacques Bruyas claimed in 1668 that these naturalized citizens of Iroquoia "have become Iroquois in temper and inclination." And French governor-general Alexandre de Prouville, seigneur de Tracy remarked in the mid–1660s, "The element of greatest strength among the Iroquois was not the Iroquois themselves"; instead, he observed, "their might resides in the large

---

cember 7, 1741, in *The Letters and Papers of Cadwallader Colden; Additional Letters and Papers, 1715–1748*, vol. 8, in *Collections of the New-York Historical Society for the Year 1934*, 67 (New York, 1937), 280–81. The Jesuit missionary Father Anthony Poncet found himself in a Mohawk lodge in 1653 under such circumstances and observed the Condolence merge into adoption: "I became aware that I was given in return for a dead man, the last mourning for whom these women were renewing,—causing the departed to become alive again in my person, according to their custom" (Thwaites, ed., *Jesuit Relations*, 50:139). The most striking example of a Jesuit's adoption, however, was the ritual adoption of Father Pierre Millet by the Oneidas and his transformation into Otassete, a member of the confederate grand council; his new kinsmen declared, "My elder brother, you are resurrected" (ibid., 64:67–107).

[71]Lafitau, *Customs of the American Indians*, 2:172.

[72]See Axtell, "White Indians," on the assimilation of European captives. Though Axtell may overstate the ability of Indians to assimilate adult white men, white women and children, and sometimes even men, were successfully incorporated into native societies with enough frequency to alarm colonists; see Alden T. Vaughan and Daniel K. Richter, "Crossing the Cultural Divide: Indians and New Englanders, 1605–1763," *Proceedings of the American Antiquarian Society*, 90 (1980), 23–99.

[73]Thwaites, ed., *Jesuit Relations*, 43:265.

number of captives,—French, Hurons, Algonquins, and those from the other Nations,—who formed more than two-thirds of the Iroquois."[74]

In the case of groups, the Iroquois could follow the precedent set by their founders. When the Cayugas had declared that their tribal organization already approximated the system proposed by Deganawidah, the prophet embraced them without annihilating their autonomy: "The delimiting bushes shall be leveled between your lands and those of the tribes who have joined the League. You shall become a member without reorganizing the internal structure of your tribe."[75] Following the Cayugas, in the seventeenth and eighteenth centuries others joined the League but maintained considerable autonomy; the process culminated in the integration of the Tuscaroras. Driven out of North Carolina following the Tuscarora Wars (1711–13), they found protection among the Five Nations, and by 1722 or 1723 their formal adoption increased the Iroquois to the Six Nations.[76] In a striking fashion, then, the Five Nations incorporated outsiders, physically and symbolically, into their longhouses and into their Longhouse, which represented their expansive universe and dynamic process of peace.

The symbols and metaphors and the institutions and ritual practices bequeathed by Deganawidah to the Five Nations provided a political and ideological structure that described and prescribed Iroquois life. Peace was never abstract or simply ideological; it was concrete and experiential. In the words of the historian Paul A. W. Wallace, "peace was a way of life, characterized by wisdom and graciousness"; it was "the Good expressed in action, that is, the good life."[77]

The Five Nations conceived of peace and enacted it in terms of a domestic harmony—within households, *owachiras*, and villages. Peace became possible only within a group cemented together by consanguinity and a common sense of moral order. More than the absence of war, peace meant a practical way of life lived face to face with other

[74]Ibid., 51:123; Tracy is quoted in 49:233. On the difficulties of assimilation as the influx of foreigners increased, see Daniel K. Richter, "Iroquois Versus Iroquois: Jesuit Missions and Christianity in Village Politics, 1642–1686," *Ethnohistory*, 32 (1985), 1–16, and Richter, "War and Culture."

[75]Lafitau, *Customs of the American Indians*, 2:172; J. N. B. Hewitt, miscellaneous unpublished notes, NAA ms. 3580; see also Parker, *Constitution*, 50–52.

[76]David Landy, "Tuscaroras among the Iroquois," in Trigger, ed., *Handbook of North American Indians: Northeast*, 15:518–20.

[77]Wallace, *White Roots of Peace*, 7.

people who found shelter, security, and strength under the branches of the Great Tree of Peace. In structuring their League on the model of the household they extended the mechanisms of domestic harmony to maintain peace throughout Iroquoia. The Iroquois kinship state was real as well as symbolic, for the clan system that wove through it, with its exogamous marriage patterns, made members of the same clans, arrayed in different nations, sisters and brothers, aunts and uncles, parents and children. And it implied that biological fathers and their children, and many cousins, aunts, and uncles would be members of different clans.[78]

The household was a domain controlled by women in their complementary relationship with men. Through the ownership of domestic property and the primary provision of subsistence, women commanded great prestige and authority. While men traveled beyond the village clearings to hunt, fight, or negotiate with outsiders, women maintained the lodges, families, and clans of the Five Nations. Women thus represented domesticity, security, prosperity, and peace; in contrast, men embodied wildness, risk, danger, and aggressiveness. In Iroquoian dualism, each sex was embued with something of the other, for women sanctioned war parties with their consent and provisions, and men promoted harmony and safety when they worked in their communities for peace.[79] When women demanded that their grief be assuaged and their kinsmen be replaced through warfare, they si-

---

[78]Iroquois social and political organization is summarized authoritatively in William N. Fenton, "Northern Iroquoian Culture Patterns," in Trigger, ed., *Handbook of North American Indians: Northeast*, 15:309–16.

[79]The sometimes misunderstood Iroquois representation of the Delawares as "women" illustrates the male/female dualism and the association of women with peace in Iroquois culture. Confusion about gender arrangements and meanings in Native American societies produced the notion that the Delawares, sometime in the 1740s, had been conquered and forced into the submissive status of women by the Six Nations of the Iroquois. In fact, as a number of scholars have noted recently, the Delawares had not been "conquered," nor were they subjects of the Iroquois in the way that a Euro-American construction of the term "woman" implied. According to David Zeisberger, Moravian missionary to the Delawares (Archer Butler Hulbert and William Nathaniel Schwarze, eds., *David Zeisberger's History of Northern American Indians, Ohio Archaeological and Historical Publications*, 19 [Columbus, Ohio, 1910], 1–173), the Iroquois and Delawares settled their differences following a long-standing rivalry by a special strategy, one that honored the Delawares; according to Zeisberger, "one nation should be the woman. She should be placed in the midst, while the other nations, who make war, should be the man and live around the woman. No one should touch or hurt the woman.... The woman should not go to war but endeavor to keep the peace with all" (34). In this fashion, the Iroquois used their own gendered, social, and spatial model of domestic life in ordering their larger world in the interest of peace. Delaware men were not actually clothed in women's garments or remade into cultivators of maize; rather, they were charged with "the preservation of peace and entrusted with the...great belt of peace and the chain of friendship which they must take care to preserve inviolate" (35).

multaneously acted aggressively like men, while, like women, they sustained and increased the population as if through childbirth. And men, when they advocated peace and sought to embrace a larger sphere of peoples in the Iroquois Longhouse, acted domestically like women, while they ventured, like men, through the forests into dangerous lands to effect the Great Peace, or to defend their communities against outside assaults.[80]

Good life among the Iroquois depended on achieving harmony, striking balance between dual principles, and among the most important dualisms that the Five Nations sought to address was the one that linked inside with outside, self with other. When it came to relations with foreigners, the Five Nations relied on the same methods that Deganawidah had used in creating their commonwealth. They pursued peace with those outside the domestic group by expanding the group boundaries themselves. Instead of constructing alliances in which negotiating parties remained fully discrete entities, they sought a complete merger; the many became one. Deganawidah's triumph was not to attach the five Iroquois nations simply to an alliance of nonaggression but to amalgamate them as one people. As a sort of midwife, the prophet attended their rebirth; as a single people—the People of the Extended Lodge—they possessed one mind and lived under one law. In this fashion the domestic model of peace became appropriate and effective in maintaining harmony in their motherland, Iroquoia.

The Five Nations continued their experimental process of peace into the colonial era, recruiting and welcoming both individuals and groups into their Great Peace. In expanding their League, they attempted to convince a wider universe of the imperatives of peace and the necessity of the Iroquois moral order to effect it. As foreigners followed the White Roots of Peace to their source, they were trans-

---

[80]Hewitt and Fenton, "Requickening Address," 82–85, discuss the dualism of female/male in Iroquois society and polity; see also Lynch, "The Iroquois Confederacy and Adoption," especially 83–84, on the relationship between male and female in Iroquois ideology and social and political order. Through the union of the male and female sides, the Five Nations achieved a "dialectical synthesis" expressed as *ne skennon'*, or "harmony" (84). For a convenient summary of Iroquois gender arrangements, see Nancy Bovillain, "Gender Relations in Native North America," *American Indian Culture and Research Journal*, 13, no. 2 (1989), 1–28; see also Elisabeth Tooker, "Women in Iroquois Society," in Michael K. Foster et al., eds., *Extending the Rafters: Interdisciplinary Approaches to Iroquoian Studies* (Albany, N.Y., 1984), 109–23. On women's role in the replacement of family members in mourning war, see Lafitau, *Customs of the American Indians*, 2:99, 154, 156; see also Du Creux, *Historia Canadensis*, 1:338–39. Iroquois League Chiefs literally represented women, as their appointment was dependent on the women holders of the league titles.

formed into kindred, allowed to dip food from the Iroquois common bowl, the "border of bushes" between lands was removed (though spatial distance remained), the way was made "to lie flat," and they became "braces" and extensions to the lengthened lodge.[81] As the Roll Call of the Chiefs proclaimed during the Condolence Ceremony:

> Then in later times they made additions
> To the great house.[82]

Despite the Five Nations' remarkable success in transforming foreigners into Iroquois, it was corrosive to their mission that many of those outside Iroquoia—especially Europeans—never assimilated into their kinship state and never embraced the Iroquois moral vision.

Deganawidah celebrated and embodied sensitivity, condolence, atonement, forgiveness, restraint, circumspection, calmness, and peace, all of which were essential to the success of the Iroquois experiment in peace. The Iroquois representation of their prophet portrayed him as the ideal model for humanity, which men and women should emulate. How successful were they, and what price did they pay?

The Jesuit Father Joseph-François Lafitau was one of the most acute observers of Iroquois life, and a rather lengthy quotation from his *magnum opus* is justified here as a means of analyzing their performance. In his chapter on political government, Lafitau wrote of the Iroquois:

> Respect for human beings which is the mainspring of their actions, serves no little to keep up their union. Each one, regarding others as masters of their own actions and themselves, lets them conduct themselves as they wish and judges only himself. I have often admired them in this respect. It must be agreed that they avoid an infinite number of quarrels by this means. They have, besides that, an admirable composure and do not know what it is to burst out into insults. I do not remember ever seeing any one of them angry. [This is the case] especially with the men, who would think themselves degraded if they showed any emotion. They go so far that a

---

[81]Fenton, "Structure, Continuity, and Change," 21; Hewitt, "Constitution," NAA ms. 3599; Hewitt, "The Laws of Adoption," NAA ms. 496.

[82]Beauchamp, *Mourning Councils,* 377.

man of composure would let himself be beaten outright by a drunk-
en man, without defending himself at all, especially if he is observed,
because he believes it unworthy to get angry and still more unworthy
to blame another for an action which he thinks the other man in-
capable of governing because he is not himself.[83]

The composure and restraint required to endure the physical assaults
of a drunken man (a man, that is, lacking composure, without sense
or reason) must have been tremendous. But it was of a piece with the
self-control required to repress anger, jealousy, grief, and rage within
a society that prohibited the open indulgence of such emotions. As
Lafitau acknowledged, "It is not that no disorder ever takes place
among them, that envy, cupidity, vengeance do not actuate them as
they do other men."[84] Deganawidah's admonitions simultaneously ad-
dressed and exacerbated the anxieties that his formula for peace had
produced.

The Condolence and Requickening, for example, expressed sensitivity to people's grief at the loss of a loved one and provided a safe
means of overcoming the dangerous insanity that bereavement in-
cited. Yet when mourning war ended in ritual torture and cannibalism
rather than adoption of the survivors, clearly restraint in dealing with
outsiders had failed dangerously. If Iroquois mourners achieved an
emotional release, internal harmony and external safety could be preserved; but if the fires of rage could not be extinguished, Iroquois
communities would suffer by being exposed to the retaliation of their
foes or the pathology of some of their own citizens.[85]

The Iroquois practice of dream guessing provided another means
of satisfying, in a nonaggressive way, the repressed "hidden wishes
of the soul." In dream festivals, Iroquois men and women recounted
their dreams and then coaxed the others to guess what they felt,

[83]Lafitau, *Customs of the American Indians*, 1:300.
[84]Ibid.
[85]Wallace, *Death and Rebirth of the Seneca*, 76–113 dealt brilliantly with these psychological
issues; he chronicled the career of Aharihon, an Onondaga war captain who captured and
tortured some forty men to avenge his brother's death (31–33, 102–13). We may wonder
whether ritual atonement was always satisfying to the injured parties; they may sometimes
have intended to take other vengeance later. The seventeenth-century observer Adriaen van
der Donck, *Description of New Netherland*, 101, wrote that tribal leaders and friends "use all
possible means, and give liberally to effect their object [atonement for murder and recon-
ciliation] when the offender is deficient in means.... A murder among them is never atoned
for without heavy payment. The nearest relative by blood always is the avenger, and if he
finds the murderer within twenty-four hours after the act, he is slain instantly; but if the
murderer can save himself until one day is past, and the avenger slays him afterwards, then
he is liable to be pursued and slain in like manner."

believed, or wanted by interpreting the dreams; it was then incumbent upon the community to fulfill their desires. The inability or refusal to satisfy the hidden wishes of the soul was a major source of ill health, but Iroquois dreams seem, generally, to have been appeased, tensions released, and social order maintained. Dream guessing seems to have been a remarkably sophisticated therapeutic practice; it institutionalized sensitivity in a society historically based on reticence and restraint.[86]

Ultimately, Iroquois men and women restrained themselves and lived, if uneasily, in harmony. They did so out of commitment to peace and for the greater good of their society, but they also knew that there would be consequences for inappropriate or aggressive behavior. When the Iroquois violated social norms, they expected retribution. That expectation produced anxiety, and this in turn bred restraint. Child abuse might result in retaliation in old age by one's children. Expressions of hostility to kinsmen or community members might lead to retaliatory witchcraft. Anger, once let loose, might be impossible to cage, devouring the man or woman who had thus lost all reason. In the ultimate exercise of restraint, or in desperation, Iroquois men and women occasionally killed themselves, finding in suicide the only means of dealing with the problems they could not confront.[87]

Most Iroquois men and women endured, however, adjusting to difficult conditions, celebrating the unique possibilities that Iroquois life offered, and overcoming in their own particular ways the obstacles that Iroquois culture had stacked against itself. To guide them in ordinary life and in their larger mission they had the myth and teachings of their prophet, Deganawidah. Whether Iroquois cultural inclinations and historical experience retrospectively generated the explanatory text of the myth, or whether the real career of Degan-

[86]J. N. B. Hewitt, "The Iroquois Concept of the Soul," *Journal of American Folk-Lore*, 8 (April–June 1895), 107–16; Wallace, *Death and Rebirth of the Seneca*, 59–75; Lafitau, *Customs of the American Indians*, 1:231–37. According to Jesuit historian Joseph Jouvency, "they believe that there are two main sources of disease; one of these is in the mind of the patient himself, which desires something, and will vex the body of the sick man until it possesses the thing required. For they think that there are in every man certain inborn desires, often unknown to themselves, upon which happiness of individuals depends" (Thwaites, ed., *Jesuit Relations*, 1: 259). See also ibid., 10:169–73, which concerns the culturally similar Hurons.

[87]See A. Irving Hallowell, "Some Psychological Characteristics of the Northeastern Indians," in Hallowell, *Culture and Experience* (Philadelphia, 1955), 125–50, esp. 134–41; William N. Fenton, "Iroquois Suicide: A Study in the Stability of a Cultural Pattern," *Bureau of American Ethnology Bulletin*, no. 128, Anthropological Papers, no. 14 (Washington, D.C., 1941), 79–138.

awidah and his chartering myth shaped the social and political culture of subsequent generations of Iroquois people, is unimportant. In any event, in the seventeenth century the text and Iroquois behavior were both factors; each helped form and reflected the other. If human action is understood as purposeful behavior of people living in accordance with a meaningful scheme, then the Deganawidah Epic and its ritual performances simultaneously reflected the material circumstances and history of the Five Nations, constituted the Iroquois interpretation of reality, and represented Iroquois action and belief.[88]

As European colonization began to achieve some success in the seventeenth century, and as contact increased between the two Old Worlds in northeastern North America, the Five Nations of the Iroquois embraced and enacted the peace they had constructed. Looking back to that distant moment, we struggle as historians to reconstruct the past, an enterprise perhaps as difficult as early seventeenth-century Iroquois efforts to imagine the implications of Dutch, French, and English penetration of their world. From the foreshortened perspective of the present, years, decades, even centuries run together and glaze the distant past with a certain timelessness. The present, or less distant past, seems to proceed from those times inevitably and inalterably. The people who lived that history, however, produced a succession of meaningful interpretations of their world in a dynamic relationship with their experiences. The Iroquois did not seem particularly awed by Europeans or their culture, material or spiritual. The Anglican missionary Henry Barclay wrote to Cadwallader Colden in 1741, "They seem always to have Lookd upon themselves as far Superiour to the Rest of Mankind and accordingly Call themselves *Ongwehoenwe* i.e. Men Surpasing all other men."[89] Nor did they envision their own decline, in the fashion that would become the cliche and myth of the Vanishing Indian.[90] Looking back on Ir-

---

[88]See Marshall Sahlins, *Culture and Practical Reason* (Chicago, 1976), viii.

[89]Barclay, missionary of the Society for the Propogation of the Gospel, to Colden, December 7, 1741, in *The Letters and Papers of Cadwallader Colden*, 8: *Additional Letters and Papers, 1715–1748, Collections of the New-York Historical Society for the Year 1934*, 67 (New York, 1937), 279.

[90]On white images of American Indians, see especially Robert F. Berkhofer, Jr., *The White Man's Indian: Images of the American Indian from Columbus to the Present* (New York, 1978) and Berkhofer, "White Conceptions of Indians," in Wilcomb E. Washburn, ed., *Handbook of North American Indians: History of Indian-White Relations* (1988), in William C. Sturtevant, gen. ed., *Handbook of North American Indians*, 20 vols. projected (Washington, D.C., 1978–), 4:522–47; Brian Dippie, *The Vanishing American: White Attitudes and United States Indian Policy* (Middle-

oquois action and thought as inscribed in the historical record, we can watch the Five Nations learning from the course of their experience. They sought to expand their League of Peace, and to embrace ever more people as kinsmen who would share the peace, prosperity, and security of the Iroquois Longhouse.

Despite Iroquois confidence, Europeans wrought enormous changes in their world, which severely taxed the Five Nations' abilities to effect and maintain their vision of peace. But the meager efforts of Europeans to establish colonies in the early seventeenth century could hardly have impressed the Iroquois or forced them to modify in any significant way their goals or strategies. Indeed, the appearance of Europeans initially required no revision of the program represented in the Deganawidah Epic. The Iroquois acted as if they expected these foreigners to behave like the other peoples they encountered at the margins of Iroquoia. Amalgamation, they supposed, would be the gradual and natural outgrowth of any sustained contact with the Five Nations.

---

town, Conn., 1982). In seventeenth-century New Netherland, the idea of the Vanishing Indian can be seen in van der Donck's concern "that after the Christians have multiplied and the natives have disappeared and melted away, a memorial of them may be preserved" (*Description of the New Netherlands*, 71–72). His concern seems to anticipate that of the nineteenth-century painter of Indians George Catlin, who devoted his professional life "to the production of a literal and graphic delineation of the living manners, customs, and character of an interesting race of people, who are rapidly passing away from the face of the earth ..., thus snatching from a hasty oblivion what could be saved for the benefit of posterity, and perpetuating it, as a fair and just monument, to the memory of a truly lofty and noble race" (George Catlin, *Letters and Notes on the Manners, Customs, and Conditions of North American Indians*, 2 vols. [New York, 1973 (orig. pub. London, 1844)], 1:3).

PART II

New Worlds

4

Settlement and Unsettlement: New Netherland, Beverwyck, and the Dutch Frontier

> Liberty to trade with the Indians was the cause of the increase of population in N. Netherland. We shall now show that it also is the cause of its ruin.... For everyone thought that now was the acceptable time to make his fortune; withdrew himself from his fellow, as if deeming him suspected and the enemy of his desire, sought communication with the Indians from whom it appeared his profit was to be derived, all contrary to their High Mightinessess' motto [*Eendracht maakt macht;* Union is strength].
>
> —*Journal of New Netherland; Written in the years 1641–1646*

In the seventeenth century, the Dutch and the other Europeans who came to America encountered radically new lands and peoples, new kinds of liberty and opportunity, and new sorts of dangers. Amid the perils and possibilities of the wilderness, they shaped a New World. In this chapter I provide a sketch of that cultural landscape, a Dutch frontier poised on the eastern and southern margins of Iroquoia. I narrate briefly the course of Dutch colonization in the region, Dutch motives, goals, and strategies, and the nature of the colonial experience for Europeans in New Netherland, especially for those who inhabited the upper Hudson settlements near present-day Albany. Despite the unsettling disorder which seemed to reign in these places, and which troubled their new Iroquois allies, partners, or "brethren," the cultural landscape of

New Netherland did possess a certain coherence, one provided by commerce.[1]

Paradoxically, the people of New Netherland attempted to keep their distance from Iroquoia, both culturally and physically, while they sought close commercial relations with the Five Nations, their major source of furs, the most valuable commodity available in the province. The Dutch-Iroquois frontier simultaneously separated and joined the two societies. Although few Dutchmen entered Iroquoia and few Iroquois paid extensive visits to Fort Orange and Beverwyck, events in each place fundamentally affected life in the other. Frontiers, by definition, exist only in relation to centers, and so we must look away from the frontier for a moment and examine the Dutch New World. Shifting the angle of vision of this Cubist history to the Dutch perspective, we now observe how New Netherlanders understood themselves, in contrast to Iroquois perceptions of them as alien and enigmatic.

In late July 1660, New Netherland's Director-General, Pieter Stuyvesant, found himself far up the Hudson River, at the trading outpost of Fort Orange and the surrounding communities of Beverwyck and Rensselaerswyck, the latter a private colony founded in 1629 by the Amsterdam diamond merchant Kiliaen van Rensselaer. Stuyvesant had just arrived from the south, along the Hudson, where his efforts to restore order in the troubled province had been crowned with an important success, the conclusion of peace with the Esopus Indians, ending—for a time—a bloody crisis that had erupted in September 1659.[2] While the people of Beverwyck and Rensselaerswyck worried that the Esopus War might entangle them as well, their immediate concern at the time of Stuyvesant's arrival was the nature and regulation of the Indian trade. Within the last month, they had been visited by a delegation of Mohawks, who complained vigorously about the ways in which Dutch brokers and traders abused them. And as the trading season opened, a vituperative exchange of petitions, insults,

---

[1]My chapter title alludes to Kenneth A. Lockridge's *Settlement and Unsettlement in Early America: The Crisis of Political Legitimacy before the Revolution* (New York, 1981); the notion of "settlement and unsettlement" might be reshaped to apply to the intercultural contest of legitimacy between the Dutch and Iroquois.

[2]The origins and development of the First Esopus War (1659–60) can be followed, from a Dutch point of view, in E. B. O'Callaghan, ed., *Documents Relative to the Colonial History of the State of New York*, 15 vols. (Albany, N.Y., 1856–87), 13:77–108, 110–12, 114–84; see 179–81 for the treaty of peace.

and charges had excited the already volatile atmosphere of commerce and competition for furs around Fort Orange. On July 22, 1660, Director-General Stuyvesant, presiding with both the courts of Beverwyck and Rensselaerswyck, promulgated another "ordinance for the regulation of the fur trade and forbidding the sale of liquor to the Indians," designed to confirm previous rules and appease their annoyed Indian clients.[3]

Certainly the trade at this outpost seemed to require regulation. In the yearly cycle of life in Beverwyck, *handelstijd,* the trading season, reigned from the first of May to the end of October. People—foreigners and outlivers, as well as burghers and local company employees—swarmed within the palisades, crowding and jostling each other for space and advantage in the bustling trade in furs.[4] Risk, opportunity, danger, excitement, intrigue, and often violence characterized these frenzied times in the annual calendar of the Dutch community. Normal social rules, imperfectly upheld during most of the year, crumbled during *handelstijd;* men and women acted in unusual ways as Beverwyck became a world turned upside down.[5] The activity in and around the community took on the appearance of ritualized disorder. In addition to the gambling, sharp trading, buying and selling, litigation, and surreptitious commercial forays beyond the town walls, inhabitants and strangers engaged in heavy drinking, contests of marksmanship (*den papegay te laten scheiten*) and other festivities, heated speech, fisticuffs, and occasionally certain sexual activity that was considered abominable by burghers and authorities alike.[6]

[3]On residents' concern about the crisis at Esopus, see the sources cited in ibid.; see also A. J. F. van Laer, trans. and ed., *Correspondence of Jeremias van Rensselaer, 1651–1674* (Albany, N.Y., 1932), 98–100, 186, 220, 227, 240. On the controversy over the employment or prohibition of Indian or Christian brokers in the fur trade, see Vice Director Johannes La Montagne to Director-General Stuyvesant, June 15, 1660, in O'Callaghan, ed., *Documents Relative to the History of New York,* 13:175; on this and other Mohawk complaints, see A. J. F. van Laer, trans. and ed., *Minutes of the Court of Fort Orange and Beverwyck, 1652–1660,* 2 vols. (Albany, N.Y., 1920–23), 2 (1657–60), 255–56, 266–70. For examples of violations of the court's rulings and its attempts to enforce them, see ibid., 278–83.

[4]Donna Merwick, *Possessing Albany, 1630–1710: The Dutch and English Experiences* (New York, 1990), 77–103, provides a brilliant description and analysis of *handelstijd.*

[5]The inversion of social order occurred at other times of the year as well, as during Shrovetide preceding Lent; authorities at Fort Orange reported in 1654 that "certain persons, on the solemn festivals of yesterday and Shrovetide evenings, in this jurisdiction, having clothed themselves in strange habiliments, and put on women's clothes, therein publicly marched as mountebanks, through the city and streets, in the sight of the inhabitants, and besides did other scandalous and unseemly things" (Jonathan Pearson, ed. and trans., *Early Records of the City and County of Albany and Colony of Rensselaerswyck,* rev. and ed. by A. J. F. van Laer, 4 vols. [Albany, 1869–1919], 1:219); see also Merwick, *Possessing Albany,* 74–75.

[6]On the court's authorization of the *papagaai-schoet* in May 1655, see Ordinary Session for

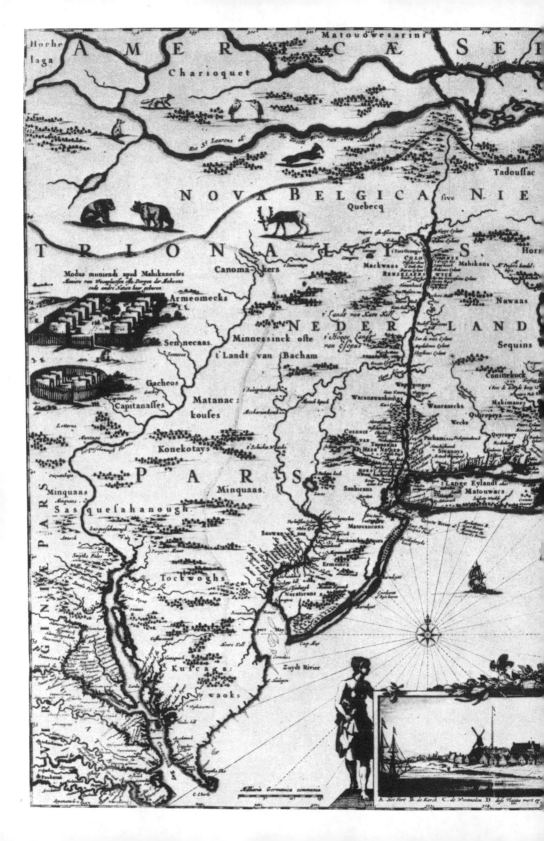

New Netherland in 1655, from Nicolas Jansz Visscher, *Novi Begii Novaeque Angliae nec non partis Virginae tabula* (Amsterdam, 1655), reprinted with permission from Oliver A. Rink, *Holland on the Hudson: An Economic and Social History of Dutch New York* (Ithaca: Cornell University Press, 1986; copyright © 1986 by Cornell University) and courtesy of the New York State Library, Albany. Visscher shows the principal European settlements while suggesting the considerable limits of Dutch knowledge about the native landscape.

Into this strange, unsettling place came a delegation of "Sinnekus," members of the Five Nations confederacy who lived far into the interior, beyond the Mohawks, and who were infrequent visitors to Fort Orange. Whether they were in fact Senecas, the westernmost Iroquois nation, or simply Five Nations people who were not Mohawk, we do not know; Dutch understanding of Iroquois society and polity remained vague, and New Netherlanders frequently lumped together the Oneidas, Onondagas, Cayugas, Senecas, and perhaps others as well, into a single generic group, the "Sinnekas." If the appearance of these "*wilden*," or Indians, struck the people at Fort Orange and Beverwyck as unusual, it is likely that the Iroquois envoys found their hosts and Dutch behavior at least as puzzling. Indeed, they had come to complain about the bizarre, irrational, inappropriate, and irritating ways of their Netherlandish "brothers."[7]

Their meeting at Fort Orange on July 25 and 26, 1660 was hardly a first encounter. By then, as each side acknowledged, their alliance—indeed their brotherhood—was of long standing. The Senecas declared that "it is now some years past since they had been at the Manhattans" and that their present purpose was merely to renew their bonds of friendship; they said, "Let us be of one mind."[8] For their part, the Dutch negotiators acknowledged the treaty of friendship and confirmed Seneca notions of Iroquois-Dutch relations by calling

---

May 11, 1655 in van Laer, ed., *Court Minutes of Fort Orange*, 1:220; see ibid., 220n45 for an explanation of *den papegay to laaten schieten*, a method of target shooting in which marksmen competed to knock a figure resembling a parrot from a pole erected within a large circle. See also Merwick, *Possessing Albany*, 79–80, and E. Hverkamp-Begemann, *Rembrandt: The Nightwatch* (Princeton, N.J., 1982), 42–44, on the annual competition of Shooting the Parrot among militia companies and on their participation in the Amsterdam *kermis*, or fair, in the seventeenth century. See Simon Schama, *The Embarrassment of Riches: An Interpretation of Dutch Culture in the Golden Age* (New York, 1987), 180–82, on the flamboyant display of *schutters* or militia brotherhoods in the Netherlands, which by mid-seventeenth century were increasingly seen as existing simply for the sake of their routs. For a sense of the raucousness of *handelstijd*, see the court record for the trading season following in 1655 (van Laer, ed., *Court Minutes of Fort Orange*, 1:218–37, 241), which chronicled a typical pattern of prosecutions for illegally tapping and drinking liquor, slandering officials as well as common people, illicit commerce, and general defiance of law and good order. During *hadelstijd* in 1658, the soldier Nicolaes Gregory Hillebrant was accused of sodomy; see ibid., 2:153–55, and "Deposition of Rutger Jacobsen against Nicolaes Gregory Hillebrant," in Pearson, ed. *Early Records of Albany*, 4:69–70.

[7]"Propositions made to us by the Sinnekus in Fort Orange, the 25th of July 1660," in van Laer, ed., *Court Minutes of Fort Orange*, 2:283–85; for an example of the indiscriminate use by the Dutch of "Sinnekans" for non-Mohawk Iroquois, see Kiliaen van Rensselaer to Wouter van Twiller, May 6, 1638, in A. J. F. van Laer, trans. and ed., *Van Rensselaer-Bowier Manuscripts: Being the Letters of Kiliaen van Rensselaer, 1630–1643, and other Documents Relating to the Colony of Rensselaerswyck* (Albany, N.Y., 1908), 401.

[8]Ibid., 2:283.

the Indians "brothers."[9] Yet the limited degree of familiarity that each party had acquired did not dissipate the overwhelming strangeness of the other. It was a discourse of confusion. The Senecas believed that the Dutch failed to reply to their measured requests, to discuss issues properly and respectfully, and to follow reasonable rules of etiquette and protocol. "We only make a little request of you and yet in asking this it is as if we ran against a stone," one Seneca spokesman complained. "You have slept until now, therefore we now wake you up again."[10] The Seneca indictment of Dutch behavior offers us a unique insight into the larger cultural landscape of Dutch New Netherland, especially at the cultural frontier of the upper Hudson.

The individualism, aggressiveness, and competitiveness displayed by the Dutch in New Netherland struck the communal, circumspect Iroquois as curious and unfortunate. Indeed, the exuberance, passion, and even violence, with which the Beverwyck farmers and traders expressed opinions and pursued self-interested goals seemed madness to the Iroquois. Compared with their own sense of hospitality, reciprocity, and kinship, the Iroquois considered the Dutch too selfish, antisocial, and uncivilized. In return for presents they had offered some years past at Manhattan, the Senecas received "not even a pipeful of tobacco"; at other times, their inquiries even failed to elicit a Dutch reply. When the Iroquois faced times of crisis, the Dutch still demanded furs in exchange for the powder and lead required, which the Senecas contended they "ought to have . . . for nothing." And when they arrived to trade with the Dutch, the Senecas suffered the heavy-handed tactics of over-zealous traders who forced them into their own houses, physically prevented their escape, and violently abused them. "Sometimes when they are in a trader's house and they wish to go to another man's house to buy goods that appeal to them," the Senecas complained, "they are severely beaten till they hardly know where their eyes are. That ought not to be and every one ought to be free to go where he pleases to buy the goods that suit him best."[11]

More than restraint of trade, such acts constituted extraordinary violations of Iroquois sensibilities because they were committed by "brothers." Kinspeople ought to agree on fair exchanges and share freely in times of want or danger, not subjecting each other to what-

[9]"Answers to the propositions made by the chiefs of the Sinnekus, dated July 26, 1660," ibid., 285–86.
[10]Ibid., 283, 284.
[11]Ibid., 283–85.

ever prices the market would bear. "The Dutch are sending so many brokers into the woods from one house, that they do not know where to go with their beavers," the Senecas declared. "Each house ought to have something. They, that is to say, the brokers, pull one hither and thither, so that one does not know where to go. That should not be tolerated, but each house ought to have something."[12] In short, the Iroquois noticed and objected to the particular form of early modern capitalism the Dutch imported from the Low Countries and cultivated in New Netherland. Although the Five Nations believed that the good life was achieved collectively, by suppressing competition and contention, expanding the domestic sphere, and sharing their resources, the inhabitants of the Dutch towns defied their High Mightinesses' motto, "union is strength," and pursued individual or family interests; this they did by competing with each other as well as with outsiders, by monopolizing or forestalling trade when they could manage it, and by serving community or national goals chiefly when such action might serve their own fortunes.

Yet the society that the Iroquois saw as chaotic and uncivilized operated according to its own logic. The Dutch in New Netherland organized their physical, social, and political landscape in ways shaped by their cultural experience. As historian Donna Merwick has suggested, its *burgerlijk* (civic, mercantile orientation) gave the province its coherence. The urbanized Dutch emphasized city over country, depended on commerce, and stressed mobility over stability, navigation over occupation; within the new world of possibility and constraint, they therefore constructed a New Netherland, more primitive perhaps, but structurally the same as its model in the United Provinces.[13] Their relationship with the Iroquois, the Dutch hoped, would be all business.

The Dutch and Iroquois worlds began to draw nearer in 1609, when Henry Hudson sailed *De Halve Maen* into New York Bay and became the first European since Giovanni da Verrazzano in 1524 to enter the mouth of the river later known as the Hudson. Although a subject of James I of England, Hudson now found himself employed by the Dutch East India Company. On its behalf, Hudson had been seeking a northeast passage to the Orient, but, turned back by foul weather

---

[12]Ibid., 285.
[13]Merwick, *Possessing Albany;* see especially her introduction, 1–5 and chap. 7, 286–95.

and impassable ice, *De Halve Maen* ventured out across the Atlantic and up the Hudson River. The voyage did not uncover a route to the East, nor did a subsequent adventure that gave Hudson's name to the great Canadian bay while costing Hudson his life. Yet the 1609 voyage brought the Dutch to the verge of Iroquoia and opened the New World to Dutch trade and colonization.[14]

In 1609 the achievement of a twelve-year truce between the Dutch Republic and Spain ended at least for a time the war that had begun with the Dutch Revolt in 1566 and dragged on for over forty years. The truce allowed Dutch merchants time to exploit the new opportunities in North America, and should a firm peace never materialize, these new lands might later provide a base for assaults on Spain's American empire. By 1614 private Dutch adventurers had founded a trading outpost up the Great North River (Hudson) on Castle Island, Fort Nassau, near the present site of Albany. After the *octroy*, or exclusive charter, of some thirteen merchants expired in 1618, a vigorous trade developed with the New World, inspired by the profits of the thirteen. As the truce with Spain lapsed, in 1621 Their High Mightinesses, the States-General, chartered the Dutch West India Company to challenge Spain and construct a commercial empire.[15]

The company—modeled on the Dutch East India Company, char-

[14]Michael Kammen, *Colonial New York: A History* (New York, 1975), provided a general overview of early New York history; see especially chaps. 1 and 2 on Dutch reconnaissance and early settlement. For the history of New Netherland see also the following important works: Merwick, *Possessing Albany;* Oliver A. Rink, *Holland on the Hudson: An Economic and Social History of Dutch New York* (Ithaca, N.Y., 1986); Alice P. Kenney, *Stubborn for Liberty: The Dutch in New York* (Syracuse, N.Y., 1975); George L. Smith, *Religion and Trade in New Netherland: Dutch Origins and American Development* (Ithaca, N.Y., 1973); Van Cleaf Bachman, *Peltries or Plantations: The Economic Policies of the Dutch West India Company in New Netherland, 1623–1639* (Baltimore, 1969); Thomas J. Condon, *New York Beginnings: The Commercial Origins of New Netherland* (New York, 1968); Allen W. Trelease, *Indian Affairs in Colonial New York: The Seventeenth Century* (Ithaca, N.Y., 1960). Among the more important recent books is Thomas E. Burke, Jr., *Mohawk Frontier: The Dutch Community of Schenectady, New York, 1661–1710* (Ithaca, N.Y., 1991). For an overview of such recent work, including studies in the historiography of New Netherland, see Eric Nooter and Patricia U. Bonomi, eds., *Colonial Dutch Studies: An Interdisciplinary Approach* (New York, 1988); see also A. G. Roeber, "'The Origins of Whatever Is Not English among Us': The Dutch-speaking and German-speaking Peoples of Colonial British America," in Bernard Bailyn and Philip D. Morgan, eds., *Strangers within the Realm: Cultural Margins of the First British Empire* (Chapel Hill, N.C., 1991), 220–83.

[15]These developments can be traced in Rink, *Holland on the Hudson,* 26–68. Rink demonstrated that the Dutch West India Company was an "enfeebled giant" and a failure as a monopoly; nonetheless, he argued convincingly, "New Netherland may be considered a successful experiment in private colonialism under the auspices of a chartered monopoly. It is the contrast between the success of New Netherland as an outpost of Dutch private capitalism and its failure as a company monopoly that makes the history of the colony a unique chapter in America's colonial past" (23). See also Condon, *New York Beginnings,* 3–61; Bachman, *Peltries or Plantations,* 3–43.

tered in 1602—held a monopoly on all Dutch trade and navigation with the Americas and West Africa; it commanded the authority to maintain naval and military forces, to make war and peace with indigenous powers, to colonize and settle the lands it acquired, and to exercise judicial and administrative functions.[16] Interests within the West India Company struggled to establish the relative importance of conquest, commerce, colonization, and its various other concerns in Africa, South America, the Caribbean, and North America. Although it did offer some dividends in furs, New Netherland often came last on the company's list; despite the impressive privileges the company officially enjoyed, New Netherland remained a place of private initiative and profit.[17]

The emphasis on private enterprise represented by the West India Company well suited the bourgeois Dutch. The company itself exercised its powers and responsibilities in a decentralized fashion. A board of nineteen directors, representing five different city or provincial chambers, along with a representative of the States-General, administered the company. Within the loosely structured corporation, the development of New Netherland became the responsibility of the wealthiest and most powerful chamber, Amsterdam. The phenomenal growth of Amsterdam in the sixteenth century made it the preeminent commercial and financial center of northern Europe in the seventeenth century.[18] The Amsterdam chamber possessed the largest number of company directors "because from thence came the most money."[19] Twenty men sat in the Amsterdam Chamber committee, a privilege bought for six thousand guilders. Outside this committee, a body of chief participants—all of whom had invested the same amount—was constituted but had no role in the daily management

---

[16]See "Charter of the West India Company," granted June 3, 1621, in van Laer, ed., *Van Rensselaer-Bowier Manuscripts*, 86–115.

[17]See especially Rink, *Holland on the Hudson.* After 1626, the company virtually abandoned the province to its Amsterdam Chamber; it reluctantly promoted private colonization; it eventually surrendered its monopoly privileges; and increasingly the company found itself transformed from a business enterprise into a government (see especially, ibid., 70–116).

[18]On the Dutch Golden Age, see J. H. Huizinga's classic *Dutch Civilization in the Seventeenth Century and Other Essays*, trans. Arnold J. Pomerans (New York, 1968 [orig. pub. Haarlem, 1941]), 9–104; Pieter Geyl, *The Netherlands in the Seventeenth Century* (New York, 2d ed., 1961); Violet Barbour, *Capitalism in Amsterdam in the 17th Century* (Ann Arbor, Mich., 1963 [orig. pub. 1950]). Simon Schama, *The Embarrassment of Riches: An Interpretation of Dutch Culture in the Golden Age* (New York, 1987) is a stimulating though controversial work. Jan de Vries, *The Dutch Rural Economy in the Golden Age, 1500–1700* (New Haven, 1974) is the standard study of that subject.

[19]Van Laer, ed., *Van Rensselaer-Bowier Manuscripts*, 46.

of the company. Nonetheless, they had considerable influence on major policy decisions, especially after they won direct representation in the Chamber in the charter revision of 1623, and some acted as individual adventurers in New World enterprises. Chief participant Kiliaen van Rensselaer, for example, became the first of these stockholders to become a Chamber director in such a fashion, and he soon increased his involvement, becoming the patroon of Rensselaerswyck in 1629.[20]

Colonization began haltingly; in the spring of 1624, the Dutch West India Company equipped a vessel of 130 lasts, the *Nieu Nederlandt*, and dispatched it under the command of Cornelis Jacobsz May of Hoorn with a company of thirty families to plant a colony in the New World. The ship entered the River Mauritius, or North River (Hudson), in May and proceeded up to the site of the abandoned Fort Nassau with about eighteen families of Walloon immigrants, speakers of a French dialect and Protestant refugees from the Spanish Netherlands. There they reestablished the post, naming it Fort Orange. Within three years Fort Orange was left to be maintained as a trading post by fifteen or sixteen men, as the company concentrated its colonists at "the Manhates," which had been settled in 1626.[21]

At least by the year 1624, the Dutch had learned something of the complex political geography of the area surrounding Fort Orange. Johan de Laet, a geographer and company director, observed in his *New World, or Description of West-India* (1625) that around Fort Orange, "on the west side of the river, . . . a nation of savages dwells called the Mackwaes [Mohawks], the enemies of the Monhicans [Mahicans]," who increasingly removed to the eastern bank. "Almost all those who live on the west side, are enemies of those on the east, and cultivate more intercourse and friendship with our countrymen than the latter."[22] The scholar and physician Nicolaes van Wassenaer, in his *Historisch Verhael* of February 1624, demonstrated an awareness

---

[20]On the organization of the Dutch West India Company, and the Amsterdam Chamber, see ibid., 46–47 and 86–115, especially 95–101. On van Rensselaer himself, see ibid., 42–85; his registration of his colony, November 19, 1629, is reprinted on 157–58.

[21]J. Franklin Jameson, ed., *Narratives of New Netherland, 1609–1664* (New York, 1909), 75–76, 83–84; A. J. F. van Laer, ed. and trans., *Documents Relating to New Netherland, 1624–1626, in the Henry E. Huntington Library* (San Marino, Calif., 1924), which contains important introductory material (xiv–xxiv) and reprints the regulations for the colonists, instructions for the director and other company officials, and an important letter from Isaack de Rasiere to the Amsterdam Chamber, dated September 23, 1626, assessing the state of the young commercial-colonial enterprise. The description of the colonists' time in New Netherland as a "sojourn" suggests the company's limited commitment to settlement (10).

[22]Jameson, ed., *Narratives of New Netherland*, 47.

of the Mohawks as a culturally and linguistically distinct group at odds with the Mahicans, who controlled access to the Hudson River. Fort Nassau on the upper reaches of the Hudson had fallen into decay and had been abandoned by the company at least in part because the Dutch found it difficult to function in the uneasy political environment that developed as the Mohawks and Mahicans struggled for supremacy.[23]

As the Mohawk-Mahican war escalated, and Dutch settlers prepared to retire and consolidate at Manhattan Island, the Dutch garrison at Fort Orange entered the conflict in support of the Mahicans. Accompanying a party of Mahicans, about a league from the fort, commander Daniel van Krieckenbeeck, six of his men, and the Mahicans encountered the Mohawks, "who fell so boldly upon them with a discharge of arrows, that they were forced to fly, and many were killed," including van Krieckenbeeck and three other Dutch men. At least one of the Dutch victims, Wassenaer reported, was "well roasted" and eaten. Within days trader Pieter Barentsz visited the Mohawks from Manhattan to atone for Krieckenbeeck's rash action and to restore the peace. The Mohawks hoped to excuse their act and explained "that they had never set themselves against the whites, and asked the reason why the latter had meddled with them; otherwise, they would not have shot him."[24]

Unlike the French after Samuel de Champlain's battles with the Iroquois, the Dutch managed to mend their rift with the Mohawks. Barentsz, who seemed to inspire confidence among the Indians, took temporary control of Fort Orange; the new director Pieter Minuit rushed up from Fort Amsterdam to assess the situation; and Bastiaen Jansz Krol earned the appointment as Fort Orange's new commissary, "because he is well acquainted with the language," as New Netherland's secretary, Isaack de Rasiere, reported on September 23, 1626 to the Amsterdam chamber of the West India Company. This debacle offered the Dutch an early lesson in their relationship with the Iroquois. De Rasiere attributed the crisis to the "reckless adventure of Crieckenbeeck" and suggested reforms to prevent such events in the future. "I find it important that the natives are well treated, each according to his station and disposition, . . . to prevent discontent and to keep all the nations devoted to us."[25]

[23] Ibid., 67–68, 70–73.
[24] Ibid., 84–85, 262.
[25] Van Laer, ed., *Huntington Library Documents,* 172–248, quotations from 175–76, 200–203.

The tenuousness of their foothold on the margins of Iroquoia and their own commercial self-interest demanded a policy of nonintervention in Iroquois affairs. De Rasiere reported, for example, that "trade at Fort Orange has been very bad, on account of the war between Crieckenbeeck and the Minquaes, so that during my stay here there have been bartered not more than 197 beavers and 60 otters." Uninterrupted, profitable trade in furs, of course, was the goal behind de Rasiere's hope that the tribes might remain at peace with each other as well as with the Dutch.[26] The Dutch forgot their hard lesson only rarely and at great cost.[27]

Nonetheless, the Dutch education in Iroquois culture and politics was protracted, and it yielded uneven results, as we have already seen in the Dutch-Seneca encounter of September 1660. Like any other people, the Dutch learned according to their particular aptitude and experience, and as seventeenth-century sojourners or colonists from the urban, commercial Low Countries, they proved better prepared to become the Five Nations' trading partners than to become their kinspeople.

By 1628 or 1629 the Mohawk-Mahican war that engulfed van Krieckenbeeck and other unfortunate Netherlanders had ended; the Mohawks defeated the Mahicans, incorporated some, and drove the remainder well to the east and north into the Connecticut River valley.[28] The Mohawk-Mahican war has often been interpreted as a commercial conflict, with the Mohawks as aggressors trying to acquire access to Dutch markets for their furs. Certainly the Dutch would

[26]Ibid., 212. In this quotation, Rasiere uses "Minquaes" to refer to the Mohawks, though in other places in the letter "Minquaes" refers, more conventionally, to the Susquehannocks or other tribes to the south (192).

[27]On the other hand, Dutch relations with other Native Americans in their North American province were not particularly distinguished by Dutch toleration, non-intervention, or good will. New Netherland's dealings with Indians on Long Island, around Manhattan, and along the lower Hudson, which exploded into disastrous war in the 1640s, are summarized in Francis Jennings, "Dutch and Swedish Indian Policies," in Wilcolm E. Washburn, ed., *Handbook of North American Indians: History of Indian-White Relations* (Washington, D.C., 1988), 4:13–19. Trelease, *Indian Affairs in New York,* is the standard treatment of the subject. The findings of Lawrence M. Hauptman and Ronald G. Knapp, "Dutch-Aboriginal Interaction in New Netherland and Formosa: An Historical Geography of Empire," *Proceedings of the American Philosophical Society,* 121 (April 1977), 166–82, seem to suggest that, globally, Dutch relations with New Netherland's Algonquian coastal and river Indians were more typical of their relations with indigenous inhabitants than was the unique relationship that developed between the Dutch and the Five Nations.

[28]Wassenaer reported the Mahican defeat in March 1630. See Jameson, ed., *Narratives of New Netherland,* 89; see also ibid., 131, 172. For a memorandum prepared by Kiliaen van Rensselaer, July 20, 1634, see van Laer, ed., *Van Rensselaer-Bowier Manuscripts,* 306. Cf. Bruce G. Trigger, "The Mohawk-Mahican War (1624–28): The Establishment of a Pattern," *Canadian Historical Review,* 52 (1971), 276–86, which analyzes the Mohawk-Mahican conflict as precursor to the so-called beaver wars.

have seen the war in these terms, though the surprise they expressed when the supply of furs at Fort Orange initially remained low or declined should caution us against interpreting Iroquois actions in these Western economic terms.[29] The scant historical records are difficult to read and limit our ability to form definitive conclusions about Iroquois or Mahican interpretation of their conflict. Kileaen van Rensselaer seemed to suggest that the Dutch themselves had upset the uneasy balance of Mohawk-Mahican peace and exacerbated the crisis. Like de Rasiere, he placed special blame in the lap of Daniel van Krieckenbeeck, who "involved and engaged these same Manhykans [Mahicans] in needless wars with the warlike nation of Maquaes [Mohawks], their former friends and neighbors."[30] Recent demographic and archaeological research suggests that epidemic disease, rather than a crushing military campaign by the Mohawks, was responsible for the displacement of the Mahicans.[31] While European materials and trade goods held great attraction for native people, the Iroquois and other Indians did not conceive of their relationships with Europeans simply in economic terms. And in the complex, changing world of seventeenth-century Native America, trade was not the motivation for alliance so much as its by-product; exchange functioned symbolically as well as materially to cement alliances between friends and kinspeople. The Dutch did not pause to consider such matters. From their perspective, the Mohawk dominance around Fort Orange signaled the beginning of a native political stability in the area that would provide a proper climate for the realization of their own economic interests.

Yet by 1628, following the turmoil of Indian warfare and factional struggles in the Netherlands and its American colony, New Nether-

---

[29]Kiliaen van Rensselaer to Willem Kieft, Director in New Netherland, May 29, 1649, in van Laer, ed., *Van Rensselaer-Bowier Manuscripts*, 483–84; see also Trelease, *Indian Affairs in New York*, 48; and see George R. Hamell and Christopher L. Miller, "A New Perspective on Indian-White Contact: Cultural Symbols and Colonial Trade," *Journal of American History*, 73 (September 1986), 311–28, for some provocative suggestions about the contrast between the meaning of "commercial" exchange for Native Americans and its meaning for Europeans.

[30]"Account of Rensselaerswyck," in van Laer, ed., *Van Rensselaer-Bowier Manuscripts*, 306.

[31]Dean R. Snow and Kim M. Lanphear, "European Contact and Indian Depopulation in the Northeast: The Timing of the First Epidemics," *Ethnohistory*, 35 (Winter 1988), 24 (Table 1), estimated that a pre-epidemic Mahican population of approximately 6,400 was reduced by the mid-seventeenth century to about 500, representing a mortality of over 90 percent. Snow and Lanphear have determined that a major epidemic afflicted the Northeast for the first time in 1616 and was followed by a disastrous plague of smallpox in 1633 (20–24). Although neither Snow and Lanphear nor Henry F. Dobyns, *Their Number Became Thinned* (Knoxville, Tenn., 1983), focus specifically on the Mahicans, they seem to agree generally about the role of disease in this crisis, even if they differ on its timing and dimensions.

land did not seem to be serving the interests of the West India Company or the United Provinces particularly well. The province remained an insignificant side show compared to the greater drama being played out in the Caribbean, the Spanish Main, Brazil, and West Africa. Only 270 people lived at New Amsterdam on the island of Manhattan, and a mere handful of traders occupied posts up the Fresh (Connecticut), North (Hudson), and South (Delaware) Rivers.[32] The planners of the Amsterdam Chamber envisioned New Netherland as a company operation. The traders, clerks, officials, soldiers, farmers, and their families were sent to New Netherland as company employees, to increase the profits of the stockholders, not to make their own fortunes.

But too few chose to venture to the New World on these terms, and company expenses in maintaining those who did outdistanced company profits. The West India Company's nineteen directors—the Nineteen—wrote to the States-General on October 23, 1629, "colonizing such wild and uncultivated countries, demands more inhabitants than we can well supply; not so much through lack of population, in which our provinces abound, as from the fact, that all who are inclined to do any sort of work here [in the Netherlands], procure enough to eat without any trouble; and are, therefore, unwilling to go far from home on an uncertainty." The people conveyed to New Netherland, the Nineteen reported, "have not been any profit, but a drawback, to this Company."[33]

The sparseness of population threatened to attract the aggressive attentions of other colonial powers (particularly the English), who might easily overrun the colony and endanger its other commercial missions. Without adjustments, especially the increase of population, New Netherland and all that it had to offer—as a source of valuable furs, as a station for West Indian and Brazilian ships, and as a supplier of grain, cattle, and provisions—would have to be abandoned. The

[32]Jameson, ed., *Narratives of New England*, 88–89.

[33]O'Callaghan, ed., *Documents Relative to the History of New York*, 1:39–40. The promoters of New Netherland attempted to solve their recruitment problems by appealing widely to Dutch men and women, to foreign nations of northern Europe, and especially to refugees of war and upheaval within the Dutch Republic. On the diverse character of the New Netherland populations, see David Cohen, "How Dutch were the Dutch of New Netherland?" *New York History*, 62 (1981), 43–60; Oliver A. Rink, "The People of New Netherland: Notes on Non-English Immigrants to New York in the Seventeenth Century," *New York History*, 62 (1981), 5–42, and Rink, *Holland on the Hudson*, 139–71. See also John O. Evjen, *Scandinavian Immigrants in New York, 1630–1674* (Minneapolis, 1916); Roeber, " 'The Origins of Whatever Is Not English among Us,' " 220–83.

Dutch would lose the chance at great profits in New Netherland and reduce their ability to deprive the king of Spain of his silver, "which was as blood from one of the arteries of his heart," as the Nineteen said.[34]

The directors of the company, Wassenaer tells us, "the better to people their lands, and to bring the country to produce more abundantly," resolved to grant "divers Privileges, Freedoms and Exemptions to all patroons, masters or individuals who should plant any colonies and cattle in New Netherland."[35] This *Vryheden,* or grant of "Freedoms and Exemptions," issued in 1628 and revised in 1629, reflected the company's decision to halt further direct investment in New Netherland and to transfer the initiative for colonial development there into private hands. The directors hoped that individuals could accomplish what the public corporation could not.

In effect, the grant of "Freedoms and Exemptions" established private colonies in New Netherland, finally encouraging directly the sort of private enterprise that had dominated the province from the beginning. Patroons, or proprietors, were invested with far-reaching privileges, which seemed to create in the New World a variant of feudalism already archaic in Europe. In fact, both the company and individual patroons hoped to put these antique structures to modern ends. Company regulation and taxation would allow it to share in the patroons' profits, which the patroons would realize more through commerce than quitrents.[36]

Kiliaen van Rensselaer quickly embraced the opportunity. Discerning the benefits of situating a colony near New Netherland's outpost on the North River, the new patroon claimed and purchased from the Indians a vast tract of land near Fort Orange. There he founded Rensselaerswyck, sending over its first group of tenants in 1630. Van Rensselaer never visited his New World domain. Like other citizens of the Dutch Republic, whether of considerable or modest means, he

---

[34]O'Callaghan, ed., *Documents Relative to the History of New York,* 1:42.

[35]Jameson, ed., *Narratives of New Netherland,* 89; for the revised "Freedoms and Exemptions" (June 7, 1629) see 90–96; see also van Laer, ed., *Van Rensselaer-Bowier Manuscripts,* 136–53.

[36]On the rights, responsibilities, and restrictions of patroons, see van Laer, ed., *Van Rensselaer-Bowier Manuscripts,* 51–52, 136–53; Rink, *Holland on the Hudson,* 94–116. See also Merwick, *Possessing Albany,* 39–45, who argues convincingly that the most successful patroon, Kiliaen van Rensselaer, ultimately "opted for mercantile over feudal ways of possessing the New World" (45); he asserted a sense of the land as fief, not because he aspired to the status of feudal lord but because this mechanism offered a right of exclusion that served his financial (not social) goals (39–40).

preferred the comforts of the fatherland to the American wilderness. But unlike other patroons, van Rensselaer alone succeeded in managing Rensselaerswyck from across the Atlantic. Few men found the prospects of colonization in New Netherland inviting. And among those who took the risk, only van Rensselaer avoided failure.[37]

Although he staved off ruin in the New World, the patroon could never count Rensselaerswyck as an unqualified success. The difficulties of carving out farmsteads and making them produce; of supplying and controlling an often unruly, contentious, and self-interested group of tenants on the margins of Dutch civilization; and of overcoming the factionalism both in New Netherland and Amsterdam; all posed major problems to van Rensselaer's enterprise.[38]

The labor problem in New Netherland posed the greatest concern. In addition to the difficulties that the West India Company and the patroons encountered in attracting people to their colonies, they found it hard to retain the newcomers' services once their contracts expired. And perhaps worse, from the patroon and the Company points of view, the farmers, laborers, artisans, even officials, too often failed to perform their contracted duties conscientiously and successfully.[39] Secretary de Rasiere complained to the company's Amsterdam Chamber in 1626 that some of the men sent to the colony "are not of much account; they are a rough lot who have to be kept at work by force." He recommended that "whenever your Honors are engaging sawyers or such-like men, it had better be done at so much per foot, or cord, or in shares; in that way your Honors cannot be

[37]See Rink, *Holland on the Hudson*, 107–16, 130, 196–200; Merwick, *Possessing Albany*, 12–67. See also van Laer, ed., *Van Rensselaer Bowier Manuscripts*, especially 40–85. The course of van Rensselaer's colony can be followed in A. J. F. van Lacr, trans. and ed., *Minutes of the Court of Rensselaerswyck, 1648–1652* (Albany, N.Y., 1922); van Laer, trans. and ed., *The Correspondences of Jeremias van Rensselaer, 1651–1674* (Albany, N.Y., 1932); and van Laer, trans. and ed., *The Correspondences of Maria van Rensselaer, 1669–1689* (Albany, N.Y., 1935).

[38]On van Rensselaer's attempts to develop commercial agricultural and extractive enterprises, which could fuel intraprovincial, intercolonial, and transatlantic trade in such items as cattle, grain, beer, butter, milk, cheese, lumber, bricks, tobacco, and even silk, see van Laer, ed., *Van Rensselaer-Bowier Manuscripts*, 196–201, 208–12, 233. Van Rensselaer's views on factionalism within the Amsterdam Chamber and in New Netherland, and its negative effects on his colonial enterprise, were set out in his memorial to the Assembly of the Nineteen of the West India Company, November 25, 1633 (235–50).

[39]For an example of such complaints about the delinquence of employees and their "impertinences," see Kiliaen van Rensselaer's "Instructions to Arent van Curler as secretary and bookkeeper of the colony of Rensselaerswyck," in ibid., 490–94, 508–15. The patroon was on occasion forced to admonish van Curler for failing to keep proper accounts (488), and he was often concerned that even his own officers profited from the fur trade at his expense (430). The unreliability of his colonists—from top to bottom—remained a major concern for van Rensselaer (630–44).

cheated, as they are in many things." Later in the same letter de Rasiere reflected, "At times I cannot sufficiently wonder at the lazy unconcern of many persons, both farmers and others, who are willing enough to draw their rations and pay in return for doing almost nothing, without examining their conscience or considering their bounden duty and what they promised to do upon their engagement." In fact, some were not so much lazy as distracted by the possibility of enriching themselves in the fur trade. De Rasiere was forced to pay high prices for furs to farmers, smiths, other artisans, and their wives in order to prevent the trade from going to "strangers"; and he attempted to corner the market on wampum, buying it up from colonists "in order to take the fur trade away from them."[40]

Even after the advent of private colonization, the simple lack of population, regardless of quality, remained a severe problem. New Netherland seemed to represent a dangerous political vacuum in colonial North America. In 1630 no more than 300 persons inhabited the province, most of them at Manhattan; by the early 1640s this number had barely increased as New Netherland suffered through Governor Willem Kieft's Indian wars.[41]

In contrast, English settlers flocked to Massachusetts Bay, approximately 3,000 arriving between 1630 and 1633. From a population of about 4,000 in 1634, the Bay Colony grew to 6,000 within a year and to 11,000 by 1638. Some 21,000 emigrant Britons crossed the Atlantic and settled in New England in the Great Migration of the 1630s; by 1641, a delegate from New England to the Dutch West India Company, the Reverend Hugh Peters, estimated its population at 40,000. Although internal migration and repatriation probably reduced this figure to approximately 13,500, it was clear that the people of New England were pushing hard against the borders of New Netherland, filling up the Connecticut Valley and pouring south along the Connecticut coast and onto Long Island.[42] To the south of New Neth-

[40]Van Laer, ed., *Huntington Library Documents*, 207–8; see also 187–88, 196–99, 236. On de Rasiere's attempt to control the trade, see 216–19; on his efforts to corner the wampum market, 248; see also 196, 215–20.

[41]See Rink, *Holland on the Hudson*, 144, 158; Kammen, *Colonial New York*, 38, reported approximately 500 in 1628. On Kieft's War and its devastating effects on New Netherland's population, see Trelease, *Indian Affairs in New York*, 60–84, 86.

[42]Evarts B. Greene and Virginia D. Harrington, *American Population Before the Federal Census of 1790* (New York, 1932), 8–9, 12–13; David Cressy, *Coming Over: Migration and Communication between England and New England in the Seventeenth Century* (Cambridge, 1987), 68–71; O'Callaghan, ed., *Documents Relative to the History of New York*, 1:567–68; see Neal Salisbury,

erland, primarily in Virginia, there were some 2,600 English people in 1629; by 1640 the number had increased to 8,100.[43] Finally, according to recent estimates, about 2,000 Mohawks lived just to the west in the 1640s, even after their numbers had been reduced by some 75 percent (from approximately 8,100) during the epidemics of the 1630s. Beyond the Mohawks were the rest of the Five Nations, and surrounding Dutch outposts in other directions were numerous other native peoples.[44] Unless the terms of settlement could be made more attractive, New Netherland would never induce people to immigrate and remain in the province in the numbers necessary to maintain its place within the native landscape and hold its position against English expansion in America.

By 1638, these problems finally attracted the interest and intervention of the States-General. Sensing that affairs in New Netherland were "retrograding more and more, to the injury of this state and its inhabitants," they posed a number of questions to the Nineteen. Regarding settlement, their High Mightinesses learned that "the Company cannot people it; because the Company cannot agree among themselves; but a plan of throwing it open, must be considered." The States-General in reply issued an implicit threat that if the company could not resolve its problems, the States-General would assume control of New Netherland.[45]

With this prodding, in 1639 the West India Company provided a "special impulse" to settlement by declaring the fur trade "free and open to every body."[46] The directors hoped that extension of the privilege of trading directly with the Indians and exporting furs to

---

Manitou and Providence: Indians, Europeans, and the Making of New England, 1500–1643 (New York, 1982), 183, 215–16, 225.

[43]Edmund S. Morgan, in *American Slavery, American Freedom: The Ordeal of Colonial Virginia* (New York, 1975), 404; see also Evarts and Harrington, *American Population*, 134–36, on the growth of Virginia in this period. Peters estimated the total English population of America at 50,000 in 1641 (O'Callaghan, ed., *Documents Relative to the History of New York*, 1:567). Jim Potter summarizes the demographic history of colonial Anglo-America, especially of New England and the Chesapeake, in Jack P. Greene and J. R. Pole, eds., *Colonial British America: Essays in the New History of the Early Modern Era* (Baltimore, 1984), 139, 142–44. While the Chesapeake colonies did not pose the same threat to New Netherland as did those in New England, the Dutch were flanked by an expanding English colonial presence in the seventeenth century.

[44]Snow and Lanphere, "European Contact and Indian Depopulation," 23–24.

[45]"Report on the Conditions of the Colony of New Netherland, in 1638," in O'Callaghan, ed., *Documents Relative to the History of New York*, 1:106–7.

[46]This measure is described in the historical summary provided by the "Report of the Board of Accounts [of the West India Company] on New Netherland," December 15, 1644, in ibid., 150.

Europe on a private basis would encourage population growth. But a new charter of Freedoms and Exemptions, issued in 1640, proved to be a more significant inducement. It restricted the grants to future patroons and offered more favorable terms of colonization to those of moderate means, creating a category of "Masters or Colonists" for those capable of transporting and maintaining but "five souls above fifteen years."[47]

By these means the company sought to increase New Netherland's population and trade, provide for its security, eliminate the company's perennial deficits, and profit from enlarged custom duties. Yet these reforms represented "the final act in the long drama" of maintaining its monopoly on trade, in the words of the historian Oliver A. Rink. Much like the English colony of Virginia, New Netherland found itself transformed from an organization into a society. Relinquishing its hold on land and trade, the West India Company lost its ability to enforce its authority on colonists; the company still shouldered the burden of government, but without the exclusive privileges, profits, or respect it had pursued since its inception.[48]

Following these reforms, New Netherland experienced its own modest "great migration," growing substantially to include as many as 2,500 persons by 1643 and perhaps 9,000 persons by 1664.[49] Meanwhile, the populations of New England and the Chesapeake continued to dwarf New Netherland; English-Dutch rivalry became increasingly explosive, especially in a series of three naval wars in 1652–54, 1665–67, and 1672–74; and in New Netherland itself old problems persisted.[50] Nonetheless, when New Netherland is seen from the vantage

[47]Ibid., 119–23. On these reforms, see also Allen W. Trelease, *Indian Affairs in Colonial New York: The Seventeenth Century* (Ithaca, N.Y., 1960), 60–61; Kammen, *Colonial New York,* 44.

[48]See Rink, *Holland on the Hudson,* 134–38. Rink noticed and commented on the parallels with the Virginia experience, classically expressed by Sigmund Diamond, "From Organization to Society: Virginia in the Seventeenth Century," *American Journal of Sociology,* 63 (1958), 457–75. A critic of the West India Company's administration of New Netherland reflected, in 1649 or 1650, that the province remained at the mercy of the English "only because we have neglected to populate the land; or, to speak more plainly and truly, because we have, out of regard for our own profit, wished to scrape all the fat into one or more pots, and thus secure the trade and neglect the population" (Henry C. Murphy, trans. and ed., *Vertoogh van Nieu Nederland and Breeden Raedt aende Vereenichde Nederlandsche Provintieu. Two Rare Tracts, Printed in 1649–1650, Relating to the Administration of Affairs in New Netherland* [New York, 1854], 30–31).

[49]Rink, *Holland on the Hudson,* 158.

[50]On the problems afflicting New Netherland during the early 1640s, especially those associated with the Indian war, see O'Callaghan, ed., *Documents Relative to the History of New York,* 1:149–56, 160–62, 179–88, and 188–214. See also the revised translation of "Journal of New Netherland," in Jameson, ed., *Narratives of New Netherland,* 269–84. On the Anglo-

point of the late 1650s rather than from the perspective of its subsequent conquest and Anglicization, the final years of the province's existence as a Dutch colony seem to have been full of promise.

Especially after 1657, a surge of immigration by families reflected New Netherland's improving reputation and transformed the province into a more prosperous place, occupied by Dutch families committed to life in the New World rather than by a motley array of single, male sojourners. As Rink concluded, New Netherland in 1664 was hardly a failed colony but rather one that seems, finally, to have turned itself around. From these beginnings, much of New York remained Dutch in character in the years following the English conquest; Anglicization would prove to be a difficult, unpleasant, and protracted process, because Dutch men and women resisted the cultural education imposed on them by their new English rulers just as firmly and subtly as they resisted the instructions of their Iroquois neighbors.[51]

Meanwhile, the Five Nations of the Iroquois learned more and more about their new Dutch brethren and became increasingly involved in provincial affairs, as in the Mohawk mediation of the Indian-Dutch conflict at New Amsterdam during Governor Kieft's war in 1645, and the Iroquois intervention in the Esopus wars of the 1660s.[52] But the Five Nations focused more typically on those settlements on the margins of their territory, Rensselaerswyck, Fort Orange, and Beverwyck (known as Albany after 1664). For the Iroquois, this frontier settle-

---

Dutch rivalry, see generally C. R. Boxer, *The Dutch Seaborne Empire, 1600–1800,* 2d ed. (London, 1966); J. S. Bromley and E. H. Kossmann, *Britain and the Netherlands,* 3 vols. (London, 1960–68); Charles H. Wilson, *Profit and War: A Study of England and the Dutch Wars* (London, 1957). The long dispute over boundaries and sovereignty in America between the Dutch and English runs throughout the documentary record; see, for example, O'Callaghan, ed., *Documents Relative to the History of New York,* vol. 1.

[51]Rink, *Holland on the Hudson,* 164–71. On the cultural, social, political, and legal contest between Dutch and English in colonial New York, see Merwick, *Possessing Albany,* especially 188–285. Jeremias van Rensselaer suggested the Dutch commitment to their own cultural order and language, and Dutch distaste for English ways and speech, in a letter to his mother in the Netherlands, June 10/20, 1668: "We did not have the least idea here that the country would remain English, since the Lord God blessed the arms of their High Mightinesses.... Now it seems that it had pleased the Lord [to ordain] that we must learn English. The worst of it all is that we have already for nearly four years been under this jurisdiction and that as yet have learned so little. The reason is that one has no liking for it" (van Laer, ed., *Correspondence of Jeremias van Rensselaer,* 403).

[52]See Trealease, *Indian Affairs in New York,* 117; O'Callaghan, ed., *Documents Relative to the History of New York,* 13:18. See also 88–89, in which a group of Mohawk sachems referred to their mediation on behalf of the Dutch and requested a similar act of friendship from the Dutch, to help mitigate tensions with the French; see also 122 and numerous documents referring to the Esopus conflict in ibid. and cited above, this chapter.

ment was the real capital of New Netherland or (later) New York. By shifting our attention to Beverwyck, Fort Orange, and Rensselaerswyck and the surrounding hamlets, we get a better view of those who had the most contact with and the largest impact on the Five Nations. Here and in the surrounding landscape the Dutch and Iroquois made a New World in common, one which, paradoxically, each understood differently.

In 1643, in the vicinity of present-day Albany, observers saw but "a miserable little fort called Fort Orange, built of logs, with four or five pieces of Breteuil cannon, and as many pedereros." The settlements around Fort Orange were "composed of about a hundred persons, who reside in some twenty-five or thirty houses built along the river, as each found convenient." The residents lived in houses built "merely of boards and thatched, with no mason work except the chimneys. The forest furnishing many large pines, they make boards by means of their mills," one traveler noted. And because their land was hilly, they were obliged to spread out their farms, occupying "two or three leagues [that is, about eight to twelve miles] of the country."[53] Until perhaps 1648, most settlers dwelled on the east side of the Hudson, in the *Greenenbosch* or Greenbush, which the patroon hoped would be the center of Rensselaerswyck. But van Rensselaer failed to impose this cluster of people just there, in a place that might have hindered their participation in the fur trade. And after the destruction by severe flooding in 1646 and 1647, the vice-director of Rensselaerswyck, Brant van Slichtenhorst, and the residents shifted to the west side of the Hudson and built a more compact settlement around Fort Orange. In 1652, in a jurisdictional conflict between the company and Rensselaerswyck that would continue to simmer, Director-General Pieter Stuyvesant intervened, setting aside all the land "within a cannon shot of the fort" and chartered it as the market town of Beverwyck.[54]

In these rude surroundings, the Dutch were decidedly self-absorbed in surviving and making their fortunes through agriculture, trade, or a combination of both. Most embraced only modest dreams—eco-

---

[53] Jameson, ed., *Narratives of New Netherland,* 261–62.
[54] These events are detailed in the introduction to van Laer, ed., *Court Minutes of Rensselaerswyck,* 18–19, 21–23, 199–200, see Merwick, *Possessing Albany,* 33, 34–39, 72–73; on the settlement of Rensselaerswyck and the creation of Beverwyck, "a town with two beginnings," 72.

nomic independence, self-sufficiency, and the production of a surplus that could be traded for some of the essentials or comforts of life. For burghers, tenants, and employees alike, the fur trade typically was a part-time and sometimes illicit occupation—the best means of earning an income that made life easier or survival possible. Most likely, few men and women anticipated wringing great wealth out of the wilderness or contemplated the great imperial issues of the mercantilist era.[55]

Their numbers remained small throughout the Dutch period, and the available land—vacated by the Mahicans after their defeat in 1628, and purchased by van Rensselaer and the company—proved sufficient to their needs. Limited settlement suited the company, which required only a ruling presence for its commercial designs, as well as the colonists, who brought an urban sensibility with them from the Low Countries. The margins of Iroquoia also hemmed in European settlement. And available lands and opportunities near Manhattan and on Long Island absorbed much of the immigration to New Netherland from the fatherland and from New England. Finally, for much of the Dutch period, most colonists dispatched by the patroon and the company and many who arrived independently came as individuals, not in family groups, and as sojourners they proved less apt to spread across the land in isolated farmsteads. These upper Hudson settlements thus avoided the crowding experienced in New England communities, where a larger number of people with burgeoning families quickly occupied nearby lands and pushed outward into Indian territory. The particular inclinations, modest needs, and small numbers of settlers kept the Dutch concentrated in the vicinity of Beverwyck and Fort Orange and delayed the deeper penetration of Iroquoia.[56]

[55]On the indispensability of the trade in pelts to common burghers, see Merwick, *Possessing Albany*, 96–97. For a family of five, in which a woman baked her own bread, according to Merwick, one beaver in trade would have provided the basic bread requirement of about thirty-six days (36). The plight of burghers was often exacerbated by high prices charged for goods imported by official and private traders; see, for example, Rink, *Holland on the Hudson*, 197–98.

[56]On the contrast between Dutch and English possession of the New World, see generally Merwick, *Possessing Albany;* Merwick, "Dutch Townsmen and Land Use: A Spatial Perspective on Seventeenth-Century Albany, New York," *William and Mary Quarterly,* 3d ser., 37 (1980), 53–78; and Alice P. Kenney, "Dutch Patricians in Colonial Albany," *New York History,* 49 (1968), 249–83; cf. Cohen, "How Dutch Were the Dutch of New Netherland?" and Stefan Bielinski, "The People of Colonial Albany, 1650–1800: The Profile of a Community," in William Pencak and Conrad Edick Wright, eds., *Authority and Resistance in Early New York* (New York, 1988), 1–26. The founding of Schenectady in 1662 represented the first, modest

The Dutch displayed a striking lack of curiosity about the Iroquois. They seemed to adopt an attitude of live and let live, which corresponded to their attitude toward one another. In spite of the powers and privileges granted to the patroon and the company, tenants and employees were allowed a remarkable freedom of conscience, and they assumed a considerable freedom of action. Authorities in these settlements achieved little success in imposing a particular way of life, morality, or set of beliefs on the inhabitants. Van Rensselaer worried about the "licentiousness and wantonness" of his colonists and complained of their "covetousness" and "unfaithfulness" as they violated and abused his ordinances and regulations.[57] Authorities thus had their hands full dealing with their European, Christian charges; they seldom attempted to impose their views or regulations on Indians beyond their jurisdictions, and they treated Indians who appeared at Beverwyck and Fort Orange with care.[58]

Few if any ethnographers emerged from Dutch settlements that might be compared to the Jesuit missionaries of New France. The occasional *Domine* of the Dutch Reformed Church who went among the Iroquois to "civilize" and Christianize was exceptional. In general, despite the patroon van Rensselaer's urging, the Dutch demonstrated little inclination to engage in such enterprises, and those ministers who did quickly gave up the effort. As two Dutch clergymen, Johannes Megapolensis and Samuel Drisius, wrote to the Classis of Amsterdam on August 5, 1657, "We can say but little of the conversion of the heathen or Indians here, and see no way to accomplish it, until they are subdued by the numbers and power of our people, and reduced to some sort of civilization; and also unless our people set them a better example, than they have done heretofore."[59]

The people of Rensselaerswyck, Fort Orange, and Beverwyck viewed the Iroquois who came among them from the Dutch perspective: they were merely *wilden* who would trade for Dutch wares and supply valuable furs. Beyond their interest in the Indians as trading partners, they showed little curiosity. Absorbed in their own lives, they knew little of Iroquois culture and did little to remedy their

penetration of the area's interior; on Schenectady as an exception to the rule of Dutch circumscribed settlement, see Trelease, *Indian Affairs in Colonial New York*, 136.

[57]Van Laer, ed., *Van Rensselaer-Bowier Manuscripts*, 686–88.

[58]As Iroquois complaints suggest, however, not all Dutch inhabitants cooperated in community and official attempts to treat Indian allies and trading partners with respect; see, for example, van Laer, ed., *Court Minutes of Fort Orange*, 2:283–85.

[59]Jameson, ed., *Narratives of New Netherland*, 399.

ignorance. The Reverend Jonas Michaelius, for example, the first minister residing in New Netherland (at New Amsterdam), showed considerable hostility toward the province's native peoples after his arrival in 1628. Michaelius complained about the Indians, "I find them entirely savage and wild, strangers to all decency, yea uncivil and as stupid as garden poles, . . . devilish men, who serve nobody but the Devil." The minister also believed that the Indian languages were very difficult to learn; communication of religious ideas in them, he suggested, would be nearly impossible. His preferred program of conversion and civilization was to separate children from parents and raise them under Dutch supervision, something never seriously considered in New Netherland.[60]

The first minister to reside at Rensselaerswyck-Fort Orange was the Reverend Johannes Megapolensis, who arrived there in 1642 and remained at the upper Hudson outpost about seven years. Published apparently without his permission in 1644 in the Netherlands, Megapolensis's "A Short Sketch of the Mohawk Indians" was a rare description of Mohawk customs. Yet it is not clear that Megapolensis ever visited Mohawk villages, mastered their language, or devoted much effort to their conversion, despite his stated intention "in process of time" to preach to them and "come to them in their own country and castles . . . when I am acquainted with their language." Given his lack of facility in the language when his account was written, we might question his ability as an ethnographer. Indeed, much of the minister's information may have been gleaned from the Jesuit missionary Isaac Jogues, to whom he offered refuge after the priest's escape from the Mohawks in 1643. The small but unknown number of Dutch fur traders who lived at least part of the time in Iroquois villages with native women represent the only exception to the rule of Dutch cultural distance from the Indians.[61]

Life at Beverwyck, Fort Orange, and Rensselaerswyck was a curious mixture of the medieval and modern, as it was in much of the fa-

<hr />

[60]Ibid., 122–33, especially 126–29; quotation from 126.

[61]Jameson, ed., *Narratives of New Netherland*, 168–80; quotation from 178. See Berthold Fernow's "Critical Essay" on New Netherland, in Justin Winsor, ed., *Narrative and Critical History of America*, 8 vols. (Boston and New York, [c. 1884]–1889), 4:420–21, on Jogues as Megapolensis's primary informant on the Mohawks. On Michaelius, Megapolensis, and other Dutch ministers in New Netherland, see Hugh Hastings and E. T. Corwin, eds., *Ecclesiastical Records of the State of New York*, 7 vols. (Albany, N.Y., 1901–16), 1:43–64, 152–57, 166–69, 187, 326–27, 398–99, 436–39.

therland that New Netherlanders had left. J. H. Huizinga's classic *Dutch Civilization in the Seventeenth Century* describes an Old World society in which the nobility had not disappeared but were weak; in which the clergy had established the Dutch Reformed Church as the state church but nonetheless commanded limited power; in which great old cities rather than the State dominated political life; and, most important, in which economic prosperity emerged from a pre-mercantilist economy, based on medieval liberty and not on "modern," capitalist arrangements. Rejecting vague explanations of Dutch success in terms of an alleged capitalistic outlook or the Calvinistic spirit of enterprise, Huizinga argued that "prosperity flowed quite naturally from the medieval system and there was never a point where the old was deliberately shaken off and the new warmly embraced." New Netherland was a new society, but it surpassed the fatherland in some ways in its attempt to achieve new, modern ends through old and even obsolete arrangements, as seen in the use of the feudal institution of patroonship to promote commercial development.[62]

Rule by the patroon and his agents or by the company vice-director and *commis* (commissary of the fort) bore little resemblance, at least in theory, to republicanism or free market capitalism. The feudal privileges of the patroon and the control of the West India Company strictly regulated the settlers' economic lives, and a consensus among the people seemed to support the close official scrutiny of weights, measures, and prices inherent in a traditional European moral economy. On the surface, the authority that their betters held over inhabitants' lives extended also to matters of religion. Each magistrate swore when taking office, "We shall help to maintain here the Reformed Religion according to God's Word and the regulations of the Synod of Dordrecht and not publicly tolerate any sect. So help us God Almighty."[63] Officials of the church, state, and company similarly believed it was their obligation to prevent vice and maintain moral standards among their citizens and employees. Inhabitants risked the discipline of the court for incontinence, excessive or ill-timed drinking, dereliction of duty, or raucous behavior.

Yet the New World presented new challenges for which no Old World precedents existed, although the fatherland itself was strikingly

[62]Huizinga, *Dutch Civilization in the Seventeenth Century*, especially 20–25; quotation from 24–25.
[63]For an example of this oath at Fort Orange and Beverwyck, see van Laer, ed., *Court Minutes of Fort Orange*, 1:269.

modern in the seventeenth century. Relatively cosmopolitan, bourgeois, and tolerant, the New Netherlanders were also self-confident
and self-interested. Like their kinsmen across the Atlantic, the men
and women who peopled this frontier outpost were very much the
products of a particular historical experience dominated by urbanism,
commerce, and mobility, and by the Dutch Revolt and the settlements
that followed the Wars of Religion.[64]

Men—and women—on the make dominated life at Fort Orange,
Beverwyck, and Rensselaerswyck. As one observer had remarked,
their inhabitants "were as many traders as persons."[65] Settlers often
ignored law and custom that proved inconvenient to them, or they
used it to their own advantage. When possible, they bent or eluded
the regulations that prevented their own commercial advancement.

While religious dissension was not publicly allowed in these settlements, officials looked the other way when rival denominations and
faiths established themselves. French Jesuit Isaac Jogues, who passed
through Fort Orange and New Amsterdam in 1643, observed that
"on the island of Manhate, and its environs, there may well be four
or five hundred men of different sects and nations: the Director
General [Willem Kieft] told me that there were men of eighteen different languages. . . . No religion is publicly exercised but the Calvinist,
and orders are to admit none but Calvinists, but this is not observed;
for besides the Calvinists there are in the colony Catholics, English
Puritans, Lutherans, Anabaptists, here called Mnistes [Mennonites],
etc."[66]

---

[64]A. M. van der Woude, "Variations in the Size and Structure of the Household in the
United Provinces of the Netherlands in the Seventeenth and Eighteenth Centuries," in Peter
Laslett, ed., *Households and Family in Past Time* (Cambridge, 1972), 299–318, argued that cities
and commerce dominated life in the Low Countries even among those living in rural areas.
Van der Woude painted a portrait of Dutch life that was decidedly urban, individualistic,
mobile, and diverse. By 1622, 54 percent of the population in Holland lived in towns, some
of them very large, and such was the distribution of urban centers throughout the country
that virtually no village was more than twenty-five kilometers (fifteen miles) removed from
one or several of them (302). While agriculture was important, it did not have "that predominance over daily life" typical elsewhere, and by the mid-seventeenth century only perhaps 18 percent of the male working population earned a living in agriculture (303).
Significantly, navigation was one of the most important employments (303). These gener-
alizations are applicable as well to many, though not all, of the non-Netherlandish immigrants
to the province. On the European background of New Netherland's colonists, see Rink,
Holland on the Hudson, 139–71; Cohen, "How Dutch were the Dutch of New Netherland,"
43–60.
[65]Jameson, ed., *Narratives of New Netherland* (New York, 1909), 274.
[66]Ibid., 259–60. Not all New Netherlanders, of course, were so tolerant, nor did most
celebrate their toleration; it was simply a necessary fact of life. On attempts by Dutch Reformed clergymen, in New and old Netherlands, to resist religious pluralism, see for example,

Against the threat of chaos engendered by the abandoned behavior of Europeans set loose in the wilderness of the New World, men like Kiliaen van Rensselaer tried to impose order. The patroon took his privileges seriously and attempted to establish a system of civil government for his colony. But his efforts to regulate life in Rensselaerswyck were as often frustrated as realized. The dispatch in 1632 of a silver-plated rapier with baldric for his chief officer, or *schout,* and black hats with silver bands for his magistrates, or *schepens,* symbolized in the end his impotence rather than his majesty. It ultimately proved to be a futile gesture, an inadequate attempt to endow his government with a dignity and authority that the inhabitants never seemed to accept.[67] Van Rensselaer experienced great difficulty in finding competent leaders and managers for Rensselaerswyck, and the men he did entrust often failed to command the deference they expected; charges of disrespect, slander, and insubordination peppered the colony's court records.

Raucous behavior, disrespect for the patroon's property, and lack of deference came together in a particularly telling case brought against one Claes Teunisz Uylenspiegel in December 1648. The director of the colony, Brant van Slichtenhorst, charged that the defendant "three several times, yes, even twice on the same day, notwithstanding the fine and the prohibition of their honors' ordinance [against racing horses in the streets], out of pure mischief and in spite of the court, has presumed to ride past the director's door as fast as the horse could run.... He has not only violated [the authority of] the honorable patroon in his high and low jurisdiction and [that of] the court here, but also [that of] the Lords States General whose place we occupy and committed the highest crime [against them]." The director demanded that Teunisz—whose nickname, *Uylenspiegel,* "the wag, or joker," seems appropriate—be publicly exposed in the

---

"Revs. Megapolensis and Drisius to the Classis of Amsterdam, Oct. 6, 1653," in Corwin and Hastings, eds., *Ecclesiastical Records of New York,* 1:317–18; for a continuation of the discussion see 320–23. Prosecutions for the performance of private religious services contrary to ordinances were recorded in Beverwyck as well; see, for example, van Laer, ed., *Court Minutes of Fort Orange,* 1:247, 251–52; see also A. J. F. van Laer, trans. and ed., *Minutes of the Court of Albany, Rensselaerswyck, and Schenectady, 1668–1685; Being a Continuation of the Minutes of the Court of Fort Orange and Beverwyck,* 3 vols. (Albany, N.Y., 1926–32), 1:233, 243, 247, for later controversies between the Dutch Reformed Church and Lutherans in Albany.

[67]Van Rensselaer was forced to experiment with a number of formulas for governing his colony, mostly as a result of the incompetence or self-interestedness of those he sent to rule. See preface to van Laer, ed., *Court Minutes of Rensselaerswyck,* 7–23. On the emblems of rule, which the patroon hoped would command deference among his employees, see van Laer, ed., *Van Rensselaer-Bowier Manuscripts,* 204, 205.

pillory and banished from the colony, "in accordance with the custom of the fatherland, where those who disobey and disregard the lord's prohibition and banishment are punished with death." Despite these harsh words, the court merely admonished and fined the defendant six guilders for each offense, in addition to the damage done to the horses.[68] Authority was hard to enforce in the face of a general pattern of disrespect toward the person and position of the director. Laws and regulations were passed *in terrorem,* with the expectation that severe penalties would be commuted; magistrates seemed unable to awe the people and showed the expected mercy because they had little choice. Inhabitants flouted the law, if not with impunity, then at least with great regularity and success.[69]

In Fort Orange, and in Beverwyck after 1652,[70] inhabitants and employees of the West India Company lived under the authority of the *commis* (later called vice director) and a varying number of *commissarissen,* or local magistrates.[71] These representatives of the company and the States-General proved similarly unable to cow local inhabitants with their authority and majesty. Mischief, violence, and vituperation were as common in these jurisdictions as in the patroon's domain. Settlers did not stop at breaking the law: they often assaulted

[68]"Court Proceedings, December 17 Anno 1648," in van Laer, ed., *Court Minutes of Rensselaerswyck,* 50–52; a short biographical sketch of Claes Teunisz is in van Laer, ed., *Van Rensselaer-Bowier Manuscripts,* 830.

[69]See Merwick, *Possessing Albany,* 182–84, on the expectation that sentences would be mitigated or never executed; Merwick explained that, in practice, "the law smothered rather than adjudicated conflict" (183). For another example of the use of mercy in judicial proceedings, see van Laer, ed., *Court Minutes of Fort Orange,* 1:240. See also Pearson, ed., *Early Records of Albany,* 3:3–23, on the nature of notorial law in the province; and see van Laer, ed., *Court Minutes of Rensselaerswyck,* 7n, and van Laer, ed. *Court Minutes of Fort Orange,* 1:8–9, on judicial practice in Rensselaerswyck and Beverwyck. Most discussions of law in colonial New York generally neglect the Dutch period, or focus primarily on the transition from Dutch to English legal practice, but see Merwick, *Possessing Albany;* Leo Hershkowitz "The Troublesome Turk: An Illustration of Judicial Process in New Amersterdam," *New York History,* 46 (October 1965), 299–310; Linda Briggs Biemer, *Women and Property in Colonial New York: The Transition from Dutch to English Law, 1643–1727* (Ann Arbor, Mich., 1983); David E. Narrett, "Dutch Customs of Inheritance, Women, and the Law in Colonial New York City," in Pencak and Wright, eds., *Authority and Resistance in Early New York,* 27–55.

[70]As the settlements in the vicinity of Fort Orange and Rensselaerswyck grew in the mid-seventeenth century, jurisdictional conflicts mounted between the patroonship, on the one hand, and the company's fort and director-general on the other. Tensions erupted into violence in February 1652 (see van Laer, ed., *Court Minutes of Rensselaerswyck,* 184–200). Finally, Director-General Stuyvesant arrested Director van Slichtenhorst and, on April 10, 1652, established a court at Fort Orange and transformed the main settlement of Rensselaer's colony—now on the west side of the Hudson River—into an independent village, Beverwyck. Despite the antagonism between authorities, the settlements under their control were quite similar and generally can be treated together, rather than as separate concerns.

[71]On these arrangements, see van Laer, ed., *Court Minutes of Fort Orange,* 1:7–9.

the reputations, and sometimes the persons, of those charged with upholding it.

Such troublemakers were not typical. Yet their lives help illustrate the unsettled new Dutch world along the upper Hudson, on the margins of Iroquoia, a world that the Five Nations found disturbing. In the chaos of Beverwyck—where each inhabitant seemed to think, selfishly, "that now was the acceptable time to make his fortune," as one chronicler complained—a clear and coherent Indian policy could not emerge. Regulations, sought by the Indians as well as by Dutch officials, could not be enforced; abuses committed by Dutch ruffians against their European compatriots and their Indian neighbors could not be punished and curbed. Such a world offered a poor soil for cultivating a new landscape of peace.

The particularly egregious record of one Herman Jansz van Valckenburg exemplifies the turmoil characteristic of the new Dutch cultural landscape. In 1655, the court pronounced a sentence on the prisoner van Valckenburg for breaking the window of Marcelis Jansz, "out of pure mischief," climbing into the house, and molesting the occupant. Van Valckenburg had then scattered fire from the hearth and started a blaze, which he had prevented Jansz and his wife from extinguishing. Moreover, as the court record tells us, the prisoner confessed "that lately when they were riding the goose, he, on the public street, (be it said without disrespect) befouled the servant, or one of the men of Mr. de Hulter, . . . thereby violating and disturbing the peace on the public highways and streets." Then, at a later time, he entered the house of Steeven Jansz and threatened to beat him. Jansz ran and obtained the help of the *commis* Joannes Dyckman, who arrested van Valckenburg. Finally, while sitting in the house of Steeven Jansz some time later, "with his feet in irons," the prisoner assaulted the prestige and dignity of the *commis* himself and his spouse, as he "declared openly that he had seen the wife of Commissary of Officer Dyckman commit adultery with several persons, showing with outstretched arms the size of the horns which he saw put on the commissary."[72]

For his various offenses, the court demanded that van Valckenburg be displayed in flogging irons, "with a few rods hanging from the post

---

[72]Ibid., 1:203–4, 206–8; Merwick, *Possessing Albany*, 74–75, which also refers to this incident and connects it with the revelry of Shrove Tuesday; "riding the goose" was a sort of bloodsport, in which men rode at full speed on horseback and attempted to pull the head from a goose suspended by its feet.

above his head and on his breast [placed] a sign with the words 'False Accuser,' " and that he be banished from the jurisdiction for six years. The sentence was much more lenient than the defendant deserved, but the court was "moved to mitigate and reduce the sentence to this extent in the hope that he may improve his conduct." Van Valckenburg was not a typical burgher of Beverwyck, yet his crimes represent an extreme example of a larger pattern of life in the settlement.[73]

The powers of the various officials who governed in Rensselaerswyck, Fort Orange, and Beverwyck, even if greater in theory than in practice, brought them into the center of the burghers' and employees' lives. These officials organized the community's defenses, built and maintained fortifications, coordinated the guard, and oversaw the burghers' maintenance of roads and bridges. They attempted to prevent the dangers of fire by issuing ordinances that required the frequent sweeping of chimneys and prohibited the piling of firewood in the streets. And town officials tried to protect the citizens from one another by outlawing the racing of horses along town thoroughfares and by banning "the practice of playing golf along the streets," which was "contrary to the freedom of the public streets," caused "great damage to the windows of the houses," and exposed people "to the danger of being injured."[74]

With an eye on both the morals of the townspeople and the state of the excise, the magistrates regulated tavern keepers. And various ordinances for the proper assize of bread governed how often, in what quantities, and at what prices bakers could bake and sell their wares to burghers. Inhabitants expressed concern that the loaves they bought were too often measured short and were of inferior quality,

[73]Van Laer, ed., *Court Minutes of Fort Orange*, 1:208. For other extreme examples of the ribaldry, mischief, and disrespect of inhabitants, see 198 n99, in which court sessions on February 2 and 23, 1655 investigated the matter of scandalous nicknames given to the houses of prominent townspeople, apparently by one Cornelis Vos. Gerrit Jansz's house was called "The House of Discord," Andryes Herpertsz's "The House of Ill Manners," and Jeremias van Rensselaer's "Spoiled Early"; Volckert Jansz's was denigrated as *de Vogelsanck*, or "The Bird Song," after a street in the city of Gouda assigned to women of ill fame. See also the prosecution in January 1678 of unruly townsmen, including a city constable, William Loveridge, Jr., detailed in Pearson, ed., *Early Records of Albany*, 1:126n and in van Laer, ed., *Court Minutes of Albany*, 2:288–90.

[74]See, for example, van Laer, ed., *Court Minutes of Albany* 1:295; 2:168, 226, 234–35. See Merwick, *Possessing Albany*, 183, on civil—rather than religious—officials in Albany even being called upon to explain the appearance of a comet to townspeople and imposing "silence on public clamour" in 1680; on this incident see also van Laer, ed., *Court Minutes of Albany*, 3:57–58. The persistent need to draft renewals and amplification of ordinances testifies to the inability of officials to enforce numerous regulations; see, for example, the court's actions (1670–71) in ibid., 1:148, 223, 279–80.

while unscrupulous bakers sold the more delectable wares to the Indians at exorbitant prices. As inhabitants at Fort Orange charged, bakers "do not act in good faith in the matter of baking bread for the burghers, but bolt the flour from the meal and sell it greatly to their profit to the savages for the baking of sweet cake, white bread, cookies and pretzels, so that the burghers must buy and get largely bran for their money."[75]

Immoral actions of another sort came under the scrutiny of the *schout* and *schepens* as they sought to curb the licentiousness of the inhabitants. In March of 1654, Commissary Dyckman hauled Abraham Crabaat into court "for having last Shrove Tuesday walked along the street in woman's clothes."[76] In August of 1658, the court at Fort Orange confronted one Nicolaes Gregory Hillebrant, a Company servant, for committing what the early twentieth-century archivist and editor A. J. F. van Laer termed "unprintable" offenses. Van Laer censored the details, but the published records nonetheless reveal that Hillebrant was discovered in the garden of Jochim Ketluyn in a compromising position with a young boy after the boy refused his advances and cried out to a passer-by. And during the winter of 1647–1648, officials had pursued the fugitive Harmen Meyndertsz van den Bogaert into Mohawk country, where he fled following "criminal offenses of a grave nature," alleged acts of sodomy with his black servant, Tobias.[77] In addition to these extraordinary cases, the courts considered it their obligation to deal with the more frequent discoveries of illicit carnal conversations "in order to avoid scandal, to prevent further mischief, to promote good order, and finally to fulfill our bounded duty."[78]

While regulating and policing the community, and prosecuting a wide variety of criminal matters, the *schout* and his agents heard civil cases that pitted citizen against citizen in a context where everything seemed unpredictable. The proceedings that most occupied the

[75]See van Laer, ed., *Court Minutes of Fort Orange*, 1:128–29; quotation from 128. See also 2:234, 166–67. On the charges brought against one baker, Jochem Wesselsen, see 1:55, 61, 241–43, 248–51, 280.
[76]Van Laer, ed., *Court Minutes of Albany*, 1:118.
[77]*Ibid.*, 2:153–55; the Hillebrant case is referred to as well in Pearson, ed., *Early Records of Albany*, 4:69–70. Van den Bogaert's escapades are detailed in J. H. Innes, *New Amsterdam and Its People* (New York, 1902), 67–74; this information is updated and corrected in the introduction to Charles T. Gehring and William A. Starna, trans. and eds., *A Journey into Mohawk and Oneida Country, 1634–1635: The Journal of Harmen Meyndertsz van den Bogaert* (Syracuse, N.Y., 1988), xxi–xxii.
[78]Van Laer, ed., *Court Minutes of Fort Orange*, 1:188–90, 197–98.

The Baker, oil on canvas, by Job Adriaensz Berckheyde (1630–93), Dutch, courtesy of the Worcester Art Museum, Worcester, Massachusetts, gift of Mr. and Mrs. Milton P. Higgins. In their new world, the Dutch townspeople of Fort Orange and Beverwyck complained that bakers "do not act in good faith . . . but bolt the flour from the meal and sell it greatly to their profit to the savages for the baking of sweet cake, white bread, cookies and pretzels, so that the burghers must buy and get largely bran for their money."

schout's and *schepens'* attention centered on property and trade. The courts spent much of their time authorizing the use, transfer, or improvement of various pieces of real property. Litigious residents seemed constantly at odds with the patroon, the company, and each other over plots of farm land and building sites and structures in the town. As Donna Merwick has shown, the Dutch in New Netherland understood and employed land in ways significantly different from those of the English in America. New Netherlanders valued land and real property not for the status it might convey but for the commercial opportunities it might promote. Such ownership was to be inconspicuous, and the transfer of real property was expected to occur frequently and discreetly. Land was a commodity, and land ownership constituted part of an investment portfolio that "purposely hid as much as it showed about the accumulation of wealth."[79]

If the strange patchwork of ownership and the peculiar use of land among the Dutch shocked their new English rulers after 1664, Dutch possession of land must have surprised and challenged the Five Nations as well, though in different ways. It may have been easy for the Iroquois to accept the occupation of Mahican lands, where the Dutch fort and town were situated, and even the transfer of land for the new village of Schenectady in the 1660s did not seem to threaten Iroquois territorial integrity. Indeed, the establishment of new European settlements—even Dutch ones—conveniently situated and bound into a larger Iroquois Longhouse by ties of friendship, reciprocity, and even kinship was consistent with the vision and historical experience of the Five Nations. Yet the concept of exclusive ownership characteristic of the Dutch, although at variance with English notions of dominion, contrasted even more sharply with the Iroquois understanding of land as symbolically a common bowl; for the Iroquois, land could be occupied, used, and shaped, but not really owned. It was shared communally, entrusted to the group as a whole and distributed temporarily according to need and use. The use of land as a commodity and the volatility of real property transfers, if observed by Iroquois visitors to Beverwyck, must have seemed amazing. In these transactions, in the litigated contentions over land, and in the hunger

---

[79]Merwick, *Possessing Albany*, especially 196–201; see also Sung Bok Kim, *Landlord and Tenant in Colonial New York: Manorial Society, 1664–1775* (Chapel Hill, N.C., 1978), who suggested in a later period that the superficially feudal, manorial estates of colonial New York were in fact strongly capitalistic in character.

for property that increased substantially with the English conquest, we can see the seeds of later European-Indian conflict.[80]

In March of 1654, the court at Fort Orange reported to the Director-General that "the colony extends far and wide and between the farms established by the patroon there are still many lands which are not yet bought or occupied by the patroon or his subjects, but are cultivated by the natives themselves." The court complained that the persistence of Indian occupation worked to "the great prejudice of this country" because the Indians tended to "imagine after a time that they [the lands] belong to them."[81] In general, the Dutch favored separation between themselves and native groups and disliked the continuing presence of some Indian people within the limited orbit of their settlement on the upper Hudson—generally Mahicans and other displaced Algonquians rather than Iroquois. The Dutch inhabitants urged Stuyvesant to purchase or authorize the acquisition of such property and thereby encourage its exclusive occupation and cultivation by Europeans. The alienation of the land in the vicinity of Fort Orange was accomplished without major incident, although it foreshadowed later trouble, could the parties have read the signs. Despite the conflict between Indian and European understanding of land ownership, the Dutch remained centered in the area near Fort Orange and Beverwyck and attempted to penetrate Iroquoia not with streams of settlers but with lines of commerce.

[80]William Cronon, *Changes in the Land: Indians, Colonists, and the Ecology of New England* (New York, 1983), especially 54–81, analyzed English and Indian ideas and practices of land ownership, and the conflicts that developed over land, in colonial New England. On the Iroquois, see George S. Snyderman, "Concepts of Land Ownership among the Iroquois and their Neighbors," in William N. Fenton, *Symposium on Local Diversity in Iroquois Culture, Bureau of American Ethnology Bulletin*, no. 149 (Washington, D.C., 1951), 15–34.

[81]Van Laer, ed., *Court Minutes of Fort Orange*, 1:125.

5

Commerce, Kinship, and the Transaction of Peace

> They [the Mohawks] say, we have been here before
> and made an alliance. The Dutch, indeed, say we are
> brothers and are joined together with chains, but that
> lasts only as long as we have beavers. After that we are
> no longer thought of, but much will depend upon it
> when we shall need each other.
>
> —Extraordinary Session of the Court
> at Fort Orange, September 6, 1659

Johan de Laet's 1625 chronicle suggests both the private, improvisational character of New Netherland and its decidedly commercial orientation. He wrote: "Our countrymen have continued to make voyages thither each year, and continuously some of our people remain there for the purpose of trafficking with the natives; and on this account the country has justly received the name New Netherland."[1] But such individual, self-interested behavior flew in the face of Iroquois expectations and social prescriptions. In this chapter I examine the peculiar, contested, hybrid discourse and practice that developed between New Netherland and the Five Nations. While the Dutch attempted to keep their distance culturally and physically from Iroquoia, they nonetheless sought the profits that only Iroquois furs could produce. And while the people of the Five Nations strove to maintain their cultural identity and political autonomy, they nevertheless hoped to merge with the Dutch, transforming New Netherlanders into allies and kinspeople. Along the Dutch-Iroquois frontier, then, we see a contest of cultures. Yet it was a contest unlike most

---

[1] J. Franklin Jameson, ed., *Narratives of New Netherland, 1609–1664* (New York, 1909), 39.

others in colonial America: despite the unruliness of Dutch inhabitants and traders, despite the seemingly unreasonable demands of Iroquois allies or "brethren," the relationship worked. In this chapter I relate and analyze Dutch attempts to "transact" peace with the Iroquois, which the Five Nations grudgingly found consistent with their own efforts to cultivate a landscape of peace and naturalize outsiders in their greater Longhouse.

In "A Dialogue Between a Patriot and a New Netherlander Upon the Advantages which the Country Presents to Settlers, &c. [1655]," Adriaen van der Donck had the anonymous colonist declare, "Our national character is well known. They delight in commerce."[2] Indeed, in the settlements of Beverwyck, Fort Orange, and Rensselaerswyck, commerce was paramount. Small farmers and artisans traded with each other and hoped to tap into the greater provincial and Atlantic markets. The Company, the patroon, and private merchants of substantial means also produced for these markets, though on a grander scale.[3] The trade in furs, the chief staple for small and large colonists alike, found its outlet through these channels into Europe. From the Dutch perspective, the fur trade began in places like Fort Orange. Yet as historians increasingly point out, the production of this commodity began in a much earlier phase, in the complex processes of hunting or trapping, skinning, tanning, and transportation to export depots.

In the fur trade, two complex industries met, one European and one Native American; the pelts that arrived at Fort Orange represented the highly processed result of an involved production phase.[4] The Dutch displayed little interest in attempting a vertical integration of the industry that would give them control of the earlier stages of production. They remained traders and merchants, content to distribute these partially processed goods to markets in Europe. Major fur dealers and smaller, part-time traders demonstrated little incli-

[2]Thomas F. O'Donnell, ed., *[Adriaen van der Donck's] Description of New Netherlands* (Syracuse, N.Y., 1968 [orig. pub. Amsterdam, 1655]), 120–33, quotation from 128.

[3]See especially Oliver A. Rink, *Holland on the Hudson: An Economic and Social History of Dutch New York* (Ithaca, N.Y., 1986), 172–213; Donna Merwick, *Possessing Albany, 1630–1710: The Dutch and English Experiences* (New York, 1990), 83–88, 88–92, described the principal *handelaars,* or merchants, their mode of operation, and the hostility they sometimes generated among small traders.

[4]See especially Francis Jennings, *The Invasion of America: Indians, Colonialism, and the Cant of Conquest* (Chapel Hill, N.C., 1975), 88–94, 96–98, for interesting suggestions and useful information on the fur trade.

nation to follow Indians into the forests and compete with native producers. Instead they opted to remain in or near their towns and allow the furs to come to them. The Dutch preference for this form of commerce kept them out of Iroquoia, but it bound them inextricably to the Iroquois.[5]

For the Dutch, the fur trade and Indian relations became virtually synonymous. New Netherlanders craved furs, and they tolerated and welcomed the Iroquois and other Indian peoples among them chiefly because they were the source of that valuable commodity. The exchange between Dutch and the Iroquois across the cultural frontier stood at the center of Dutch economic life, and the interactions of colonists and Indians thus became one of the most important concerns of public policy. Control or prohibition of the trade in liquor, and regulation of forestalling tactics, especially the employment of Indian or Christian "brokers," loomed largest among officials' concerns as they tried to stabilize commerce with the Iroquois and other Indians. Because this business relationship involved a powerful foreign nation, one that could threaten the province militarily as well as economically, authorities paid even greater attention. The survival of the entire settlement—not merely the economic health of individual residents—depended on the maintenance of good relations with the Five Nations.

Yet the freedom, disorder, and volatility that characterized life in general at Beverwyck, Fort Orange, and Rensselaerswyck governed the Dutch encounter with their Iroquois partners as well. In these settlements, no particular officer or agent handled Indian affairs exclusively. The task was as diffuse as Indian policy itself, which was never clearly articulated. Indian policy existed only as tentative and often ineffective commercial regulation, as improvisational and sometimes reluctant negotiation. Authorities administered the rules of the patroon and the company, which were designed primarily to conserve their own privileges and maintain the peace that made trade possible.

Yet the individual initiatives of private traders affected Indian-European affairs at Fort Orange and its environs at least as much. For the most part, large and small traders looked to their own interests. They viewed their relationship with Indians narrowly, demonstrating more concern for the personal encounters than for the greater political relationship between their two nations. Only when forced—

[5]Although Dutch traders often went into the woods to coax Indian traders to their own trading houses or to seek other advantages in competition with fellow Dutch traders, they seldom ventured all the way to Iroquois villages or engaged directly in trapping.

in times of general Indian unrest, in the face of new competition from the French or English, or when Iroquois sachems appeared in their settlements with propositions that could not be ignored—did they adopt a wider view.

Indian affairs at Fort Orange were democratized as they were improvised. Regulation of the trade was effective only when it won community support. Traders effectively nullified ordinances—such as those against commerce in liquor or employment of brokers—with which they did not agree or which seemed to threaten their livelihood.[6] Competition was fierce, as a Jesuit visitor, Father Isaac Jogues, noticed in 1643: "Trade is free to all; this gives the Indians all things cheap, each of the Hollanders outbidding his neighbor, and being satisfied provided he can gain some little profit."[7]

Competition did not confine itself to matters of price. Many obstructed regular trade within the town by illegally intercepting Iroquois traders on their way to market. In April 1649, officials at Rensselaerswyck served notice on three Dutch traders: "You have license to carry on lawful trade, but in no wise to carry on any illegitimate trade, as is daily done by you in running into the woods to meet savages who come with beavers and in promising them presents of stockings, hatchets and other goods if they come to your houses to trade, and after ... giving them a little note to tell other savages where you dwell and such presents as will induce them to come to you to trade." The defendants promised to reform, but in receiving their reprimand one of them—Cornelis Teunisz van Breuckelen, former colony commissioner—added this qualification: "provided those of the fort do likewise, as heretofore they have not done."[8] Traders willingly submitted to regulations only when they were convinced that

[6]On the traffic in liquor and attempts by authorities on both sides of the cultural frontier to control it, see Allen W. Trelease, *Indian Affairs in New York: The Seventeenth Century* (Ithaca, N.Y., 1960), 93–94. The trade was first prohibited in 1643, and ordinances against it were frequently renewed, though apparently with little effect. On the unscrupulousness of some tapsters and the dangers caused by drunkenness of Indians at Rensselaerswyck, see A. J. F. van Laer, trans. and ed., *Minutes of the Court of Rensselaerswyck, 1648–1652* (Albany, N.Y., 1922), 97; for similar prosecutions at Fort Orange and Beverwyck, see van Laer, trans. and ed., *Minutes of the Court of Fort Orange and Beverwyck, 1652–1660*, 2 vols. (Albany, N.Y., 1920–23), 1:286–91. For Mohawk complaints about the liquor trade, see 2:211, 212. For one of many ordinances against the traffic in wine, brandy, strong liquor, or beer, see 281–83; see also A. J. F. van Laer, trans. and ed., *Minutes of the Court of Albany, Rensselaerswyck and Schenectady, 1668–1685*, 3 vols. (Albany, N.Y., 1926–32), 1:69, 237–38, 245–47, 281, on the renewal of prohibitions following the English conquest.

[7]Jameson, ed., *Narratives of New Netherland*, 262.

[8]Van Laer, ed., *Court Minutes of Rensselaerswyck*, 70–71.

others would have to abide by similar rules. And conflict over jurisdictions between Fort Orange and Rensselaerswyck, between classes and factions, and between burghers and outsiders added fuel to the fires.[9]

In response to rumors of war with the Mohawks in September 1650, Fort Orange and Rensselaerswyck worked together to correct trade abuses that had antagonized the Indians. Secretary Anthony de Hooges wrote for the court of Rensselaerswyck, "It has occurred to us that it is very necessary that the running into the woods, the delivery of notes and the sending of brokers (a source of mischief, quarreling and discord) be stopped.... As this can not be done properly and decently without the consent of the inhabitants of Fort Orange, [the court therefore obtained a confirmation of their] good intentions and inclinations."[10] Burghers and tenants from both jurisdictions agreed, because the present crisis demanded a reform that left no one with an unfair advantage.

The sense of crisis faded, but competition between traders continued to grow. The decline of Rensselaerswyck relative to Beverwyck after 1652 ultimately helped to end jurisdictional conflicts, though some rivalry lingered. Authorities nonetheless found it difficult to control traders in the context of cut-throat competition; there was widespread violation of the ordinances as individual traders strove to maintain or increase their own shares of the market. Some argued that

[9]In May of 1645, the officers at Fort Orange and the court at Rensselaerswyck had cooperated in issuing a joint ordinance concerning the fur trade; it set prices, outlawed trade at night or at "unseasonable hours," designated the proper place in which trade could be conducted, and prohibited "enticing" Indians from the house of the *commis* or in any other way interfering with free trade; see A. J. F. van Laer, trans. and ed., *Van Rensselaer-Bowier Manuscripts: Being the Letters of Kiliaen van Rensselaer, 1630–1643, and Other Documents Relating to the Colony of Rensselaerswyck* (Albany, N.Y., 1908), 722–23. On the participation of outsiders and transients in the fur trade at Beverwyck during *handelstijd*, see Merwick, *Possessing Albany*, 77–78.

[10]The rumors were reported at a special meeting, September 21, 1650, recorded in van Laer, ed., *Court Minutes of Rensselaerswyck*, 127–30. On September 23, one prominent Fort Orange inhabitant and translator experienced in Indian affairs, Jan Labatie, refused to cooperate (129), but common action, including the dispatch of a special delegation to the Mohawks, was arranged (129–30). In general, cooperation was possible only in times of considerable economic or military peril, for example, when the van den Bogaert commercial embassy was sent to the Iroquois in the winter of 1634–1635 to restore the fur trade; see Charles T. Gehring and William A. Starna, trans. and eds., *A Journey into Mohawk and Oneida Country, 1634–1635: The Journal of Harmen Meyndertsz van den Bogaert* (Syracuse, N.Y., 1988); other examples were the missions to the Mohawks, in the 1640s, to ransom captive French Jesuit priests or to help the Indians fortify their castles against anticipated French attacks; see depositions of Simon de Groot and Labatie in Lawrence H. Leder, ed., "The Livingston Indian Records," *Pennsylvania History*, 23 (January 1956), 143–46.

fur trade regulations represented an attempt by the magistrates to reserve the entire traffic for themselves.[11] The wealthier and more established members of the community may well have enjoyed competitive advantages under the tighter trading regimen established by company and town ordinances. And smaller, part-time fur traders and commercial sojourners may have been less concerned about the dangerous effect of their illicit trading practices on Indian affairs.

In June 1659, the substantial trader and influential townsman Philip Pietersz Schuyler defended himself against charges that he had ventured into the woods illegally to forestall trade that should have taken place within the town or fort. The vice-director and *schout* claimed that Schuyler had given one Indian a new coat as a bribe to deliver five Indians and their furs to his trading house. After denying that the coat was such a bribe, Schuyler went on to declare that "he gave a present to the Indians and if he did wrong in that, ... not a single beaver is bartered in the Fuyck [Beverwyck, the area of settlement surrounding the old trading post of Fort Orange] but it is done contrary to the ordinance."[12] Schuyler's violations both reflected and encouraged the pattern of widespread abuse of fur trade regulation, and the controversy over brokers that emerged in that year showed the burghers and traders at Beverwyck at their most chaotic. Schuyler simply did what others were doing. His ability to avoid prosecution antagonized those who conformed to the rules or commanded less power, and his active disregard for ordinances spurred others to further violation of the law.

Defendant Cornelis Bosch spoke with frustration and contempt when, according to a witness, he said that "he would go into the woods and let everyone see it and ... he wiped his ... [omitted in original] on the ordinance." According to other witnesses, Bosch said "that if Philip Pietersen [Schuyler] and Pieter Hartgers, who were caught, were not punished first, that he wiped his ... on the ordinance.... I do not care a thing about the magistrates and shall go into the woods and let them see it, and they are a lot of perjurers if they do not punish those." Hartgers merely replied to Bosch and the court, which had apprehended him on a similar offense, that he believed he should be allowed to employ Indians as brokers, or forestalling agents, "be-

[11]Van Laer, ed., *Court Minutes of Fort Orange*, 1:223–24.
[12]Ibid., 2:191.

cause the ordinance according to his opinion should have been re-pealed in the same way as last year."[13]

Indeed, the actual rules governing the fur trade changed from year to year, despite the persistence of ordinances prohibiting various practices. Community pressure effectively nullified unpopular restrictions. In 1659, authorities at Fort Orange once again gave way in the face of popular resistance and replied to Hartgers's argument weakly, declaring that they would "take the matter under advisement."[14] It is an irony, however, that strict regulation of the commerce in furs came only through the initiative of the Iroquois. Organized Iroquois pressure lent a reason and sense of urgency to efforts by the magistrates to curb abuses and regulate the trade. The events of 1660 may serve as a case study.

As the trading season approached on May 25, a group of prominent petitioners noticed "that the Christians are again about to run into the woods as brokers in order by their subreptive and improper ways to get the trade entirely into their hands, which can only tend to the general decline and utter ruination of Fort Orange and the village of Beverwyck; yes, what is more, the said running in the woods is accompanied by many excessive and shameful irregularities for which God the Lord would punish such a place, all of which has no other motive than greed." The petitioners asked that everyone be allowed to employ Indian brokers, to the exclusion of Christian ones. Prohibiting "Christians," that is, the common farmers and townspeople of Beverwyck, from entering the woods to forestall trade would have given substantial fur traders—who could afford to employ Indian brokers—a competitive advantage. In addition, the prohibition would have promoted greater cultural separation between Indians and Europeans, and because the trade would then take place within the Dutch settlement, magistrates and prominent burghers could monitor the Iroquois-Dutch relationship more closely. On the last day of May, the court heard testimony from various members of the community on the issue. It decided, in accordance with an ordinance issued in 1654 and renewed each year thereafter, "that no brokers, whether Christian

---

[13]Ibid., 2:201–3; see also 189, 221, 225 on Bosch's encounters with the law and with more substantial traders.

[14]Ibid., 2:203; for a somewhat different interpretation of this controversy, see Merwick, *Possessing Albany*, 88–94.

or Indian, shall be employed, but that Indians without being called or solicited shall be allowed to trade their beavers where they please."[15]

After a number of violations and prosecutions, on June 15 the court bowed to community pressure and granted to all burghers the right to employ Indian brokers, but not Dutch ones, while it again prohibited traders from sending presents ahead into the woods.[16] But in an extraordinary session on June 17 the court heard a petition submitted by a group of smaller traders, who called the petition of May 25 "a pretext for no other purpose than to divert the trade to themselves [the larger dealers] and inspired by greed." The petitioners, claiming to represent a majority of the inhabitants, asked the court to consider that "many a poor person could earn a beaver and the community would be better served." They took issue with earlier attempts to characterize them as "rabble" and argued that "the least [of the citizens] has as much right as the most [important one], since the country must exist by them." The eighty inhabitants who signed the petition requested that all be allowed "to do the best they can with Christians and with Indians," that is, that everyone be allowed to hire Indian or Christian brokers.[17]

In response, the court capitulated once again. "Although of dangerous consequences," the practice of using Dutch brokers could not be prevented "without causing great mischief." The court thus ruled that the use of brokers would be left to the discretion of individual traders, "protesting meanwhile their innocence of all mischief that may result therefrom, the more so as some of the petitioners have said that they would do it anyway, whether it was permitted or not." Although the community was torn by this controversy over the proper methods for conducting the Indian trade, Dutch traders great and small were nonetheless generally satisfied with the existing commercial chaos, which, however, some Dutch officials and the Iroquois criticized. The officials hoped for an order that would supply the stability and profits they required; the Iroquois wanted a wide distribution of resources and an order based on reciprocity, one that could promise important nonmaterial rewards.[18]

The matter did not end there. Nine days later the Mohawks ap-

[15]Van Laer, ed., *Court Minutes of Fort Orange*, 2:255–56.
[16]Ibid., 266; on various violations and prosecutions see 261–65.
[17]Ibid., 266–68.
[18]Ibid., 268.

peared at Fort Orange to protest the trading practices of the Dutch and demand reforms. Their spokesman complained "that the Dutch when they are in the woods to fetch Indians beat them severely with fists and drive them out of the woods." The Mohawks charged that Dutchmen greatly maltreated them and that "presently ten or twelve of them surround an Indian and drag him along, saying: 'Come with me, so and so has no goods,' thus interfering with one another, which they fear will end badly."[19]

Vice-Director Johannes La Montagne disingenuously replied that they had not heard of such violence occurring before, but now that it had come to light the court would take action to prevent it. Yet in an extended conference with the Mohawks in September of the previous year (1659), the Dutch had been warned to "leave off their wickedness and not beat them [the Mohawks] as much as they have done heretofore." Officials were concerned enough to promise the Mohawk delegation that Stuyvesant himself would respond to their complaints, or that "Dutch sachems will go into the country." With Stuyvesant downed by illness, a special delegation representing Beverwyck, Fort Orange, and Rensselaerswyck made the difficult journey to Caughnawaga, the first "castle", or fortified town, of the Mohawks, and presented their considered response to the Mohawk propositions on September 24, 1659. Finally, back in Beverwyck after satifying their Iroquois partners at least temporarily, on September 27 La Montagne and the magistrates declared, "Having received several complaints about the insolent treatment of the savages in beating them and throwing things at them, which tends to dangerous consequences, . . . they expressly do forbid hereby, all residents of this jurisdiction to molest any savage, of whatever nation he may be, on pain of arbitrary correction." La Montagne's statement of ignorance about such matters in 1660, including the difficult episode of the previous year, simply lacks credibility.[20]

To correct the persistent abuses, which were "contrary to the welfare and peace of this place," and to prevent the disaster that the annoyed Mohawks threatened, that is, "war between us and the Maquas," the court once again reversed itself and imposed restrictions on Christian brokers.[21] An ordinance promulgated by Director-General Stuyvesant

[19]Ibid., 268–69.
[20]Van Laer, ed., *Court Minutes of Fort Orange,* 2:211–19 (quoted Mohawk complaint from 212).
[21]Ibid., 269–70.

and the local magistrates combined the stricter regulations on July 22, 1660, anticipating similar complaints by other Iroquois nations.[22] A recapitulation of earlier ordinances, the law prohibited the use of all brokers, of any nation, prevented traders from confiscating Indian pelts or in any way inhibiting free trade, and renewed the restrictions on trafficking in liquor.[23]

Even from the perspective of mid-seventeenth-century Beverwyck, and deprived of the hindsight of history, it would be difficult to look on these reforms with great optimism. Burghers would continue to violate ordinances while they engaged in the frenzy of free trade. Ironically, Iroquois entreaties, threats, and actions seem to have had a greater effect on the volatile Dutch townspeople than did the orders and regulations of their own employers and governors. Without Iroquois pressure and support, company officials and town magistrates could hardly control the rambunctiousness of their charges. Yet despite the chaos of Indian affairs at Fort Orange, Beverwyck, and Rensselaerswyck, the Dutch managed to avert disaster in their relationship with the Five Nations; a fundamental disruption of peace with the Iroquois was in no one's interest.

If the Dutch at these commercial outposts lived to trade, and if Indian affairs for the Dutch were a function of commercial interests, the Five Nations nonetheless demanded that their commercial relationship with the people of New Netherland become something more; the Iroquois saw their commerce with the Dutch as but one aspect of a more complex friendship. Despite their efforts to maintain a social and cultural distance from the Iroquois, the Dutch at Fort Orange and Rensselaerswyck by necessity entered into a political and social alliance based on reciprocity, mutual obligation, and some aspects of kinship, which the Five Nations demanded. The Dutch often failed to grasp the Iroquois meaning of the relationship, and what they did understand they did not always like. The Five Nations were often unsatisfied with the Dutch performance in the relationship, and they attempted continually to apprise the Dutch of their obligations and to demand that they satisfy them. Together, the Iroquois and the Dutch made the imperfect and often misunderstood alliance work.

For the people of New Netherland, life in the American wilderness

---

[22]On these complaints by the "Sinnekus," see ibid., 283–86.

[23]Ibid., 281–83. It is worth noting that Dutch "free trade" almost inevitably violated the freedom of Indians to trade as they chose. "Free trade" was a culturally specific concept.

was best lived apart from its native inhabitants. Prohibitions against employing Christian brokers represented more than a mere interest in preventing unfair commercial advantage. They feared the effects the savage woods would have on Christians. Even those who ventured out on the "Maquaes path" as brokers seldom continued on to Iroquois villages. Rumors of imminent attack by the Iroquois in September 1650 provoked expressions of anxiety and hostility at Rensselaerswyck, displaying the Dutch sense of cultural distance from the Iroquois that made their physical proximity so terrifying. One man wrote, "The insecurity of our lives and property oppresses us continually, living as we do under the unrestrained domination of inhuman people and cruel heathen." Although some argued for "recourse to arms and resistence," officials opted instead for diplomacy, taking the extraordinary action of commissioning an embassy to the Mohawks "to renew the former alliance and bond of friendship."[24]

By the late 1650s few Dutch had traveled into Iroquoia beyond Mohawk lands, and it is unlikely that any had advanced beyond Onondaga. The commercial mission led by Harmen Meyndertsz van den Bogaert in the winter of 1634–1635 may represent the deepest Dutch penetration of Iroquoia until the 1660s. While the trader-diplomats journeyed as far as Oneida, the easternmost territory of the Five Nations beyond Mohawk lands, the party's ignorance of the geography and culture of Iroquoia and the difficulty of their travel suggests that no one from Fort Orange, or other Dutch settlements, had been farther west. The Mohawks' amazement at the appearance of the Dutch in their towns further indicates that this visit was unprecedented; van den Bogaert reported, for example, that "they crowded in on us so much that we could barely pass among them.... They pushed one another into the fire in order to see us."[25]

On the diplomatic mission of September 1659, representatives of

[24]Van Laer, ed., *Court Minutes of Rensselaerswyck*, 128–29.

[25]Bogaert, *Journey into Mohawk Country*, 9. On the other hand, Jean (or Jan) Labatie claimed in a 1688 deposition (when he was seventy-four years old) that he had been sent to "ye Sinnekes Countrey as far as Jagaro" by the West Indian Company in 1638 (see Leder, ed., "Livingston Indian Records," 145). "Jagaro," or "onjagaro" [onyagaro], apparently referred to Niagara, the area around the Niagara River in present-day western New York and including the eastern tip of Ontario's Georgian Peninsula (see the gazetteer in Francis Jennings et al., eds., *The History and Culture of Iroquois Diplomacy: An Interdisciplinary Guide to the Treaties of the Six Nations and Their League* [Syracuse, N.Y., 1985], 220, 222). If so, such a trip would have constituted a very deep, early penetration of Iroquoia by the Dutch. It is not clear, however, that Labatie can be trusted (Labatie's claims conveniently served British imperial interests in establishing dominion over these lands), nor is such a journey—if it occurred—anything but exceptional.

Director-General Stuyvesant and of Fort Orange complained about going into Iroquois territory: "We can not come here every day, as the roads are so bad." In response to an Iroquois request for horses to help in repairing their palisades, the Dutch replied that horses were little use in country so steep and that they themselves "can not carry it out as they become sick merely from marching to this place, as you can see by looking at our people."[26] Most residents preferred the security of their own villages and only journeyed far into the forests with reluctance and trepidation.

The first patroon, Kiliaen van Rensselaer, showed concern that his young cousin and one of his officials, Arent van Curler, spent too much time in the woods. Writing on May 13, 1639, he cautioned van Curler "above all be careful not to mix with the heathen or savage women, for such things are a great abomination to the Lord God and kill the souls of the Christians when they debauch themselves with them."[27] The patroon believed that one of the sources of ruin in his colony was "the unchastity with heathen women and girls," and instructed that severe fines and punishment be imposed on "whoever is found to have intercourse with them."[28] In 1647, analysts in the Netherlands had also argued that Indian troubles during Governor Willem Kieft's administration (1638–1647) in New Netherland stemmed from "altogether too much familiarity with the Indians." Such familiarity engendered contempt, "usually the father of hate," they commented. The colonists, "not being satisfied with merely taking them [Indians] into their houses in the customary manner," attracted the Indians "by extraordinary attention, such as admitting them to the table, laying napkins before them, presenting wine to them and more of that kind of thing."[29]

Just as the Dutch attempted to control the arena of intercultural

[26]"Proposition made at the first castle of the Maquaes," September 24, 1659, in van Laer, ed., *Court Minutes of Fort Orange*, 2:216–17.

[27]Van Laer, ed., *Van Rensselaer-Bowier Manuscripts*, 442; for later letters see 486, 511. Others, less typical, were not so hostile to this sort of intercultural mixing; Adriaen van der Donck commented that Indian women "are well favoured and fascinating. Several of our Netherlanders were connected with them before our women came over, and remain firm in their attachments" (Thomas F. O'Donnell, ed., *[Van der Donck's] A Description of New Netherlands* [Syracuse, N.Y., 1968 (orig. pub. 1655)], 73). It seems likely that these unions represented migrations across the cultural frontier by natives into Dutch settlements rather than acculturation of Dutchmen into native towns. Van der Donck suggested the direction of this acculturation by his comment that followed: "Now there are native-born Christians also" (73).

[28]Van Laer, ed., *Van Rensselaer-Bowier Manuscripts*, 442, 694.

[29]Jameson, ed., *Narratives of New Netherland*, 273.

exchange and to insulate themselves from native influences, they demonstrated little desire to inject Dutch culture or religion into Indian lives. Missionary efforts, as we have noticed, were haphazard and carried out with little zeal. The Iroquois seemed to appreciate this disinterested approach, in stark contrast to the meddling and proselytizing of the French Jesuits. A Mohawk man told Father Isaac Jogues, who made the sign of the cross in his presence, "There is what we hate; that is what we killed thy comrade [René Goupil] for, and will kill thee too. Our neighbors, the Europeans [that is, the Dutch], do not make it."[30] Indeed, the Protestant townspeople and clergymen of New Netherland neither made this distinctively Roman Catholic gesture—one easily interpreted by Indians as a malevolent act—nor pressed the Christianity it represented on the Iroquois.

Difference in language represented a significant barrier to cultural understanding and exchange, and the Dutch did little more than was absolutely necessary to overcome it. In 1628, the Reverend Jonas Michaelius, the first minister in New Netherland, characterized the native tongue he heard as "a made-up, childish language; so that even those who can best of all speak with the savages, and get along in trade, are nevertheless wholly in the dark and bewildered when they hear the savages talking among themselves."[31] By 1644, the Dutch had made little progress in bridging the language gap. The Reverend Johannes Megapolensis reported that the Mohawks spoke

a very difficult language, and it costs me great pains to learn it, so as to be able to speak and preach in it fluently. There is no Christian here [at Fort Orange or Rensselaerswyck] who understands the language thoroughly; those who have lived here long can use a kind of jargon just sufficient to carry on trade with it, but they do not understand the fundamentals of the language.... When I observed that they pronounced their words so differently, I asked the commissary of the company what it meant. He answered me that he did not know, but imagined they changed their language every two or three years; I argued against this that it could never be that a whole nation should change its language with one consent;—and, although

[30]John Gilmary Shea, trans. and ed., "The Jogues Papers," in *New-York Historical Society Collections*, 2d ser., vol. 3, part 1, 227.

[31]Jameson, ed., *Narratives of New Netherland*, 128; see also Lois M. Feister, "Linguistic Communication Between the Dutch and Indians in New Netherland, 1609–1664," *Ethnohistory*, 20 (Winter 1973), 25–38.

he has been connected with them here for twenty years, he can afford me no assistance.[32]

The Dutch understanding of Iroquois society and politics was so rudimentary that the most experienced among them apparently failed to identify the several different Iroquois tongues with the several tribes of speakers that composed the Five Nations; of course the "Maquas," or Mohawks, would speak differently from the "Sinnekes," and the "Sinnekes" themselves spoke at least four distinctive tongues (Oneida, Onondaga, Cayuga, and Seneca). Occasionally an official, clergyman, or a trader managed primitive communication with the Iroquois in their native languages, but lack of linguistic skill must have prevented any sharing of complex cultural knowledge by either the Dutch or the Iroquois. Nonetheless, New Netherlanders tried to control intercultural discourse by conducting it in Dutch or through their own interpreters, by centering it in their own towns, and by focusing the conversation on matters of business.

In spite of Dutch efforts to maintain a business relationship with the Iroquois, they found that they had become "old friends" and, eventually, "brothers" to the Iroquois.[33] When the need arose to negotiate with their Iroquois trading partners, the Dutch were forced to endure what had become, at least by 1657, "the usual ceremonies."[34] Although we cannot determine with absolute certainty what such ceremonies comprised, it is likely that the Dutch participated with the Five Nations in a form of the traditional Condolence. When the Iroquois began any important meeting of kinspeople, especially the annual league council at Onondaga, they condoled with each other

[32]Jameson, ed., *Narratives of New Netherland*, 172–73. Megapolensis apparently did not make a sustained effort to learn the Mohawk language; any preaching he did was most likely in the Dutch language, in Dutch settlements. Megapolensis himself, during his stay in Rensselaerswyck, lived on the eastern side of the Hudson, in the area most removed from Iroquoia and the trails connecting it with the upper Hudson colony.

[33]On the Dutch designation as "old friends" by the Iroquois, see Van Laer, ed., *Court Minutes of Fort Orange*, 2:45; see also 211–12, in which the Iroquois referred to the Dutch as their "brothers...joined together with chains" (211). The Dutch acknowledged their "brotherly union" with the Iroquois (213).

[34]Ibid., 45. This kind of ceremony—most likely the Iroquois Condolence, applied to matters of diplomacy—is indicated at least as early as the winter of 1634–1635, during the embassy led by van den Bogaert; see Bogaert, *A Journey into Mohawk Country*, especially 12–17, 43–48; see also "Propositions made by certain sachems (sachimas) of the Mohawks before...the respective courts of Fort Orange and the colony of Rensselaerswyck," November 19, 1655, in Jonathan Pearson, trans. and ed., *Early Records of the City and County of Albany and Rensselaerswyck*, rev. ed., by A. J. F. van Laer, 4 vols. (Albany, N.Y., 1869–1919), 1:237, the format of which clearly suggests the Iroquois Condolence.

for those who had died since the last convocation, recited and reenacted their history, and celebrated their union. The Five Nations
expected that the Dutch as their brothers would participate in such
a ritual.

They patiently educated their European allies and kinsmen in their
obligations and in proper etiquette, complaining at times about Dutch
failure to act appropriately and generously when they met to renew
their bonds, to confer, or to trade. In 1655, the Mohawks complained
to the magistrates and burghers that "we [the Dutch] did not entertain
them in such a manner as they entertained us when visiting their
land." Dutch officials and townspeople "did not provide the least thing
for and mend their guns or other things, except they were asked for
payment and seewant [wampum] therefore; with other trifles of the
like kind: they held that it was not altogether brotherly."[35]

The court minutes of Fort Orange reported another lesson in manners and obligations in 1659. An Iroquois embassy instructed that
whenever an Iroquois "dies and one of the Dutch is his partner, he
ought to give to the relatives of the deceased one or two suits of
cloth."[36] The meaning and significance of this request is clear only if
we place it in the context of the Iroquois Condolence, recalling that
such presents functioned to bind together the actors as kinspeople in
a display of mutual concern during moments of crisis precipitated by
death, and to return order to their universe. In treaty negotiations,
the Iroquois ritually offered symbolic gifts—usually "seawan," or
wampum—after each of their propositions, to signify the importance
of their words and to serve as mnemonic aids.[37] The failure to furnish
gifts of condolence was not merely unfeeling and rude but uncivil
and hostile, and the absence of presents to support the words exchanged in negotiations deprived them of their credibility and import.
The Dutch misunderstood such gifts, seeing their function more in
material than in symbolic terms. They carefully recorded the value
of each present as it was offered, hoping that some day they might
receive a return on their investment, and grumbling perhaps about

---

[35]Pearson, ed., *Early Records of Albany*, 1:237.

[36]Van Laer, ed., *Court Minutes of Fort Orange*, 2:213.

[37]On the role and importance of wampum in Iroquois culture and politics, see especially
Mary A. Druke, "Iroquois Treaties: Common Forms, Varying Interpretations," in Jennings
et al., eds., *The History and Culture of Iroquois Diplomacy*, 88–90, and Michael K. Foster, "Another
Look at the Function of Wampum in Iroquois-White Councils," ibid., 99–114.

the hidden expenses of commerce with Indians.[38] Dutch negotiators accepted and provided gifts, and took part in traditional Iroquois social and political ritual, not out of any particular cultural sensitivity or appreciation but simply out of necessity, as the cost of doing business with the Five Nations.

The kinship relationship that the Iroquois attempted to build with the Dutch continually challenged New Netherlanders' conception of their alliance with the Five Nations. The chroniclers of New Netherland, unlike those of New France, did not preserve the rich, evocative language of the Iroquois that described their expectations so well. Yet in the records of Iroquois-Dutch negotiations, one can notice nonetheless the other aspects of the relationship that the Five Nations held paramount and insisted upon; from their viewpoint, their alliance with the people of New Netherland implied spiritual and emotional as well as material support.

Iroquois bonds entailed concrete obligations of mutual aid and protection. They expected the Dutch to provide help in repairing village fortifications, to offer military assistance, and to shelter their women and children in times of peril.[39] It puzzled the Iroquois that the Dutch apparently failed to understand, or refused to perform, their brotherly duties even to their own Netherlandish countrymen. During an outbreak of trouble between New Netherland and Indians at Esopus in 1659, a Mohawk spokesman chided the Dutch at Fort Orange for failing to intervene on behalf of their Dutch brethren of the lower Hudson: "You say you have no war and that you do not wish to go to war against any savages." Yet, he continued, "you and the Manhatans [Dutch at New Amsterdam] are one. Suppose the Esopus savages came now or in the spring to kill the country people [at Fort Orange], what would you do then? You have no sense."[40] The Iroquois expected the Dutch to come to the defense of their European kinsmen, just as the Five Nations would have done. Retrieving strings of wampum they had given the men at Fort Orange, the Mohawks themselves

---

[38]See, for example, the Dutch-Iroquois meeting of June 16, 1657, in van Laer, ed., *Court Minutes of Fort Orange*, 2:45.

[39]Ibid., 2:45, 212–13; see also deposition of Symon Groot (Simon de Groot), July 2, 1688, in Leder, "Livingston Indian Records," 144, de Groot said that he and another man, "upon ye Maquase Request [were] Sent to ye Maquase Countrey with horses to Ride Timber to make there Castles Strong . . . & were at work 14 days" (apparently in the late 1650s).

[40]Van Laer, ed., *Court Minutes of Fort Orange*, 2:222–23.

intervened on behalf of their Dutch brothers, dispatching a mediator to arrange a peace between the Esopus and New Netherland.[41]

As we have seen, this was not the first time the Mohawks acted as peacemakers. They had intervened to arrange a settlement between the Dutch and various Algonquian Indians in 1645 and saw themselves as brokers of peace ever after. The Iroquois understood their alliance with the Dutch as a way of extending their universe of peace, in the fashion prescribed by their prophet Deganawidah and informed by their social and political history. By expanding their sphere of kinship, the Iroquois League and its constituent members could use the mechanisms bequeathed by Deganawidah—especially adoption and amalgamation, Condolence and Atonement—to plant and nurture peace in a wider area. The various nations that became "props" to the Iroquois Longhouse were obliged to work towards a common harmony. Mohawk mediation and pacification of the Esopus in 1659 thus constituted an act of civility, a successful attempt to defend their Dutch brethren and maintain the integrity and peace of their expanding world.

At the same time, the Iroquois expected the Dutch to mediate on their behalf, as a function of their alliance and kinship with them. Following the conclusion of an Iroquois-French peace in 1653, the Mohawk delegate Stick Stiggery appeared before officials at Fort Orange and Beverwyck to request that the Dutch endorse the peace and affirm Iroquois good intentions in a letter to be dispatched to Canada. Writing to the governor of New France, Jean de Lauson, the commissary of the Fort, Joannes Dyckman, communicated these messages, although somewhat reluctantly. Dyckman also diffidently conveyed some Mohawk suggestions, for example, that the French should remain neutral in the event of fighting between the Iroquois and New France's Indian allies. In conclusion the commissary wrote apologetically, "We could not do otherwise than promise them [to write] and which we therefore do hereby."[42]

In August 1658, while addressing the magistrates at Fort Orange, the Mohawks made the implications and expectations of alliance and kinship even more explicit, when they asked for further Dutch assistance in establishing peace with New France. Requesting the aid of an interpreter, the spokesman for a delegation of fifteen Mohawk

[41]Ibid., 223.
[42]Ibid., 1:90–92 (quotation on 91).

sachems "explained that at the time of the war with the Indians [in 1645] they had gone down to the Manhatans and done their best to bring about peace and that it was our duty to do the same in such circumstances for them, promising in the future to do their best between us and other Indians."[43] Yielding to the desires of the Mohawks, and thereby acknowledging the extracommercial nature of their relationship with the Five Nations, the officials at Fort Orange composed a letter of peace on behalf of the Iroquois and subsidized the diplomatic mission of one Henderick Martensen to New France. Like other members of the Iroquois Longhouse, the Dutch were expected to share in the cultivation of peace.[44]

Repeatedly the Dutch failed in their attempts to confine their relationship with the Iroquois to simple commerce. When they tried to treat the Five Nations merely as trading partners, letting the principles of supply and demand dictate the nature of their commerce, the Iroquois responded by imposing their own principles of kinship, hospitality, and reciprocity. In September 1659, for example, the Mohawks complained, "The Dutch, indeed, say we are brothers and are joined together with chains, but that lasts only as long as we have beavers. After that we are no longer thought of, but much will depend upon it [the alliance] when we shall need each other."[45] Given the precarious nature of Dutch existence in America, wedged as it was between the powerful forces of England and France and dependent economically on commerce with the Five Nations, the magistrates and burghers at Beverwyck and Fort Orange quickly took these words to heart. As we have seen, a special delegation made the difficult journey to Kaghnuwage (or Caughnawaga), the first castle of the Mohawks, to reassure the Iroquois of their commitment, concern, and friendship. The Dutch envoys declared to those assembled, "Henceforth you will have no occasion to doubt that we shall be and remain brothers"; Netherlanders and Iroquois "shall all be and remain as if we had lain under one heart."[46] The Five Nations' power, and its eco-

---

[43]Ibid., 2:149–52 (quotation on 150).

[44]At an Extraordinary Session at Fort Orange on October 8, 1658, Mohawk sachems again appeared before the magistrates to request that the Dutch write another letter, informing the French that the Iroquois had not killed a prisoner, Louis Paraget, who had apparently escaped. The Dutch wrote the letter and hired the soldier Jacob Begyn, who was competent in the French language, to carry it to New France on behalf of the Mohawks (see ibid., 2:161–62).

[45]Ibid., 211.

[46]The resolution to send a delegation to the Mohawks emerged from the court's extraordinary session held at Fort Orange, September 16, 1659, ibid., 214. On the propositions

nomic and military importance to the Dutch, forced New Netherland to indulge its Indian brethren in their peculiar vision of Iroquois-Dutch relations.

To the puzzlement of the Dutch, the Five Nations did not function according to Western economic principles. In a free market economy, one would expect the increased value of a commodity to stimulate its production. In seventeenth-century North America, European trading goods became increasingly abundant, especially amid the fierce competition in places like Beverwyck and Fort Orange. This abundance caused a decrease in the price of such goods relative to beaver pelts. And as furs became more dear, the Dutch expected that the Iroquois—now able to make more money in the transaction—would bring more of them to their trading posts. Yet, surprisingly, the anticipated influx of furs failed to materialize.[47]

The secretary of the West India Company at New Amsterdam, Issack de Rasiere, wrote in 1626 to the Amsterdam Chamber of the Company that an abundance of trade goods and perhaps some gentle instruction in proper business behavior among the Indians would generate a lucrative trade for both Dutchman and native: "The Indians will be all the more diligent in hunting when they see that when they have skins they can get what they want, about which the Maquaes do not hesitate to complain bitterly, saying: 'Why should we go hunting? Half the time you have no cloth.' "[48] De Rasiere misunderstood the Mohawks and underestimated the complexity of the commerce in furs. The Iroquois, like other native peoples encountered by the Dutch, understood the process of exchange, and the meanings and values of exchanged goods, in their own particular ways. The Dutch scholar and New World investor Johan de Laet wrote of the native

---

carried to the Mohawks, see 215–18. Quotations are on 216, 215. Caughnawaga here refers to the original settlement of that name in Mohawk territory; in the 1670s, Caughnawaga would emerge as a Christian Iroquois (mostly Mohawk) community on the St. Lawrence River under the auspices of the Jesuits of New France. For a brief history of this community, see William N. Fenton and Elisabeth Tooker, "Mohawk," in Bruce G. Trigger, ed., *Handbook of North American Indians,* gen. ed., William C. Sturtevant, 20 vols. projected (Washington, D.C., 1978–), *Northeast,* 15:466–80, especially 469–71.

    [47]On the early inflationary pressures on the value of furs, which continued throughout New Netherland's history, see Isaack de Rasiere to the Amsterdam Chamber of the West India Company, September 23, 1626, in A. J. F. van Laer, trans. and ed., *Documents Relating to New Netherland, 1624–1626, in the Henry E. Huntington Library* (San Marino, Calif., 1924), 216–20; de Rasiere complained that inhabitants "outbid one another, each trying to get hold of as many skins as possible" (220), which pushed up the price of furs in disturbing fashion for the company.

    [48]Ibid., 231.

Sychnecta, a young Mohawk man, as he appeared in an exhibition in Amsterdam in 1764 at the Blauw Jan Inn, drawn from life by Pieter Barbiers and etched by A. Smit (Gemeentelijke Archiefdienst Amsterdam). The portait of Sychnecta is perhaps the earliest ethnographically reliable representation of an Iroquois man, despite Sychnecta's Dutchlike features and the incongruous palm tree (symbolizing his exoticism, as *Een Wilde*) etched in the background (bottom right).

people living in 1615 near the mouth of the Quinnipiac River (in the vicinity of present-day New Haven, Connecticut), "They take many beavers, but it is necessary for them to get into the habit of trade." If the Iroquois had already acquired the habit, they had not necessarily done so in a way that the Dutch found reasonable and convenient.[49]

The Iroquois showed preferences in trade that sometimes confounded inexperienced or uniformed merchants. De Rasiere noted that different bands and tribes sought different items, and he informed the Amsterdam chamber that Indians demanded cloth of certain colors ("blue and standard grey," for example) and rejected others: "The rest of [the duffels] which I have are all red, whereof I can hardly sell a yard, because the Indians say that it hinders them in hunting, being visible too far off. They all call for black, the darker the color the better, but red and green they will not take."[50] De Rasiere went on to specify the company's need for strung coral beads, especially in black and white, which were "much sought after" by both Indians and colonists, who could use them to buy maize, fish, and various other things from the natives. Finally, de Rasiere observed that some distinctions important to Europeans meant little to Indians. Perhaps Europeans would expect to pay more for copper kettles, but the West India Company's native trading partners would not: "We also have here a number of copper kettles, which cannot be traded here without spoiling the natives; moreover, they would not give more for them than for the others, which would not make good the cost."[51]

While Europeans focused on the utilitarian advantages of the goods they provided, Indians viewed traded items in broader terms, considering both the supernatural and material potential of the substances they obtained. In fact, European manufactured items underwent a sort of transubstantiation as they passed to native peoples and became Native American artifacts. "Nonutilitarian" trade goods— the things disparaged as "baubles," "trinkets," and "trash"—were valuable to Indians not for their novelty but rather for their similarity to native substances, charged with ideological and symbolic meaning. And even articles considered useful on European terms were often integrated into Indian lives in surprising ways. Copper pots, for example, were dismantled for their parts and used as raw material, which could be fashioned into arrowheads, fishhooks, or amulets, rather

[49]De Laet's *New World* (1625, 1630), in Jameson, ed., *Narratives of New Netherland*, 44.
[50]Van Laer, ed., *Huntington Library Documents*, 223, 224–27, 228; quotation on 228–31.
[51]Ibid., 232, 223.

than used as Europeans had intended. But as metal objects became more available, native peoples increasingly used kettles and other items in the ways intended by Europeans. And it is clear that some items of European technology and material culture, like guns, would reshape native life in important ways. In their discourse of words and deeds with the Dutch, the Iroquois made the strange familiar, integrating both the people and products of New Netherland into their culture, but on their own terms.[52]

While the Dutch reluctantly became the Iroquois' "brothers" in order to trade, the Five Nations traded in order to acquire the Netherlanders as kinsmen and maintain peace and prosperity in their new world. The Iroquois were not unconcerned about matters of price in their commerce with the Dutch. Difficult terms implied a lack of hospitality and challenged the reciprocity implicit in their relationship. Although they had some interest in enriching their lives through the acquisition of European manufactured goods, their behavior was not governed by the market. They participated in it only to satisfy their collective social, political, and material needs. For the Iroquois, people's essential emotional and material requirements should govern exchange, not the impersonal forces of the market or the individual, self-interested quest for riches.[53]

This behavior confused the Dutch merchants. Kiliaen van Rensselaer wrote in 1640, "I can not get over my surprise as to the changes which are said to have occurred in the fur trade at Fort Orange." Though nothing seemed to have affected the potential supply of furs,

---

[52]See especially Christopher L. Miller and George R. Hamell, "A New Perspective on Indian-White Contact: Cultural Symbols and Colonial Trade," *Journal of American History*, 72, (September 1986), 311–28; Calvin Martin, "The Four Lives of a Micmac Copper Pot," *Ethnohistory*, 22, no. 2 (1975), 111–33; Martin, *Keepers of the Game: Indian-Animal Relationships and the Fur Trade* (Berkeley, Calif., 1978); James W. Bradley, *The Evolution of the Onondaga Iroquois: Accommodating Change, 1500–1655* (Syracuse, N.Y., 1987), especially 130–65; see figure 13 (131) for a graphic illustration of the recycling of a copper kettle.

[53]E. E. Rich, "Trade Habits and Economic Motivation among the Indians of North America," *Canadian Journal of Economics and Political Science*, 26 (1960), 35–53, discredited the simplistic interpretation of Native Americans as Western "economic men." The important work of Arthur J. Ray has subsequently added subtlety and sophistication to the analysis of Native American economic motivation and behavior; see Ray, *Indians in the Fur Trade: Their Role as Hunters, Trappers, and Middlemen in the Lands Southwest of Hudson Bay, 1660–1870* (Toronto, 1974); "The Hudson's Bay Company Fur Trade in the Eighteenth Century: A Comparative Economic Study," in James R. Gibson, ed., *European Settlement and Development in North America: Essays on Geographical Change in Honour and Memory of Andrew Hill Clark* (Toronto, 1978), 116–35; and especially Ray and Donald B. Freeman, *"Give Us Good Measure": An Economic Analysis of Relations Between the Indians and the Hudson's Bay Company before 1763* (Toronto, 1987). Ray made clear that both sides—native and European—adjusted to make the trade mutually acceptable and profitable.

fewer pelts appeared at the fort and in his colony. He acknowledged that his colonists may have bid up prices in their competition with the inhabitants of Fort Orange, "but such outbidding does not divert the fur trade, but causes a greater supply," he reasoned. "Now, as far as I can see, the trouble is not with the price [offered for furs] but with the quantity [traded by Indians], which is a great paradox to me."[54]

Once sufficient quantities of European goods became common among the Iroquois, the Five Nations required less in trade with the Dutch to maintain them in their new style of life. With higher fur prices, the Iroquois could buy what they needed with fewer pelts, and so they carried a smaller number of them to Fort Orange and Beverwyck. The Five Nations' ability to satisfy their needs more cheaply, and perhaps their annoyance with the sharp trading tactics that came to light in the 1650s, help to solve van Rensselaer's paradox.

Just as high prices should not spur trade, low prices should not halt it, the Five Nations believed. The reciprocal relationship between brothers, which the Iroquois understood their alliance with the Dutch to be, implied that need should govern exchange. Reluctantly, the Dutch responded, though out of a respect for Iroquois power and their own long-term self-interest, rather than out of any deep understanding of Iroquois culture.[55]

In a telling incident in July 1654, the court of Fort Orange and Beverwyck called together its most well-disposed citizens to appeal for their support and to requisition goods to send as presents to the Mohawks. Conditions beyond Fort Orange's control had delayed an expected merchant ship, and merchandise was in short supply. "The savages, on account of the scarcity of merchandise, have been obliged to give much more than ordinarily for the goods which they bought by the measure," officials noted.[56] But Dutch explanations of the dif-

---

[54]Van Laer, ed., *Van Rensselaer-Bowier Manuscripts*, 483–84. Van Rensselaer wrote at a time before the population of beavers in Iroquoia had been dramatically reduced. See Bruce G. Trigger, *The Children of Aataentsic: A History of the Huron People to 1660*, 2 vols. (Montreal, 1976), 2:618–21, on the exhaustion of beavers; in refutation of George T. Hunt, *The Wars of the Iroquois: A Study in Intertribal Trade Relations* (Madison, Wis., 1940), 33–35, Trigger concluded, "there is no proof" that the supply of beavers in Iroquoia was depleted "as early as 1640" (620). Thus the supply of finished pelts reaching Dutch towns, rather than a dwindling population of beavers, was the problem for men like van Rensselaer; the problem was cultural rather than ecological.

[55]Dutch merchants, of course, would have had some experience with less formal kinds of exchange—favors, patronage, premiums, gifts—that occurred alongside more formal market transactions. But the Dutch understood these supplementary, often covert, payments simply as baksheesh; the payments were not a response to the obligations of reciprocity or condolence felt by the Iroquois.

[56]Van Laer, ed., *Court Minutes of Fort Orange*, 1:170–71 (quotation on 170).

ficulty apparently failed to satisfy the Mohawks. Just as New Netherlanders failed to look deeply into the interior, into Iroquoia where
the furs they defined as commodities were produced, so the Iroquois
seemed uninterested in focusing their gaze much beyond New Netherland, beyond the Atlantic, and into the mercantile network that
brought them things. For both the Dutch and the Iroquois, face to
face on their cultural frontier, local issues were most immediate and
important.

Responding to the painful reality that market pricing could not be
strictly applied to their Iroquois partners, the Dutch sent along some
goods as a show of faith and "to renew the old alliance and friendship
between both sides." To their own citizens, the magistrates promised
to divide proportionately among all contributers the gifts the Mohawks would inevitably send in return.[57] While both sides were satisfied in the end, they construed the exchange in different ways. The
Mohawks received what they felt was their due, and they, in turn,
would cement the old friendship and kinship with material offerings
infused with symbolic meaning. The Dutch meanwhile transformed
this symbolic exchange into a material and commercial one: they
hoped that each burgher's investments would pay dividends.

In a similar spirit, the Senecas informed the Dutch in 1660 that
narrow economic concerns, such as a low exchange value of beaver
pelts, should not prevent the Iroquois from obtaining the supplies
they needed, especially in their times of peril. The delegation of Iroquois sachems who appeared at Fort Orange that July forced the
Dutch to confront their responsibilities within the friendship that
bound the two peoples together. In frustration, the headmen had
declared, "We only make a little request of you and yet in asking this
it is as if we ran against a stone." They told the Dutch, "We are now
engaged in a great war [with the Susquehannocks], and we can get
no powder or lead unless we have beavers and a good soldier ought
to have powder and lead for nothing."[58]

The Seneca disregard for Dutch economics emerged also, we have
seen, in their confusion and displeasure over the tactics of Dutch
brokers. The furious quest for individual gain reflected in forestalling

[57]Ibid. The exorbitant profits taken by independent traders, or by the patroon, in times
when European goods were in short supply at the upper Hudson settlement were apparently
not gained at the expense of the Iroquois, who—unlike common Dutch inhabitants—could
enforce lower, more brotherly prices. On the high cost of trade goods and commodities at
these settlements, see Rink, *Holland on the Hudson*, 209–11, which suggests, ironically, that at
least for a time the chief victims of colonialism were more apt to be Dutch than Iroquois.
[58]Van Laer, ed., *Court Minutes of Fort Orange*, 2:283, 284.

practices clashed with Iroquois ideas about cooperation in the interest of the common good. The Iroquois persistently criticized and attempted to reform the self-interest, competitiveness, and inhospitality they perceived in Dutch commercial activity. An Iroquois proposition in 1655 contained the complaint that the Dutch "did not entertain and satisfy them as fully as they did us." In reply, the magistrates argued, "If one, two, or three of them came as we did they should be properly lodged and accommodated, but that justice and law provided in this respect that none should be compelled to do so, since every person being free, must earn his own maintenance, and that no one was holden to be another's servant for nothing." The Dutch argued in vain "that such being the custom among us, no more complaints were to be made about it,"[59] but the Iroquois continued to question the legitimacy of Dutch "free" trade and to seek private and official Dutch commitment to their particular, corporate vision of peace.

New Netherlanders were hardly prepared to abandon their economic beliefs, or to alter radically their economic practice. Yet in 1655 they attempted to act more hospitably, and in 1660 they worked to correct the abuses of brokers and mitigate the difficulties inherent in their pricing system. After both negotiations, they provided the Iroquois delegates with substantial gifts of powder. Once again, the Dutch used gifts to respond to Iroquois concerns, but they offered them on Dutch terms, not as normal, legitimate components of business, but merely as indulgences, as exceptional grants or rebates to maintain the channels of commerce. But neither the Dutch nor the Five Nations were dominant enough to dictate fully the terms of the discourse along the Dutch-Iroquois cultural frontier.

Fundamental conflicts in definition and expectation riddled the ambiguous relationship between New Netherland and the Five Nations. Each side conceived of the alliance in terms of its own world view and historical experience. The feisty citizens of the Dutch Republic and the self-confident heirs of Deganawidah both adjusted to the strange people each group faced across the cultural frontier. Each bowed to the other without ever fully confronting the lack of mutual understanding and cultural appreciation. The motives they ascribed to each other and the kinship terms that they tacitly accepted allowed the two

[59]Pearson, ed., *Early Records of Albany*, 237.

peoples to delude themselves that they understood each other. Yet, strangely, the Iroquois-Dutch relationship worked. The Five Nations patiently accommodated the New Netherlanders without compromising Iroquois ideas and goals; they endured Dutch imperfections and failures and taught their "brethren" how to become "props" in the Iroquois Longhouse. In the end they expected to prevail. Certainly the Dutch responded outwardly to Iroquois pressure, and they watched their own narrow, commercial relationship with the Five Nations take on broader dimensions.

Nonetheless, New Netherland's accommodation with the Five Nations remained merely pragmatic. The Dutch never altered their ideas and goals; after all, both new-world and old-world Netherlanders were not unaccustomed to contradictions. They nonchalantly mixed medieval institutions with modern purposes, aristocratic or patrician government with republicanism, an established church with de facto toleration, mercantilism with free trade, nationalism with individual self-interest. New Netherlanders sought no vast territorial empire and found it difficult to people the limited one it had acquired. No massive swarm of Dutch settlers spread out from Fort Orange to found agricultural communities of saints, and no bands of zealots wandered into the Iroquois wilderness to gather the heathen into God's flock. Commerce reigned supreme. The people of the Five Nations, active as fur traders and secure in their homeland, were more valuable to the Dutch than were Iroquois lands or Iroquois souls. As residents pursued their own self-interests, and as their public officials struggled to keep them in line, the Dutch posed little threat to Iroquois power and autonomy. A de facto "policy" of benign neglect toward the Five Nations seemed most desirable to burghers and officials alike. The Dutch got along with the Iroquois by keeping their distance. Their toleration and respect for the Five Nations did not stem from cultural approval or admiration but from an appreciation of Iroquois power and the role it played in Dutch security and prosperity.

6

False Starts and Failed Promises: New France and the French Frontier

At length, this last war will plant Peace and the Lilies
in all our forests, to make Cities of them if it be desired, and to convert a land of Savages into one of
Conquest for Jesus and for France.
    ... In short, the cry is raised on every hand, "Send
aid; save bodies and souls; destroy the Iroquois, and
you will plant the Faith throughout a territory of more
than eight hundred leagues in extent."
                            —*Jesuit Relations* for 1660–61

In the remarkable fall of 1654 in Quebec, and before the last ships
left the St. Lawrence and ice began to seal off New France from the
Atlantic world, Marie de l'Incarnation, the mother superior of the
Ursuline nuns, hurriedly penned her stunning news to her son,
Claude Martin, in France. "I cannot let the vessels depart without
telling you something of what has happened in this new Church since
last year," she wrote. In a dramatic reversal, the bright promise of
peace had replaced the vicious warfare of only a few months earlier.
L'Incarnation reported that the Iroquois nations had sought peace
and demonstrated their sincerity, ransoming captives at their own
expense, maintaining French observers among them, whom they
"loved and cherished ... extraordinarily," soliciting letters from the
Dutch at New Netherland to attest to their earnestness, and entreating
so insistently for peace that their petitions could not be rejected. The
authorities at Quebec dispatched the Jesuit missionary Father Simon
le Moyne on a tour "throughout the five nations to ascertain whether
they all concurred in the desire for peace." He returned in triumph.
L'Incarnation wrote, "It is not believable how overjoyed the French

and our Savages were at his return and at the happy outcome of his journey"; and plans were developed to found a mission in the heart of Iroquoia.[1]

As these promising exchanges between New France and the Five Nations took place, Iroquois ambassadors and visitors to Quebec sought out the Ursulines and their native charges. According to l'Incarnation, "they wondered at our Savage seminarians, whom they heard singing God's praises in three different tongues. They were delighted to see them so well dressed in the French style. But what touched them most," the nun observed, "was to see that, though these girls were nothing to us, we held them in great affection, loving and caressing them as mothers love and caress their children."[2] This otherwise insignificant meeting and others like it reveal a contradiction inherent in the encounters at the French-Iroquois cultural frontier. Each party came away from the meeting encouraged, all the while basing its favorable response to its counterpart and its optimistic assessment of future relations on its own peculiar and contrasting interpretation of the other. The encounter allowed, indeed, encouraged the growth of misunderstanding and laid the groundwork for later frustration, anger, and conflict; the peace celebrated by l'Incarnation was short lived.

The numerous meetings between the Iroquois and French colonial world took place at a variety of settings: Quebec, Trois Rivières, and Montreal; more frequently, and often with violence, they occurred along trade routes, in the lands of native allies of the French, or in Iroquois country, when missionaries or soldiers pursued their particular colonial campaigns. In this chapter I sketch briefly the new French cultural landscape that emerged on the northern margins of Iroquoia

---

[1]L'Incarnation to her son, September 24, 1654, in Joyce Marshall, trans. and ed., *Word from New France: The Selected Letters of Marie de l'Incarnation* (Toronto, 1967), 211–17; quotations from 211, 212, 215. On the crisis of 1654 preceding the peace, see Percy J. Robinson, trans., and James B. Conacher, ed., *The History of Canada or New France by Father François Du Creux, S.J.* [Paris, 1664], *Publications of the Champlain Society*, 30, 2 vols. (Toronto, 1951) (hereafter cited as *Historia Canadensis*), 2:653–54. Du Creux claimed, for example, that conditions had deteriorated to the point that "there was every probability that those of the French who remained [in Canada] would collect their belongings and embark as quietly as they could and return to France" (653). *Historia Canadensis* was the official summary of the *Jesuit Relations*, covering a period from 1625 to 1658; Du Creux nonetheless made use of other sources, omitted material from the *Relations*, and added his own interpretive gloss. In short, it is a valuable source in itself, despite its derivative quality.

[2]Marshall, ed., *Word from New France*, 213–14; the ambassadorial visits to Quebec by Iroquois men and women, and their visits to the Ursulines, are also described in Du Creux, *Historia Canadensis*, 2:698–702, especially 699–700.

and relate in some detail the course of French colonization in Canada, which proceeded through a number of false starts and which, from the French perspective of the late seventeenth century, must have seemed a great disappointment, if not a failure. For much of this period, the intercultural discourse between the Iroquois and French was characterized by hostility and bloodshed. Yet for the Five Nations and those French colonists most frequently in contact with them—the Jesuit missionaries—peace and the transformation of the other were the greatest goals.[3] Examining French motives, objectives, and strategies and analyzing the nature of the colonial experience for French officials, soldiers, *habitants,* and priests will help us understand how and why the French-Iroquois exchange sank into frustration and violence.

The meeting of French colonial and Iroquois worlds must be seen from both sides of the cultural frontier and understood as a complex interaction of real people in particular places. Each side possessed its own experience, ideology, and world view; and the conjunction of these two worlds produced a third evolving structure. As counterpoint to our discussion of Iroquoia and New Netherland, then, I paint another perspective into this Cubist history by analyzing New France as a world that its European inhabitants constructed in the wilderness, and that itself helped mold their perceptions and influenced their actions.

The Five Nations, as will be seen, encountered little of continental France in their New World. What they met was a peculiar extension of that old European society, one increasingly detached from the Old World context. And to make matters more complex, the lodging of this French fragment in North America significantly altered the intricate Native American political geography of the northern woodlands and Great Lakes. The Iroquois thus encountered not only a New France but new Indian worlds as well.[4]

---

[3]The group of French colonists who had the most contact with the Iroquois, after the Jesuits, were the regular and militia soldiers of New France; they were ultimately bent on achieving "peace" through the military subjugation of the Five Nations.

[4]On the "fragmentation" of European cultures through overseas colonization, see Louis Hartz, *The Founding of New Societies: Studies in the History of the United States, Latin America, South Africa, Canada, and Australia* (New York, 1964). Richard Colebrook Harris has refined Hartz's argument, especially in his analysis of early Canada; see especially Harris, "European Beginnings in the Northwestern Atlantic: A Comparative View," in David D. Hall and David Grayson Allen, eds., *Seventeenth-Century New England, Publications of the Colonial Society of Massachusetts,* 63 (Boston, 1984), 119–52, particularly 133–35; quotation from 134. And see Harris, "The Extension of France into Rural Canada," in James R. Gibson, ed., *European*

The Five Nations' sense of their encounter contrasted with the French experience for two reasons: first, because the Iroquois were allowed to see only a portion of that European colonial society; second, the Iroquois world view, cumulative experience, and goals differed markedly from those of the French. The role of the Jesuit order—the Society of Jesus—in New France, for example, was perceived by the Iroquois to be much more important than the *habitants* of New France themselves perceived it to be. Nonetheless, the differences between the Five Nations and New France could appear insignificant or at least surmountable to both parties. Each apparently believed that the other, despite previous antagonism, might ultimately join its larger program. For New France, this meant pacification and "French-ification," which of course implied conversion to their One True Faith. For the Five Nations, this meant the enlargement of their League of Peace and the incorporation of the French as naturalized Iroquois.

Trying to make sense of these strange people on their northern frontier, the Iroquois on their visits to Quebec in the mid-1650s would have found paradoxes that were at once instructive and deceptive. Gender arrangements among the transplanted French differed considerably from those of Iroquois society. Yet in the separate Ursuline residence and seminary, Iroquois visitors would have found autonomous and powerful women whom Iroquois observers could equate with their own matriarchs. Moreover, the motherly love and affection that the Ursulines bestowed on their neophytes seemed not unlike that which Iroquois matrons showered on their own *owachiras* [female lineages] or even on those outsiders adopted into their families. Finally, the Ursulines appeared to be fluent in the traditional Iroquois ceremonial discourse based on kinship and reciprocity.

Marie de l'Incarnation's account in 1655 reveals the Ursulines' insight: "We regaled them splendidly twice in their style, for it is thus one must attract them."[5] One exemplary Huron girl of ten or eleven years, seminarian Marie Arinadsit, begged a member of a Seneca delegation to send Iroquois girls to be instructed at the seminary, promising that they would be treated as sisters. Her appeals were well received. One woman chief was particularly moved; she promised to send her own daughter, and meanwhile hugged Marie in a manner

---

Settlement and Development in North America: Essays on Geographical Change in Honour and Memory of Andrew Hill Clark (Toronto, 1978), 27–45.

[5] Marshall, ed., *Word from New France*, 222.

Marie de l'Incarnation (1599–1672), first superior of the Ursulines of New France. Oil painting completed in 1672, attributed to Hugues Pommier (ca. 1637–86), courtesy of the Archives des ursulines de Québec, Quebec. L'Incarnation's *Lettres*, published in 1681, are among the best sources for the early history of New France.

"quite extraordinary among the Savages." This delegation of Senecas soon formed "a little movable church," in l'Incarnation's words, as it led the missionary Chaumonot into Iroquoia. The Seneca women passed on their favorable impressions, and other Iroquois came to visit the Ursulines. They too were feasted and given "presents to their taste." "You would be surprised," l'Incarnation wrote, "at the skills one needs to draw these lost souls to the Faith."[6] Such skills were carefully cultivated and purposefully employed to effect the conversion of the Iroquois, but to native visitors the apparent willingness and facility of the French as they engaged in such discourse probably suggested an openness to Iroquois culture and practice, perhaps even a readiness to accept a place under the spreading branches of the Iroquois Tree of Peace.

Certainly the Ursuline nuns, Jesuit priests, and government officials had different motives and understood the Iroquois visits differently. Deep suspicions commingled with sincere hopes, less than benevolent objectives—carefully concealed from their Iroquois guests—mixed with benevolent ones. And the very humanitarianism of men and women missionaries constituted an aggressive, although covert, colonial project. "Ah, how we long to see a group of Iroquois girls in our seminary! How we should cherish them for the love of the One that spilled his blood for them as for us!" l'Incarnation wrote. Yet, she continued, "it is important that we have some of their girls as hostages." In the negotiations that followed, the French offered a present to achieve this objective, but they tried to obscure one of its real purposes while emphasizing another: "It did not witness, however, that the girls would serve as hostages, but that they should be instructed in the Faith, which is indeed the principal motive."[7] The Ursuline nun's sincerity about her religious purpose need not be questioned, but a neophyte and hostage is hardly a sister or a daughter. The complexity of this cross-cultural encounter with its troubling

---

[6]Ibid., 223; see also Du Creux, *Historia Canadensis*, 2:699. The two versions of the meetings vary; it is possible that different, though quite similar, encounters are being described. Du Creux's Marie exclaimed, "I accept the name [daughter]; I am glad to take you as mother; are you taking me as daughter? . . . Send me as many of my Iroquois sisters as you can; I will be their older sister; I will teach them." On the provision of gifts, and the Ursulines' use of the young Huron neophyte to affect a traditional Iroquois discourse, see 700: "This apparently amusing incident [the presentation of gifts "adorned" with words] had its effect in laying the foundation of Christianity among the Iroquois."

[7]Marshall, ed., *Word from New France*, 223.

double meaning must be left at the edge of the French-Iroquois cultural frontier for a moment in order to trace the beginnings and to
assess the nature of the new French world in Canada, a world whose
inhabitants could understand the apparently hostile act of hostage
taking as fundamentally humanitarian.

France was late in joining the European expansion into the New
World. Failing to follow through on early initiatives and advantages,
the French planted a permanent settlement in North America only
in 1608, established a modicum of stability there only after 1632, and
became secure in their Canadian colony only in the 1660s. The French
colonial enterprise in some ways resembled that of the Netherlands.
Yet there were profound differences in national politics and objectives, in economy, religion, and geography between New France and
New Netherland. Over the course of the seventeenth century, the
Five Nations of the Iroquois came to grips with these differences,
eventually adapting their traditional vision of peace to the new circumstances created by a New France poised on the northern margin
of Iroquoia.

Even before the 1524 voyage of discovery by the Florentine navi-
gator Giovanni da Verrazzano, in which he mapped the east coast of
North America and claimed it for France, Norman, Breton, and
Basque fishermen found individual riches in the fecund waters off of
Newfoundland.[8] Jacques Cartier, the Saint-Malo pilot, searched for
gold and a northwest passage in two voyages, during the years 1534–
36. He found neither but instead discovered the St. Lawrence River,
that "Great Highway into the Continent."[9] Under the joint direction

[8]On the European penetration of the New World, the many works of David Beers Quinn
provide an excellent starting point. See especially *North America from Earliest Discovery to First
Settlement: The Norse Voyages to 1612* (New York, 1977), 108–36, 152–90, 240–61, 347–68,
417–28, 465–89, for Quinn's analysis of French efforts. See also Carl Ortwin Sauer, *Sixteenth-
Century North America: The Land and People as Seen by the Europeans* (Berkeley, Calif., 1971);
Olive Patricia Dickason, *The Myth of the Savage and the Beginnings of French Colonialism in the
Americas* (Edmonton, Alberta, 1984); Cornelius J. Jaenen, *Friend and Foe: Aspects of French-
Amerindian Cultural Contact in the Sixteenth and Seventeenth Centuries* (New York, 1976); Bruce
G. Trigger, *Natives and Newcomers: Canada's 'Heroic Age' Reconsidered* (Kingston and Montreal,
1985). See also the beautifully produced volumes in the *Records of Our History* series, published
by the Public Archives of Canada; Andre Vachon, ed., *Dreams of Empire: Canada before 1700*
(Ottawa, 1982) presents the earliest period.
[9]This phrase is from Marcel Trudel, whose important work informs my own analysis. See
The Beginnings of New France, 1524–1663 (Toronto, 1973). In addition to this and the works
cited in the previous note, I have found the following works by William J. Eccles indispensable:
Essays on New France (Toronto, 1987); *France in America* (New York, 1972); *The Canadian
Frontier, 1534–1760* (New York, 1969); *Canada under Louis XIV, 1663–1701* (Toronto, 1964);
Frontenac: The Courtier Governor (Toronto, 1959).

of Jean-François de La Rocque, seigneur de Roberval, and Cartier, a group embarked in 1541 with the aim of colonizing the St. Lawrence. But within two years the New World's harsh elements, which included a distinct lack of cooperation by the indigenous inhabitants, coupled with hostility in France toward the effort led to the abandonment of the colonizing experiment. With this failure, as Marcel Trudel has written, the "veil of mystery fell once more about the great river of Canada, not to be raised again for half a century."[10]

During the turmoil of religious war that distracted France for the rest of the sixteenth and into the seventeenth century, French adventurers looked elsewhere in the New World. Backed by the Huguenot Admiral Gaspard de Coligny, the first minister of Henri II, French Protestants attempted to establish colonies in Brazil and Florida. These too failed. And further efforts were hindered as religious conflict in Europe grew more bitter. But after the accession of Henri IV and the end of the wars of religion, the French renewed their interest in America. Authorities granted commissions that provided vice-regal authority and conveyed monopolies on fishing and fur trading as an inexpensive means of encouraging the exploitation and settlement of New World domains. The opposition of merchants and fishermen to these powers and privileges and the great expense and difficulty of founding colonies again prevented the establishment of a New France.[11]

. In 1603 Pierre Du Gua, sieur de Monts, received a commission as lieutenant general for the vast region that would become Canada, with the right to grant land in seigneurial tenure and a ten-year monopoly of the fur trade. Although early efforts by de Monts and his associates proved feeble, and although his monopoly was soon broken, they managed to hang on. Acknowledging the difficulties of maintaining his exclusive privileges against interlopers and the vulnerability of his settlement on the Atlantic coast in Acadia, de Monts directed his associate, Samuel de Champlain, to erect a post on the upper St. Lawrence, at Quebec, in 1608. Here de Monts could hope

[10]Trudel, *Beginnings of New France*, 53. Nonetheless, contact between indigenous Canadians and the French hardly ceased, and French influence continued directly or indirectly by virtue of their material culture; see Trigger, *Natives and Newcomers*, 111–63 and 303–4. James W. Bradley, *The Evolution of the Onondaga Iroquois: Accommodating Change, 1500–1655* (Syracuse, N.Y., 1987), 74–80, 82–83, 98–103, argues that European goods found their way into Iroquoia by the second quarter of the sixteenth century, though southern channels were more important than northern ones.
[11]Trigger, *Natives and Newcomers*, 303–8.

to attract Indian furs from a vast inland territory before Indian traders reached other European traders. The members of Champlain's outpost lived a precarious existence. Only eight of twenty-eight men survived the first winter. And only the indulgence of the Indians and the meager and unreliable support of France allowed the colony to endure.[12]

Quebec's and New France's success in these years, as well as some of its difficulties, was a result of Champlain's initiative and perseverance.[13] Nurturing the fragile colony, exploring little-known lands, penning geographical and promotional tracts, traveling between the new and old worlds, and playing courtier to royalty in native America and France, Champlain managed to keep his dream and New France alive. In October of 1614, after two years of negotiation—between Champlain, the new viceroy, Henri de Bourbon, prince de Condé, and the merchants of rival ports Rouen and Saint-Malo—a charter established the Compagnie de Canada. The new company won a monopoly on trade in the St. Lawrence for eleven years (until 1624) in return for transporting six families to begin a settlement, maintaining the viceroy's lieutenant, Champlain, and providing an annual payment to Condé. On this new footing, New France, or at least the portion known as Canada, hoped to prosper.[14]

Canada encountered further local difficulties as a result of intrigues in France. Survival, many believed, depended on colonization. Yet, as with the Dutch, many who sought the profits of commerce were unwilling to endure the expense of settlement and the potential competition from colonists. And settlement financed by grants of monopoly antagonized less-favored commercial interests. As in New Netherland, commercial and colonial interests faced each other in a debilitating contest that both were destined to lose. The opposition

[12]Eccles, *France in America*, 20; Trigger, *Natives and Newcomers*, 306–8, 312–13.

[13]Bruce G. Trigger credits François Gravé Du Pont, soldier, navy captain, merchant, with much of New France's success during these years: "Although far less information is available about him, he appears to have played a role in dealing with native peoples that was at least as important as Champlain's during the first three decades of the seventeenth century" (*Natives and Newcomers*, 305). In general, Trigger is convincing in his deflation of Champlain's historical reputation. See, for example, 316–19.

[14]See Trudel, *Beginnings of New France*, 93–106. In New France, Acadia was a separate concern, though also under the dominion of the viceroy. See also, Trigger, *Natives and Newcomers*, 312–13. This was not the first time that settlement had been mandated in such an agreement; indeed, the handful of settlers required in exchange for these privileges represented a moderate demand. Champlain was disappointed by the failure to require extensive colonization, especially when even the meager colonization program never bore fruit (313).

of private commercial interests, on the one hand, with those of the province and the growing French empire on the other, would continue to play an important role in the development of New France.[15]

Late in 1617 or early in 1618, Champlain was again in France and presented a comprehensive plan for colonization to the Chamber of Commerce. He proposed that 300 families and 300 soldiers be dispatched to the St. Lawrence to establish an agricultural and commercial settlement. Within four years, Champlain believed, the colony would attain self-sufficiency and begin to pay great dividends from its fisheries, forests, mines, fur resources, and farms on the modest investment of the Chamber or the king. In addition, French coffers might be filled by trade with Asia, if a passage to the East was ever located. And the government could expect revenue from taxes and duties levied on a prosperous New France. Not least among the many advantages of Champlain's colonization plan was the anticipation that countless souls could be redeemed by the Church.[16]

The Chamber of Commerce carefully studied Champlain's memorandum and, without pledging its own financial support, passed it along to the king as something he should sponsor. In turn, King Louis XIII pronounced his approval, backed the plan, and confirmed Champlain's command. But the king was distracted by matters closer to home and would not commit his material support, nor did he attempt to coerce the Company of Canada to implement it. By the end of 1618, Champlain finally succeeded in winning a commitment from the company for a modest program of settlement in which eighty families would be dispatched to the St. Lawrence. More internal wrangling in the Company of Canada placed obstacles in Champlain's path. By the end of 1620 Canada was in a sorry state, with Quebec inhabited year round by perhaps sixty people continually on the brink of starvation.[17]

In November of 1620, the merchants of Saint-Malo and Rouen lost their monopoly and were replaced by a new Compagnie de Montmorency pour la Nouvelle-France directed by the sieurs de Caen. Little changed, however. Indeed, the rivalry between merchant

---

[15]Trigger, *Natives and Newcomers*, 315–25, discusses the struggle between colonizers and traders during the first two decades of the seventeenth century.

[16]See Trudel, *Beginnings of New France*, 125–26. Trigger, *Natives and Newcomers*, 321–23, analyzes the plan, argues convincingly that it was unrealistic, and successfully challenges Champlain's reputation as a visionary colonizer.

[17]Trudel, *Beginnings of New France*, 129.

groups added to the turmoil in New France. By 1625 less than seventy
persons occupied Quebec, and fewer than fifteen acres were being
cultivated.[18] In the year 1625 five members of the Society of Jesus
appeared in Canada. As the king and French merchants were reluctant or unable to back colonial settlement in New France, the Church
and its zealous followers assumed the initiative.

Missionary efforts had begun in 1614, after French bishops endorsed Champlain's request by sending to New France four members
of the Recollet order of the Minor Friars. Almost immediately upon
arriving in Canada, two of the Recollets set out for Tadoussac and
Huronia to begin their work with the Indians. But the mendicant
Recollets lacked the necessary resources, seemed ill-suited to this missionary work, and were too few to make a large impact.[19] The advent
of the Jesuits in 1625 began a new era in the Indian mission and more
generally in the history of New France. The determined, disciplined,
highly trained, and militant members of the Society of Jesus were the
shock troops of the Counter Reformation. Encouraged by victories
over the Protestants in Europe, they were bent on expanding their
work to include missions to the New World; they eagerly focused
attention on Canada. Armand-Jean Du Plessis, Cardinal de Richelieu,
now the king's first minister, proved an ardent supporter of the Society
and of a revitalized New France.[20]

The redemption of the pagan peoples of Canada was a major goal,
but a related and more immediate objective was to place New France

[18]Eccles, *Canadian Frontier*, 32; Trigger, *Natives and Newcomers*, 323–25.
[19]Trigger, *Natives and Newcomers* treats the mission of the Recollets extensively; see especially 200–203, 316–25. See also James Axtell, *The Invasion Within: The Contest of Cultures
in Colonial North America* (New York, 1985), especially 36–38, 49–54. The Recollets' ideas
about and actions in their Canadian mission can be followed in Gabriel Sagard, *Histoire du
Canada et Voyages que les Frères Mineurs Recollects y ont Faicts pour la Conversion des Infidèles depuis
l'an 1615*, 4 vols. (Paris, 1866); George M. Wrong, ed., H. H. Langton, trans., *Sagard's Long
Journey to the Country of the Hurons* [1632], *Publication of the Champlain Society*, 25 (Toronto,
1939); Chrestien Le Clercq, *The First Establishment of the Faith in New France* [1691], ed. and
trans. John G. Shea, 2 vols. (New York, 1881), a polemical pastiche written by others and
attributed to Le Clercq (apparently without his knowledge or permission), and which should
therefore be used with some caution; W. F. Ganong, ed. and trans., *Le Clercq's New Relation
of Gaspesia, with the Customs and Religion of the Gaspesian Indians* [1691], *Publications of the
Champlain Society*, 5 (Toronto, 1910).
[20]William V. Bangert, S. J., *A History of the Society of Jesus* (St. Louis, 1972) provides a
comprehensive account of the Society; Lynn A. Martin, *The Jesuit Mind: The Mentality of an
Elite in Early Modern France* (Ithaca, N.Y., 1988) focuses on France. The Jesuit missionary
program for New France can be traced in previously cited works by Trudel, Eccles, Axtell,
and Jaenen. See also Jaenen, *The Role of the Church in New France* (Toronto, 1976); for a
recent brief synthesis and revision see Trigger, *Natives and Newcomers*, 325–41.

on a firm foundation. As Richelieu and his zealous fellow subscribers complained,

> Those to whom we had entrusted the care of the colony were so little interested that, to date, there is but one settlement ... in which are maintained forty or fifty Frenchmen favouring the interests of the merchants rather than the ... King; so badly maintained have they been ... that if yearly provisions had been delayed ... the small group would have starved to death.... The disorders have reached such a point that ... to assist in the conversion of the indigenous inhabitants and to establish a prosperous colony ... New France should be, once and for all, made a part of the King's domain.[21]

To accomplish both his political and his religious goals, Richelieu formulated a grand colonial program of consolidation and expansion. For Canada he formed a new Compagnie de Nouvelle France in 1627 to develop and exploit its natural resources, to establish self-sufficient agricultural settlements, and to encourage the conversion of the heathen, while preventing the encouragement of heretics by banning the Huguenots. This Compagnie de Cent-Associés—so called because over one hundred officeholders, merchants, and members of the clergy and nobility subscribed with investments of at least 3,000 *livres*—assumed monopoly privileges and seigneur title to France's lands in North America. Although the company was a private rather than a state enterprise, its investors acted more out of religious devotion and patriotism than out of a simple concern for profits. In the context of growing nationalism and imperial rivalry in Europe, and inspired by the revival of religious enthusiasm in France, these associates tried to construct a New France that previous adventurers could not or chose not to create.[22]

The novelty and the remarkable privileges of the company's charter had an enormous impact on the history of New France. King Louis XIII cleared the way for the participation of nobles and ecclesiastics by granting an exception to traditional restrictions against commercial enterprise for these estates. In the Company of the Hundred Asso-

---

[21]"Establishment of the Company of the Hundred Associates," 29 April 1627, *Édits et Ordonnances*, in Cameron Nish, ed. and trans., *The French Regime, Canadian Historical Documents Series* (Scarborough, Ont., 1965), 1:18.

[22]Ibid., 18–19; Trudel, *Beginnings of New France*, 169–72; W. J. Eccles, *France in America* (East Lansing, Mich, rev. ed., 1990 [orig. pub. New York, 1972]), 27–29; Eccles, *Canadian Frontier*, 32–33.

ciates, they were allowed to venture on an equal basis with merchants and yet not forfeit their rank and privileges. The king's exception brought new men and women into the field, private investors with greater concern for the advancement of the Catholic church and the glory of the French nation in the new age of mercantilist competition. These new noble and ecclesiastic subscribers provided the substantial funds necessary to make the grand settlement project successful. They agreed that any profits from the enterprise would not be distributed for the first three years. The profits would instead be added to each of the 107 investors' original capital. Thereafter, subscribers could withdraw no more than one-third of their yearly profits. In this fashion, the colony was assured of stable and abundant funds, especially in the early years of weighty expenses and meager returns.[23]

The concern for profit was not completely eliminated. Both the investors and the king hoped that the enterprise would pay, and they supposed that colonial profits would not compromise but rather enhance the interests of the French state in the mercantilist climate of the day. Business in New France, though private, was ultimately under the control of the king, by means of the company. The chief commodity that would help maintain the colony—fur—showed promise of also enriching company subscribers. Yet the turmoil of private enterprise that ultimately distinguished the New Netherland fur trade was not anticipated and did not develop in New France, not at least, until the changes wrought in the 1670s under the administration of Louis de Buade, comte de Frontenac.[24]

The king supported the company and its settlements by granting it a monopoly over the fur trade that would continue even after other exclusive rights expired. These arrangements would not prohibit inhabitants from bartering with the Indians on their own behalf, but individual traders were required to sell their furs to the company at a fixed price. This restriction, applied with relative success, regulated the trade and maintained company control and profits. But fixed French prices often meant that the Indian suppliers received lower returns than they could obtain elsewhere—at Fort Orange, for instance. The French therefore depended all the more on maintaining good relations with their Indian allies, and, by inclination and necessity, they approached the Indians with a more calculated, self-

---

[23]"Establishment of the Company of the Hundred Associates," in Nish, ed., *French Regime*, 18–19; Trudel, *Beginnings of New France*, 169–72.
[24]See especially, William J. Eccles, *Frontenac: The Courtier Governor* (Toronto, 1959).

conscious, and centralized policy than did their Dutch rivals to the south.

The king also demonstrated his state support of this private enterprise by granting a fifteen-year monopoly on all commerce except fishing, and permitting all trade between France and the colony to proceed duty-free for the first fifteen years. Moreover, he encouraged the emigration of commoners to the New World by granting them extraordinary concessions in New France. After six years' service, any settler who had practiced a trade in Canada could return to France as a "master craftsman," with the right to keep an "open shop." The offspring of immigrants in the New World would be considered "French-born" and entitled to enjoy any privileges available to their countrymen in France. These concessions extended even to Indians who were baptised and became French subjects. The king, his ministers, and the Hundred Associates anticipated the creation of a new French and Catholic society in the New World, a society with natural resources and native people molded by French ideas and personnel. The grand vision of France could not have contrasted more sharply with that of the Five Nations, who anticipated that the process of assimilation would proceed in the opposite direction.

The Hundred Associates obliged themselves to settle 4,000 colonists—all French, all Catholic—in New France within fifteen years, by December 1643, and to provide for their initial material and spiritual existence. Taking up its mission, the company dispatched four ships and 400 settlers to Quebec in April 1628. These colonists represented an unprecedented investment on behalf of New France. They were to join a scant population of 107 people, 60 to 80 of whom lived in Quebec, and only about 20 of whom could be considered permanent inhabitants. In contrast, New England already contained some 300 settlers, who increased their number to about 4,000 by 1634 and to about 11,000 by 1638; Virginia was occupied by some 2,000 English people; and even New Netherland, experiencing its own difficulty in populating its province, had about 500 settlers in 1628.[25]

---

[25]Eccles, *France in America*, rev. ed., 28–29; Nish, ed., *French Regime*, 157, reported a population of seventy-six in 1628. On the population of New England, see Evarts B. Greene and Virginia D. Harrington, *American Population Before the Federal Census of 1790* (New York, 1932), 8–9, 12–13; David Cressy, *Coming Over: Migration and Communication between England and New England in the Seventeenth Century* (Cambridge, 1987), 68–71; on Virginia, which contained approximately 2,600 white settlers in 1629, see Edmund S. Morgan, *American Slavery, American Freedom: The Ordeal of Colonial Virginia* (New York, 1975), 404; on New

European conflict interfered with the Hundred Associates' plans. In the spring of 1627, the English Duke of Buckingham came to the assistance of the Huguenot rebels besieged at the French port of La Rochelle. The Huguenots failed to hold, and Buckingham was defeated; but France and England were enmeshed in war. In England, the Kirke family—privateers or buccaneers, depending on one's perspective—plotted to invade New France. With Huguenot aid, Sir David Kirke intercepted and captured the company's colonial convoy, and in the following year Kirke, his brothers, and the Scotsman Sir William Alexander conquered Canada and Acadia, thereby evicting France from mainland North America.

But the history of New France does not end in 1629. France and England settled their differences in the Treaty of St. Germain-en-Laye in 1632, and France retrieved its North American territory. In the same year they returned to the St. Lawrence Valley and began to reconstruct New France almost from scratch. The province's development continued as before, under the peculiar French system of private enterprise and the guiding hand of the emerging French State and the Catholic Church. The distractions of national and international politics in France—the Thirty Years' War and the Fronde—meant, however, that the king would continue to give the colony moral rather than material support.

Under the auspices of the Hundred Associates, which had lost much of its original investment in 1629, settlement began again in 1634. The company recruited colonists and provided the administrative framework for its Laurentian province. Its lands were divided into fiefs, with impressive feudal privileges, and offered as *terre de qualité*, that is, to persons of quality. These nobles and notables, in turn, were to recruit and settle people on their domains who would become their *censitaires*. This apparently feudal regime, was, in practice, no less modern, no more medieval, and no more successful in peopling the province than were the patroonships of New Netherland. Although elaborated with the formal paraphernalia of *foi et hommage* (fealty and hommage), honorary rights of *haute justice,* and traditional dues and impositions, the seigneurial system in Canada functioned primarily as an "instrument of good order." The wide availability of cheap land, Canada's remoteness from Atlantic markets, and the resulting weak-

---

Netherland, see Oliver A. Rink, *Holland on the Hudson: An Economic and Social History of Dutch New York* (Ithaca, N.Y., 1986), 38.

ness of commercial pressures on agricultural land insured that *censitaires* would hardly be serfs. Canadian society was mixed and mobile. Wages were at least five times higher in Canada than in France, the historical geographer R. Cole Harris concluded, and the price of cleared land in the colony was five to ten times lower. Permanent tenant farmers were rare except near Montreal and Quebec later in the century, and, sooner or later, most immigrants to New France settled on their own farms.[26] Nonetheless, the seigneurial regime provided at least the forms of hierarchy, social order, and political stability necessary for France's colonial enterprise in the American wilderness.[27]

Despite an influx of immigrants in 1634, and the foundation of a new habitation upriver from Quebec at Trois Rivières in that year, settlement of the Laurentian colony lagged well behind the projections of the Hundred Associates' charter of 1627. In 1641, almost a decade after resettlement resumed, only about two hundred French men and women occupied the colony. This number fell far short of the envisioned three thousand.[28] By 1642, with the foundation of Montreal, Canada extended still farther up the St. Lawrence. Although it seemed to be an illogical overexpansion of the scantily settled, underdeveloped colony—its detractors termed it that "insane enterprise"—Montreal was founded with great enthusiasm and hope by its devout and zealous backers, *les Messieurs et Dames de la Société de Notre-Dame de Montréal pour la conversion des Sauvages de la Nouvelle France.* As Montreal's establishment graphically demonstrated, the greatest initiative in the settlement and development, as well as the evangelizing of New France in the first half of the seventeenth century, came from the Church.[29]

[26]Harris, "Extension of France into Rural Canada," 36–37.

[27]On Canada's seigneurial regime and the French rural society that emerged in seventeenth-century New France, see Harris, *The Seigneurial System in Early Canada: A Geographical Study* (Kingston and Montreal, 1966); Harris and John Warkentin, *Canada Before Confederation: A Study in Historical Geography* (New York, 1974), especially 3–63; Harris, "Extension of France into Rural Canada"; Allan Greer, *Peasant, Lord, and Merchant: Rural Society in Three Quebec Parishes 1740–1840* (Toronto, 1985), 3–19; Trudel, *Beginnings of New France*, 186–87, 246–52.

[28]Trudel, *Beginnings of New France*, 187. Eccles, *Canadian Frontier*, 38, estimated the European population at 359 for 1640 and for a decade later at 675; Eccles, "The Role of the Church in New France" [1975], in Eccles, ed., *Essays on New France* (Toronto, 1987), 28, revised his 1640 estimate downward to 356 persons, including members of families, individuals, soldiers, Jesuits, and other religious personnel. These higher totals nonetheless fell well short of the projected 3,000.

[29]On the foundation of Montreal, see Trudel, *Beginnings of New France*, 187–89, 231–54; see also Eccles, *France in America*, rev. ed., 49–54; Eccles, *Canadian Frontier*, 39–42. François Dollier de Casson wrote a contemporary account, "Histoire du Montréal," which has been

The religious revival that swept through France in these years spilled over into Canada. Zealous like the New England Puritans but in their own fashion, the religiously inspired subjects of France hoped to create a "New Jerusalem, blessed by God and made up of citizens destined for heaven."[30] Members of the Society of Jesus—unlike their Protestant counterparts in New Netherland or New England—labored diligently among the Indians, hoping to incorporate them within this elect citizenry. The populous, horticultural, and sedentary Hurons seemed to offer the best prospects. By 1649, eighteen Jesuit priests and over thirty of their assistants evangelized in Huronia, and thousands had been baptised.[31]

In the 1630s, Indian boys received training as Catholics and Frenchmen in a Jesuit seminary removed from the influences of their native villages. And the Jesuits established a reserve at Sillery near Quebec where nomadic Indians could live, away from the distractions of both native and French societies, and transform themselves gradually into proper Catholic citizens. To provide for the medical care of their Indian and French charges, the Jesuits appealed to France for the endowment of a hospital, and in 1639 three Hospitalière nuns disembarked at Quebec to begin this work. Ursuline nuns arrived on the same ship, answering the call to provide instruction to Indian girls.[32]

While guiding the native inhabitants of America on their path toward civilization and salvation, the Jesuits did not neglect France's immigrants in the New World. In 1635 they founded a college for the education of French boys. To maintain the spiritual and moral health of the colony, the Jesuits considerably involved themselves in colonial administration. The journals and letters of the Jesuit fathers in America, collected and published in France, chronicled and most vigorously promoted the entire colonial enterprise in New France during the seventeenth century. And, as the province still had no

edited and translated as Ralph Flenley, ed., *A History of Montreal, 1640–1672 from the French of Dollier de Casson* (Toronto, 1928). Gustave Lanctôt, *Montreal under Maisonneuve, 1642–1665,* trans. Alta Lind Cook (Toronto, 1969) is a dated, romantic account that can be useful if approached with caution; some relevant primary sources are reprinted in its appendices. Other primary documents (including brief passages from Dollier de Casson) are excerpted and translated in Nish, ed., *French Regime,* 27–31.

[30]Eccles, "Role of the Church in New France," 27.

[31]Trudel, *Beginnings of New France,* 237–40; Eccles, *France in America,* rev. ed., 44–46. Bruce G. Trigger, *The Children of Aataentsic: A History of the Huron People to 1660,* 2 vols. (Montreal, 1976) is the classic ethnohistorical account of the Hurons; the Jesuit mission to Huronia is treated mainly in vol. 2.

[32]See especially Axtell, *Invasion Within,* 33–127.

bishopric, the mission Church in New France, which was monopolized by the Jesuits, ministered to the spiritual needs of all inhabitants. The Society of Jesus's preeminence in this regard went unchallenged until members of the rival Society of St. Sulpice joined the Jesuits in 1657, and until the advent of secular clergy in 1659 replaced the missionaries in the new parish of Quebec.[33]

The Church maintained its power in New France because colonization was for many a religious and humanitarian endeavor. Substantial financial and moral support came from devout men and women in France, some of whom came themselves to work for the conversion of pagan North America. After Champlain's death in 1635, governors of the province—many of whom belonged to a knightly religious order, the Knights of Malta—matched or exceeded his concern for morality and religion. The habitation of Ville Marie, created as a center for proselytizing the Indians, best symbolized the religious motivations of New France. On the island of Montreal, well beyond even the Laurentian outpost of Trois Rivières and closer to the potential Indian neophytes, the "Montrealists" hoped to establish an isolated puritanical religious community for its resident French men and women. In such a setting, they believed, conversion would be most effective. Settlement began in May of 1642, and the good fortune that smiled on the habitation seemed to confirm the nobility of its purpose. Yet enthusiasm gradually dimmed, development stalled, and the original purity of life at Montreal was eventually sullied. New recruits failed to appear, and deaths offset the natural increase of births. By 1651 the number of men available to defend the outpost stood at approximately fifty.[34]

In 1653, some one hundred colonists arrived at Montreal, apparently to breathe new life into the community. But this influx was not followed up by others. Indeed, the tale of these sorry immigrants simply underscores the fact that most French people felt a deep aversion toward Canada and showed an extreme reluctance to emigrate from France to the St. Lawrence Valley. Their story tells of disap-

[33]See Trudel, *Beginnings of New France*, 231–37; Eccles, "Role of the Church in New France," especially 27–28; Eccles, *France in America*, rev. ed., 40–42, 56–57. On the attempt by the Jesuits to promote colonization and support of New France through their *Relations*, see Thwaites, ed., *Jesuit Relations and Allied Documents*, 73 vols. (Cleveland, 1896–1901), 8:9–13; 9:185–91; and see Peter N. Moogk, "Reluctant Exiles: The Problems of Colonization in French North America," *William and Mary Quarterly*, 3d ser., 46 (July 1989), 466.
[34]Trudel, *Beginnings of New France*, 187–91; Eccles, *France in America*, rev. ed., 49–54; Lanctôt, *Montreal under Maisonneuve*, 54.

pointment and failure rather than new hope. In France, 153 men had
signed on for a five-year term, at good wages and a cash advance, but
49 fled before their ship could sail. When the leaky vessel began to
take on water, its captain sequestered the colonists (or sojourners) on
an island off the coast of France to prevent their escape. Nonetheless,
some were so desperate that they were willing to attempt the difficult
swim back to the mainland "to save themselves, for they were like
madmen and believed that they were being led to destruction," wrote
one observer. In retrospect, the recruits' fears were not misplaced:
eight died en route to Canada, and another twenty-four were killed
by Indians. This unfortunate saga is an illustration of some of the
difficulties New France experienced in peopling its Canadian colony,
despite the opportunities that existed there and despite the series of
crises in seventeenth-century France that made life so difficult for
common people.[35]

By 1663, Montreal's population stood at 596 persons. Yet this substantial increase was not made up of inhabitants who matched the
devotion and zeal of early Montrealists but rather of men and women
enamored of commerce. Well situated for gathering in Christ's flocks
to the Church, Montreal was as well located for the collection of
precious furs. The rise of Montreal, and the corruption of its original
vision, presents a vivid symbol for the history of New France in the
seventeenth century.[36]

Despite the religious idealism and activism of New France, *seigneurs*
and *habitants* looked for profits in the fur trade. The Hundred Associates also expressed concern that their spiritual and material investments in Laurentia at least not leave them a continuous burden
of debt. In 1645, with the development of the colony stalled and trade
sluggish, the Hundred Associates was persuaded to transfer control
to the Communauté des Habitants, a local oligarchy of the most prominent seigneurs in Canada. The Communauté assumed the fur trade
monopoly, as well as the company's obligations and responsibilities.
Although administration of New France thus passed to Canada itself,
the transfer did not ring in a period of republicanism. The new company was governed by a consortium of perhaps fifteen persons, most

[35]Moogk, "Reluctant Exiles," 469–70, describes the ordeal of these fearful recruits and,
in general, provides a good analysis of the problems experienced in effecting the emigration
of French people to France's American colonies; contemporary observer quoted in ibid., 469.
[36]Trudel, *Beginnings of New France*, 189–91; Eccles, *France in America*, rev.ed., 51, 53–54;
Trigger, *Natives and Newcomers*, 332–33.

of whom were related by blood or marriage. A revival of the fur trade, which accompanied a short-lived peace with the Iroquois, immensely benefited the Communauté in 1645 and 1646.[37]

But prosperity was fleeting. Renewed war between New France's Indian allies and the Five Nations clogged the channels of trade. Simultaneously, a Communauté prohibition on individual participation in the fur trade, which the Hundred Associates had allowed since 1627, antagonized the inhabitants, and charges of the Communauté's mismanagement and corruption led to a series of reforms. By 1648, the King's Council had modified the agreement between the Hundred Associates and the Communauté and had established a new administrative structure for Canada.[38]

Despite these innovations, New France continued to struggle. The province depended heavily on the fur trade and prospered only when a climate of peace allowed Canada's Indian trading partners to reach Laurentian posts. In the early 1650s, hostility with the Five Nations prevented these happy circumstances. With trade closed off, Canada's economy staggered. New France was on the very brink of destruction. In 1650, Marie de l'Incarnation, writing from the Ursuline Convent at Quebec, saw the Iroquois as the chief threat to the survival of Canada. Lacking new help from France, she believed, "we must... either die or return to France." If Iroquois assaults continued, she wrote, "there will be nothing for the French to do here. It will not be possible to carry on trade. If there is no trade, no more ships will come here. If ships no longer come, we shall lack all things necessary for life."[39] The Communauté and New France confronted a woeful state of affairs. Its warehouses empty, its burden of debt growing, the Canadian company was unable to meet its obligations, and residents feared for their very lives.

The astonishing peace initiated by the Five Nations in 1653—mentioned at the outset of this chapter—seemed to promise a way back from the precipice. But the Communauté suffered a serious loss when one of its vessels fell prey to privateers and three other supply ships

[37]Trudel, *Beginnings of New France,* 210–12; Eccles, *Canadian Frontier,* 42–44; Trigger, *Natives and Newcomers,* 334, 338.
[38]Trudel, *Beginnings of New France,* 212–17; Eccles, *Canadian Frontier,* 43–44. See "Judgment by which his Majesty Approves the Agreement... between the Company of New France and the Inhabitants of New France, of March 6, 1645 [Paris, July 3, 1651]" and "Decree for the Council of New France, 1647," excerpted and translated in Nish, ed., *French Regime,* 37–41.
[39]Marshall, ed., *Word from New France,* 184–85.

failed to reach the St. Lawrence. Moreover, peace with the Iroquois did not hold, and this once again disrupted the fur trade. These disasters persuaded the Communauté to offer the fur trade monopoly back to the Hundred Associates. They quickly declined. New reforms instituted by the king brought the Hundred Associates back into colonial administration and created an additional administrative apparatus to supervise the Communauté and the trade in 1657. But the Communauté's continued inability to perform its function and meet its obligations led finally to a fundamental reorganization after 1661, when King Louis XIV began to rule as well as reign.[40]

New France drifted, as a result of the instabilities of private colonial enterprise and the confusing matrix of administration that developed through the end of the 1650s. Colonization by private companies failed because of several factors: insufficient investment, international rivalry and hostility, low profits, and the extreme reluctance of French men and women to emigrate.[41] Self-government suffered from some of the same problems and from many of its own creation. The Church had done all it could, subject as it was to the ebb and flow of religious enthusiasm among its backers, and it was gradually overwhelmed by those in New France who were more concerned with profits than with proselytizing and religious purity. Following the death of Cardinal Giulio Mazarin, Louis XIV began to rule directly over his nation and empire; using as his agent Jean-Baptiste Colbert, former treasurer of the late cardinal's household and now controller-general of finances and minister of the marine, the king sought to construct a new mercantilist order. Colbert attempted to reorganize France's colonial empire, rationalizing its administration, encouraging its diversification and development, sealing it off from rival powers, and rendering it self-sufficient, prosperous, and powerful.[42]

Louis XIV revoked the Hundred Associates' charter in 1663, and New France became a royal colony under the jurisdiction of Colbert

[40]Trudel, *Beginnings of New France*, 223–25, 227–28.

[41]See Moogk, "Reluctant Exiles," especially 463–70, 503, on the failure of publicity, recruitment, and transportation efforts to compensate for the too weak "push" of difficult conditions in France and the too weak "pull" of potential opportunities in New France. Philip Boucher, "French Images of America and the Evolution of Colonial Theories, 1650–1700," in Joyce Duncan Falk, ed., *Proceedings of the Sixth Annual Meeting of the Western Society for French History* [San Diego, Calif., 9–11 November, 1978] (1979), 220–28, also assesses the poor record of France in its settlement of its New World colonies.

[42]See Raymond Birn, *Crisis, Absolutism, Revolution: Europe, 1648–1789*, 2d ed. (Fort Worth, Tex., 1992), especially 52–57, for a brief analysis of Colbertine mercantilism that places it in a wider context.

and the Department of Marine. Louis's minister observed the success England and the Netherlands had achieved on the basis of their commercial empires, and he hoped to compete with and surpass them. According to mercantilism national strength came through economic self-sufficiency and overseas commerce centered upon the metropolis. In a closed world system, each power competed for colonies that would provide the wealth that led to power. Mercantilists saw the mother country as both head and heart of the imperial body and the colonial possessions as its appendages, existing not for their own sake but to nourish the greater nation. Colbert accordingly set out to make New France self-sufficient so that it could serve its imperial function. His criticism and reorganization of New France in 1663 gives us a lens through which to evaluate the French colonial enterprise in Canada in the first half of the seventeenth century.[43]

In place of the confused and meandering administration that preceded, Colbert constructed a strong, more centralized system of government for New France. His model was military; a clear chain of command began at the top, with the king, and proceeded down through the minister of marine in France to the governor and *intendant* in Canada, who ruled through the Superior Council of Quebec.[44]

With this administrative structure in place, Colbert hoped to effect a diversification of New France's fur-based economy. He advocated the further development of fishing, tanning, brewing, lumber production, and mining. To enhance France's commercial position, Colbert attempted to stimulate the production of naval stores and ship building, and he encouraged intracolonial shipping and commerce, after the example of the "triangle trade" of Holland and England. For several reasons Colbert failed. Fishing suffered from competition and from a lack of salt, which was necessary as a preservative. The inaccessibility of St. Lawrence ports both winter and summer—even in the summer they lay "almost a thousand shoal-ridden and often foggy miles from the open ocean," the historical geographer R. Cole Harris tells us—as well as the competition of Dutch shipping reduced Canada's role in intracolonial trade. When mercantilist regulations

[43]"Colbert's colonies" from 1663 to 1685 are traced in Eccles, *France in America*, rev. ed., 63–94. See "Instructions for [the Royal Commissioner,] Sieur Gaudais sent by the King to Canada," Paris, 1663, in E. B. O'Callaghan, ed., *Documents Relative to the Colonial History of New-York*, 15 vols. (Albany, N.Y., 1856–87), 9:9–13. Related documents are excerpted and translated in Nish, ed., *French Regime*, 46–48.

[44]"Edict Creating the Superior Council of Quebec, Paris, April 1663," in Nish, ed., *French Regime*, 51.

later excluded Dutch ships from New France, neither colonial vessels nor vessels from France filled the gap.[45] Labor shortages, high wages, and a lack of skilled workers hampered lumbering, naval stores production, and shipbuilding; consequently, Canada remained a dispersed, underdeveloped province, where the fur trade and, especially, subsistence agriculture drew most inhabitants away from these and other recommended economic endeavors.[46]

These attempts at diversification and development suggest in retrospect the nature and state of the Canadian economy, and they tell us about French objectives in New France before and during the 1660s. Nonetheless, Canada developed, although not as quickly as many hoped, and it became an important part of the French empire, though for reasons that were, ultimately, more strategic than economic.[47] Sincere religious motives cooperated and competed with commercial concerns in New France's development. The state, involved and concerned from the beginning, guided that development with an increasingly firm hand.

As in New Netherland, so in New France the small number of people continued to be a major problem. After 1662, the crown assumed responsibility for populating the colony, expending on average some twenty-five thousand *livres* per year between 1662 and 1671, when royal subsidies lapsed, to recruit and dispatch the managers, settlers, indentured workers, and marriageable women necessary to ensure New France's existence and prosperity. By 1663, the population stood at slightly more than three thousand people. In contrast to the modified feudal system of patroonship in New Netherland, *seigneurs* usually lived in the New World. But like New Netherland

[45]Harris, *Canada Before Confederation*, 21. Harris, "Extension of France into Rural Canada," 37, observed that Quebec was twice as far as Boston from the West Indies by ship. Moogk, "Reluctant Exiles," 465, noted the lack of interest in Canada among French high-seas traders and asked, "What might the Netherlanders have done for Canada had they not been excluded from French colonial trade in the eighteenth century?" After the failure of French merchants and royal ships to deliver colonists alive and in good condition to Canada, the crown chartered Dutch vessels in 1664, as did the *Compagnie des Indes Occidentales* in 1665 (469).

[46]See Harris, *Canada Before Confederation*, 55–57; see also Harris, "Extension of France into Rural Canada." For a glimpse of *Intendant* Jean Talon's attempts to implement Colbert's program, see "Talon to Colbert, Quebec, November 13, 1666" and "Memoir of Talon on the Present State of Canada, 1667," in Nish, ed., *French Regime*, 54–56.

[47]W. J. Eccles, "The Fur Trade and Eighteenth-Century Imperialism," *William and Mary Quarterly*, 3d ser., 40 (July 1983), 341–62, makes this point convincingly for the eighteenth century. See also Eccles, "New France and the French Impact on North America," in Eccles, *Essays on New France* (Toronto, 1987), 14: Canada, Acadia, and Louisiana were "liabilities on the [eighteenth-century] French balance sheet," but they were maintained for their political and military importance.

patroons, they often failed to meet their obligation to develop settlement. Less than one-third of 1 percent of seigneurial lands had been conceded to settlers in 1645, and by 1663 still less than 1 percent of Canadian lands had been distributed and developed by their *seigneurs*. In population New France thus lagged well behind New Netherland which comprised some nine thousand persons by 1664—about the same number as the Five Nations. And by 1660 it was dwarfed by the burgeoning English colonies in New England and the Chesapeake, which comprised some 33,000 and 35,000 people respectively.[48]

Between 1662 and 1671, the efforts of the crown and the Compagnie des Indes Occidentales delivered approximately 2,500 "personnes," some women as well as men, according to the estimates of the historian Peter N. Moogk. But "a worker delivered ... was not a settler established." The king's subsidy should have increased the colony's male population by some 1,700; yet to Colbert's surprise, the 1668 census found a *total* of only 1,568 European men in Canada capable of bearing arms. A recount in 1676 documented a total population of adults and children, both native-born and settlers, of only 7,832.[49] Moogk concluded that, during the entire French regime, fewer than 300 lay persons emigrated independently and voluntarily from France to Canada. Colonization depended instead on sponsored emigrants, who came to the St. Lawrence less willingly and under arrangements that often entailed some form of temporary bondage. From the 1640s through the 1670s, some four thousand men and women entered Canada as "reluctant exiles" because of the efforts of private companies, *seigneurs*, religious groups, merchants, and the crown. Over two-thirds of the transported single men returned to France, and many others would have joined this mass repatriation

[48]Trudel, *Beginnings of New France*, 251–52. Appendix A of Nish, ed., *French Regime*, 157, provides the following estimates: 1663—2,500; 1665—3,215; 1668—6,282; 1679—9,400. "Abridged Census of the...Families in New France, 1666," 57, reported a total of 3,418 Europeans living in Canada, of whom 1,344 were "men capable of bearing arms between the age of 16 and 50." See also O'Callaghan, ed., *Documents Relative to the History of New-York*, 9:57–58, 61. On New Netherland's population in 1663, see Rink, *Holland on the Hudson*, 158. Jack P. Greene, *Pursuits of Happiness: The Social Development of Early Modern British Colonies and the Formation of American Culture* (Chapel Hill, N.C., 1988), 178–79, provides a convenient population chart for (Table 8.1) 1660, 1710, and 1760. On Iroquois population, see Table 3 in Daniel Karl Richter, "The Ordeal of the Longhouse: Change and Persistence on the Iroquois Frontier, 1609–1720," Ph.D. diss., Columbia University, 1984; Richter estimates a Five Nations' population of 7,600–8,400 in 1661 and 8,960–9,360 in 1665.

[49]Moogk, "Reluctant Exiles," 481. If the same proportion of men capable of bearing arms existed in the total population in 1668 as in 1666 (based on census figures in Nish, ed., *French Regime*, 57), the total European population of New France stood at a mere 3,983 in 1668.

had they been able to elude the restrictions designed to tie them to Canada.[50]

This meager population was strung out thinly in *côtes*, coasts or lines, of farmsteads primarily along the St. Lawrence River. As late as 1749, the Swedish traveler and botanist Peter Kalm could describe Canada as "one continued village" that began at Montreal and ended at Quebec, a distance of more than 180 miles.[51] In the mid-seventeenth century, the *côtes* were fainter and more frequently interrupted by unsettled lands. And finally, at the western terminus of the *côtes* at Montreal, about 150 to 200 miles away to the southwest (as the crow flies), lay the heart of Iroquoia.[52]

Colonists clung roughly to three centers of habitation: the region of Quebec, containing about 65 percent of the total population; or near Trois Rivières with 15 percent; and Montreal with 20 percent. Only Quebec could be considered a town by European standards; the other settlements were little more than crude outposts. Wilderness intervened between the habitations; each was isolated, rough-hewn, and, by necessity, self-sufficient. By 1663, almost 40 percent of the inhabitants were Canadian-born. First-generation Canadians came mainly from Paris and the French Atlantic provinces, but a number of other regions contributed immigrants; within New France there seems to have been no clustering by particular province.[53]

---

[50]Ibid., 497–98. Moogk revises Mario Boleda's net migration estimates (see Boleda, "Les migration au Canada sous le regime français," Ph.D. diss. Université de Montréal, 1983) but essentially affirms Boleda's striking conclusions about the magnitude of the flight of migrants back to France. Of at least 27,000 people who emigrated to Canada during the French regime, according to Boleda, only 31.6 percent became permanent residents; that is, nearly 70 percent returned to France (see Moogk, "Reluctant Exiles," 462–63, 502–3).

[51]Adolph B. Benson, ed., *Peter Kalm's Travels in North America,* 2 vols. (New York, 1966), 2:416–17.

[52]On the distance of these Laurentian settlements from Iroquoia, and the ways that French troops would approach it in the 1660s, see "Papers Relating to De Courcelles' and De Tracy's Expeditions against the Mohawk Indians, 1665–6," in E. B. O'Callaghan, ed., *The Documentary History of the State of New York,* 4 vols. (Albany, 1849–51), 1:60–64. Missionary and envoy Father Simon le Moyne took some nineteen days to return from Onondaga to Montreal in 1654. He followed the normal route, north to Lake Ontario (about 90 miles, in 8 days), then north and east along the St. Lawrence to Montreal (190 miles, in 11 days). Le Moyne's progress was delayed, not untypically, by bad weather and good hunting (see Du Creux, *Historia Canadensis,* 2:673). All but the Mohawk lands—reached via the Richelieu River, Lake Champlain, Hudson River corridor—were most easily connected to New France by this Lake Ontario–St. Lawrence route.

[53]Trudel, *Beginnings of New France,* 252–60. See also Harris, "Extension of France into Rural Canada"; Harris, *Canada Before Confederation,* 32–63, is a fine historical-geographical synthesis of the settlement of the St. Lawrence lowlands during the French regime; figure

In this regionally mixed population,[54] Canadians were young and disproportionately male in the year 1663. Some 80 percent of the immigrants who arrived between 1632 and 1662 were male. About one-half of the residents were under twenty years of age in 1663, and only 37 percent were female. The imbalance between the sexes was especially severe among people of marriageable age. Apart from the women who were members of religious communities and those who were already married, so few marriageable women lived in Canada that about six men could have competed for each woman. In these circumstances, disparity in age between spouses and frequent remarriage were typical. But the difficulties experienced by young, single men as they sought wives and stable family life helped to make them largely sojourners rather than permanent settlers in New France.[55]

Family ties and prompt grants of land, tended to keep former indentured workers in the colony. The Montreal Associates were mindful of the power of these attachments when they recruited families and marriageable women for their settlement in 1659. But, in general, old world families pressured emigrants to return to their homeland. French relatives argued that colonization was unnatural, selfish, and immoral, and that it violated family obligations.[56]

Between 1662 and 1673, under the auspices of royal colonization, the crown did sponsor the emigration of 774 *filles du roi*, women who came from a charitable hospice in Paris or from the countryside to marry and settle in New France. Frequently older or disadvantaged by the loss of a parent, they found new opportunities in Canada and became true immigrants. But too few *filles du roi* embarked from France. Christianized Native American women—potential brides for French colonial men under a religious and social "Frenchification" program—similarly failed to appear in great numbers. And various dowries, pensions, and punitive measures directed at bachelors re-

---

2–4 graphically illustrates the *côtes* of settlement. See also R. Cole Harris, ed., *Historical Atlas of Canada* [vol. 1]: *From the Beginning to 1800* (Toronto, 1987), plates 45 and 46.

[54]Moogk, "Reluctant Exiles," 502–3, observed that Canadian workers and soldiers contained in addition a sprinkling of Flemings, Germans, Swiss, Italians, and Iberians. Moreover, he commented on the diversity even among the French: "It would be anachronistic to refer to Bretons, Basques, Flemings, Alsatians, Provencaux and speakers of French dialects as 'the French people'" (504).

[55]Trudel, *Beginnings of New France*, 260–62; Moogk, "Reluctant Exiles," 482. Moogk argues that in the 1660s there were more than twelve unmarried males in the 16–30 age group for every eligible female in the same age group.

[56]Moogk, "Reluctant Exiles," 483–87.

sisting marriage did not produce enough marriages and stable families to increase the French population or prevent the exodus back to the sojourners' *patrie*.[57]

Finally, the crown achieved some success in its colonization attempts by inducing French soldiers, like the Carignan-Salières regiment sent to Canada in 1665 to deal with the Iroquois, to stay and settle. Prompt discharges, settlement grants, and attractive severance payments persuaded over a thousand soldiers to become settlers in the seventeenth century, and in the eighteenth century they constituted the principal source of Canadian immigrants. In fact, some might have suspected that troops were dispatched to Canada as much to help populate the colony as to defend it. Marie de l'Incarnation, noting in another letter to her son the beneficial effects of immigration by the king's soldiers, wrote, "they are men broken from the king's service that His Majesty wished sent to this country. They have all been put in Bourg-Talon two leagues from here, to settle and people it."[58] Nonetheless, by 1680 the population of New France had grown only to about ten thousand—roughly equivalent to the population of the Five Nations—and it lagged well behind English America, which was about to embark on a period of even more vigorous growth with the colonization of Pennsylvania and the middle Atlantic region.[59]

Ironically, in the midst of these volatile conditions, a distinctive agricultural individualism centered on the family unit emerged in Canada during the seventeenth century. People derived their rude but adequate subsistence predominantly from the soil, and, increasingly, few engaged in the fur trade; as the seventeenth century pro-

[57]Ibid., 475–76, 482–83. Marie de l'Incarnation noted the beneficial effects of immigration by the king's soldiers and *filles du roi* in a letter, October 1669, to her son (Marshall, ed., *Word from New France*, 353–54). The best analysis of the various "Frenchification" programs is Axtell, *Invasion Within;* on the Recollet and Jesuit program, see 38–39, 53–70. On French attempts to retain and produce colonists in New France through gratuities and punitive measures, see M. Colbert to M. de Courcelles, St. Germain, 9 April 1670, in O'Callaghan, ed., *Documents Relative to the Colonial History of New-York*, 9:63. See also "Decree of the King's Council for the Encouragement of Marriage...in Canada, April 1, 1670," and related documents in Nish, ed., *French Regime*, 57–58, 61–62. See also Vachon, *Dreams of Empire*, 109–10, 120, 127, 144; reproductions and excerpts of various important documents follow each section of the book.

[58]Marshall, ed., *Word from New France*, 345.

[59]Moogk, "Reluctant Exiles," 500–503; Eccles, *France in America*, rev. ed., 80–83. Despite his interest in providing French inhabitants for Canada, Colbert had limits. He refused to empty the prisons, for example, though petty criminals were transported to Canada in small numbers in the eighteenth century (see Moogk, "Reluctant Exiles," 467–68, 498–99). Moreover, "even granting that there were no other concerns and that resources of the Kingdom ...could be applied to Canada," Colbert wrote, "it would not be prudent to depopulate his Kingdom...to populate Canada" Nish, ed., *French Regime*, 57).

gressed, very few living east of Trois Rivières participated in that trade and by 1700 no more than 2 percent of all Canadian men were in the West—that is, the vast interior of the continent beyond Montreal—as fur trappers or traders in any given year. Though they clustered near the major habitations, no more than one in four *habitants* lived within Canadian villages or towns; in contrast to the town focus of New Netherland with its *burgerlijk*—its civic and mercantile spirit—New France was settled in a dispersed and fragmented fashion, with weak links between discrete rural farmsteads and town cores. Attempts by Colbert and his *intendant* to gather inhabitants into nucleated settlements failed. At the end of the French regime, only six nucleated villages and four hamlets had developed to complement Quebec, Trois Rivierès, and Montreal. All ten of these settlements had emerged since 1700. In Canada during this era, R. Cole Harris concluded, "farm families lived in rough sufficiency, their lives dominated by the seasonal rhythms of the land, not by the more powerful people who lived in other ways.... Institutionally Canadian rural society was simple enough: nuclear families spread across the land in small subsistent farms with few and weak institutional constraints on their independence." The *habitants* enjoyed a better life than their countrymen in France. In the relatively simple economy and comparatively open, egalitarian society of New France, Canadians could more easily achieve the humble prosperity that eluded so many desperate men and women in their crisis-ridden homeland. Yet, as we have seen, the advantages of life in Canada never were sufficient to overcome the social, familial, cultural, and structural obstacles that prevented any sustained immigration from developing.[60]

In response to the problems facing French colonization before 1663, Louis XIV and Colbert therefore initiated a program that inaugurated a new era in Canada. Yet the continuity across this apparent historical divide is also striking. Many of the same maladies that plagued New France would continue to fester in the province. By 1663 many of the basic patterns of life in New France were established, among them war with the Five Nations of the Iroquois. Colbert's response represented a variation on earlier French colonial themes.

Canada in the mid-1660s must have been a great disappointment

---

[60]Harris, *Canada Before Confederation*, 32–63 (the limited success of attempts to impose nucleated settlement is treated on 39–42); Harris, "Extension of France into Rural Canada," 36–37, quotation from 43. See Moogk, "Reluctant Exiles," and Boucher, "French Images of America," on the problems of French emigration.

to the metropolis, as well as to many officials, religious workers, and *habitants* in Laurentia. Although its fur trade was somewhat profitable, the colony fell well short of realizing the mercantilist goals of the French state. It was economically backward; for example, furs were its only marketable commodity, yet Canada exported virtually no pelts from about 1662 to 1675. Concentration on the fur trade, moreover, was in conflict with New France's plans for diversification of trade. The colony was a financial and military drain on France, which was about to embark on a course of expensive military adventurism in Europe. The king and Colbert were unwilling to allow Canada to siphon off population vital to France, and by the early 1670s they had abandoned their immigration policy, leaving New France to grow through natural increase alone.[61]

Moreover, Canada's religious mission was in disarray. The crown of the Jesuit mission in Huronia was destroyed, and new ventures into the *pays d'en haut* (the far west, literally the upcountry beyond Montreal) were modest and tentative, Jesuit missionary tactics were in disrepute, and factional struggles pitted the Jesuits against other religious orders as well as the civil government. By the end of 1668, Marie de l'Incarnation's Ursuline convent could boast of only one resident Native American student. Despite their labors, only eight girls were sufficiently transformed to qualify for religious vocations, and none of them were ultimately permitted to take their vows; no Native American girl or woman entered the Ursuline order in the seventeenth century. Nor did the *Jesuit Relations* mention the ordination of a single Native American man.[62]

As we have seen, few emigrants willingly embarked for Canada, which was perceived in France to be an unpromising, wretched place, a place of "exile," "purgatory," or, even worse, death. Indeed, when the townspeople of La Flèche learned that forty respectable women were about to leave for Canada in 1659, they assumed the worst. Unable to imagine that the emigration was voluntary, the good people of La Flèche attempted to prevent the women's departure. French men and women were repelled by tales of bitter Canadian winters, ferocious mosquitoes, and venomous rattlesnakes. Inhabitants of New

---

[61]See Harris, ed., *Historical Atlas of Canada*, plate 48, on the limited commerce of New France, as well as the lack of beaver exports, 1662–75; see plates 45 and 46 on the nature and magnitude of Canadian immigration and population growth.

[62]Dickason, *Myth of the Savage*, 261, 263–64.

France endured such hardships, but they were at one with their countrymen in France in fearing "the Iroquois, our enemies."[63]

For the king and his counselors, for provincial administrators, priests, nuns, and *habitants* alike, the Iroquois made a perfect scapegoat for the problems of New France. A myth of the savage Iroquois formed and gathered force in people's minds, and like all myths it derived its power from its ability to explain the world to its believers. A seemingly endless Iroquois campaign of terror, bloodshed, and destruction throughout the second half of the seventeenth century made believers out of most French colonists. We do not know how many potential colonists were frightened by tales of Iroquois atrocities and so stayed in France, or wandered to other parts of Europe, instead of venturing to Canada, nor do we know precisely how many settlers were persuaded to leave New France by the Iroquois peril. The common people of New France (some 95 percent of the population) had practically no role in formulating or implementing French policy toward native inhabitants, and their opinions about that policy are largely lost to us. But they could not avoid its repercussions. Most *habitants* preferred the peace and independence of their *côtes*, well away from governors and *intendants, seigneurs* and priests. But their world at the French-Iroquois cultural frontier was repeatedly embroiled in warfare. They had not created the strife; they simply endured it. Some sought refuge in France, others stayed; all grew to know and fear the Iroquois as treacherous savages.[64]

Such an interpretation of the Five Nations, based on the world view, assumptions, and experience of colonial French men and women, is hardly surprising or unreasonable. The colonial French representation of themselves, their colony, and their enemy—the Iroquois—stood in sharp contrast to the counterpart Iroquois representations. Neither assessment negated that of its adversary, nor should we now attempt to replace either perspective with a single omniscient view. More to the point, we should recognize that while the common people

[63]On the poor reputation of Canada, see Moogk, "Reluctant Exiles," 463, 465–66; quotation from Pierre Boucher, *Histoire Véritable et Naturelle des Moeurs & Productions du Pays de la Nouvelle France* (Paris, 1664), 465. Though intended as a promotional account, Boucher's *Histoire* described in great, horrifying detail Iroquois torture and cannibalism. See also Philip Boucher, "French Images of America," especially 221, 225–26.

[64]Calling the French perception of the Iroquois as savages a "myth" does not imply that, for the French, such a characterization was inappropriate or "untrue." It may have been appropriate for seventeenth-century Canadians (and many who followed). I do hope, however, to point out the cultural and historical specificity of such "truths," questioning their universal status.

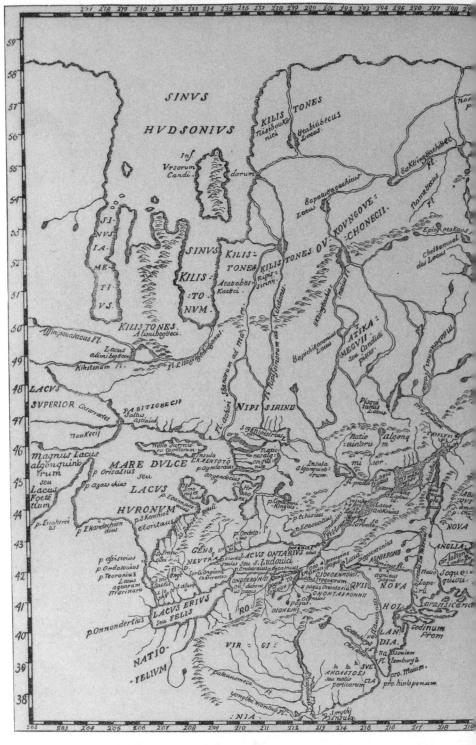

Tabula Novae Franciae, Anno 1660, from François Du Creux's *Historiae Canadensis* (Paris, 1664), reproduced in facsimile in Reuben Gold Thwaites, ed., *The Jesuit Relations and Allied Documents*, 73 vols. (Cleveland, 1899–1901), vol. 46, frontispiece, courtesy of Special Collections, Knight Library, University of Oregon. Du Creux's map of New France emphasizes the expansion of New France into the Great Lakes and beyond and the strategic Iroquois position that could menace such plans.

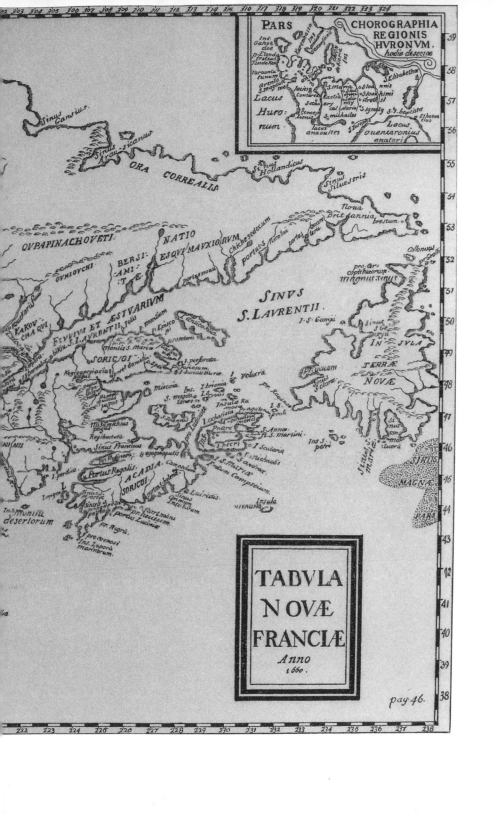

PARS

CHOROGRAPHIA
REGIONIS
HVRONVM.
hodie desectae

 Int.
Gahoé
doe
p.Etanda
fretus
Tandaket

Vanrabata

Tarumia
tunum
amel.
S.magdal
not

Iacilg
Contarea
Secuari
ary
Someru
lionu
S.michaelis

S.maria
iata
cal Odaria

S.Iod
S.Ioannis
S.Ioachimi
dreth
S.Igrely

SEliakethá

S.ignely
S.I.baptiste

Lacus

Huro-

rum

lacus
anaouites

S.Iofeph

Lacus
ouentaronius
anatari

Ethoua
rius

OVPAPINACHOVETI:

NATIO

BERSI-
:AMI-
:T:E:

ESQVIMAVXIORVM

Chichesedecum

portus

Tirolas

portus
lenri

S.Brus
Hollandicus

Sinus
Siluestris

Noua
Brittannia,
brestum.

Collonnas
pro.Ars
copithacorum
magnus sinus

SINVS
S.LAVRENTII.

J.S.Georgi

Sinus
S.Ge
urgu

IN·SVLA
TERRÆ

NOVÆ

FLVVIVS ET ÆSTVARIVM

SORICOI

Sinus Francius

ACADIA
SORICOI.

Portus Regalis.

TABVLA
NOVÆ
FRANCIÆ
Anno
1660.

SIRTIS
MAGNÆ

PARS

of New France encountered the Iroquois primarily as savages, the Iroquois encountered New France, *not* as a quaint, peculiar fragment of early-modern, rural France, but as an intrusive enterprise of zealous missionaries, occasional traders, and marauding soldiers.

The New France that the Five Nations knew, then, was not the world of the *habitants,* even though that world affected them and the way they would be interpreted by history. Face to face, they encountered a Canada of priests and warriors, each of whom proved determined to destroy the Iroquois vision of peace. Although Jesuit missionaries still held out hope that they could subdue Iroquoia through their "invasion within," by the mid-1660s military conquest of the Five Nations had become official policy.[65]

[65]This characterization of the Jesuit program comes from Axtell, *Invasion Within;* see especially 71–127. On the French policy of dealing with the Iroquois through military means, which emerged clearly with the dispatch of the 1,200-man Carignan-Salières regiment in 1665, see Eccles, *France in America,* rev. ed., 69–70; Trigger, *Natives and Newcomers,* 284. See also "Instructions to Gaudais, Paris, May 7, 1663," in Nish, ed., *French Regime,* 47: "The principal menace to the inhabitants being the Iroquois, who at all moments attack the French ... and massacre them cruelly, ... the King has resolved, if it is necessary, to send next year some regular troops to the country." See also Vachon, *Dreams of Empire,* 226, 227, who quotes the Jesuit priest Paul le Jeune, writing to the king in 1662, "These perfidious people [the Iroquois] will rob your crown of one of its jewels if your powerful hand does not act.... Your salvation is perhaps wrapped up with the salvation of so many people which will be lost if they are not succoured by Your Majesty's attention" (excerpt of *Jesuit Relations* reproduced 227). On the French campaigns against the Mohawks, see "Papers Relating to De Courcelles' and De Tracy's Expeditions against the Mohawk Indians, 1665–6," in E. B. O'Callaghan, ed., *The Documentary History of the State of New York,* 4 vols. (Albany, 1849–51), 1:57–84.

7

Kinship, Conversion, Conquest, and the French-Iroquois Discourse of Frustration

These poor Barbarians feel like fathers, brothers, children, and nephews toward us when we call them by those names.
>   —Jesuit Superior Jean de Quen among the
>   Iroquois (1657)

If you love, as you say you do, our souls, love our bodies also, and let us be henceforth but one nation.
>   —Iroquois plea to French missionaries

The "Black Robes," the Jesuit missionaries of New France, willingly accepted the name "father" from their new Iroquois flock. Indeed they expected the title, as well as the role and authority that it implied in the Catholic, European world they represented. But the meaning of kinship, together with its arrangements and terminology, varied across the French-Iroquois cultural frontier. Jesuit priests, despite their apparent cooperation with Iroquois objectives and their respect for native culture, never intended to become Iroquois kinsmen. And few among the Five Nations were inclined to submit to the Jesuits' assimilationist plans. The French and the Five Nations each sought the transformation of the other, on terms dictated largely by themselves. In this chapter I detail the discourse of confusion and frustration that emerged as New France and Iroquoia met and clashed during the seventeenth century. Although their aims were mutually exclusive, each group worked to incorporate the other in its distinctive program of civilization and peace. Given the conflicting objectives, the self-confidence, and the zeal of each, cooperation was seldom possible. Indeed, in retrospect, violence and bloodshed seem to have been inevitable.

But the disaster of French-Iroquois relations did not seem preordained to many people of the Five Nations or to some French colonists, most notably the missionaries of the Society of Jesus. After a brief look at the late 1650s and the early 1660s—a turning point in the French-Iroquois discourse—I return to the earlier part of the century and narrate the course of Iroquois peace efforts with the French and New France's Indian allies. Persistently, the Five Nations attempted to bring about kinship and peace with the Canadians, both natives and European newcomers. And just as persistently, for its own reasons, New France obstructed the Iroquois program of peace. Although the Jesuits, unlike most officials and *habitants,* could imagine Iroquois conversion and subordination without violence, by the 1660s they joined their more cynical colonial colleagues in a firm consensus, agreeing that the Five Nations required humbling by force. After experiencing the military assaults of New France, and still facing unstable frontiers to the east and south in the 1660s, the Iroquois were a people in crisis. How they faced that crisis by drawing creatively on their history is the subject of the book's epilogue.

By 1643, the French Jesuit scholar François Du Creux was hard at work in Bordeaux, having been selected by his superiors to write a history chronicling the apostolic labors of the Society of Jesus in New France. Some twenty years later, in 1664, the *Historia Canadensis* was published in Paris by Sebastien Cramoisy (publisher of the *Jesuit Relations*) in a sumptuous quarto edition of more than eight hundred pages. Du Creux took his history, in ten books, through the year 1656. Perhaps with the realization that he would never compose another ten, he felt compelled to mention, at the very end of his master work, an event beyond its chronological scope. "Before, however, I do conclude I must warn the reader in anticipation that Christianity among the Iroquois was almost destroyed in the next year on the feast of St. Joseph [1658].... The Iroquois had formed a base plot,... and had determined to destroy utterly the French, both priest and laymen, as many as were among them, and to spare none." But the French uncovered the alleged conspiracy, foiled its apparent intention with their escape, and so "the cruelty of the still faithless tribe was mocked." After an auspicious beginning, with the surprising peace of 1653, and the advent of the Jesuit mission among the Iroquois, the barely averted St. Joseph's Day massacre was a serious blow to Jesuit dreams. Yet Du Creux reserved judgment and the hope, indeed the "certainty[,] that Faith still lives in some of them, who are perchance to be the seed which the Lord God of Sabaoth has left that the whole race may not perish as Sodom."[1]

Du Creux wrote with confidence and determination regarding the Iroquois mission and published the *Historia Canadensis* before French frustration with the Five Nations had hardened into a policy of violent conquest. The Jesuits, in contrast to other French metropolitans and colonials, remained less willing to see the Five Nations as a people chronically and irredeemably savage. Nonetheless, in the same year that the *Historia* appeared, Louis XIV's chief minister Jean-Baptiste Colbert, the controller-general of finances, wrote to the new bishop at Quebec, François de Laval, "His Majesty has decided to send a good regiment of infantry to Canada at the end of this year or in February to crush the Iroquois." In the previous year the governor of Trois Rivières, Pierre Boucher, had pleaded with the king and Colbert for relief from the Iroquois fury. By November 1664 the minister of war, Michel le Tellier, ordered the troops sent, and in the summer of 1665 a force of some 1,200 men, the entire Carignan-Salières regiment under the leadership of Louis's lieutenant-general, Alexandre de Prouville, marquis de Tracy, arrived in Canada with the specific instructions to attack and pacify the Five Nations, indeed "to carry war even to their firesides in order to exterminate them."[2]

---

[1] See introduction, Percy J. Robinson, trans., and James B. Conacher, ed., *The History of Canada or New France by Father François du Creux, S.J.* [Paris, 1664], Publications of the Champlain Society, 30, 2 vols. (Toronto, 1951) (hereafter cited as *Historia Canadensis*), 1:ix–xxvii, especially ix–xiii, for an analysis of Du Creux and his work. The final passages quoted are from ibid., 2:753–54. The "plot" and dramatic escape of the missionaries were narrated in Reuben Gold Thwaites, ed., *The Jesuit Relations and Allied Documents*, 73 vols. (Cleveland, 1896–1901), 44:213–17; and see l'Incarnation to her son, Quebec, October 4, 1658, in Joyce Marshall, trans. and ed., *Word from New France: The Selected Letters of Marie de l'Incarnation* (Toronto, 1967), 229–32.

[2] On the Carignan-Salières regiment and its role in the emerging French policy of dealing with Iroquois through force, see W. J. Eccles, *Canada under Louis XIV, 1663–1701* (Toronto, 1964), 24–25, 39–44; Eccles, *France in America*, rev. ed. (East Lansing, Mich., 1990), 69–70. The campaigns can be traced in "Papers Relating to De Courcelles' and De Tracy's Expeditions against the Mohawk Indians, 1665–6," in E. B. O'Callaghan, ed., *The Documentary History of the State of New York*, 4 vols. (Albany, N.Y., 1849–51), 1:57–84. Revealing and indispensable are the letters of the Ursuline nun in Quebec, Marie de l'Incarnation; see Marshall, ed., *Word from New France*, 307–28; Colbert to Bishop Laval is quoted in Eccles, *Canada under Louis XIV*, 22. The king's instructions to his new *intendant*, Talon, from which the quotation is drawn, characterized the Iroquois as "perpetual and irreconcilable enemies of the Colony." Their extermination was, for the king and his ministers, "a suitable remedy.... Having no

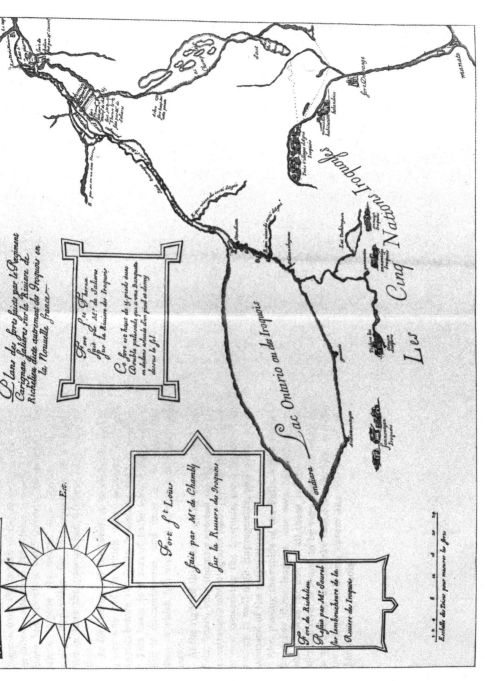

The Iroquois country and plan of forts on River Richelieu, from the *Relation* of 1664–65, in Reuben Gold Thwaites, ed., *The Jesuit Relations and Allied Documents*, vol. 49, courtesy of Special Collections, Knight Library, University of Oregon. This military map, appearing in the Jesuits' chronicles, suggests the implicit alliance between the sword and the cross against the Five Nations.

Arriving too late in the season, and exhausted from the journey, the regiment was forced to put off the invasion until the next year. But in February 1666 the French commenced their assault on the Mohawks, deemed to be the most intransigent of the Five Nations. Although this was a disastrous campaign for the French, it was followed up by another in July; but the French turned back when they met a delegation of Mohawks, led by the great Iroquois leader, the so-called Flemish Bastard, en route to New France to return French captives and sue for peace. Despite these Mohawk (and other Iroquois) peace overtures, in mid-September 1666 a massive force (1,400 men) of regular soldiers, locally raised militia, Christian Indians, and four Catholic priests set out for the Mohawk country in a campaign of devastation and terror. Before it was done, four or five villages were plundered and burned; the food destroyed was "enough to nourish all Canada for two entire years," wrote Marie de l'Incarnation. The Mohawks had offered no resistance, but instead fled into the forests, so the French had no one to kill. Certainly the puzzling lack of armed resistance—which the French attributed to cowardice—made the campaign a triumph for New France. While the French may not have actually shot or impaled a single Mohawk man or women, surely their invasion cost numerous Iroquois lives, as l'Incarnation certainly knew. "What will become of them?" she wrote in a letter to her son. "Where will they go? Their villages have been burned; their country has been sacked. The season is too advanced for them to rebuild their villages. The little grain that remains from the firing of their crops will not be enough to nourish them . . . If they go to the other nations, they will not be received for fear of causing famine." L'Incarnation nonetheless concluded, "God has destroyed them without there being a single one of them lost. Perhaps he has humbled them only for their salvation."[3]

The events of 1665–1666 suggest the essential consensus about the Iroquois that existed between Church and State in seventeenth-

---

guarantee in their words, . . . they [the Iroquois] violate their faith as often as they find the inhabitants of the Colony at their mercy." See E. B. O'Callaghan, ed., *Documents Relative to the Colonial History of the State of New-York*, 15 vols. (Albany, N.Y., 1853–87), 9:24–29; quotation from 25. For indications of the earlier identification of the Iroquois as "the principal menace to the inhabitants" of New France, and a developing consensus on the need for military action, see 9–13; the instructions ordered the commissioner to investigate the feasibility of "invading them [the Iroquois] in their fastnesses, and exterminating them in their own country . . . should it be deemed necessary" (11). The instructions are excerpted as well in Cameron Nish, ed. and trans., *The French Regime, Canadian Historical Document Series* (Scarborough, Ont., 1965), 1:47.

[3]Marshall, ed., *Word from New France*, 321–28 (quotations from 323–25, 328).

century New France, notwithstanding the contentiousness that set the Jesuits against other religious orders and the royal government. And they provide a graphic illustration of the nature of the New France that the Five Nations encountered—an intrusive, threatening regime of missionaries and soldiers. Secular authorities, as well as other missionary orders, questioned Jesuit loyalties, motives, and tactics, and they were especially skeptical about the Jesuits' conviction that Christianization might precede "Frenchification"; but it was clear that the Jesuits were one with Louis XIV and Colbert, with *Intendant* Talon, Governor Daniel de Remy, sieur de Courcelle, and General de Tracy when it came to the Iroquois. Two Jesuits, Charles Albanel and Pierre Raffeix, as well as a Sulpician priest and the regiment's regular chaplain, accompanied Tracy's invading force in the autumn of 1666.[4] And Jesuit missionaries proved as thankful for the devastation of the Iroquois, and as quick to celebrate it, as the Ursuline nun Marie de l'Incarnation.

Spiritual if not material partners in the military enterprise, the Jesuits received their first dividends in 1667 as the Iroquois mission reopened. Like Father Jacques Bruyas, toiling among the Oneidas, the Jesuit missionaries appreciated that "the [Mohawk] Campaign of monsieur de tracy among their neighbors has aided not a little in their conversion." And they realized that, as Jesuit superior in Canada François le Mercier wrote, "these blessings will continue so long as peace continues, and the latter so long as the Iroquois are kept in a state of fear." The governor, le Mercier reported, was making "strenuous exertions" to this effect, using the terror of new marches and disasters to subdue the Five Nations; "he keeps the Iroquois at peace by the fear of war." And the *intendant* too, attempting to implement Colbert's policies, cooperated in the effort to transform the apparently pacified Iroquois, and other Native Americans, into Catholics and French peasants, if not necessarily in that order.[5]

Finally, the partnership of the French sword and cross becomes

[4]Ibid., 323, 416n3.

[5]On the reopening of the Iroquois mission in 1667, see Thwaites, ed., *Jesuit Relations,* 51:81–85, 159, 175, and passim. Bruyas's statement is quoted on 131; le Mercier quotation from 169–71. On the cooperation of the military, civil, and religious establishments on Iroquois matters, see 131, 159, 169–73. The Jesuits remained aware that the conversion of the Iroquois would be a difficult task, one that would become impossible without French incentives and persuasion: gifts and military force; see, for example, the statements of Jesuit missionary among the Iroquois Jean Lamberville in 1673 (ibid., 57:127–29).

clear in the events following the 1666 invasion, when advancing Jesuit priests could assume the role of "good cops" to the Iroquois, positioning themselves against the "bad cops" represented by Tracy's regiment. In July 1667, the Fathers Jacques Fremin, Jean Pierron, and Jacques Bruyas set out to evangelize among the lower Iroquois—the Mohawks and Oneidas. "The whole country of the Iroquois was at that time so overcome with fear of a new French army," they reported, "that for several days fourteen warriors had been constantly on the watch. . . . But, by great good fortune for them and for us, instead of being enemies to them, we were Angels of peace."[6] The Mohawk party willingly became the Jesuits' porters and led them to the edge of their main village, where they "were received . . . with the customary ceremonies, and with all imaginable honor." Perhaps without realizing it, the missionaries had entered into the Iroquois discourse of peace. Once they were ushered into the village and the cabin of the principal chief, the inhabitants crowded in to gaze at the priests, "quite delighted to see among them Frenchmen, so peaceably inclined, who not long before had made their appearance there as if infuriated, setting fire to everything."[7]

The alternatives made available to the Mohawks and the rest of the Five Nations were presented clearly: to accept the "Angels of peace" or to suffer the angels of death. The Jesuits carefully represented themselves to the Iroquois as having no complicity with the military while in Iroquoia.[8] Yet the particular dualism of the Iroquois world view—in which, conceptually, good and evil could be thoroughly integrated may have allowed them to understand the union of French military and religious aims more clearly than the missionaries intended. More important, the Jesuits, even if associated with marauding French soldiers, seemed to offer the Five Nations a measure of hope, in their apparent nonviolence, in their rhetoric of kinship, and

[6]Thwaites, ed., *Jesuit Relations*, 57:185.

[7]Ibid., 185–87; quotations from 187. Note that the Mohawks here welcomed the Jesuits in a traditional fashion; it seems apparent that the pause "within three quarters of a league" from the village occurred as the opening rite of greeting in the Condolence. On the structure and function of the Condolence, see Elisabeth Tooker, "The League of the Iroquois: Its History, Politics, and Ritual," in Bruce G. Trigger, ed., *The Handbook of North American Indians: Northeast*, vol. 15 in William C. Sturtevant, gen. ed., *Handbook of North American Indians*, 20 vols. projected (Washington, D.C., 1978–), 437–40, especially 439. The remainder of the ritual encounter is described opaquely as "the customary ceremonies."

[8]Bruce G. Trigger, *Natives and Newcomers: Canada's "Heroic Age" Reconsidered* (Kingston and Montreal, 1986), 291, observed that "most Iroquois viewed the Jesuits as a pro-Iroquois faction among the French," and therefore their presence was valued, for political if not religious reasons.

in their willing participation in traditional Iroquois ceremonial discourse of words and actions.[9] The Iroquois could imagine an alternative to both French invasions, whether military or religious, and they could accept the Jesuits and other French colonists as potential converts to their own peace program.

The French policy of violence against the Five Nations may have emerged clearly only in the 1660s and become for the first time, as historian Cornelius J. Jaenen suggested, a form of interracial rather than simply intertribal warfare.[10] But the enmity between New France and Iroquoia had much deeper and longer roots.

Beginning with the career of Samuel de Champlain, indeed even before, France placed itself in the center of the intricate political and commercial networks of native North America. These French-Indian relationships were highly personal and ritually established. From the native points of view, they constituted an extension of friendship and reciprocity between people, an extension that was neither fundamentally commercial nor military, although trade and the exchange of military aid played important roles. Champlain and his colleague François Grave Du Pont, who was more sensitive and skilled in Native American affairs, first cemented ties with the Indian groups of the St. Lawrence Valley and then pushed into the interior to reach the great trading confederation, the Hurons. These Indian nations provided New France with the furs, neophytes, and allies required to make its colonial enterprise prosperous. Canadian officials and missionaries made New France the mediator between its Indian allies, maintaining peace, coordinating activity, and holding the balance of power. Because many of New France's native allies had been traditional enemies of the Five Nations, the Iroquois remained conspicuously absent—indeed were excluded—from the French orbit. But

[9]Indeed, in 1656 and 1657, Jesuits even acted to persuade the Huron refugees in their midst to accept Iroquois propositions to join the Five Nations and their Huron kinspeople in Iroquoia (provided that the Jesuits accompanied them). Such action by the Jesuits must have seemed a powerful confirmation of the Five Nations' expansive vision. See Thwaites, ed., *Jesuit Relations,* 44:73–77; Trigger, *Natives and Newcomers,* 279, 290.

[10]Cornelius J. Jaenen, *Friend and Foe: Aspects of the French-Amerindian Cultural Contact in the Sixteenth and Seventeenth Centuries* (New York, 1976), 136. Francis Jennings, *The Ambiguous Iroquois Empire: The Covenant Chain Confederation of Indian Tribes with English Colonies* (New York, 1984), suggested the genocidal implications of the French decision to deal with the Iroquois by force after 1664 when he referred to Louis XIV's new policy, aptly, as "a final solution to Canada's Iroquois problem."

France's entrance into native political geography solidified these rivalries and made them more dangerous.[11]

The political landscape proved too small to accommodate the French and the Iroquois in the seventeenth century. The Iroquois entrance into the alliance constructed by New France threatened to destroy its balance and endanger the New World vision of the French. On the one hand, the French believed that an agreement with the Iroquois might antagonize their current Indian allies. On the other hand, peace with the Five Nations might upset New France's own position in the alliance it had built. Canadian officials feared that the Iroquois might replace them as the guiding force in the alliance, that the Five Nations would seduce their allies, divert the fur trade to New Netherland (or New York), undermine New France's religious mission, and impose its own barbarous regime.[12]

Yet Iroquoia beckoned to the priests and fur traders of Canada. It appeared to be fertile ground for planting the Church's seed, and no people so much as the Iroquois seemed to require the evangelizing and civilizing work of the Jesuits. Iroquois hostility and their reputation as fierce cannibals only seemed to inspire the missionaries of New France to further efforts. The difficulty of Iroquois conversion represented a challenge that Jesuit pride could not resist. And given the missionaries' willingness to accept, even to embrace, martyrdom among the "savages," few places more promising than Iroquoia existed in the New World. Father Jacques Buteux, among the Algonquins and Montagnais in 1652, confided to his native charges that he had no "dread of the fire of the Iroquois." Buteux remarked, "I should think myself fortunate to be reserved for the fire; their cruelty is great and to be burned by slow fire is indeed horrible torture, but there is nothing that the grace of God cannot overcome." Unperturbed and with "no sign of fear on his face," according to Jesuit historian Du

[11]The best recent treatment of the native political geography of New France and the geopolitical context of French-Iroquois relations is Trigger, *Natives and Newcomers*, especially 172–200, 226–343. Although I disagree with some of its interpretation, which is more economically determined than I find convincing, I greatly admire the depth and sophistication of its analysis.

[12]See ibid., 182–83, 200, 311–12, 319. Although New France saw the Five Nations as its chief enemy, and although Champlain, as early as the late 1620s, advocated their extermination or subjugation, that policy was not only impossible to execute but was deemed by others to be undesirable. French traders especially saw the Mohawks and other Iroquois nations as important barriers to the development of trade between the Montagnais and Algonquins, on the one hand, and the Dutch on the other (311–12, 319). See also W. J. Eccles, *France in America*, rev. ed. (East Lansing, Mich., 1990), 48.

Creux, Father Buteux later had his chance and paid the ultimate price as a martyr among the Iroquois.[13]

Others in New France also felt an attraction to Iroquoia. Fur traders believed that the Iroquois might become valuable suppliers of pelts and contribute to New France's prosperity—or at least profit individual Frenchmen—if they could be drawn away from Dutch and English markets.[14] These possibilities coaxed some in New France to try peace with the Five Nations. But in the end, the failure of such religious and economic experiments confirmed the generally held position that New France's policy toward the Iroquois should be one of hostility.

Until the 1640s, Iroquois-French conflict never assumed the major dimensions that would characterize it throughout the rest of the seventeenth century.[15] As we have seen, as early as 1609 Champlain skirmished with the Mohawks when he accompanied a band of Algonquins near Lake Champlain. Other battles followed in which the French and the Iroquois—most often the Mohawks—fought on opposite sides. Yet these early instances of hostility did not result in much loss of life, nor did they determine the course of Iroquois-French relations.[16] In 1622, two Mohawks appeared at Quebec to

[13]Countless examples of the Jesuit quest for martyrdom, especially among the Five Nations, pepper the contemporary sources, but see Du Creux, *Historia Canadensis*, 2:622–23, which includes a description of Buteux's death at the hands of the Iroquois and a eulogy; quotation from 623.

[14]See Trigger, *Natives and Newcomers*, 190, 315, and especially 319–20. In 1634, a Dutch surgeon, Dutch West India Company official, and momentary diplomat, Harmen Meyndertsz van den Bogaert, reported that French traders had visited the Oneidas in their homeland in an attempt to form a commercial relationship, one that would have been considered as illegal in New France as it was in New Netherland. See Charles T. Gehring and William A. Starna, trans. and eds., *A Journey into Mohawk and Oneida Country, 1634–1635: The Journal of Harmen Meyndertsz van den Bogaert* (Syracuse, N.Y., 1988), 12–13. The Gehring and Starna edition supersedes that published as the "Narrative of a Journey into the Mohawk and Oneida Country, 1634–1635," in J. Franklin Jameson, ed., *Narratives of New Netherland* (New York, 1909), 148, 149.

[15]For a general understanding and alternative interpretations of Iroquois-French relations in the first half of the seventeenth century see the following: George T. Hunt, *The Wars of the Iroquois: A Study in Intertribal Trade Relations* (Madison, 1940), an important work, though flawed by the ethnocentric ascription of Western economic thought and behavior to the Five Nations; Bruce G. Trigger, *The Children of Aataentsic: A History of the Huron People to 1660*, 2 vols. (Montreal, 1976); Trigger, *Natives and Newcomers*, Jennings, *Ambiguous Iroquois Empire*, a lively revisionist history of the Iroquois, which is more convincing in its analysis of the eighteenth than the seventeenth century. While I greatly admire Jennings's work, it tends, perhaps inadvertently, to perpetuate an image of the "imperial" Iroquois.

[16]This skirmish is described by Champlain in W. L. Grant, ed., *Voyages of Samuel de Champlain, 1604–1618, Original Narratives of Early American History*, gen. ed., J. Franklin Jameson (New York, 1907), 157–66; later expeditions, in 1610 and 1615, are narrated on 178–85 and 285–96. See also Trigger, *Natives and Newcomers*, who argued that between 1608 and 1615,

begin informal negotiations of peace. That peace with the Five Nations was a distinct possibility became clearer in 1623, and the French worried about the implications of such a concord, especially if it were concluded between their Indian allies and the Iroquois without French mediation. Recollet Fathers Joseph le Caron and Nicholas Viel and Brother Gabriel Sagard hurried to Huronia to prevent peace between the Iroquois and Hurons, concerned that such a pact would divert Huron furs through Iroquoia, away from Canada. Nonetheless, the Iroquois journeyed to Trois Rivières in the summer of 1624 and agreed to a general peace. The Iroquois demonstrated their commitment to peace by overlooking, after French mediation, a murder committed by a Montagnais delegate on an earlier mission to Iroquoia.[17]

The 1624 peace did not last, and the skirmishes the French called collectively *la petite guerre* returned to the Iroquois-French frontier. During this time, the Iroquois continued to pursue the hope of peace, while the French confused the Iroquois with their inconsistency and frustrated their vision. The Five Nations did not press their advantage against the Canadian Indians after their victory over the Mahicans, or during the period of instability in Canada following the Kirkes' temporary conquest of New France in 1629. This apparent "failure" to consolidate their military gains suggests that the Five Nations were not engaged in a course of conquest. They continued to participate in a cycle of feud, a traditional form of warfare that also included the possibility of a traditional Iroquois peace. Prisoner exchanges and armistices punctuated periods of small-scale raiding. While Champlain, desperate in the face of isolation and starvation in 1629, first contemplated seizing a Mohawk town and then, in 1633, formulated plans to invade and conquer Iroquoia, independent French fur traders ventured to the lands of the Oneidas and Onondagas to open peaceful channels of commerce. By 1633 the Iroquois again approached the Indian allies of New France with offers of peace.[18] In

despite Champlain's involvement in attacks on them, the Iroquois displayed little hostility to the French (181–82); see also 308–9.

[17]Hunt, *Wars of the Iroquois*, 69–70. See also George M. Wrong, ed., H. H. Langton, trans., *The Long Journey to the Country of the Hurons by Father Gabriel Sagard* [Paris, 1632], *Publications of the Champlain Society*, 25 (Toronto, 1939). Sagard made no mention of this purpose, but that goal is mentioned in Pierre François Xavier de Charlevoix, *History and General Description of New France* [1744], ed. and trans. John Dawson Gilmary Shea, 6 vols. (New York, 1866–72 [micropub. in Western Americana: Frontier History series, New Haven, Conn., 1975, reels 103–4]), 2:34–35.

[18]The confusion of signals sent by the French to Iroquoia can be seen in Trigger, *Natives*

his 1634 report, Jesuit Superior Paul le Jeune requested two additional priests for the Huron mission in anticipation of this accord, which might open Iroquoia to French missionaries: "If they [the Hurons] make peace with the Iroquois, for I am told that it is being negotiated, a number more will be needed, as we must enter all the stationary tribes. If these people receive the faith, they will cry with hunger, and there will be no one to feed them."[19]

By 1635 the Iroquois had established peaceful relations with New France's Indian allies. In Laurentia, the eastern tribes of the Iroquois worked out an understanding with the Algonquins and Montagnais, while in the west the Senecas enjoyed relative harmony with the Hurons. In the spring of 1634 the Hurons had attacked the western Iroquois, but they were repulsed. Instead of pressing their advantage, the Senecas made peace.[20] New France seems not to have been involved officially in these accords, and it expressed suspicion about them. "Those best informed," reported le Jeune, "believe that this is a ruse of those [the Five Nations] who . . . are striving to divert, through their agency, the Hurons from their commerce with our French."[21]

When this interlude of peace finally ended later in the 1630s, the Hurons, not the Iroquois, caused the breach. The historian George T. Hunt concluded, "It is quite evident that the Iroquois, far from 'throwing off the mask' and invading Huronia, were remaining religiously at home."[22] Nevertheless, the Hurons attacked Iroquoia; in response, the Iroquois ventured into Huronia only to conduct the traditional forms of retaliation characteristic of the feud, meanwhile continuing their efforts to construct peace. As the Five Nations pursued peace on their traditional terms, the French, negotiating on their own behalf and for their Indian allies, demanded a peace "so vague as to give the Iroquois no privileges at all," according to Hunt. Rebuffs by New France and the Hurons finally pushed the Iroquois in the

---

and Newcomers, 200. The visit by French traders is recorded in Bogaert, *Journey into Mohawk Country,* 12–13. These traders operated on their own behalf, circumventing controls of French officials and the Hundred Associates. On Iroquois efforts to arrange peace with New France's Indian allies in 1633, see Thwaites, ed., *Jesuit Relations,* 5:209.

[19]Thwaites, ed., *Jesuit Relations,* 6:57.

[20]Ibid., 8:115–16.

[21]Ibid., 8:61.

[22]George T. Hunt, *Wars of the Iroquois,* 73. Hunt was quick to accuse the Iroquois of belligerence, which he attributed (I think ill advisedly) to their quest for middleman status in the fur trade. Nonetheless, here he challenged the eighteenth-century French Jesuit historian Charlevoix (*History and General Description of New France,* 2:93–94), who argued that the Iroquois threw off their masks, making their alleged treachery known and felt, as they supposedly invaded Huronia.

1640s to begin what Hunt called the "long and desolating wars of the Iroquois." In 1645, looking back regretfully on the Huron failure of nerve and the forfeited chance for peace in 1640, Iroquois orator Kiotsaeton asked the Hurons, "It is five days ago [that is, five years] since you had a pouch filled with porcelain beads and other presents, all ready to come and seek peace. What made you change your minds? That pouch will upset, the presents will fall out and break, they will be dispersed; and you will lose courage."[23]

And so the *petite guerre* developed into something greater and more destructive, a conflict debilitating enough for the French and Hurons to make them more interested in Iroquois peace efforts. In 1645, New France took the initiative, sending Iroquois prisoners home with a proposal for negotiations. An Iroquois delegation appeared at Trois Rivières in July to begin negotiating the first formal treaty of friendship between the French, their Indian allies, and the Iroquois.[24] These efforts reflected the long-standing interest of the Iroquois in achieving peace in their world.

From July 5 to 15, the Iroquois led the French and Indians—Algonquins, Montagnais, and Hurons—through negotiations taking the traditional form of the Condolence Ceremony. In a masterly ritual performance by Mohawk spokesman Kiotsaeton, the Iroquois presented a series of proposals symbolically underscored by gifts of wampum. They sought to forgive and forget the causes of previous hostility, end the cycle of revenge, smooth the paths between their countries, and bind the various people together in peace. At one point Kiotsaeton took a Frenchman and an Algonquin by the arm, and as the three were joined together he intoned, "Here is the knot that binds us inseparably; nothing can part us. Even if the lightning were to fall upon us, it could not separate us; for, if it cuts off the arm that holds you to us, we will at once seize each other by the other arm."[25] In such a manner, the Mohawk spokesman dramatized the amalgamation of these former enemies.

What the Iroquois had in mind might have become clearer to the French when the Mohawks complained about the escape or abduction of French captives among them. If François Marguerie and Thomas Godefroy had remained in Iroquoia, Kiotsaeton remarked, "they would be married by this time; we would be but one Nation, and I

[23] Ibid., 74–75; Thwaites, ed., *Jesuit Relations*, 27:263.
[24] The Jesuit description of these involved proceedings in 1645 is in ibid., 27:229–305.
[25] Ibid., 7:261.

would be one of you."[26] When the Iroquois departed from Trois
Rivières on July 15, Kiotsaeton bade the French, "Adieu my brothers;
I am one of your relatives. I am going to carry back good news to *our*
country." As quoted in the *Jesuit Relations*, the diplomat Kiotsaeton
referred to Iroquoia as "notre pays" ("our country"), rather than as
"mon pays" ("my country"): did the former term imply Iroquoia's
collectivity—including the French as well as Kiotsaeton's kinspeople—
and suggest that the Iroquois-French peace was meant to construct a
single people and a single country? In a follow-up diplomatic exchange, the Iroquois reaffirmed their intention to merge their country
with the French and their native allies: "All the country that lies
between us is full of Bears, of Deer, of Elk, of Beaver, and of numerous
other animals. . . . This present invites you to hunt, we shall benefit by
your skill; we shall roast the animals on the same spit, and we shall
eat on one side, and you on the other."[27]

In that return visit to Trois Rivières in September, representatives
of the Iroquois confirmed the peace and invited Indian and French
delegates to Iroquoia, where the Five Nations would provide the hospitality reserved for friends and kinsmen: soft mats, a warm fire, good
food, and soothing ointment to heal wounds. The Iroquois indicated
their commitment to peace by invoking these symbols of social life,
conversation, and harmony, and they declared their aversion to warfare by stating metaphorically "that the Iroquois chiefs did nothing
but smoke in their country, and that their calumets were always in
their mouths." Again they assured the French that they would find
wives in Iroquoia.[28] And when the proceedings concluded so agree-
ably, a Christian Huron, Jean Baptiste Atironta, proclaimed sentiments he shared with the Iroquois: "It is done. We are brothers. The
conclusion has been reached; now we all are relatives,—Hiroquois,
Huron, Algonquins, and French; we are now but one and the same
people."[29]

Significantly, no one in these negotiations mentioned trade, although many historians see the treaty as an attempt by the Iroquois
to serve their commercial interests. The point of these negotiations

[26]Ibid., 263.

[27]Ibid., 272–73; quotation from 273, my emphasis; the French is given on 270. The
quotation from the follow-up meeting appears on 289–91.

[28]Ibid., 279–91 (quotation from 285). These presents and words came through a Frenchman, whom the Iroquois returned to New France, and they were followed up by additional
gifts and remarks by the leader of the Iroquois delegation.

[29]Ibid., 289.

for the Five Nations was to condole and forget former injuries, end the cycle of feud and bloodshed, and bind the various people together into one commonwealth, as the prophet Deganawidah had prescribed. The particular treaty proceedings of 1645 must be seen as part of a much larger process to extend the Iroquois domain of peace, one that had begun in earlier times with the formation of each of the five nations and the League itself, and that continued beyond into the seventeenth century.

The Hurons, culturally Iroquoian neighbors of the Five Nations, appeared to be the most important new recruit for the Iroquois League of Peace. Warfare with the Hurons had developed out of the disappointment and frustration caused by their refusal to join the Iroquois confederation and by their threats to the Five Nations' experiment. Despite Iroquois hopes, the Hurons found the Five Nations' invitation unappealing. They had formed a confederation of their own, by much the same process of village fusion that brought the Iroquois League into existence. Satisfied with their autonomous way of life and their separate prosperity, and hard-pressed by New France to reject peace with the Iroquois, they snubbed the Five Nations in favor of New France's affections. Consequently, the Huron-Iroquois conflict continued, amid numerous attempts by the Five Nations to effect a peaceful amalgamation, until the Hurons were eventually devastated by poor harvests, famine and disease, French-induced factionalism, and, by 1649, Iroquois assaults.[30]

Much has been made of the "secret proceedings" during the peace negotiations in 1645 between the French and Iroquois, in which the French are said to have abandoned those of their Indian allies who

---

[30]Trigger, *Natives and Newcomers*, 250–73, detailed the destruction of the Hurons. Trigger, however, attributed escalating hostilities in the 1640s to Iroquois aggression, which he then attempted to explain in economic terms. While I respect Trigger's position, I believe the alleged aggressiveness of the Iroquois is problematic and open to alternative interpretations, and I am not convinced that Iroquois actions in these hostilities stemmed from economic concerns. See W. J. Eccles's critique of Hunt's economic interpretation, and of Trigger's more sophisticated revision, in Eccles, *France in America*, rev. ed., 46–47. According to Eccles, the Iroquois sought neither to become middlemen in the fur trade, nor to obtain furs by raiding and pillaging activities: "Both of these hypotheses are refuted by the fact that, of 147 recorded Iroquois raids on the Hurons and French between 1626 and 1666, on only seven occasions were furs or other goods seized. On most occasions the furs were left to rot" (46). Persistent Iroquois efforts to effect peace with the Hurons are interpreted ungraciously by Trigger as treacherous attempts to divide members of the Huron confederation. Nonetheless, as Trigger shows, a pro-Iroquois group developed among the Hurons which took Iroquois peace overtures seriously and advocated accepting them (see Trigger, *Natives and Newcomers*, 263–65).

had not converted to Catholicism.[31] The nature of a separate, secret agreement between the governor, Charles Huault, chevalier de Montmagny, and Kiotsaeton—if it occurred at all—remains obscure. Legendary or real, harmless or sinister: who can now say? It is not surprising that the Iroquois would choose to negotiate with the several native groups one-by-one, hoping to bring them into their League individually. And it is unreasonable to expect that the Iroquois would simply defer to French authority and mediation when such peoples could make treaties on their own behalf. It was not clear that the unconverted Indians of New France were merely subjects of the French Crown. Could the governor of New France be trusted to speak for those over whom he held such ambiguous jurisdiction? The peace of 1645 did not hold for long, but we do not know which side—or sides—broke it. If we can infer motives from later behavior, we can agree with Hunt: "Everything considered, the peace seemed to have been made in earnest by the Mohawks."[32]

The peace of 1645 disintegrated in the fall of 1646, marked by the martyrdom of Jesuit Father Isaac Jogues. Jogues traveled to Iroquoia in May 1646 and again in September of that year. While among the Mohawks, he antagonized them and seemed to pose a serious threat to the health and vitality of the communities he visited. Mohawks believed his prayers were sorceries that destroyed the success of their hunting and planting. From the Iroquois perspective, the "wizard" Jogues brought disease and destruction to Mohawk villages.[33] Even the Jesuits had to acknowledge the connection between their missions and epidemics: "It is true that, speaking humanely, these Barbarians have apparent reasons for thus reproaching us,—in as much as the scourges which humble the proud precede us or accompany us wherever we go."[34] After refusing to participate in hunts and other subsistence tasks, annoying townspeople with his incessant criticism and religious harangues, disrupting their rituals, engaging in mysterious

[31]See Francis Jennings et al., eds., *The History and Culture of Iroquois Diplomacy: An Interdisciplinary Guide to the Treaties of the Six Nations and Their League* (Syracuse, N.Y. 1985), 153, for a reprinted account of the "secret articles"; see also 134 for Mary A. Druke's analysis; Hunt, *Wars of the Iroquois*, 80–81; Francis Jennings, *Ambiguous Iroquois Empire*, 92–95.

[32]Hunt, *Wars of the Iroquois*, 81.

[33]On Jogues's mission to the Iroquois and his death at their hands, see Thwaites, ed., *Jesuit Relations*, 29:51–53; 31:73–75, 121–23; 43:291. Pertinent documents are also assembled in the "Jogues Papers," New-York Historical Society, *Collections*, 2d ser., 3:194–228.

[34]Thwaites, ed., *Jesuit Relations*, 31:121–23.

sorceries, and inflicting famine and pestilence upon them, Father Isaac Jogues was eventually killed by the Mohawks.

Following the death of Jogues, the Iroquois, French, and New France's Indian allies were again enmeshed in war. The "Beaver Wars" or "Wars of the Iroquois" have been thoroughly chronicled from the time they occurred. And in most accounts the Five Nations appeared as bloody aggressors, intent on commercial gain and empire. Yet one might as easily note the persistent attempt by the people of the Iroquois League to maintain or establish peace.

The allegedly intransigent and bellicose Mohawks, for example, "repeatedly offered to make peace with the French" throughout the 1640s, as Bruce Trigger has noted, and only in 1650 did they finally initiate an attack on New France. Other Iroquois tribes also sought peace with the French, and simultaneously they worked to create harmony and an amalgamation with the Hurons, perhaps New France's most important native allies. By 1647, among the deeply factionalized Hurons, traditionalists favored the expulsion of the Jesuits—whom they blamed for the fractious divisions and the devastating epidemics that afflicted them—and urged that Iroquois overtures of peace be accepted. Increasingly, these traditionalists advocated alliance and amalgamation with the Five Nations over continued attachment to the Jesuits and New France. Canadian missionaries and officials viewed such developments with mixed emotions and ultimately with alarm. On the one hand, they craved the relief that peace with the Five Nations might produce, but on the other hand, they imagined the implications of such a Five Nations' diplomatic victory for their own religious, economic, and political program. The French therefore worked against the Huron-Iroquois accords, preferring to see the construction of aggressive anti-Iroquois coalitions (including the Susquehanocks and other traditional foes of the Five Nations) and the division of the Iroquois League by the isolation of individual tribes, especially the Mohawks. Meanwhile, the French turned their own backs on Iroquois peace missions to New France.[35]

[35]Trigger, *Natives and Newcomers*, 336, 264–66. Trigger argues that the Mohawks' peace with France "did not include the Indian tribes that traded with the French"; the Mohawks hoped to encourage a position of neutrality for the French which resembled that of New Netherland (336). It strikes me as reasonable, consistent, and hardly diabolical that the Five Nations would seek to deal with various groups—French and native—separately, or that French neutrality or disengagement would be sought during Iroquois negotiations with native groups considered allies or satellites by New France. And given the Iroquois overtures to

Another, more bloody round of warfare ensued in which the Hurons were dispersed and New France faced an unprecedented peril. In the midst of their travail, the French continued to pursue solutions of war rather than of peace. And as if to underscore the complicity of Church and State, cross and sword, in 1650 New France dispatched Father Gabriel Druillettes, then a Jesuit missionary among the Abenakis of northern New England, to negotiate a military and trade agreement in Boston. While affecting an interest in intercolonial commerce, the French had something else in mind. The fundamental purpose of the pact was conquest, that is, the construction of "a league offensive and defensive . . . against the Iroquois," a people who—the French attempted to persuade the English—"ought to be our common Enemies." Though initially optimistic about the responses of New England's leaders, Druillettes and his French colleagues did not see their efforts bear any fruit, and the fury surrounding New France only seemed to grow.[36]

Yet once again in the early 1650s, the Five Nations refused to press their advantages in war and instead attempted to follow their prophet, Deganawidah, in the pursuit of peace. By examining this fragile moment, when the Five Nations sought to apply the lessons of their culture and history to the dangerous context of the New World they shared with Europeans, we can see Iroquois belief and ideology in action.

How might an Iroquois have made sense of the circumstances that surrounded the Five Nations in the mid-seventeenth century, especially as he or she contemplated those strange neighbors to the north in New France? North America in the 1650s was as much a New World for the people of the Five Nations as it was for the people of Europe. An earlier way of life had been irrevocably altered by the advent of Christian Europeans, who disturbed whatever fragile bal-

---

the Hurons, which many Hurons found relatively appealing, and which the French viewed with concern, the Five Nations appear as the primary architects of peace during the period. See Thwaites, ed., *Jesuit Relations,* 33:71–73, 117–27, 229–33.

[36]Thwaites, ed., *Jesuit Relations,* 36:75–81, 83–111; Council of Quebec to the Commissioners of New England, Quebec, 20 June 1651, in O'Callaghan, ed., *Documents Relative to the History of New York,* 9:5–6; quotation is from 5: See also "Extract from the Registers of the Ancient Council of this Country [20 June 1651]," 6; "Commission to the Rev. Father Druillettes and Mr. Jean Godefroy as Ambassadors to New England," 6–7. The devastation and terror of the Iroquois, which encircled New France at this time, is apparent in the entries of the "Journal of the Jesuit Fathers, in the year 1651," in Thwaites, ed., *Jesuit Relations,* 36:113–49.

ance had existed in the universe that contained Iroquoia. The Iroquois had painstakingly constructed an internal harmony out of the chaos that had ruled their lives in an earlier time. The political mythology of the Iroquois told of the coming of a great prophet, Deganawidah, who ended the bloodshed between nations and kinspeople and who provided a charter of peace known as the Great Law. Now, in the 1650s, though the Five Nations found themselves in new circumstances, they recognized the older dangers they had faced in the past: chronic, bloody, crippling warfare; the terror of vulnerability to total war; the specter of death, unbearable grief, and the resulting insanity that bred further killing. How might a lost balance be recovered and peace be established in this new world? The most obvious and available solution was near at hand, embodied in their social and political structures, in their ritual practices, in their potent history and mythology; they would adhere to the teachings of Deganawidah.

"At last we have peace," proclaimed Father François le Mercier, Superior of the Jesuit mission in New France, in the summer of 1653. "It is the Iroquois that have made peace. Or, rather, let us say it is God; for this stroke is so sudden, this change so unexpected, these tendencies in Barbarian minds so surprising, that, it must be admitted, a genius more exalted than that of man guided this work." Indeed, during what seemed to be New France's darkest hour—as the missions lay in ruin, with the fur trade completely shut down, and as "a Mohawk storm howled" about Montreal and Trois-Rivières—a new day suddenly dawned. Each of the Five Nations approached the French "to learn whether the hearts of the French would be inclined to peace."[37]

Why did the Iroquois suddenly seek peace? The development so shocked the priests and nuns of New France that they could explain it only in terms of divine intervention. Historians since have eschewed that explanation, but they have not been much more successful in deciphering Iroquois motivation.[38] The Iroquois wanted and actively sought peace in the way they thought most reasonable—a way based on a model of domestic harmony, within the confines of an expanding

[37]Thwaites, ed., *Jesuit Relations*, 40:157, 89. On the perceived perils that New France faced due to the Iroquois, see letters of l'Incarnation in Marshall, ed., *Word from New France*, 181–87, 196–210.

[38]Cf. Hunt, *Wars of the Iroquois*, 176–81; Bruce G. Trigger, "Early Iroquoian Contacts with Europeans," in Trigger, ed., *Handbook of North American Indians: Northeast*, 15:354; Trigger, *Natives and Newcomers*, 337–38. For a contemporary explanation of these events in terms of God's providence, see l'Incarnation to her son in Marshall, ed., *Word from New France*, 211–17.

kinship state. The soldiers, missionaries, and *habitants* of New France could never be incorporated into the League in that manner, and so dreams of peace were frustrated. But the failure of the peace does not imply that Iroquois attempts were disingenuous, or tainted with treachery. Indeed, much of the treachery ascribed to the Five Nations may have been a French projection of their own fears, based on their sense of vulnerability, and their mindfulness of their own schemes to purge themselves of the source of their inner terror—their external foes, the Iroquois.[39]

The seventeenth-century Jesuit historian François Du Creux, for example, wrote about the peace negotiations of 1654: "They [the French] saw that it was unsafe to place any confidence in the deceitful and treacherous Iroquois; that the object of the Annierronons [Mohawks] and the Onnontaerronnons [Onondagas] was the extermination of the French; what terms were possible with those who under the cloak of sincerity plotted treason? It seemed the least of two evils to dissemble with dissemblers."[40] Rumors of Iroquois attacks circulated widely in New France, as they did among the Hurons, Algonquins, the Montagnais, and other natives allied with the French. Though often unfounded, such rumors inspired fear far and wide. Yet, as the historian John Dickinson has shown, during the half-century from 1608 to 1666, fewer than two hundred French colonists were actually killed by the Iroquois in warfare or in captivity. All but ten were men. Very few actually met their fate while alone, at the hands of "skulking" Iroquois raiders. And most died during the warfare of 1650–53 and 1660–61.[41]

Du Creux's telling and inappropriate charge of "treason" implied a violation of the subjects' obligations to their king, and it assumed that the Iroquois, like other natives in the French sphere, somehow owed allegiance not only to the French Crown but to French civilization and Catholicism as well. The Five Nations' ability to reject this colonial embrace and extend their own program proved deeply troubling to New France, which viewed with exaggerated fears the in-

[39]The sharp insights of Karen Kupperman, "English Perceptions of Treachery, 1583–1640: The Case of the American 'Savages,' " *The Historical Journal*, 20 no. 2 (1977), 263–87, are also applicable to the French colonial experience in Canada; see also Kupperman, *Settling With the Indians: The Meeting of English and Indian Cultures in America, 1580–1640* (Totowa, N.J., 1980).

[40]Du Creux, *Historia Canadensis*, 2:657.

[41]John Dickinson, "La guerre iroquoisie et la mortalité en Nouvelle-France, 1608–1666," *Revue d'Histoire de l'Amerique Française*," 36 (1982), 31–54; see Axtell, *Invasion Within*, 340n22.

dependence—even arrogance—of the Five Nations. The French felt vulnerable in their isolated province, and their own developing scheme to eradicate the Five Nations (and perhaps a latent sense of guilt about the propriety of such a scheme) also informed French views of the Iroquois. French anxiety, guilt, and treachery seem ultimately to have been projected on their enemy and in a circular, self-justifying—if unconscious—way helped to legitimize the aggression that New France contemplated.

In the summer of 1650, for example, we can see such projection in the actions of a Christian Huron party, which were recorded approvingly by a Jesuit chronicler. The Hurons encountered what they took to be a band of Iroquois warriors. To their surprise, the Iroquois came with words and gifts of peace and "to invite the remnants of the Hurons, who were dying of hunger, to take refuge among them, so that in the future they might be but one people." The Huron protagonist of the Jesuit tale feigned belief and acceptance while remaining convinced of Iroquois treachery. Cooperating with the peace delegation, he helped to arrange a celebration, and after luring some thirty Iroquois into the Huron fort he and others "seized and killed the treacherous enemies, who were biding their time to carry out the same plan, but were forestalled," according to the Jesuit narrator, Paul Ragueneau. While Jesuits were predisposed to question the sincerity and good intentions of the Iroquois, their rivals and enemies, there is good reason to take Iroquois peace initiatives seriously, to indict the Hurons and French for the very crimes they ascribed to the Iroquois, and to see some of their charges of treachery and aggression against the Five Nations as self-fulfilling prophecies. Nonetheless, despite a long history colored by the frustrations and fears of New France, the Iroquois accord of 1653–58 was not a peace with a diabolical purpose; instead it was a genuine effort by the Five Nations to make their moral vision of peace manifest, just as Deganawidah had in an ancient time.[42]

Through a series of councils at Quebec and Onondaga, the Iroquois and French constructed and reaffirmed a real if short-lived peace. The presents that accompanied Iroquois words suggest the seriousness of the negotiations, for, as the Jesuits realized, gifts, "among all these Barbarous tribes, have the same use that writing and contracts have with us." Using the traditional form of the Condolence, the

[42]Thwaites, ed., *Jesuit Relations*, 36:181–87; quotations from 183 and 187.

Iroquois continually sought "to make bright the Sun, darkened by the clouds and disturbances of so many wars, . . . to wipe away the tears that are commonly shed upon hearing of the brave warriors killed in battle," to provide "a draught to counteract whatever bitterness might remain in the hearts of the French, because of the death of their people," to cover and bury the dead and smooth the earth so "that nothing might ever issue from their tombs that could sadden their relatives, and arouse any feelings of revenge in their bosoms."[43]

The French willingness to participate in conventional Iroquois discourse, and to do so skillfully, encouraged the Five Nations and gave them hope that a true commonality was growing between the League and New France. A series of councils between the constituent members of the Iroquois confederacy and the French in Quebec reinforced the emerging sense, in similar meetings in Onondaga and Mohawk country, that the Iroquois and the Europeans and Indians of New France might become one people. In these years hostilities did not fully cease, but in contrast to the recent past, quarrels became exceptional rather than typical.[44]

The Iroquois used the words and rituals of Condolence because they saw them as appropriate, that is, appropriate among parties who would occupy the same extended lodge. The Five Nations pushed for

[43]These words are taken from the councils at Quebec in September 1653 involving the French, Onondagas, and Mohawks (see Thwaites, ed., *Jesuit Relations*, 40:165–69, 185–91), but such sentiments echo throughout the record of the 1653–58 peace. In ibid., 42:55 a passage described the symbolic planting of what a Jesuit writer termed a "May-tree," but what clearly represented for the Iroquois the Great Tree of Peace. The relation explained, "by this they meant that the center of the Peace, and the place for general reunions, would be in that house [constructed at Sainte Marie among the Onondagas], before which should be erected this great May-tree, so lofty that it could be seen from every direction, and all Nations, even those most distant, could come to it."

[44]Marshall Sahlins, *Islands of History* (Chicago, 1985), analyzing early encounters between the English and Sandwich Islanders (Hawaiians), suggests that "customary kinds of acts can precipitate social forms," not merely the reverse (xi). In the context of Iroquois-French relations, one might follow Sahlins in seeing an event (or series of events) like the peace negotiations between the two "not simply [as] a phenomenal happening, even though as a phenomenon it has reasons and forces of its own, apart from any given symbolic scheme. An event becomes such as it is interpreted. Only as it is appropriated in and through the cultural scheme does it acquire historical significance" (xiv). The negotiations that brought the Iroquois and French together thus acquired different meanings for each side, as the events were interpreted differently, through contrasting French and Iroquois symbolic schemes. Sahlins suggests that something peculiar develops as the two sets of actors and two sets of interpretive systems come together in such events: interposing between structure and event is "the situational synthesis of the two in a 'structure of the conjuncture'" (xiv). Among the Iroquois and French, as among the Iroquois and Dutch, new forms of discourse were thus constructed, which were neither fully Iroquois nor fully French, and which were constantly contested as each attempted to make its own meaning and purpose the single, accepted one.

a real amalgamation by the formation of kinship ties based on French and Huron residence among them and a mixing of blood. It is in this context that we must understand the Five Nations' earnest requests for a French colony and mission among them.

In September of 1653, the Mohawk representative Andioura made the first appeal of many to the governor-general at Quebec for a French settlement among the Five Nations. At Montreal in May of 1654, the Onondagas likewise asked for the "Black Robes" to come among them. Father Simon le Moyne journeyed to Onondaga that summer and received a warm reception. He commented that among his hosts, "one calls me brother, another uncle, another a cousin; never have I had so many kinsfolk." Such greetings were probably meant to be less metaphorical than le Moyne realized, as were the words of an Onondaga civil chief who spoke for all of the Five Nations assembled in council: "Place yourself in the heart of the country, since you [the French] are to possess our hearts."[45]

In September 1655, the superior at Quebec dispatched Fathers Pierre-Joseph-Marie Chaumonot and Claude Dablon to Onondaga after a preliminary council with the four upper Iroquois nations confirmed the peace. As the ritual of Condolence dictated, the Iroquois met the priests at the forest's edge and conducted them into the village, where over the next few days a great council of peace took place. Though the Jesuit missionaries remained unaware of or unsympathetic to the implications of these proceedings, Iroquois participants ritually reenacted, in a traditional fashion, Deganawidah's mythic mission of peace and consolidation. Again, constituent members of the Iroquois League stressed their kinship with the French. The Oneidas and Cayugas argued that, as now the French and Onondaga were one, and as they were younger brothers or nephews of the Onondaga, they must occupy the same position relative to the French.[46] A final song concluding the council intoned, "Today the great peace is made. Farewell, war; Farewell arms! For the affair is entirely beautiful. Thou upholdest our Cabins, when thou comest among us."[47]

The French missionaries and envoys may not have understood the full meaning of the words. The Iroquois conceived of their commonwealth as a longhouse, or a bark dwelling, which they expanded by removing the end-wall and adding additional hearths when the

[45]Thwaites, ed., *Jesuit Relations,* 40:185; ibid., 41:75, 99, 117.
[46]Ibid., 42:49–57, 67–95, 99, 117–21.
[47]Ibid., 117.

new families joined them through marriage or adoption, a practice observed since the fifteenth century, archaeology tells us. As the nineteenth-century linguist and ethnologist Horatio Hale observed in *The Iroquois Book of Rites,* "Such was the figure by which the founders of the confederacy represented their political structure, a figure which was in itself a description and an invitation. It declared that the united nations were not distinct tribes, associated by a temporary league, but one great family, clustered for convenience about separate hearths in a common dwelling." The Five Nations invited the French to become additions or supports to their Longhouse, that is, to assimilate into their League, to become, in effect, Iroquois. One Jesuit writer noticed that the Five Nations hoped for a fundamantal amalgamation: "Were one to believe them, either New France would be almost entirely Iroquois, or one would no longer have any French except among the Iroquois."[48]

The priests stayed in Onondaga through the winter of 1655–56, but the Iroquois grew frustrated by the delay—now stretching to three years—in establishing a French colony and mission among them. At a council held in February, an Oneida delegate thanked one of the priests, with words symbolically supported by wampum, "for adopting them as his children and compatriots" and exhorted him "to be a veritable Father, not one in words, but also in reality, as indeed he was expected to be."[49]

As the Jesuit "Fathers" were beginning to realize, the Iroquois desired a more literal consummation of their relationship. Yet the Jesuits were hesitant; they did not share with the Five Nations a common conception of their place in Iroquois communities. For the Iroquois, real men lived in matrilineal households and helped to produce children for matrilineal families and clans. Adoption began the process of amalgamation, but naturalized members of the group would plant firm roots in Iroquois society only if their intercourse was sexual as well as social and symbolic. And though the missionaries were pleased to be called "father" by the Iroquois—a designation they found familiar and unexceptional—they might have reflected further on the particular meaning and position of fathers in this matrilineal society. Of course, among the matrilineal Iroquois, fathers were not central figures. Men lived as fathers within the matrilocal households and

---

[48]Horatio Hale, *The Iroquois Book of Rites,* ed., William N. Fenton (Toronto, 1963 [orig. pub. Philadelphia, 1883]), 75–76; Thwaites, ed., *Jesuit Relations,* 44:63.
[49]Thwaites, ed., *Jesuit Relations,* 42:191.

matrilineal clans of their wives and children. They remained members of their own mothers' clans, and they performed their most important roles within them. A man's most critical functions within the Iroquois kinship and household system, then, were carried out in his role as son, brother, or uncle, *not* as father. Adopted men, even among the inclusive Five Nations, would have lacked the roots, the standing, and the authority that their children would achieve through birth into an Iroquois family and clan. The Jesuit missionary fathers, therefore, had taken an important step into the Iroquois domestic world, but they had not assumed the particular fatherhood that they anticipated and desired, nor had they satisfied their increasingly frustrated hosts.

As Father Dablon wrote in his journal, "They urge on our settlement in their Country, and reproach one another for not making us come." They "never cease to press the matter vehemently, and to threaten us with their enmity unless we speedily become their Compatriots." Dablon made the difficult trip to Montreal to convey the message of Iroquois impatience, arriving on March 30, 1656. Yet not until the summer of 1657 did the French begin to fulfill their obligations to the Iroquois, to come, "uphold their cabins," and live among them.[50]

On July 11, 1657 the French mission, led by Jesuit Superior François le Mercier, and including Dablon and Chaumonot, two other priests, two lay brothers, and forty *habitants,* arrived at the shores of Onondaga Lake to found Sainte Marie de Gannentaha. They completed the difficult tasks of constructing the mission despite mosquitoes and sickness; if their hosts had not supplied game, fish, and vegetables, hunger would have been yet another hardship. The French then settled into life among the Onondagas. Writing after le Mercier's journal, the interim Superior Jean de Quen reported that "those poor Barbarians feel like fathers, brothers, children, and nephews toward us when we call them by those names." And as kin, the Onondagas rendered to the French the same considerations and services that other members of the society received. When two Frenchmen died, a sympathetic chief called on le Mercier to console him, saying, "The Elders of our country have the custom of wiping away one another's tears when they are afflicted by any misfortune. We come Achiendase [le Mercier], to perform that friendly duty toward thee. We weep with thee, because misfortune cannot touch thee without piercing us by the same blow." In such a fashion, the Iroquois instructed and naturalized their new

[50]Ibid., 201–3.

brethren, even as the Jesuits began to implement their own project of transformation.[51]

The missionaries proved difficult, stubborn, and willful pupils, and they used their new positions within the Iroquois domestic world effectively to deliver their subversive message of Christ. One priest wrote about the Jesuits' clever manipulation of Iroquois life:

> God makes use of their superstitions and false piety to derive his glory from them. He gives us the means of sanctifying their tendency to practice some Divine worship and to perform some ceremonies of Religion; we make them change the object of these, and address to the true God the invocations and words of adoration which they formerly employed in their sacrifices. . . . The custom observed by these Nations, of giving one another each year friendly presents in the Councils and public Assemblies, will afford us . . . a favorable opportunity for explaining our mysteries, instead of reciting things that are passed and are the most remote from memory, as they do in performing these ceremonies.
>
> In the same manner, also, we take advantage of the custom followed by the relatives and elders, of meeting during the night after a funeral, to relate stories of olden times. We turn their curiosity to advantage on such ocassions.[52]

Penetrating Iroquois belief and practice wherever and whenever possible, the Jesuits sought to insinuate themselves and their religion into Iroquoia. As one missionary reported, "imperceptibly, and at leisure, we cast the seeds of the Faith into their souls."[53]

Initially their relentless work seemed to pay great dividends. Jesuit optimism was unbounded, as they reported more Iroquois converts within two months than had been won among the Hurons in several years. Soon they widened the focus of their mission by sending priests to the Oneidas and Cayugas, which they were obliged to do, as the Father Superior explained, "to make our kinship more useful and more desirable to them." The expanded reach of the mission coincided with a more intense, less indulgent approach to Indian conversion as the Jesuits "openly declared war against Paganism."[54]

[51] Ibid., 43:277–79. The foundation of this mission among the Onondagas is also described by Marie de l'Incarnation; see Marshall, ed., *Word from New France*, 224–28.
[52] Thwaites, ed., *Jesuit Relations*, 43:285–87.
[53] Ibid., 287.
[54] Ibid., 283, 307, 297.

But as the glowing accounts of God's enormous successes among the Iroquois poured into New and old France, trouble flared along the French-Iroquois cultural frontier. All of New France did not share in the Jesuits' optimism or faith that the Iroquois were sincere and deserving of trust. And for those cynical about Iroquois intentions, events seemed to confirm their view. Instances of Iroquois treachery were apparently observed throughout the period of peace, in a series of incidents ranging from petty thefts and the destruction of property to the murder of Father Leonard Garreau, a Jesuit priest on a mission to the West. By 1656, many had turned against the Jesuits, among them Paul de Chomedey de Maisonneuve, the governor of Montreal, who successfully appealed to France for priests of the Sulpician order who might challenge the Jesuits' Canadian monopoly. The governor of New France, Jean de Lauson, who had backed the French-Iroquois accord, returned to France in the same year, leaving administration of the province in the hands of his son. But in 1657 Charles de Lauson also left Canada, and the acting governor, Louis d'Ailleboust de Coulonges, charted a new, less indulgent, and more hostile course in New France's Iroquois policy, a course that would mark yet another descent into violence.[55]

A major point of contention between New France and the Iroquois League was the status of the native peoples allied with the French, especially the position of the Huron refugees living then in Canadian reserves. Continually, the League and its constituent nations tried to effect a relocation of the Hurons to Iroquoia, which New France perceived as a plot to subject the Hurons to new cruelties and oppressions, and which they feared might undo whatever progress the Hurons had made toward conversion to Christ. The Iroquois, on the other hand, saw Huron resettlement in their country as a natural culmination of their attempt to bring the Hurons into the Great Peace. Ironically, despite their reservations, Jesuit missionaries seemed to encourage the Huron relocation and amalgamation as a way of gaining access to Iroquois villages—and of planting native Christians among them. One priest wrote, with more confidence and hope than sorrow,

[55]On the tensions that continued during this interlude of peace in the mid 1650s, see l'Incarnation in Marshall, ed., *Word from New France*, 217–35. See also Thwaites, ed., *Jesuit Relations*, 42:237–39, 263; 43:35–37, 43, 61, 67, 109–13. Rumors of Iroquois treachery run throughout these relations; see 43:67, 109, 179. Du Creux described the "Glorious death of Father Leonard Garreau," in *Historia Canadensis*, 2:742–45. See Trigger, *Natives and Newcomers*, 339, 280–81, on the advent of the Sulpicians and the change in New France's administration and policy. And see Thwaites, ed., *Jesuit Relations*, 44:191–97.

"*Bene omnia fecit* [He did all things well]. In truth, my Reverend Father, the judgments of God are wonderful. I have seen the flower of the Huron Congregation carried away into captivity by the Infidels, with many others whose devotion would appear extraordinary even in a Cloister. Praise be to him forever, since *bene omnia fecit*." This action on the part of the Jesuits—sending the Hurons off to become kinspeople of the Five Nations—must have been read (inaccurately) as a powerful endorsement of the Iroquois vision of peace.[56]

Embedded in the confused Iroquois-French discourse was an even larger problem, however, which was obscured by the hopes of both sides, but which nonetheless emerged fitfully by the end of the 1650s and doomed the Iroquois-French peace. Even those in New France who were most sanguine—the missionaries of the Society of Jesus— failed to understand and could never embrace the kind of peace envisioned by the Five Nations, one based on the Iroquois model of kinship and domestic harmony. Europeans understood peace between nations in fundamentally different terms. Nations constructed non-aggression and cooperation agreements and transferred property, but they remained discrete, sovereign political entities.

In the New World colonial context, the French were less prepared to treat "savages" with the same respect they accorded their European rivals. As a result, the activities of missionaries represented a means toward a larger program of subjugation and transformation of the indigenous inhabitants, as they saw it, in the interest of French civilization and the One True Faith. As long as Iroquois power demanded it, the French tendered their respect and negotiated locally with the Five Nations, though not in the fashion of statecraft but rather in the modes of colonialism. Native peoples could be considered *nations,* ethnic groups geographically circumscribed, but not *états* (states), organized, sovereign governments with coercive powers. New France itself remained a colonial periphery clearly tied to a European me-

---

[56]Trigger, *Natives and Newcomers,* 278, argues that the Iroquois pursued their assimilationist goal relative to the Hurons in the 1650s in order to prevent the Hurons from regrouping and posing new threats to the Five Nations in the West, and to deny the French allies skilled in guerrilla warfare. Nonetheless, as Trigger notes, Hurons were generally treated well and were fully naturalized into Five Nations' societies. On the Jesuit apparent acceptance and even encouragement of Huron resettlement with the Five Nations, see ibid., 278–79. These complex negotiations and violent confrontations over the Hurons, which sometimes even set Iroquois tribes momentarily against each other, are narrated throughout Thwaites, ed., *Jesuit Relations,* 43; quotations from 123.

tropolis: it could never contemplate its own absorption into a Native American core—that is, into the League of Peace—on Iroquois terms. And the celibate and self-satisfied Jesuits themselves could never provide a satisfactory response to the Iroquois request, "If you love, as you say you do, our souls, love our bodies also, and let us be henceforth but one nation."[57] In effect, the Five Nations and New France pursued the same ethnocentric goal—to assimilate the other—and the building storm of fear and exasperation in Canada and Iroquoia reflected and aggravated this conflict in expectations, producing a confused discourse of frustration.[58]

As an atmosphere of mistrust continued to envelop New France during the peace, rumored depredations, especially when attributed to Mohawk warriors, magnified the impact of real ones. On October 25, 1657, for example, word reached Quebec that three Mohawks had robbed a certain Monsieur Pinguet, "even to his shirt, while he was fishing for eels a little above Cap rouge." But the report proved false, as did the one received a few hours later that the Mohawks were massing in force in that vicinity.[59] Too many times, however, incidents did occur that compromised the peace. Robberies, assaults, acts of intimidation, even murders, were perpetrated by men from all sides of the complex, shifting cultural frontier. The Five Nations, Hurons, Algonquins, Montagnais, and the French could all share the guilt for committing deeds that jeopardized peace, especially because they did not necessarily share a common understanding of these acts or concur about the appropriate responses to apparent violations. The history of enmity and fear that had separated these groups for so long proved

[57]Quoted in Wallace, *The White Roots of Peace* (Philadelphia, 1946), 45. The fact that warriors frequently abstained from sexual relations before battle, in order to build their stores of power, may also have informed Iroquois suspicions of celibate Jesuits and caused them to question Jesuit motives. On a number of levels Jesuit celibacy proved puzzling and troubling to Iroquois people.

[58]See Cornelius J. Jaenen, "Characteristics of French-Amerindian Contact in New France," in Stanley H. Palmer and Dennis Reinhartz, eds., *Essays on the History of North American Discovery and Exploration*, The Walter Prescott Webb Lectures, no. 21 (College Station, Tex., 1988), 79–101. Jaenen provides an insightful and generally convincing analysis of the "*genie coloniale* thesis," which argues that the French displayed a particular gift for getting along with native peoples. His sophisticated revision of the thesis demonstrates that it was generally true for New France. Yet the Five Nations must be considered a prominent exception to the rule. That France could "exercise her sovereignty in North America through independent Amerindian 'nations,' " using "native self-government" as "an instrument of French power" (86), did not satisfy the Five Nations, which asserted its own sovereignty through an alternate form of self-government, and which had its own ideas about alliance and amalgamation.

[59]Thwaites, ed., *Jesuit Relations*, 43:67.

Novae Franciae Accurata Delineatio 1657, attributed to the Jesuit François-Joseph Bressani, courtesy Département des cartes et plans, Bibliothèque Nationale, Paris. The engraving in the lower right is among the earliest depicting the horrible martyrdom suffered by Black Robes at the hands of the Iroquois. Other scenes on this interpretive map are designed to suggest the piety of Huron converts and the tragedy of the destruction of the Jesuit mission and its Huron neophytes. Such representations clearly show New France's terror and its increasing hostility toward the Five Nations.

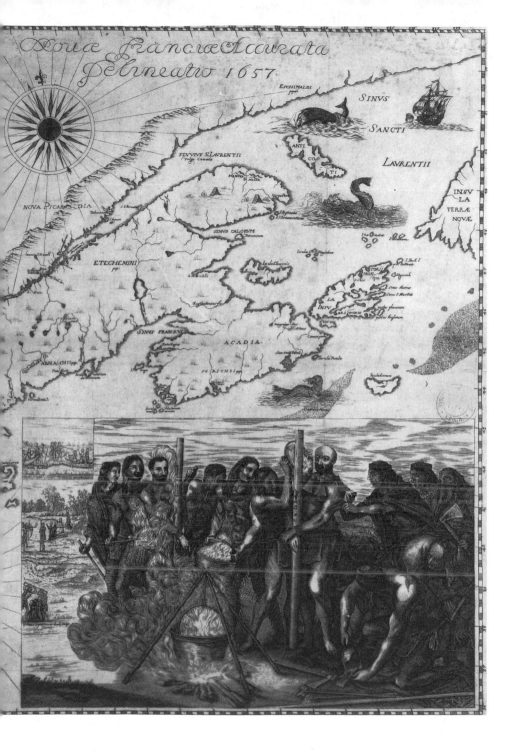

Nouæ Franciæ Accurata
Delineatio 1657.

EPCHIMALDI
ppet.

SINVS
SANCTI

LAVRENTII

ANTI
CO.
TI.

FLVVIVS S.LAVRENTII
vulgo Canada

NOVA PICARDIA

ETECHEMINI
ppt.

SINVS CALORVM

SINVS FRANCISCI

ACADIA

TO RICHESI

INSV
LA
TERRÆ
NOVÆ

difficult to overcome, and misunderstandings too often resulted in bloodshed.[60]

Within the Iroquois Longhouse the means existed to deal with such problems and settle disputes that otherwise might threaten to tear the society apart. But in so loosely woven an alliance, in a relationship which lacked real consummation and in which the French and Iroquois never shared the same social and moral vision, or the same customs and law, traditional Iroquois mechanisms proved ineffectual. For example, the French found the Five Nations' response to the Jesuit Leonard Garreau's death woefully inadequate, because the Iroquois offered at Montreal but "two wretched little presents, according to their custom . . . to show their regret at the accident . . . and to dry our tears and assuage our grief."[61] Following the unfortunate death of a young Huron man in May of 1657 near Quebec, apparently at the hands of an Onondaga youth acting in violation of Iroquois as well as Huron and French codes of behavior, French officials disparaged an Onondaga attempt to atone and condole; suspicious, they suggested that the Iroquois envoy only "pretended not to approve the deed."[62] The governor-general called for a stepped-up defense against the "insolence of both the upper and lower Iroquois," in spite of the Onondagas' words and presents which said, "Onontio, we do not approve the murder committed upon the Huron by our Youth, on the Way. Onontio, we pay for the damage which our Youth have done to the french settlements through robberies and killing the cattle."[63]

In another troubling incident, a small party of Oneida men, acting independently, apparently slew three Frenchmen near Montreal on October 25, 1657. In response, the French arrested an Onondaga hunting party in the vicinity. Soon an Oneida delegation of three appeared at Montreal to condole and atone for the murders. But, observing the treatment given to the Onondaga captives and unsure of how their mission was being received, they slipped away. Their flight only served to confirm the French view of Iroquois duplicity. On November 1, 1657, the acting governor-general, Louis d'Ailleboust de Coulonges, ordered the imprisonment of all Iroquois present in

---

[60]For a sense of the stream of misunderstandings, disagreements, and depradations among these groups, see ibid., 27, 29, 35–37, 41–43, 47, 55–61, 65–69.
[61]Ibid., 42:237.
[62]Ibid., 43:43.
[63]Ibid., 61.

French settlements. Two days later, an Algonquin man killed and scalped an Onondaga hunter on his way to Richelieu Islands. The slain man's companion escaped to Montreal, only to be arrested and placed in irons. Fear spread among the Onondagas that the French were preparing with the Algonquins for a war on the Iroquois.[64]

Each party in the escalating conflict, despite some minor transgressions, could argue that it acted appropriately, according to its own perspective, while its opponents behaved outrageously. The condolence and atonement procedures that calmed dangerous rifts within Iroquois society could not perform the same function in French-Iroquois relations. Implying their own solidarity with the grieving French, their prospective kinsmen, a Mohawk delegation memorialized the dead: "*We* have been killed in the persons of the French, whom we come to bury."[65] These Iroquois envoys conveyed their sympathy and their own sense of loss, as they sought to apply the traditional mechanisms of domestic peace to their new world. But the French governor d'Ailleboust replied with contempt, "Thou thinkest to beguile me with a collar of porcelain [wampum]. The blood of my brethren cries out very loud; and, if I be not soon appeased, I will render satisfaction to their souls.... Drop thy treachery, and let us make war if thou wilt not have peace."[66]

Earlier, in April 1656, the Mohawks had pledged themselves to the peace and, to end the cycle of feud, had promised to hold the French above suspicion. But they asked that the French show them the same confidence: "If any Frenchman be found killed in a secluded place, do not accuse the Agnieronnon Iroquois of it. Our hands will be innocent of it, and will not betray our hearts, which breathe but Peace." Amid the joy in Quebec following this council, many still harbored a deep distrust of the "treacherous spirit of the Agnieronnon." In hindsight, after Iroquois war broke out anew, the Jesuit de Quen appended this to his account: "Would to God it [the distrust] had been greater."[67] The fears, accusations, and dire predictions of Iroquois treachery became a self-fulfilling prophecy; in a sense, New France and the Five Nations had much to fear from fear itself. Nonetheless, after large-

---

[64] Ibid., 44:193–201.
[65] Ibid., 203 (emphasis added). The "we" is meant by the Mohawks to be broadly inclusive here, referring not only to themselves and the larger Five Nations, but also to their newer brethren, the French.
[66] Ibid., 211.
[67] Ibid., 43:109–13.

scale hostilities erupted once again, Iroquois cynicism and enmity were, with hindsight, inferred by the French, and Iroquois motives and goals would be interpreted in ways that still influence the historiography.

Finally, on an inclement night in March 1658, even the most optimistic and faith-filled of the French succumbed to fear and distrust as they slipped away from their mission at Sainte Marie, fearing for their lives. Increasing hostility to their message and the dangers that factionalism within the Iroquois posed to them convinced the missionaries that a rumor of their planned massacre was true. We will never know. Yet the missionaries correctly sensed that, despite their successes, they were a growing irritant to some Iroquois men and women, and a severe disappointment to others.[68] The Five Nations were never persuaded that the French took seriously their obligations to uphold the Iroquois cabin. It became increasingly clear that the French were not assimilating into Iroquois society, and, indeed, they seemed to widen the dangerous fissures opening within Iroquoia. Still, from the Iroquois point of view, it was not any action of theirs but the sudden abandonment of the mission by the French, that signaled the end of the mission at Gannentaha and the end of peace itself. Although the Iroquois and many of the French entered into the accord sincerely, and although numerous individuals on each side worked bravely and diligently, the confusions of their intercultural discourse—real cultural differences, divergent visions of the social and moral order, and, ironically, the similarity of their incorporative agendas—ultimately spelled defeat for the Iroquois-French peace. In the mid-seventeenth century, no Deganawidah emerged among the Iroquois or French who could transform the horrible chaos into a world of peace.

After the French deserted their mission at Sainte Marie de Gannentaha, the Five Nations did not abandon their quest for peace, nor were they quick to accept d'Ailleboust's invitation to war. Recovering from their shock at the priests' sudden departure, the Iroquois sent a series of delegations to New France to learn what had happened,

---

[68]In discussing the problems they encountered in their mission, the Jesuits showed their awareness of Iroquois objections to their methods. Most Iroquois wanted to be left alone, as one Jesuit noted. He wrote that, unlike the Dutch, who "have preserved the Iroquois by allowing them to live in their own fashion, . . . the black gowns [Jesuits] have ruined the Hurons by preaching the faith to them" (Thwaites, ed., *Jesuit Relations*, 43:291).

to secure the release of their countrymen, confined in chains, and to reestablish peace. The Jesuit Father Simon le Moyne, who had remained among the Mohawks, returned to Quebec in May, 1658, conveying some French captives and bringing with him the "voice of the Agneerronons [Mohawks]." They told the French, "Thou seekest a quarrel: and say not that it is I. . . . I have nothing crooked in my thoughts. I wish to be thy Brother. . . . Do like the dutchman, who interferes not in the wars of the Wolves.[69]

During the summer, relations between the French and Five Nations teetered upon the narrow ridge separating war and peace. A new governor-general, Pierre de Voyer, vicômte d'Argenson, arrived in July and displayed a fresh militance in dealing with the Iroquois. The French interpreted almost any Iroquois presence near their settlements as hostile. Soon after his arrival, d'Argenson sallied forth in pursuit of what he believed to be an Iroquois raiding party. When two Iroquois envoys appeared at Trois Rivières in August, d'Argenson chased them away, and when a group of twenty Mohawks approached the habitation—whether they were marauders, hunters, or peace ambassadors is not known—they were "roughly used," though they claimed that they had come to effect a general peace. Ten were captured as they made their appeal, and seven of them were then sent on to Quebec as prisoners.[70]

Trying whatever might work, the Five Nations appealed to their Dutch brethren to help them maintain peace with the French. The eldest sachems of the Mohawks approached Fort Orange on August 13, 1658, asking for the assistance of the court in exchanging captives and reasserting peace with New France. French hostility to Iroquois advances made such extraordinary measures necessary. In a letter to the Canadian governor, Fort Orange magistrates explained their role: the Five Nations desired peace, but "as they dare not do it personally, they have asked us to assist them."[71]

On September 7, 1658, "Atogwatkwann, called La Grande cueillière

[69]Thwaites, ed., *Jesuit Relations*, 44:97.

[70]Ibid., 227–33, 315, 107. The governor would not give way to appeals "from all directions" to release the Iroquois prisoners until the Iroquois agreed to deliver to the French the children of their chief men—children who would be kept in seminaries, reared as Christians, and held as hostages.

[71]A. J. F. van Laer, trans. and ed., *Minutes of the Court of Fort Orange and Beverwyck, 1657–1660*, 2 vols. (Albany, 1920–1923), 2:149–51. The minutes of the extraordinary session recorded that the Mohawks wished to deliver one Lowies [Louis] Parraget and two other Frenchmen to the governor in exchange for some six of their own men taken prisoner at Trois Rivières, "wishing at the same time to make a general peace with the French" (150).

[the large spoon], chief of the 7 Annieyer'onons captured at 3 Rivers," was at Quebec ritually addressing the French and their allies, the Hurons and Algonquins, and supporting his words with the appropriate gifts: "I come to lay my head at the feet of Onnontio [the governor], in full confidence that what Achiendase [Father le Moyne] said on his behalf . . . is true—namely, that false rumors could never alter the thoughts of peace between Him and us." A second present sought "to dispel The distrust that we might feel toward each other," and a third inquired whether "our people whom You have put in irons are still Alive." Finally, the Mohawk diplomat attempted to "clear the minds of the hurons, that in the future they may not circulate false rumors, either on one side or on the other."[72] In reply, the French governor cast blame on the Iroquois and asked, "What else shouldst thou deserve but fire"? Yet after invoking the sword, *in terrorem,* he offered mercy and the olive branch, while making it clear that New France would have peace on its own terms. In particular the governor stressed the inseparability of the French, Hurons, and Algonquins, an alliance that confounded the Five Nations' vision of their own Great Peace, centered firmly in Iroquoia and radiating outward.[73]

Father Chaumonot, whose journal recorded this exchange, did not elaborate on the Mohawks' reception of these hard words. But at almost the same moment, the Onondaga sachem Garakontié, displaying great personal courage and commitment to peace, was in Montreal, returning two French captives and appealing once again for an end to the bloodshed and for the construction of peace. It was a perilous time; that month eleven Onondagas had been taken prisoner at Montreal, and two had been killed. Five Oneidas had been captured near Trois Rivières, and three others lost their lives in the fracas.[74] Garakontié invoked the traditions of Deganawidah, symbolically wiping away the tears and opening the throats of the French.

[72]Ibid., 107. It is not clear whether this peace delegation, or a later one that reached Quebec on November 20, 1658, was the one that included the Dutch representative, one Henderick Martensen (or Henri Martin), dispatched after the August 13 extraordinary session at Beverwyck. The latter is more likely; the "Journal of the Jesuit Fathers" reported that this delegation of six Mohawk ambassadors was accompanied by "a Dutchman from New Holland, to assure them that the french would do them no harm. Their object is to obtain the release of their people who are prisoners, and to make peace, (so they say) with all Alguonquins And hurons" (121). On the other hand, the Mohawks had promised the Dutch that they would return Martensen within forty days—that is, some time in early October, or even late September—yet this peace mission only arrived at Quebec in late November. See van Laer, ed., *Court Minutes of Fort Orange,* 2:150.
[73]Thwaites, ed., *Jesuit Relations,* 44:107–9.
[74]Ibid., 109–11.

He cleaned the blood where it had spilled, and he administered an elixir to calm the hearts of New France. He replanted the Tree of Peace at Montreal, invited the French to return to Onondaga, and assured them that their mission still stood at Gannentaha. Finally, Garakontié informed the French that the Mohawks had rebuked the Oneidas who committed the earlier depradations, and assured them that the Iroquois would not avenge the deaths of those who had died by French hands: "I place stones on their grave, so that no more may be said about it."[75]

In October and November these diplomatic exchanges continued, along with sustained tensions on each side. The Iroquois urged the French to maintain the peace: "We are 7 [8] allied nations,— The sonnontwerronnon [Senecas], The oiogwen [Cayugas], The ononntag{e}ronnon [Onondagas], The frenchman of Gannentaa, The onneiout [Oneidas], The Anniege [Mohawks], The Mahingan [Mahicans], and the dutchman. Withdraw not from our alliance."[76] Although French interpreters rendered the term "alliance" to describe the bonds between these groups, the Iroquois meaning may have been quite different. The Mohawk spokesman considered the French and Dutch as tribes having equality with the individual nations of the Iroquois confederation; all together were to form one people. Only later, after the Five Nations endured the frustrations and failures of numerous attempts to establish Deganawidah's peace, would the French term "alliance" more closely describe the nature of Iroquois-European relations. Iroquois ambassadors reasoned that troubles inevitably arose between "allies," but that such disturbances need not cause a fundamental breach of the peace.[77] Understanding their alliance metaphorically as their Longhouse—an expanding household encompassing members of an extended Iroquois family—the Five Nations believed that the traditional practices of condolence and atonement could maintain peace, and that all within the Iroquois Longhouse—including the French and Dutch neophytes—had the obligation to work toward domestic harmony.

---

[75]Ibid., 111–15. Garakontié, however, reserved the right to maintain an independent foreign policy, including the right to initiate military action against the Five Nations' foes. He referred here specifically to the Algonquins and "the nation of Fire," the Shawnees, Miscoutens, or more generally other Algonquian peoples in the West, especially those of the lower Michigan peninsula. On identifying the Fire Nation, see Trigger, ed., *Handbook of North American Indians: Northeast*, 634, 671, 741–42.

[76]Thwaites, ed., *Jesuit Relations*, 44:123.

[77]Ibid., 125.

While the anxious period of quiet continued, an Oneida peace embassy traveled to Quebec, arriving on April 3, 1659.[78] Once again, the Iroquois appealed to the French in the traditional terms of their condolence. Finally, speaking for the Onondagas, the Oneidas reminded the French

> that you [the French and Onondagas] had clasped each other by the arm; that you had bound yourselves with iron bonds. It is thou, frenchmen, who hast broken the Bond by departing from my country without my knowledge, and by abandoning thy dwelling.... The onontageronon [Onondaga] takes thee once more by the arm, and renews friendship with thee more strongly than Ever.[79]

Although the Iroquois made their case, accusing the French and calling them back to the Longhouse, the people of New France continued to see events their own way and to look upon Iroquois peace initiatives with suspicion. Diplomatic missions shuttled between Iroquoia and Canada during 1659, and they continued intermittently into the next decade.[80] But no real peace grew out of these efforts. Indeed, the *petite guerre* between the French, their native allies, and the Five Nations persisted and threatened to erupt into a grand conflagration. Jesuit Father Jerome Lalemant echoed popular opinion when he declared in 1660 that all treaties made by the Five Nations "are proof of their perfidy; for they have never kept a single one."[81]

Nonetheless, a nervous period of relative calm continued along the Iroquois-French frontier, despite Jesuit reports of a battle between a band of Hurons, Algonquins, and Frenchmen and what the writer called "an army of 700 yroquois, who had been mustered to come to Quebek" on June 8, 1660. Whether the composite group of Onondagas and Mohawks in question constituted an invading "army" is debatable; the Jesuit chronicler acknowledged that the Onondagas were hunters rather than soldiers, who were returning from their

[78]The proceedings of this negotiation, including description of the words and presents that Father Simon le Moyne was delegated to deliver in Oneida country, are chronicled in ibid., 55:81–95.

[79]Ibid., 85.

[80]Ibid., 95, 99–105; even after the eruption of large scale warfare in 1660, some efforts to negotiate by the Iroquois continued; see 161.

[81]Ibid., 211. Though most historians have been quick to agree with Lalemant and have heaped blame for the hostilities on the Iroquois, the *petite guerre* was initiated from numerous directions. See 85–93, 97–99, 109, 113, 117–19, 153, 155–57.

winter hunt when they discovered an ambush set for them by their French and Indian foes. Predictably, they responded in kind to this aggression. The Onondagas were later reinforced by some five hundred Mohawks, and together they overpowered the Huron, Algonquin, and French force, after the latter had violated a tentative cease fire and peace parley. It is significant that the Iroquois tried to settle the fight with negotiation, and the Algonquins and Hurons "seemed inclined to give them a hearing," but, the Jesuit Lalement observed, "our French know no such thing as peace with those barbarians," and they undercut such an effort, even as they charged the Iroquois with treachery. After a ten-day siege, the Algonquins and Hurons apparently overruled their French compatriots and sued for peace; their envoys entered the Iroquois camp "with fine presents of porcelain [wampum], which are used in this country on all great occasions of Peace and War," and they were well received by the Iroquois. Almost all but the Frenchmen deserted their fort to accept the peace, but as the Iroquois and Huron envoys approached, "our Frenchmen, placing no confidence in all these parlays, fired on them unexpectedly, stretching some of them dead on the ground and putting the rest to flight." It is not surprising that the Iroquois reacted aggressively to this apparent betrayal, ultimately killing or capturing the entire force and subjecting many of those who survived to ritual torture. Despite the violence of this encounter, however, the common assumption in New France that the Five Nations planned an attack on Quebec seems unfounded. Although *habitants* felt the Iroquois presence as bands moved silently about Canadian habitations and blocked channels of trade, the anticipated Iroquois invasions never materialized.[82]

Panic nonetheless mounted in New France. Finally the storm broke in 1661, when a rash of Iroquois attacks left more than seventy Frenchmen dead. "This year deserves to be counted among those of calamity & doom," wrote Father Paul le Jeune.[83] These assaults were the product of years of frustration, during which time the French snubbed one Iroquois peace initiative after another. Yet to New France, the attacks were simply a manifestation of the inherent cruelty and savagery of the Five Nations, who by nature committed deeds so nefar-

---

[82]Ibid., 157, first noted the deeds of the Iroquois "army." A fuller and more dramatic narrative of the battle is given in 245–61; quotations from 249, 253.

[83]Ibid., 46:202–20.

ious that Jesuit writers could find "no ink black enough to describe them."[84]

The French sense of crisis grew out of face to face encounters with death and destruction, and it intensified as frightening tales circulated among them and magnified their horror. The Iroquois peril was real for New France, yet the situation was not as grim as terrified *habitants*, priests, and officials believed. The Iroquois storm that battered New France was less a hurricane than a series of squalls, punctuated with periods of calm. For the most part, in the 1660s all but the Mohawks stayed away from Canada. Different concerns distracted the other four nations, and even the Mohawks concentrated more on events to the east and south.

On the southern borders of Iroquoia, the Five Nations faced the Susquehannocks, who in 1659 or 1660 attacked the Senecas with Maryland's encouragement, renewing a conflict that continued into the 1670s.[85] Beginning in 1658 and continuing until 1664, a new Esopus Indian war engulfed New Netherland along the Hudson below Fort Orange. The Iroquois, especially the Mohawks, once again assumed a mediating, peace-making role. To the east and north of Iroquoia, the Mohawks, Oneidas, and Onondagas, found themselves locked in combat with the Abenakis and Sokokis of New England, who, the Iroquois were convinced, aided Canadian Indians in their attacks against Iroquoia. Indeed, since the early 1650s, the Jesuit Gabriel Druillettes had worked to detach the New England Algonquians from their friendship with the Iroquois and to set them against the Five Nations, just as he had worked to include New England in an anti-Iroquois alliance. By the early 1660s, for complex reasons, the peace

---

[84]Ibid., 45:213.

[85]See especially Jennings, *Ambiguous Iroquois Empire*, 113–30, on the relationship between the Susquehannocks and the Five Nations; during the 1660s, the Mohawks and Susquehannocks remained at peace while the Susquehannocks were at odds with the other Iroquois nations. Although historians have often portrayed such divisions as signs of the League's weakness, I would argue that they could represent strength. As Claude C. le Roy Bacqueville de la Potherie later noticed, the Iroquois could use their divisions to great advantage, employing them to escape humiliating and disastrous defeats; when things went badly, the faction or nation not so immediately involved could initiate peace discussions, even before hostilities ceased. See Bacqueville de la Potherie, *History of the Savage Peoples Who Are Allies of New France* [1753], in Emma H. Blair, ed., *The Indian Tribes of the Upper Mississippi Valley and Region of the Great Lakes*, 2 vols. (Cleveland, 1911–12), 2:44. This process need not be seen cynically as a form of treacherous manipulation, but instead it can be viewed through the perspective of Iroquois history as a means of aiding kinspeople and realizing or maintaining the larger cultural ideal—that is, peace.

and stability that had characterized Iroquois relations with the native peoples of New England was shattered. Nonetheless, relatively quickly after the rupture occurred, by the summer of 1664, the Mohawks believed they had worked out a peace agreement, but those hostile to the accord massacred a Mohawk delegation sent to ratify the peace. Abenakis, Pocumtucks, Sokokis, even Mahicans, have been suspected as the murderers; but the Iroquois had little doubt about who was responsible and included the Mahicans among their chief suspects. Consequently, the Mahicans and other New England nations renewed their old hostilities with the Iroquois, perhaps inspired by the English who planned an invasion of New Netherland; breaking a peace that had lasted over thirty years, they embarked on a course of depredations against Iroquoia and New Netherland.[86]

Regional unrest became all the more pronounced in September 1664, when England invaded New Netherland and forced the capitulation of the province, now renamed New York. In the early 1660s the problems of reverses in warfare, diplomatic isolation, famine, and epidemic disease afflicted the Five Nations. Crisis within Iroquoia forced the Five Nations to undertake new efforts in the interest of their original goal, peace. The frustrations of both peace and war perhaps caused the Iroquois League to fear that an accord based scrupulously on Deganawidah's prescriptions could not be established. Yet the Five Nations pressed on, hoping to keep alive their traditional dreams.

While periods of calm alternated with flurries of turmoil along the French-Iroquois frontier, New France noticed that the Iroquois at-

[86]Neal Salisbury, "Toward the Covenant Chain: Iroquois and Southern New England Algonquians, 1637–1684," in Daniel K. Richter and James H. Merrell, eds., *Beyond the Covenant Chain: The Iroquois and Their Neighbors in Indian North America, 1600–1800* (Syracuse, N.Y., 1987), 61–73, especially 63–68, provides the best analysis of the Five Nations' relations with their neighbors—English and Algonquian—in New England and the complex diplomatic and military events along the eastern margins of Iroquoia during this period. See also Colin G. Calloway, *The Western Abenakis of Vermont, 1600–1800: War, Migration, and the Survival of an Indian People* (Norman, Okla., 1990), especially 72–73 on the complex events of 1664; Jennings, *Ambiguous Iroquois Empire*, 109–12, 125–26, 129–30, 133–34; and see Allen W. Trelease, *Indian Affairs in Colonial New York: The Seventeenth Century* (Ithaca, N.Y., 1960), 127–28. See Jeremias van Rensselaer to Oloff van Cortlandt, 17 July 1664, in A. J. F. van Laer, trans. and ed., *Correspondence of Jeremias van Rensselaer, 1651–1674* (Albany, N.Y., 1932), 355–56, on the troubles resulting from the complex hostilities along the Hudson River, and to the east and west of it, which pitted various European and native groups against each other. On French efforts to enlist New England Algonquians against the Five Nations as early as 1651, see Thwaites, ed., *Jesuit Relations*, 36:101–3. On the problems faced by the Five Nations that encouraged their efforts for peace with New France, see 47:105–7.

tacks they endured seemed to come predominantly from the Mohawks, while the other nations showed less interest in war.[87] New
France began to formulate a strategy to humble the Mohawks and
thereby reduce the entire League. A Jesuit writer speculated in 1660
that "if the Agnieronnons [Mohawks] were defeated by the French,
the other Iroquois Nations would be glad to compromise with us, and
give us their children as hostages of their good faith."[88] And by 1661,
a strategy of conquest began to be articulated even more explicitly.
New France increasingly believed that no more than "a little handful
of Agnieronnons" stood in its way. The missionary Jerome Lalemant
justified their destruction "at the hands of France, as being the sacrifice
of irreconcilable enemies of the Faith and of the French, [which] seems
now to be the will of divine Justice." The holy war, he argued, would
"plant Peace and the Lilies in all our forests, to make Cities of them
if it be desired, and to convert a land of Savages into one of Conquest
for Jesus Christ and for France.... In short," he wrote, his view of
the hated Mohawks expanding to indict the entire Five Nations, "the
cry is raised on every hand, 'Send aid; save bodies and souls; destroy
the Iroquois, and you will plant the Faith throughout a territory of
more than eight hundred leagues in extent.' "[89]

Despite various peace initiatives by the Iroquois—including the
feared Mohawks—and exchanges of envoys and prisoners, New
France proceeded with its developing plans.[90] Finally, in January
1666, the governor-general, Daniel de Rémy, sieur de Courcelle, led
an assault on the Mohawks, who had been absent from the most recent
round of peace negotiations. The invasion proved disastrous to the
French and inflicted little damage on the Mohawks.[91] Still, in July the
Mohawks sent word to New France that they too wished to participate
in the peace established with the rest of the Iroquois League.[92]

During the unsettled summer that followed, Mohawk sachems appeared at Albany to confer with their new English allies, who had

[87] Ibid., 105–7.

[88] Ibid., 45:215.

[89] On the strategy to isolate the Mohawks and to reduce the Iroquois through violent
conquest, see Thwaites, ed., *Jesuit Relations*, 47:107–15; quotations from 113, 115.

[90] On Iroquois peace initiatives during this period, see ibid., 47:93–105, 139–53, 174–219;
48:75–81, 249; 49:139–41.

[91] This campaign is documented in O'Callaghan, ed., *Documentary History of the State of New
York*, 1:57–84, especially 65–67, 71–74.

[92] Ibid., 67–68, 74–76. And see O'Callaghan, ed., *Documents Relative to the Colonial History
of New-York*, 10:45–47. The Mohawks approached the French through Oneida ambassadors,
"apprehensive of bad treatment at our hands," according to a French source (46).

replaced the Dutch. The governor of Canada had sent out two detachments of men to Iroquoia. They were recalled, but not before some of them had engaged the Iroquois. Concerned Mohawk envoys warned Albany of the French advances and asked for English help. They pleaded self-defense against the French and expressed doubts about the sincerity of later French peace offers:

> We fear that we will get ourselves into much trouble, but we await the decision of our Brethren, for the French have let us know through the Senecas that they want to make peace with us. We do not believe this, for they come with all their might. If they really wanted or intended to make peace, they certainly would come to talk with us, but not with all their power, nor would they all come. Therefore, this is certainly a signal that they want to fight.[93]

In August, the Mohawks met with a French envoy at Albany. Through English mediation, Mohawk spokesmen asserted again that they wanted "a good lasting peace made between them and the French." They agreed to a preliminary exchange of delegations and prisoners, with further exchanges once "brotherhood is settled upon." The sachem informed Monsieur Cousture "that they had led the way, that they threw their guns away, and that they would not begin any trouble. The Maquase will keep the peace."[94] The Mohawks proved more faithful than the French.

In the autumn of 1666, the military commander of New France, Alexandre de Prouville, marquis de Tracy, led his crack regular troops—the Carignan-Salières regiment, sent to New France specifically to deal with the Five Nations—and local militia on another invasion of Mohawk lands. Although the Mohawks never engaged this force, choosing to preserve themselves by fleeing, they suffered enormous devastation when Tracy burned their villages and destroyed their stores of food.[95] After another series of diplomatic exchanges, the French were finally prepared to accept peace with the people of the Five Nations, and by 1667 a general peace was arranged.[96]

---

[93]Lawrence H. Leder, ed., "The Livingston Indian Records," *Pennsylvania History*, 23 (January 1956), 30. See also Carl Bridenbaugh, ed., *The Pynchon Papers*, 2 vols. (Boston, 1982–85), 1 [Letters of John Pynchon, 1654–1700], 57, 58–59.

[94]Leder, ed., "Livingston Indian Records," 31–32.

[95]See Thwaites, ed., *Jesuit Relations*, 50:143–45; O'Callaghan, ed., *Documentary History of the State of New York*, 1:44–49.

[96]Thwaites, ed., *Jesuit Relations*, 51:167–77.

Although the Iroquois thus achieved peace with New France, their accord was not yet the peace that the Five Nations envisioned and sought. And while the French seem to have pacified the Iroquois and forced them to accept French terms—a peace of capitulation—many in New France were still unwilling to accept the accord. French suspicion of the Iroquois persisted. Projecting their own motives on the Five Nations, New France believed that the Iroquois merely sought a temporary respite in the accord until they could embark on further destruction. The historian George T. Hunt wrote that Canadian officials "coolly prepared to fracture the peace themselves, should a favorable opportunity present itself." The *Intendant* Jean Talon argued, "Between us and them there is no more good faith than between the most ferocious animals."[97] Despite the state of peace that continued to exist between the Iroquois and French, Talon could nonetheless report to the king in 1670, "In my opinion it would be prudent to anticipate them [the Iroquois] by attacking them in their own country."[98] In response to the perceived treachery of the Five Nations, New France was poised to commit its own perfidious acts.

The peace established in 1667 held better than the French expected. By 1668, Jesuits had placed themselves among all five of the Iroquois nations, and they remained there into the late 1670s, when the French-Iroquois accord eventually deteriorated. During these years, the Black Robes made their greatest impact on the Five Nations. The Jesuit presence in Iroquois villages, and the new circumstances that the Iroquois faced—a population decline and social disintegration in the face of an increasing European strength in North America—forced the Five Nations to reexamine their original goals and to adapt their strategies, while conserving the fundamentals of Iroquois traditions. The myth of Iroquois invincibility notwithstanding, in the second half of the 1660s the Five Nations were a people in crisis, and only a creative mix of fresh and traditional approaches to their problems allowed them to survive in their New World.

[97]Hunt, *Wars of the Iroquois*, 135; Talon to de Tracy and de Courcelles, in O'Callaghan, ed., *Documents Relative to the History of New-York*, 9:52–54; quotation from 54.
[98]"Extracts from the Addition to the present Memorial [to the king], 10 November 1670," in ibid., 66.

Epilogue

Iroquois Reconstruction

Brother Corlaer [governor of New York], the Governor of Canada calls us children which we now know is
not so. Therefore may the tree of peace remain
planted here [Albany] steady and straight and may it
not grow sideways so that we can really trust it, and
there will not be any evil found in this house.
> —Mohawk and Oneida sachems to New York
> governor Thomas Dongan, June 17, 1687

In March 1984, a group of scholars convened at Williamsburg, Virginia to assess "The 'Imperial' Iroquois." Laying to rest a myth that
had endured some 250 years, they declared, "The emperor has no
clothes."[1] Nonetheless, they were prepared to admit that, despite the
defeats and disappointments endured by the Iroquois, the Five Nations, though not imperial, achieved a kind of preeminence in colonial
North America, based on their "extraordinary ability to adapt familiar
customs and institutions in response to novel challenges, to convert
weaknesses into strengths, and to forge alliances among themselves
and with others that helped preserve native political and cultural
autonomy." The editors of a volume presenting some of these important papers concluded, "By making a virtue of necessity, the Iroquois may not have won themselves an empire, but they did win the
respect, even fear, of native and European peoples near and far."[2]

I too have attempted to challenge the idea of the imperial Iroquois

---

[1]See Daniel K. Richter and James H. Merrell, eds., *Beyond the Covenant Chain: The Iroquois
and Their Neighbors in Indian North America, 1600–1800* (Syracuse, N.Y., 1987), which published
revised versions of some of the papers presented at Williamsburg, and which represents
collectively an important revision of Iroquois history. "The emperor has no clothes" was
Richter's clever formulation of the point.
[2]Ibid., 7–8.

while acknowledging their strength, tenacity, creativity, and resilience.[3] From the earliest moments of their history, from their very origins as a people, the Iroquois ingeniously adapted traditional ideas and practices to new circumstances, converted weaknesses into strengths, and constructed new relationships that turned enemies into friends—even kinspeople; they revitalized themselves, promoted peace and their own survival, and maintained their cultural integrity and autonomy.

My story ends where most begin. The real crisis among the Five Nations, most historians now believe, emerged in the years following the 1667 peace with New France: the politically isolated Five Nations faced continuing pressures from native neighbors; turmoil enveloped the province of New York, caught in a transition from Dutch to English rule; disease continued to attack Iroquois bodies; and Jesuits conducted their most troubling campaign within Iroquoia against Iroquois beliefs, customs, and practices. Nonetheless, the Five Nations endured, just as they had before, and just as they would again, when they faced ever greater crises after the close of the colonial period.

In another sense, the closing of my story coincides with the demise of a different American "empire," that of the Netherlands. The 1664 English conquest and the firm establishment of British dominion after the brief reassertion of Dutch control, for fifteen months during 1673–1674, ended the history of New Netherland. Yet, as the province became New York and as Beverwyck became Albany, the Dutch presence on the margins of Iroquoia continued. Especially in the remote habitations along the upper Hudson and Mohawk Valleys, the impact of the English conquest was blunted, and anglicization proceeded more gradually than in New York City, or so, at least, many historians conclude. The people of "New Albany," according to one writer, "continued to practice their crafts and to trade for furs"; "life was business as usual" under the Duke of York's benign neglect. Dutch settlers followed their inclination to dismiss public affairs, concentrating instead on the centuries-old private traditions of family, craftsmanship, and religion. Dutch culture would endure privately in America, es-

---

[3]In contrast to Richter and Merrell, eds., *Beyond the Covenant Chain*, which denies the Iroquois an empire by means of challenging the results but not so much the alleged imperial design of Iroquois expansion, I have emphasized that the Five Nations never sought an imperial role.

pecially through the maintenance of the Dutch Reformed Church and the Dutch language.[4]

Yet the difficulty and pain of anglicization, even in isolated Albany, easily can be underestimated. A disappointed Jeremias van Rensselaer, director of Rensselaerswyck, for example, complained in 1668 of the unpleasantness and indignity of having to learn English, as he scurried to protect the family's rights and possessions in the New World. Riots accompanied the establishment of English garrisons in New York City, Bergen, and Esopus. Even in Albany, Donna Merwick argues, the English occupation was "pervasive and harsh." And English soldiers and officials questioned the loyalty of their new Dutch subjects in Albany and Schenectady, who were poised, not only along the new English-Iroquois frontier, but also along a new strategic front where the empires of England and France met in North America.[5]

Captain John Baker, English commander of the fort at Albany, for example, believed that Arent van Curler, the original patroon's cousin and one-time official and now a resident of Schenectady, was conspiring with the French to assist an invasion in the summer of 1666. John Pychon at Springfield, Massachusetts wrote Connecticut governor John Winthrop, Jr. that van Curler "is preparing provisions for them [the invading French force], and Capt. Baker is preparing powder and bullet for them." Soon after, on July 11, 1666, Pynchon

---

[4]On the conquest and its impact, see Donna Merwick, *Possessing Albany, 1630–1710: The Dutch and English Experiences* (New York, 1990), which represents a revision of the works listed below; Patricia U. Bonomi, *A Factious People: Politics and Society in Colonial New York* (New York; 1971); Robert C. Ritchie, *The Duke's Province: A Study of New York Politics and Society, 1664–1691* (Chapel Hill, N.C., 1977); Alice B. Kenney, "Private Worlds in the Middle Colonies: An Introduction to Human Tradition in American History," *New York History*, 51:1 (January 1970), 5–31; Stephan Bielinski, "The People of Colonial Albany, 1650–1800: Profile of a Community," in William Pencak and Conrad Edick Wright, eds., *Authority and Resistance in Early New York* (New York, 1988), 1–26; quotation from 4. Ironically, the English conquest helped to create a "Dutch" identity among the "mixed multitude" of Dutch, Flemings, Walloons, Germans, Scandinavians, Scots, Frenchmen, and others who, despite their diversity, shared a common history and an otherness relative to the English newcomers.

[5]A. J. F. van Laer, trans. and ed., *Correspondence of Jeremias van Rensselaer, 1651–1674* (Albany, N.Y., 1932), 403. On the popular discontent and political violence associated with the English conquest, see John M. Murrin, "English Rights as Ethnic Aggression: The English Conquest, the Charter of Liberties of 1683, and Leisler's Rebellion in New York," in Pencak and Wright, eds., *Authority and Resistance in New York*, 56–94, especially 58–60; Donna Merwick, "Becoming English: Anglo-Dutch Conflict in the 1670s in Albany, New York," *New York History*, 62 (October 1981), 389–414; quotation from 393; see also Merwick, *Possessing Albany*, especially 134–87. On the strategic situation of Albany and Schenectady, between English and French America, and the events culminating in the Schenectady massacre of 1690, see Thomas E. Burke, Jr., *Mohawk Frontier: The Dutch Community of Schenectady, New York, 1661–1710* (Ithaca, N.Y., 1991), 68–108.

confided to Richard Bellingham, the governor of Massachusetts Bay, that "the Dutch at Albany do much rejoice in the French, and make provisions for them to entertain them friendly." According to Pynchon, they "do speak slightly and contemptuously of the English there and say they shall be masters over the English very speedily."[6] Van Curler's particular loyalties and plans are not clear and cannot be reconstructed, and his accidental death in the summer of 1667, while enroute to New France, removed him from the scene. In a sense, both the French and the English competed for the allegiance, if not the hearts and minds, of the Dutch in this remote but vital town. While some continued for a generation to question the residents' leanings, and though the larger province suffered a violent upheaval in Jacob Leisler's Rebellion in 1689—an ethnic Dutch reaction to the English conquest and the new political forms it spawned—the English, in the end, successfully anglicized the residents of the upper Hudson.[7]

They accomplished the task in part through their efforts, at least initially, to provide generous terms, to respect local customs and autonomy, and to limit their own expectations. Captain Baker's official instructions, issued in 1668, included the charge, "Lett not your eares bee abused with private storyes of ye Dutch, being disaffected to ye English, for generally wee can not expect they love us."[8] Indeed, the Dutch did not love the English, and they were prepared to treat the new government with the same disregard or disdain that they showed the old, as they pursued their own profits through trade. In addition, increasingly caught between the colliding French and English empires, the Dutch settlers of the upper Hudson and Mohawk Valleys, like the Iroquois, would fall into the arms of the English, not out of any particular affection, but rather in an effort to avoid the devastation threatened increasingly by a hostile New France and its Indian allies. The sack of Schenectady in 1690, which left sixty dead, confirmed their sense of membership and dependancy in English New York.[9]

After the conquest of New Netherland and their forced peace with New France, the Five Nations faced military attack and warfare as the

[6]Carl Bridenbaugh, ed., *The Pynchon Papers: Letters of John Pynchon, 1654–1700*, Colonial Society of Massachusetts, *Collections*, 2 vols. (Boston, 1982), I, 57–59; quotations from 57 and 59.
[7]Murrin, "English Rights as Ethnic Aggression."
[8]J. Munsell, ed., *The Annals of Albany* (Albany, N.Y., 1856), 7: 98–101; quotation from 99.
[9]See Burke, *Mohawk Frontier*, especially 83–108.

most obvious, if not the most severe, threats to Iroquoia. Historians possess limited information on the number of casualties suffered in battle by the Five Nations. Rumors that circulated, on both sides of the seventeenth-century cultural frontier, about spectacular losses suffered by the Iroquois or their opponents, in battles that may or may not have been fought, provide little help in making estimations.[10] While Iroquois casualties in battle were sometimes exaggerated by contemporaries and can easily be overstated by historians, this loss of men must have been a serious drain on population and disruptive to social life.

Moreover, after Tracy's assaults on the Mohawks in 1666, which resulted in the destruction of entire villages and vast stores of food, it became clear that the French would practice a kind of total war, as great a threat to Iroquois women and children as to Iroquois men. The Mohawks suffered tremendously in 1666, even though few Iroquois people died in actual combat. Having fled into the forests to avoid French soldiers, they returned later only to face starvation and exposure. Father François le Mercier observed that "those familiar with these Barbarians' mode of life have not a doubt that almost as many will die of hunger as would have perished by the weapons of our soldiers, had they dared await the latter's approach."[11]

The Iroquois weathered this particular crisis, though they remained vulnerable and suffered similar assaults again in the seventeenth and eighteenth centuries.[12] The Five Nations were fortunate in suffering fewer defeats than many Native American peoples. But, creating

[10]Keith F. Otterbein determined that an Iroquois army lost approximately 340 men, and the Hurons 780, in the extraordinary fighting in March 1649 that destroyed Huronia. Leroy V. Eid attempted to corroborate Ojibwa legend, claiming that the Ojibwas and their allies "utterly crushed" the Five Nations in a massive, three-pronged assault some time in the 1690s. See Henry F. Dobyns, "Native American Population Collapse and Recovery," in W. R. Swagerty, ed., *Scholars and the Indian Experience: Critical Reviews of Recent Writing in the Social Sciences* (Bloomington, Ind., 1984), 24–25; Leroy V. Eid, "The Ojibwa-Iroquois War: The War the Five Nations Did Not Win," *Ethnohistory*, 36 (Fall 1979), 297–324. Eid's thesis is not persuasive. While his use of oral history in the absence of conventional sources documenting the event (perhaps absent for good reason) is laudable, he must notice that Ojibwa and Iroquois oral histories conflict. Eid favored Ojibwa sources, while simultaneously undermining the credibility of his informant, who, Eid admitted, "misconstrued" in an earlier work and who "cannot be considered the last word" (314–15).

[11]Reuben Gold Thwaites, ed., *The Jesuit Relations and Allied Documents*, 73 vols. (Cleveland, 1896–1901), 50:145.

[12]The final military campaign of destruction, and the most devastating series of raids to afflict Iroquoia, came in the summer of 1779 during the American Revolution, under the direction of General John Sullivan. "Sullivan's Raid" is described in Barbara Graymont, *The Iroquois in the American Revolution* (Syracuse, N.Y., 1972), 192–222, and in Anthony F. C. Wallace, *Death and Rebirth of the Seneca* (New York, 1970), 141–44.

much of their good fortune, they sought preservation in peace and, even in war, attempted to minimize casualities by emphasizing raiding and small-scale attacks. Because women, and men of peace, controlled Iroquois society and polity, the absence of Iroquois soldiers and their death in warfare disrupted Iroquois life somewhat less than was the case among societies which organized themselves in a patriarchal fashion. And because the economy of the Five Nations was based on the horticulture of women, warfare outside of Iroquoia proved less damaging to Iroquois subsistence.

Death and destruction visited Iroquoia more frequently through disease. Like the other indigenous inhabitants of the Americas, the Five Nations could not escape the effects of deadly European pathogens.[13] Old World maladies may have begun to penetrate Iroquoia in the shadowy period even before the Iroquois encountered Dutch or French people face to face. The experience of epidemic affliction was first recorded among the Five Nations by the Dutch surgeon and trader Harmen Meyndertsen van den Bogaert in the winter of 1634–35, who learned at one Mohawk village that "many Indians here in the castle had died of smallpox." At another Mohawk settlement, he observed, "I could see nothing else but graves," and on his return from Oneida he witnessed the transfer of a vast quantity of wampum among the mourning relatives of those who had succumbed to the epidemic.[14]

This documented epidemic only presaged the onset of many others, recorded and unrecorded. In 1647, following Father Isaac Jogues's

[13]On the impact of disease on indigenous inhabitants of the Americas, see the monumental work of Sherburne F. Cook and Woodrow Borah, *Essays in Population History*, 3 vols. (Berkeley, 1970–79); Sherburne F. Cook, "The Significance of Disease in the Extinction of the New England Indians," *Human Biology*, 45 (1973), 485–508; Alfred W. Crosby, "Virgin Soil Epidemics as a Factor in the Aboriginal Depopulation of America," *William and Mary Quarterly*, 3d ser., 33 (1976), 289–99, and Crosby, *The Columbian Exchange: Biological and Cultural Consequences of 1492* (Westport, Conn., 1972); William H. McNeil, *Plagues and Peoples* (Garden City, N.Y., 1977); Henry F. Dobyns, "Estimating Aboriginal American Population," *Current Anthropology*, 7 (1966), 395–449; Dobyns, "Native American Population"; Cornelius J. Jaenen, *Friend and Foe: Aspects of French-Amerindian Cultural Contact in the Sixteenth and Seventeenth Century* (New York, 1976), 98–108. On the controversy of whether bubonic plague entered the New World before the twentieth century, see Darrell A. Posey, "Entomological Considerations in Southeastern Aboriginal Demography," *Ethnohistory*, 23 (Spring 1976), 147–60, who concluded that the plague "is suredly as old in [this] country as any in the European heritage" (155). Dean R. Snow and Kim M. Lanphear, "European Contact and Indian Depopulation in the Northeast: The Timing of the First Epidemics," *Ethnohistory*, 35 (Winter 1988), 15–33, is the best recent statement of this demographic disaster.

[14]Charles T. Gehring and William A. Starna, trans. and eds., *A Journey into Mohawk and Oneida Country, 1634–1635: The Journal of Harmen Meyndertsz van den Bogaert* (Syracuse, N.Y., 1988), 4–5, 32n27, 21, 49n126.

mission and martyrdom, the Mohawks were "afflicted with a general malady, which caused great numbers of them to die."[15] In the mid-1650s, infections accompanied Jesuit missionaries once again. Many of those souls harvested for Christ soon departed the world as a result of "a great mortality [that] has prevailed in the country since we have been here," the Black Robes reported.[16] In the early 1660s, epidemic disease returned again to devastate the Five Nations. Hundreds perished. Jesuit Jerome Lalemant reported in 1663 that the affliction "wrought sad havoc" among many Iroquois, leaving "their villages nearly deserted, and their fields only half-tilled."[17] Missionaries continued to report contagions and death among their charges in Iroquoia, once they returned in 1667—the Senecas in 1668, the Mohawks in 1673, and the Senecas again in 1676.[18] Louis de Buade, comte de Frontenac, the governor-general of New France, called smallpox the "Indian Plague" and suggested the desolation it caused among the Iroquois in 1679: "They think no longer of Meeting nor of Wars, but only of bewailing the dead, of whom there is already an immense number."[19]

The march of disaster in the form of deadly disease continued through the rest of the seventeenth and into the eighteenth century. Population declined radically among the Five Nations, especially as a result of epidemic affliction. Among the Mohawks, about whom we have the most information, population diminished by approximately 50 percent from 1640 to 1670, from a base that had already been decreased by earlier devastation. In 1660, contemporary estimates placed Mohawk population (in terms of fighting men) at approximately 500. By 1677 the number of Mohawk men had dwindled to about 300. If the ratio of men capable of bearing arms to the total

[15] Thwaites, ed., *Jesuit Relations*, 30:229, 273; 31:121.

[16] Ibid., 44:43.

[17] Ibid., 47:193, 205; 48:79–83; 49:147–49; John Duffy, *Epidemics in Colonial America* (Baton Rouge, La., 1953), 70–71; Francis Jennings, *Ambiguous Iroquois Empire*, 129; Hunt, *Wars of the Iroquois*, 134.

[18] Daniel K. Richter, "War and Culture: The Iroquois Experience," *William and Mary Quarterly*, 3d ser., 40 (October 1983), 537. See also Duffy, *Colonial Epidemics*, 187, on the "general influenza" outbreak of 1676, which carried off sixty children and many adults within a single month.

[19] Duffy, *Colonial Epidemics*, 71; in October 1679, the Onondagas and Oneidas excused themselves for missing a council with Virginia's Colonel William Kendall, claiming "ye Sicknesse of feavor and Small Pox Reigning soo Violently in our Countrey hath been...a great obstruction to our Comeing" (Lawrence H. Leder, ed., "The Livingston Indian Records," *Pennsylvania History*, 23 [January 1956], 51, 55). Note the suggestion here and in Frontenac's statement of the employment of traditional mechanisms in addressing the crisis of death; mourning and condolence would precede requickening, revitalization.

population was 1:4, then the Mohawks numbered approximately 2,000 in 1660 and about 1,200 in 1677.[20] These figures pale in comparison to the pre-epidemic population estimations of William Starna and others. Employing archaeological and historical material to estimate postepidemic population levels for the Mohawks, Starna projected (using mortality rates of 50 to 70 percent, and estimating a family size of 4 to 5) that from 8,258 to 17,111 Mohawks lived in aboriginal America.[21] Much remains uncertain in these estimates, but of the destruction wrought by Old World disease on the people of the Five Nations there is little doubt.

The Iroquois responded to population loss in a traditional fashion—through adoption. On a grand or modest scale, they followed Deganawidah's prescriptions and incorporated outsiders into their longhouses, clans, villages, tribes, and League. By transforming enemies into friends, foreigners into Iroquois, they fulfilled Deganawidah's injunction to "strengthen their house." The Five Nations sought to "remove the bushes" and "level the ground" separating them from surrounding nations. They persuaded outsiders to amalgamate with them and become one people, sheltered by the branches of the Great Tree of Peace. As the scourges of disease and warfare endangered the Iroquois and other Indian people, the absorption of outsiders left some Iroquois villages with "more strangers among them than pure Iroquois," Jesuit observers discovered. They noted in 1657, for example, that some Iroquois settlements "now contain more Foreigners than natives of the country. Onnontaghe [Onondaga] counts seven different nations, who have come to settle in it; and there are as many as eleven in Sonnontouan [among the Senecas]."[22]

Yet the Five Nations proved remarkably capable of naturalizing such foreigners as full citizens of Iroquoia. Father Jacques Bruyas

[20]Richter, "War and Culture," 542–43; see also Richter, "The Ordeal of the Longhouse: Change and Persistence on the Iroquois Frontier, 1609–1720," Ph.D. diss. Columbia University, 1984, 595–600, which includes two convenient population tables. See also table of "Iroquois Population Estimates by Fighting Men, 1660–1779," in Elisabeth Tooker, "The League of the Iroquois: Its History, Politics, and Ritual," in Bruce G. Trigger, ed., *Handbook of North American Indians: Northeast* (Washington, D.C., 1978), 15:421. Snow and Lanphear, "European Contact and Indian Depopulation," 23–24, confirm these estimates. Snow and W. A. Starna have corroborated these findings through extensive archaeological work in the Mohawk Valley and are beginning to publish some of the results of their work.
[21]William Starna, "Mohawk Iroquois Populations: A Revision," *Ethnohistory*, 27 (1980), 371–82. See also Snow and Lanphear, "European Contact and Indian Depopulation," 23–24, which estimated a decrease in Mohawk population of some 75 percent between 1633 and 1660.
[22]Thwaites, ed., *Jesuit Relations*, 43:265.

reported that those adopted by the Oneidas—former Algonquins and Hurons, who made up two-thirds of their village in 1668—"have become Iroquois in temper and inclination."[23] And as some Hurons informed Tracy, "the element of greatest strength among the Iroquois was not the Iroquois themselves." Instead, "their might resided in the large number of captives,—French, Hurons, Algonquins, and those from the other Nations,—who formed more than two-thirds of the Iroquois Nations."[24] The Iroquois willingness to adopt and transform outsiders into Iroquois belies the claim of some historians that the Five Nations saw themselves as a "master race."[25] Those adopted became full members of their new communities. The Iroquois "yoke" was hardly oppressive. As Francis Jennings has aptly concluded, "No multitude groaned under the hobnailed moccasin."[26] The Five Nations' success in assimilating their rivals, or the refugees of other conflicts, indeed contributed mightily to their cultural strength and enhanced their power in colonial North America.

Yet as the numbers of the adopted grew among the Five Nations, it became more difficult to assimilate them. The Jesuits saw an opportunity when the remnants of their former flocks—especially from Huronia—began to reside in Iroquoia in increasing numbers. Father Jacques Fremin found a number of Hurons who had been instructed in the Faith living among the Senecas when he established his mission in one Seneca village in September 1669.[27] Father Étienne de Carheil preached to Hurons and Susquehannocks, as well as to Cayugas, at his mission in the latter's country.[28] The Black Robes' presence not only inhibited a speedy and thorough assimilation of these outsiders but also encouraged the formation of a divisive Christian faction of native Iroquois that began to coalesce around the Jesuits' non-Iroquois neophytes. By the late 1660s, the traditional practice of adoption—for so long an asset to the Five Nations and a monument to Deganawidah's vision—emerged as a threat, rather than a prop, to the Iroquois Longhouse.[29]

[23]Ibid., 51:123.
[24]Ibid., 49:233.
[25]See Allen W. Trelease, *Indian Affairs in Colonial New York: The Seventeenth Century* (Ithaca, N.Y., 1960), 21.
[26]Jennings, *Ambiguous Iroquois Empire*, 94. Nonetheless, in contrast to my interpretation of the Iroquois goals, Jennings seems willing to argue that the Iroquois sought an empire, even if they were never able to construct one.
[27]Thwaites, ed., *Jesuit Relations*, 54:81–83.
[28]Ibid., 52:179.
[29]The best treatment of the process of Jesuit subversion and the rise of factionalism based

As the Iroquois kept alive the hope of expanding their universe of peace in the 1660s, they embraced the Black Robes as ambassadors and potential kinsmen, if not as teachers of an alien and unwelcome faith. But the Iroquois-Jesuit association of the 1660s, 1670s, and the years beyond proved disastrous for the Five Nations. Besides the contagions unwittingly carried by the missionaries, the Iroquois endured a cultural, social, and political assault staged by the members of the Society of Jesus. Alternating subtle with blatant attacks, the Jesuits hoped to undermine the spiritual foundation of Iroquois culture.[30] When Jesuit missionaries attacked the Iroquois belief in dreams, for example, and the rituals expressing such beliefs that maintained health and good fortune, they antagonized the Iroquois men and women and exposed themselves as dangerous sorcerers. In acting to prevent traditional cures, once their own evil spells, as some believed, had produced pestilence or other misfortunes, they compounded the damage and justified the Iroquois sense that the Black Robes sought the Five Nations' ruin.

While most Iroquois people found the Jesuit message unpersuasive and unappealing, the priests of New France enjoyed enough success, especially among newly incorporated Iroquois, to spark troubling debate and to exacerbate Iroquois factional tendencies. A single convert within a longhouse could upset social arrangements and prevent others from satisfying collective ritual obligations. Iroquois culture emphasized the achievement of domestic harmony, even if it entailed individual repression of disagreement or hostility. For this reason, missionaries among the Five Nations and other Iroquoian people often overestimated the success of their evangelizing. They later discovered, when promising neophytes apostasized, that the Christian message had been only superficially embraced. Eventually, priests required greater evidence of sincere belief among converts, or they baptized only those so close to death that backsliding became impossible (which for the Iroquois further confirmed the Jesuits' association with evil and death). Among the Oneidas in 1668, Father Jacques

---

especially on the incomplete naturalization of outsiders is Daniel K. Richter, "Iroquois Versus Iroquois: Jesuit Missions and Christianity in Village Politics, 1642–1686," *Ethnohistory*, 32 (1985), 1–16.

[30]One of the prime objects of their crusade was the Iroquois "Divinity of Dreams, which is the source of all their errors, and the soul, as it were, of their Religion," reported Father Étienne de Carheil from among the Cayugas in 1668 (Thwaites, ed., *Jesuit Relations*, 54:65). This campaign represented a fundamental challenge to Iroquois world view. The definitive work on this subject is Wallace, *Death and Rebirth of the Seneca*, 59–75.

Bruyas observed, "I have Never seen them become angry, even On occasions when our Frenchmen would have uttered a hundred oaths."[31] Yet such calm politeness, in the interest of communal harmony, broke down when some members of lodges and villages sincerely embraced Catholicism and, with the zeal of converts, defended it against their kinsmen.[32]

The worst fears of the Iroquois were realized when Oneida and Mohawk converts followed the Jesuits to a mission settlement on the Saint Lawrence at La Prairie de la Madeleine in the late 1660s and 1670s. By 1670, twenty Iroquois families resided there, and in 1673 the Mohawk leader Kryn led some forty Mohawks to the Saint Lawrence. So many Mohawks had migrated from a particular town in the Mohawk Valley that the new mission settlement they occupied came to be called "Caughnawaga," after the village they had abandoned. Jesuits reported in the same year that now more Mohawk warriors lived at Caughnawaga than in the Mohawk homeland.[33]

Finally, an event that occurred in the late 1680s perhaps best exemplified the dangers posed by French and Jesuit penetration of Iroquoia—the adoption of Father Pierre Milet by a noble Oneida family, who ritually resurrected the priest as Otassete, an Oneida League sachem.[34] As a representative in the Grand Council of the Iroquois League, Father Milet symbolized the grave threat from within to Iroquois culture, society, and politics. Who could lead a pro-French, Christian faction more effectively than a member of the Society of Jesus? And who would be less able or willing to make Deganawidah's dream manifest in the Iroquois New World?

It became clear during these decades that the French would never assimilate, on Iroquois terms, into Iroquois society, and the Five Nations themselves risked being absorbed or ruined by the spread of French religion and culture. Jesuit priests certainly showed no signs

---

[31]Thwaites, ed., *Jesuit Relations*, 51:129.

[32]When an important headman like Onondaga sachem Garakontié converted, the disruptions within Iroquois communities, and within the entire confederation, could be enormous. If family and clan members followed the lead of respected converts, villages could be dangerously split between Christian and traditional, pro- and anti-French, factions. Christian leaders among the Iroquois sometimes refused to perform traditional ceremonial functions, thereby upsetting the stability and endangering the effective operations of a society and polity based on consensus. See especially Richter, "Iroquois Versus Iroquois." And cf. Stephen Saunders Webb, *1676: The End of American Independence* (New York, 1984), 251–302.

[33]On Caughnawaga, see William N. Fenton and Elisabeth Tooker, "Mohawk," in Trigger, ed., *Handbook of North American Indians*, 15:469–71; Richter, "Iroquois Versus Iroquois," 10–11; Thwaites, ed., *Jesuit Relations*, 63:179.

[34]Thwaites, ed., *Jesuit Relations*, 44:67–107.

of establishing explicit kinship bonds with Iroquois people. The priests' celibacy was difficult for the Five Nations to comprehend, as Father Bruyas noted: "When they are told that there are men, and even women, In France who Never marry, it appears so Extraordinary to them that they can hardly Believe it."[35] Yet they were obliged to believe it after the missionaries refused to join with them as one people, to love Iroquois bodies as they loved Iroquois souls.

The devastation to Iroquois culture, religion, society, and polity mounted with the prolonged Jesuit presence in Iroquoia, and a new French expansionist policy in the west took shape during the administration of Louis Buade, comte de Frontenac, which ruined Iroquois hopes for peace with the western Indian nations and made the maintenance of peace with New France more difficult. And as the Iroquois struggled to stabilize their southern and eastern frontiers and define their relationship with their new English allies, they recognized that a mechanical application of traditional formulas would not allow them to construct the peace they sought or to maintain the autonomy their survival demanded. Holding firmly to the essence of Deganawidah's dream, and forging new mechanisms to make it manifest in their world, the Iroquois began to develop a new *foreign* policy. Accepting fictive, or symbolic, over literal kinship, and social separation rather than amalgamation, the Five Nations increasingly expected less of their allies, and sought more self-consciously to preserve their own autonomy.

The so-called Covenant Chain, or chains, that emerged most clearly in the eighteenth century represented, then, a less ambitious set of intercultural alliances, which attached discrete peoples and provinces to the Iroquois in a fashion designed to promote their mutual interests while preserving their autonomy. No longer would the Five Nations seek to make literal kinsfolk of their European neighbors, nor would they so willingly risk the dangers presented by unassimilable Europeans in their midst. As it became clearer that the Iroquois Longhouse would not continue to lengthen, the Five Nations increasingly strengthened its sides and endwalls, making them permanent rather than temporary. In the heralded "Grand Settlement of 1701," this is essentially what occurred: the dual treaties with Albany and Quebec

[35]Ibid., 51:127.

signaled that the Iroquois would pursue not neutrality so much as autonomy—paradoxically, in a context of interdependency.[36]

Ironically, as the reality of kinship between allies became more tenuous, the vocabulary and ritual of kinship in diplomatic discourse became codified. The ritual of condolence, bequeathed by Deganwidah, continued to facilitate peaceful interaction between the Five Nations and their allies, who were now considered links in covenant chains but not actual members of the Iroquois Longhouse. Europeans may have misunderstood or disregarded the implications of diplomatic ceremonies and molded the conventional words and procedures to fit their own purposes. And the Iroquois accommodated new circumstances while maintaining the symbolic meaning of the sacred pledges between "brethren." The Covenant Chain was a hybrid form, a multicultural creation which each side believed reflected the design of the other, and which each sought to shape to its own advantage. Although the Dutch-Iroquois links preceded and contributed to its development, the Covenant Chain was primarily a product of the new English–Five Nations relationship established after the conquest of 1664. It represented a new "structure of the conjuncture," in the anthropologist Marshall Sahlins's terms, which joined the Iroquois and English worlds and organized their discourse, but which did not merge them, instead leaving each of them discrete. The English-Iroquois relationship did not conform to the Iroquois expectations, which they had expressed to the Dutch and French in an earlier time. Diplomacy had replaced domesticity and kinship. Nonetheless, the chain did not signify a fundamental abandonment of Iroquois tradition; the new "silver chains" that bound the English and the Five Nations to each other were plated, their precious metal merely overlaying ancient cords first constructed by Iroquois people in a long forgotten time.[37]

---

[36]Anthony F. C. Wallace, "Origins of Iroquois Neutrality: The Grand Settlement of 1701," *Pennsylvania History*, 24 (1957), 223–35, is the classic presentation. Recently, however, historians have somewhat minimized the particular importance of this series of events, have challenged the notion that the Five Nations remained neutral or have revised their characterizations of that neutrality, and have questioned the mastery of the Iroquois in balancing England and France against each other. See especially Richard L. Haan, "The Problem of Iroquois Neutrality: Suggestions for Revision," *Ethnohistory*, 27 (1980), 317–30, and Haan, "Covenant and Consensus: Iroquois and English, 1676–1760," in Richter and Merrell, eds., *Beyond the Covenant Chain*, 41–57. See also Richter, "Ordeals of the Longhouse," in ibid., 26.

[37]See Mary A. Druke, "Linking Arms: The Structure of Iroquois Intertribal Diplomacy," in Richter and Merrell, eds., *Beyond the Covenant Chain*, 29–39. It may even have been the

In a series of complex negotiations between 1675 and 1677 involving the Five Nations, other Indian groups, and the English colonies
in New York, New England, and on the Chesapeake, the Iroquois
began to formalize their new approach to foreign relations. Following
earlier parleys with Sir Edmund Andros of New York and with Henry
Coursey of Maryland, the Five Nations met in February 1677 at Shackamaxon (later, Philadelphia) with the English, Susquehannocks, and
Delawares, and entered into a treaty that brought most of the defeated
Susquehannocks into the Iroquois League. In the spring, the English-
Iroquois alchemy transformed their alliance into a "Silver" Covenant
Chain, according to Francis Jennings, when the Five Nations joined
in a treaty with New York, Massachusetts, and Connecticut, and with
other Indian groups of the Hudson Valley. And in July and August,
another silver Covenant Chain treaty emerged at Albany in negoti-
ations involving the Five Nations, other interested tribes, New York,
Maryland, and Virginia.[38]

In the Covenant Chain alliance, each party promised aid and assistance to the other, while each in theory worked to maintain a general
peace within the Chain's bounds. For the English, New France's exclusion was important, since English America depended on the Five
Nations as a shield against French incursions, a discouragement to
French westward expansion, and a source of auxiliary (or even primary) troops in the English-French imperial conflict in North America.
And English colonial officials turned Iroquois kinship terms—still
prevalent in treaty negotiations, though now clearly symbolic rather
than factual—to their own purposes, as they asserted their sovereignty
over the Five Nations and their clients. Despite lofty claims, English
dominance was merely conceptual. The Iroquois retained their au-

---

case in some treaty minutes that this silver covenant chain was unilaterally imposed by English
scribes as a symbol or metaphor for the English-Iroquois relationship, ignoring and replacing
the more traditional Iroquois metaphor of "clasped hands." See Haan, "Covenant and Consensus," 45.

[38]On the so-called Silver Covenant Chain treaty at Albany, see Leder, ed., "Livingston
Indian Records," 42–48. See Francis Jennings et al., eds., *The History and Culture of Iroquois
Diplomacy: An Interdisciplinary Guide to the Treaties of the Six Nations and Their League* (Syracuse,
N.Y., 1985), 157–208, for a "Descriptive Treaty Calendar," which lists these and other treaties.
The foremost historian of the Iroquois Covenant Chain, especially in its eighteenth-century
manifestation, is Francis Jennings, *Ambiguous Iroquois Empire;* Jennings argues that a single,
monolithic Covenant Chain emerged in 1677 (167). Haan, "Covenant and Consensus," 44–
45, however, argues persuasively that no such Silver Covenant Chain existed at least for
another decade, that numerous separate chains were constructed independently by the Iroquois (and even by the English), and that the relationship between the Iroquois and English
"was even *more* ambiguous than we thought" (42).

tonomy and worked to promote their own interests within the structure of the Covenant Chain.

While the English attempted to retain the Iroquois as their exclusive client, the Five Nations sought an advantageous peace with New France. English officials discouraged Iroquois peace overtures to Canada, but the Iroquois themselves recognized the benefits of an alliance shorn of the liabilities of earlier models, one that would establish a lasting peace and allow them to survive and prosper as an autonomous people. Yet demonstrating that the Iroquois also saw themselves as equal partners in the alliance, as interdependent with the Europeans but hardly in a state of dependency, two Onondaga sachems delivered this statement to officials at Albany in November 1685: "We are . . . of the opinion yt. it is farr ye best to be in Peace, & not to warr wt any Christians, But Corlaer [the governor of New York] must likewise take care that they be in Peace over ye Great water, yt Soe wee may all live in Peace & Tranquility together."[39] Two Seneca sachems similarly expressed their resolve to seek peace with the French and boldly urged the English to effect a peace across the Atlantic that might aid the Iroquois in their quest for neutrality: "Take Courage and Cause all ye Commotion there to cease. . . . [Y]e Christian sachims yt live over ye great water, ought also to live in Peace wt on[e] anoyr."[40]

Such a peace between all these parties was not to be in this century, despite Iroquois efforts. Frustrations ultimately led to warfare between New France and Iroquoia, and the Covenant Chain alliance, especially its English links, provided less help than the Five Nations had hoped. The Iroquois discovered that the English were undependable as allies, when French troops, militia, and Indian auxiliaries invaded their homeland five times during the last two decades of the seventeenth century. When peace finally emerged from the chaos of these years, the Iroquois obtained from the French something more, and from the English something less, than they had earlier enjoyed: a tenuous neutrality. In the "Grand Settlement of 1701" between the Five Nations, English America, and New France, the Iroquois constructed a new balance of peace that allowed them the measure of isolation, internal harmony, and autonomy necessary for survival, prosperity, and revitalization in their New World.

[39]Leder, ed., "Livingston Indian Records," 93.
[40]Ibid., 94.

Index

Abenakis, 230, 252–53
Acadia, 187
Achiendase, 237. *See also* le Mercier, François; le Moyne, Simon
Agrippa, Henry Cornelius, 33
Albanel, Charles (S.J.), 218
Albany, 119, 127, 139, 140, 254–55, 258, 259, 268, 270, 271. *See also* Beverwyck; Fort Orange
Alexander, Sir William, 194
Algonquins, 69–72, 77–78, 108, 221, 222, 224–26, 232, 241, 245, 248, 250–51, 265
Amsterdam, 128. *See also* Dutch West India Company
Andioura (Mohawk), 235
Andros, Sir Edmund, 270
Anglicization, 139, 258–60
archaeology, 14–15
Arinadsit, Marie (Christian Huron), 183–85
Atironta, Jean Baptiste (Christian Huron), 226
Atogwatkwann (Mohawk), 246–47
atonement. *See* Five Nations of the Iroquois: murder and atonement
Axtell, James, 22, 92, 107

Baker, Captain John, 259–60
Barclay, Henry, 114
Barentsz, Pieter, 130

Bartram, John, 30, 40, 41
Beauchamp, William M., 97
"Beaver Wars," 229–30. *See also* "Wars of the Iroquois"
Beverwyck, 120, 121, 139–40, 141, 142, 158, 159, 162, 165, 170–72, 176; becomes Albany, 258; created as market town, 140; life in, 121, 140, 143–53, 155; settlement described, 140
Bellingham, Richard, 260
Bogaert, Harmen Meyndertsz van den, 38, 41, 69, 150, 164, 262
Bosch, Cornelis, 159
Boston, 230
Boucher, Pierre, 215
Bracque, Georges, 4
Bradford, William, 15, 17
Brant, Joseph, 83
Breuckelen, Cornelis Teunisz van, 157
Brillat-Savarin, Jean Anthelme, 89
Bruyas, Jacques (S.J.), 107, 218, 219, 264–8
Buckingham, Duke of, 194
burgerlijk (civic, mercantile life), 125, 207
Buteaux, Jacques (S.J.), 221–22

Caen, sieurs de, 189
Carheil, Étienne de (S.J.), 265

Carignan-Salières regiment, 206, 215–16, 218, 219, 255

Cartier, Jacques, 186–87

Caughnawaga, 162, 171, 267; Christian Mohawk settlement on the St. Lawrence (Kahnawake), 267

Cayugas, 53, 62–63, 94, 95, 108, 124, 167, 235, 238, 249, 265. *See also* Five Nations of the Iroquois

Champlain, Samuel de, 40, 69–74, 130, 187–90, 197, 220, 222, 223

Chaumonot, Pierre-Joseph-Marie (S.J.), 185, 235, 237, 248

"clash of cultures" model, 3–4, 9–10

Colbert, Jean-Baptiste, 200–202, 203, 207, 215, 218

Colden, Cadwallader, 6, 114

Coligny, Admiral Gaspard de, 187

Communauté des Habitants, 198–200

Compagnie de Canada, 188–89

Compagnie de Cent-Associés (the Hundred Associates), 191–95, 198–200

Compagnie de Montmorency pour la Nouvelle-France, 189

Compagnie des Indes Occidentales, 203

Condé, Henri de Bourbon, prince de, 188

Condolence Ceremony, 64, 77–82, 90–91, 94–95, 101–3, 111, 112, 167–68, 225–26, 233–34, 238, 244, 245, 248–49, 250, 269. *See also* Deganawidah Epic; Five Nations of the Iroquois: diplomacy

Connecticut, 259, 270

Cooper, James Fenimore, 6

Courcelle, Daniel de Rémy, sieur de, 218, 254–55

Coursey, Henry, 270

Cousture (Coûture), Guillaume, 77, 255

Covenant Chain(s), 3, 268–71; "silver" chains, 269, 270

Crabaat, Abraham, 150

Cronon, William, 42

"Cubist" history, 4–5, 120, 182. *See also* historical method

cultural frontiers: concept, 2–3; Dutch-Iroquois, 120–21, 154–55, 177, 178–79; English-Iroquois, 259–60, 268–69; French-Iroquois, 181–83, 204, 209–12, 213–14, 218, 220–21, 223, 239, 241–46, 250, 253

Curler, Arent van, 165, 259–60

Dablon, Claude (S.J.), 235, 237

d'Ailleboust de Coulanges, Louis, 239, 244, 245

d'Argenson, Pierre de Voyer, vicômte, 247

Deganawidah, 5, 7, 64, 75, 81–82, 85–115, 170, 178, 227, 230, 231, 233, 235, 246, 248, 249, 253, 264, 267, 268, 269. *See also* Deganawidah Epic

Deganawidah Epic, 7, 77, 81–115, 231, 235; and Great Law, 7, 85, 94–110, 231; sources for, 81–84, 103; symbols and metaphors of, 8, 59, 64, 78, 87–88, 94–95, 98–103, 110–11, 185, 225–26, 234, 248–49, 264. *See also* Deganawidah

Delawares, 270

Denonville, Jacques-René de Brisay, marquis de, 27, 32

Dickinson, John, 232

disease and depopulation, 67, 89, 92, 107, 132, 137, 227, 228, 253, 256, 258, 262–65

Donck, Adriaen van der, 18, 26, 36–38, 155

Drisius, Reverend Samuel, 142

Druillettes, Gabriel (S.J.), 230, 252

Du Creux, François, 214–15, 221–22, 232

Dunlap, William, 83

Du Pont, François Grave, 220

Dutch, the. *See* New Netherland; Netherlands, the

Dutch East India Company, 127–28

Dutch West India Company, 127–38, 141, 147–53, 172, 174; administration in New Netherland, 128–29, 130, 147–48, 150–52; problems in colonizing, 133–34, 136–38; problems in controlling employees and inhabitants, 147–53, 158–63; relations with Indians, 130–32, 172–79

Dyckman, Johannes, 148, 150, 170

English, the, 3, 133, 136, 152–53, 206; as allies of Five Nations, 254–55, 268, 269–71; rivalry with Dutch, 133, 138, 258–59; rivalry with French, 259–60, 270–71

Esopus Indians, 120, 169–70, 252; and conflicts with Dutch, 120, 139, 169–70, 252

Fenton, William N., 84

Fire: as ecological factor, 35–36; European attitudes toward, 33, 149; Native American attitudes and practices, 33–35

Five Nations of the Iroquois: adoption, 89, 105–8, 170, 237, 264–65; agriculture, 25–32, 44–45; archaeological sites, 54, 59, 60, 65 (*see also* Owasco: archaeological sites); cannibalism, 68, 77, 85, 87–90, 106, 112; chiefs, 74, 80, 86, 94–98, 104, 105; composure, restraint, and self-control among, 112–13, 249, 266–67; conceptions of trade, 171–79; cosmology and worldview, 20–25, 91–92, 100, 110, 219; crisis of late seventeenth century, 258–71; death, grief, and mourning, 74, 77, 79–81, 86, 90, 97, 101–5, 106, 109–10, 113, 231, 234, 262, 263 (*see also* Condolence Ceremony); diplomacy, 8, 79–81, 109–11, 114–15, 124, 131–32, 167–72, 180–83, 225–27, 228, 249, 253, 256, 268–71; dreams and "dream guessing," 49–50, 71, 112–13, 266; and ecology, 41–42; and fire, 32–36; formation of, 59, 64, 66–68, 88, 110; fortifications, 54, 66, 165, 169; gender arrangements, 28–31, 36–40, 50–52, 85, 87, 95, 104, 109–10, 183–85, 236–37, 262; health and healing, 93, 113, 266; hunting, 38–41; images of, 6, 67, 229, 257–58; incorporation and transformation of outsiders, 8–9, 65–68, 89–90, 105–8, 110–11, 131–32, 175, 264–68; internecine warfare and its prevention, 53–59, 65–68, 81, 85,

87–89, 101–5, 231; kinship ideas and organization, 59–62, 80–81, 95–96, 104, 108–11, 183, 213, 236–37; League of Peace, 53, 59, 65–68, 82–108, 227, 231, 236, 270; Longhouse as symbol of peace and Iroquois League, 7, 8–9, 60, 94, 97, 108, 110–11, 152, 155, 170, 171, 179, 235–36, 249, 264, 265, 268, 269; longhouses, 7, 46–48, 54, 60–63; men, 36–40, 87, 106, 109–10, 236–37; murder and atonement, 104–5, 170, 244, 245, 249; myth of Imperial Iroquois, 6, 67, 229, 256, 257–58; and peace, 6 9, 43–44, 53–59, 65–68, 74–75, 76–77, 81–88, 94–115, 178, 213–14, 256, 261; peace among Iroquois defined, 108–9; political structure, 95–100, 236; and politics of consensus, 95–96; population, 137, 203, 206, 263–64; rumors of French attacks, 245; settlement patterns, 26, 28, 36, 40–41, 53–59, 62–65; shamans, 91–92; soul, conceptions of, 101, 112–13; subsistence, 26–28, 36–41, 54, 109; suicide, 113; torture, 89–90, 106, 112, 251; views of history, 7, 81–82, 86, 88–89, 114–15, 231; warfare, 65–74, 97–98, 109–10, 129–32, 177, 262; witchcraft, 25, 77, 86, 90–94, 113; women, 27–31, 80, 85–86, 95, 104, 106, 109–10, 183–85. *See also constituent nations*: Cayugas; Mohawks; Oneidas; Onondagas; Senecas

—domestic model of peace, 108–11, 115, 154–55, 170; applied to Dutch, 154–55, 163, 167–72, 176, 249; applied to French, 183, 213–14, 219–20, 225–27, 231–40, 244–46, 249–50, 267–68; applied to New France's Indian allies, 225–27, 233–34, 239–40

—and Dutch, 8–10, 120–26, 130–32, 167–79; instruction of Dutch in protocols, 168–71; peace mediators on behalf of Dutch, 169–71, 252; seeking of Dutch mediation with

Five Nations of the Iroquois,
—and Dutch (*cont.*)
  French, 170–71, 247; views of
    Dutch, 124–26, 148, 152, 163, 166,
    167–72
—and English (after 1664), 260, 268–
  71
—and French: attempts to establish
  peace with New France, 180–81,
  199, 214, 217, 219, 222–28, 229–
  50, 254, 255–56, 271; disappointment with French failure to assimilate,
  246, 266–68; views of French, 166,
  183, 209–12, 213–14, 219; warfare
  with New France, 199, 223–25,
  229–30, 232, 241–56, 260–61, 271
—and Hurons, 223–34, 239–40, 248,
  251, 265
—and Indians of New England, 252–
  53
Flemish Bastard (Mohawk),
  217
Fortescue, Sir John, 22–23
Fort Nassau, 127, 129, 130
Fort Orange, 120, 121, 124, 129,
  130–2, 134, 139–40, 142, 143–53,
  155, 158, 159, 160, 162, 163, 166,
  168–72, 175, 176, 192, 247, 252;
  surrounding settlements described,
  140–41
France: colonial expansion and
  imperial rivalry, 186–87, 191, 194,
  208, 268; economic competition
  with Dutch in New World, 201–2;
  and immigration to New France,
  188, 189, 193, 202–9; mercantilism,
  192, 200–202, 208; rivalry with
  England, 194, 200, 259–60, 270–71
Fremin, Jacques (S.J.), 219, 265
Frontenac, Louis de Buade, comte de,
  192, 263, 268
fur trade, 155–56, 172–76. *See also*
  New Netherland: and Indian trade;
  New France: and fur trade

Garakontié (Onondaga), 248–49
Garreau, Leonard (S.J.), 239, 244
Godefroy, Thomas, 225
Goupil, René, 166

Grande Cruelliére, La (Large Spoon).
  See Atogwatkwann
"Grand Settlement of 1701," 268–69,
  271
Great Chain of Being, 22–25
Great Law. *See* Deganawidah Epic:
  and Great Law
Greenbush (Greenenbosch), 140. *See
  also* Rensselaerswyck

Hale, Horatio, 83–84, 97, 236
Hall, David D., 25
handelstijd (trading season), 121
Handsome Lake (Seneca), 92
Harris, R. Cole, 195, 201, 207
Hartgers, Pieter, 159–60
Heckewelder, John, 82
hell, 33, 34
Henri II, 187
Henri IV, 187
Hewitt, J. N. B., 21
Hiawatha (Mohawk), 82–83, 85–91,
  94, 101. *See also* Deganawidah Epic
Hillebrant, Nicolaes Gregory, 150
Historia Canadensis, 214–15
historical method, 1–5, 9–10, 13–15,
  41–42, 113–15, 120
Hooges, Anthony de, 158
Hospitalière nuns, 196
Hudson, Henry, 126–27
Huizinga, J. H., 144
Hundred Associates. *See* Compagnie
  de Cent-Associés
Hunt, George T., 67, 224–25, 228,
  256
Hurons, 27, 67–68, 69–72, 77–79, 90,
  91, 108, 190, 220, 223, 238, 239–
  40, 241, 242–43 (map), 244, 248,
  250–51, 265; and destruction of
  Huronia, 227, 230; Jesuit mission
  among, 196, 208, 224, 229, 238,
  239–40, 242–43, 265; hostility to
  Five Nations, 227, 233, 250–51. *See
  also* Five Nations of the Iroquois:
  and Hurons

Iroquoia: landscape of, 13, 18–25, 32,
  36, 40–41, 64–65, 74; as cultural
  landscape, 20, 32; as gendered
  landscape, 28–31, 36; as spiritual
  landscape, 20–25; territory of the

Iroquoia (*cont.*)

Five Nations, 7, 13, 16 (map), 19 (map), 141, 148, 164–65; transformation of, 26–42, 64–65, 86–87
Iroquois. *See* Five Nations of the Iroquois

Jaenen, Cornelius J., 220
Jansz, Marcelis, 148
Jansz, Steeven, 148
Jemison, Mary, 106
Jennings, Francis, 265, 270
Jesuits, 34, 68, 91–92, 101–3, 107, 142, 166, 183, 190, 196–97, 214–15; idea of history, 1, 214–15; and Iroquois assimilation program, 213, 219–20, 234–38, 239, 267; and military assault against Iroquois, 216 (map), 217–20, 230, 252, 254; and martyrdom, 92, 221–22, 228–29, 243; missionary activities among the Five Nations, 91–92, 166, 180–86, 213, 214–15, 218–20, 221–22, 224, 228–29, 235–41, 246–47, 256, 258, 263–68; missionary program, 196, 208, 214–15, 218, 221, 224; subversion of Iroquois beliefs and customs, 238–41, 246, 258, 265–68; understanding of kinship and gender roles, 213, 236–37, 267–68. *See also individual priests*
Jikonsahsch (Neutral), 85
Jogues, Isaac (S.J.), 92, 143, 145, 157, 166, 228–29, 262–63
Jouvency, Joseph (S.J.), 34

Kahnawake. *See* Caughnawaga
Kalm, Peter, 204
Ketluyn, Jochim, 150
Kieft, Willem, 136, 139, 145, 165
Kiotsaeton (Mohawk), 77–80, 91, 225–26, 228
Kirke, Sir David, and family, 194, 223
Krieckenbeeck, Daniel van, 130–31
Krol, Bastiaen Jansz, 130
Kryn (Mohawk), 267

Laer, A. J. F., 150
Laet, Johan de, 17, 129, 154, 172–74

Lafitau, Joseph-François (S.J.), 69, 72, 106–7, 111–12
Lalemant, Jerome (S.J.), 250–51, 254, 263
La Montagne, Johannes, 162
landscape: cultural, of New Netherland, 119–20, 125–26, 140–41, 152–53; cultural and political, of New France, 181–83, 189–90, 204–7; definition of, 17, 20; European views of, 15–18, 30; and Native American agriculture, 18, 31–32. *See also* Iroquoia
La Prairie de la Madeleine. *See* Caughnawaga
Lauson, Jean de, 170, 239
Laval, Francois de, 215
Law of Atonement. *See* Five Nations of the Iroquois: murder and atonement
Le Caron, Joseph (Recollet), 223
Leisler's Rebellion, 260
Le Juene, Paul (S.J.), 224, 251
Le Mercier, François (S.J.), 76, 218, 231, 237, 261
Le Moyne, Simon (S.J.), 180, 235, 247, 248
Le Tellier, Michel, 215
l'Incarnation, Marie de, 180–85, 206, 208, 217, 218; portrait of, 184
Longfellow, Henry Wadsworth, 83
Loskiel, George H., 33
Louis XIII, 189, 190, 191
Louis XIV, 200, 206–9, 215, 218

Magritte, René, 1
Mahicans, 129–32, 141, 152–53, 223, 249, 253
Manhattan (Manhates), 129, 130, 133, 136, 145, 169, 171. *See also* New Amsterdam
Maisonneuve, Paul de Chomedey de, 239
Marguerie, François, 225
Martensen, Henderick, 171
Martin, Claude, 180, 217
Maryland, 252, 270
Massachusetts Bay Colony, 136, 259–60, 270
May, Cornelis Jacobsz, 129

Mazarin, Cardinal Giulio, 200
Megapolensis, Reverend Johannes, 142–43, 166–67
Merwick, Donna, 126, 152, 259
Michaelius, Reverend Jonas, 143, 166
Milet, Pierre (S.J.), 92, 267; as Otassete (Oneida), 267
Minuit, Pieter, 130
Mohawk-Mahican War, 129–32, 141
Mohawks, 40, 52, 54, 69–72, 77, 82, 83, 92, 94, 95, 120, 124, 129–32, 137, 143, 158, 161–62, 164, 167–72, 176, 177, 217–19, 222, 223, 225, 228, 229, 231, 232, 234, 235, 241, 245, 247–55, 261–63, 267. *See also* Five Nations of the Iroquois
Monsieur Pinguet, 241
Montagnais, 34, 69–72, 221, 223–25, 232, 241
Montmagny, Charles Huault, chevalier de (Onontio, or Big Mountain), 78–79, 228
Montreal, 181, 195, 204, 205, 207, 208, 231, 235, 237, 239, 244, 245, 248, 249; foundation and early history of, 195–98
Monts, Pierre Du Gua, sieur de, 187
Moogk, Peter N., 203
Morgan, Lewis Henry, 67, 93
myth of Imperial Iroquois. *See* Five Nations of the Iroquois: myth of Imperial Iroquois
myth of the Vanishing Indian, 114

Native American agriculture, 18, 31–32
Netherlands, the, 127–28, 133, 141, 144–45, 147, 165, 179, 186; rivalry and warfare with Spain, 127, 129, 134, 145; States-General, 127–28, 133, 137, 146
New Amsterdam, 133, 143, 145, 169, 172; becomes New York, 258. *See also* Manhattan
New England, 136, 141, 193, 203, 230, 259, 270
New France: Canadian colonization, 182–209; church sponsorship of colonization, 190–98, 200; and colonialism, 240–41; commissions, charters, privileges granted by

crown, 187–200; effects of warfare on trade, 199–200, 208; and Frenchification, 9, 183, 193, 205, 218; and fur trade, 188, 192, 198–200, 206–7, 208, 221–22, 223, 231; gender arrangements, 183–85; immigration and settlement, 188, 189, 193, 195, 197–98, 200–208, 209; impact of religious developments in France, 187, 191, 196, 197, 200; missionary activity, 189, 190–91, 195–98, 208, 214–15, 218, 221, 231, 239 (*see also* Jesuits: missionary activities among the Five Nations); place in French colonial empire, 200–202, 208; and political geography of native North America, 220–21, 228, 268; population of, 189–90, 191, 193, 195, 197, 198, 202–6; relations with allied Indians, 192–93, 220–21, 227–28, 232, 240–41, 248, 268; role of French state in colonization and administration, 191–93, 194, 200–203; seigneurial system, 194, 202–3; understanding of peace, 240–41; women, 205, 208
—and Five Nations, 9–10, 180–83, 207–14, 220–56, 271; attitudes toward Five Nations, 209–12, 215, 220–22, 232–33, 245–46, 247, 251–52, 256; obstruction of Iroquois peace initiatives, 214, 223, 227, 229–30, 252, 268; peace initiatives toward Five Nations, 225; policy of military conquest of Five Nations, 215–20, 222, 230, 233, 254–56, 261, 271; rumors of Iroquois depredations, 239, 241, 246, 248, 251, 252, 261; suspicion of Five Nations, 209–12, 214, 224, 232–33, 239–40, 241, 244–56; warfare with Five Nations, 27, 69–74, 182, 199, 200, 207, 209, 215–20, 223–33, 247–56, 261, 271
New Haven, Connecticut, 174
New Netherland: administration and regulation, 128–29, 144–53, 156, 160–63, 165; attitudes toward and use of land, 152–53; charters and

New Netherland (*cont.*)

privileges granted, 127–29, 134, 137, 142; colonists characterized, 135–36, 141–53, 155; colonization and settlement, 126–40, 188; and commerce, 120–21, 125–26, 127–28, 131, 136, 137, 144, 145, 154–63, 171–79; conquest by English, 139, 152–53, 253, 258–60; and Indian language barrier, 143, 166–67; and labor problems, 135–36; life in its settlements, 140–41, 143–53, 155; missionary work among Indians, 142–43, 166, 179; patroonships, 134 35, 202–3, population, 133, 136, 138, 140, 193, 203; relations with Indians, 120, 136, 139, 153, 155 58, 252, 253; religious diversity and toleration, 145, 179; violation of laws and regulations by inhabitants, 145–50, 157, 159–63; Walloon settlers, 129; warfare with Indians, 120, 130–33, 136, 139, 252, 253
—and Five Nations: Dutch attempts to maintain cultural distance, 163–72, 179; Dutch views of Iroquois, 124, 130–31, 142–43, 163–69, 177–79; Iroquois complaints about Dutch, 121, 124–26, 130, 154, 161–63, 168, 171, 172, 177–78; relations, 8–10, 120–26, 130–32, 154–58, 160–79; warfare, 130–33
—and Indian trade, 131–32, 136, 137, 141, 142, 148, 150, 154–63, 171–79; and competition among Dutch, 157–63, 177–78; and forestalling tactics, 157–63, 177–78; and Indian preferences, 174–75; and official regulation, 120, 136, 137–38, 148, 156–63, 178
New World(s), concept of, 2–3, 119, 126, 140, 186, 230–31
New York, 253, 270; Dutch inhabitants and resistance to English, 139, 258–60
New York City, 258, 259. *See also* New Amsterdam
Norton, Major John (Teyoninho-karawen), 83–84

Oneidas, 53, 69, 94, 95, 124, 164, 167, 218, 219, 223, 235, 236, 238, 248–50, 252, 262, 264, 266–67
ongwe', 21
Onondagas, 27, 41, 53, 83, 86, 94, 95, 103, 107, 124, 164, 167, 223, 232–35, 237, 244, 245, 249, 250–52, 264, 271; foundation of tribe, 53–62
Onontio (Big Mountain), 79. *See also* Montmagny, Charles Huault, chevalier de; *and other governors of New France*
orenda, 79, 91, 101
Owasco, 13, 42, 43–53, 88–89; archaeological sites, 46–47, 50; and clans, 48–49; exchange networks, 48–49; expansion, consolidation, and amalgamation, 46–52; ritual objects, 49–50; settlement patterns, 45–48, 52; structures, 46–47; subsistence, 44–46, 48, 50–52; transformation into Iroquois, 43–44, 46–53, 88–89; warfare and defense, 46–52

Parker, Arthur C., 15
Parkman, Francis, 6
peace, idea and practice of: among Dutch, 154–55, 156, 163–64, 178–79; in New France, 140–41. *See also* Five Nations of the Iroquois: and peace
peace negotiations: Iroquois-Dutch, 124–26, 130, 162, 164, 171–72, 176–78; Iroquois-French, 76–79, 81, 91, 103, 170–71, 180–86, 219–20, 225–28, 231–36, 245, 246–50, 254–56
Peters, Reverend Hugh, 136
petite guerre, le, 223, 225. *See also* cultural frontiers: French-Iroquois; New France: and Five Nations
Pierron, Jean (S.J.), 219
Pocumtucks, 253
Pynchon, John, 259–60
Pyrlaeus, Reverend Christopher, 82–83

Quebec, 77, 180, 181, 183, 187, 189, 191, 193, 195, 197, 199, 204, 207,

Quebec (*cont.*)
    222–23, 233–35, 241, 244, 245,
    247, 248, 250, 251, 268
Quen, Jean de (S.J.), 101, 237, 245
Quinnipiac River, 174

Raffeix, Pierre (S.J.), 218
Ragueneau, Paul (S.J.), 233
Rasiere, Isaack de, 130–32, 135–36,
    173–74
Recollets (Recollet Order of the Minor
    Friars), 190, 223. *See also individual
    priests and lay ministers*
Rensselaer, Jeremias van, 259
Rensselaer, Kiliaen van, 120, 129,
    132, 134, 140–2, 146, 165, 175–76
Rensselaerswyck, 120, 121, 129, 134,
    139–40, 143–53, 155, 162, 163,
    166; advent of, 134–35;
    jurisdictional conflicts with Fort
    Orange and Beverwyck, 140, 158;
    settlement described, 140
Richelieu, Armand-Jean Du Plessis,
    Cardinal de, 190–91
Rink, Oliver A., 138, 139
Roberval, Jean François de La
    Rocque, seigneur de, 187

Sagard, Gabriel (Recollet), 27, 223
Sahlins, Marshall, 269
Sainte Marie de Gannentaha, 237–38,
    246
St. Lawrence River, 186–87, 189, 204
Sauer, Carl O., 31
Schenectady, 152, 259, 260
Schuyler, Philip Pietersz, 159
Senecas, 41, 53, 62–63, 65, 94, 95, 97,
    106, 107, 124, 167, 177, 183, 224,
    249, 252, 255, 264, 271
Shackamaxon, 270
Shakespeare, 25
Shimony, Annemarie Anrod, 93–94
Slichtenhorst, Brant van, 140, 146
Society of Jesus. *See* Jesuits
Society of St. Sulpice, 197, 218, 239
Sokokis, 252–53
Song of Hiawatha, 83
Standish, Miles, 17
Starna, William, 269

Stick Stiggery (Mohawk), 170
"structure of the conjuncture," 269
Stuyvesant, Pieter, 120–21, 140, 153,
    162, 164–65
Susquehannocks, 177, 229, 252, 265,
    270

Tadoussac, 190
Talon, Jean, 218, 256
Teyoninhokarawen. *See* Norton,
    Major John
Thadodaho (Onondaga), 86, 90–95.
    See also Deganawidah Epic
Tillyard, E. M. W., 24–25
Tobias, black servant of Harmen
    Meyndertsz van den Bogaert, 150
Tracy, Alexandre de Prouville,
    marquis de, 107–8, 215, 218, 219,
    255, 261, 265
Trigger, Bruce G., 229
Trois Rivières, 77–79, 80, 91, 181,
    195, 204, 207, 215, 223, 225, 226,
    231, 247, 248
Trudel, Marcel, 187
Tuck, James A., 58
Tuscaroras, 108

Ursuline nuns, 180–86, 196, 199, 218;
    attempts to convert native girls and
    women, 183–85, 196, 208. *See also*
    l'Incarnation, Marie de
utgon, 91
Uylenspiegel, Claus Teunisz, 146–47

Valckenburg, Herman Jansz van,
    148–49
Verrazzano, Giovanni da, 126, 186
Viel, Nicholas (Recollet), 223
Vimont, Barthelemy (S.J.), 76–80, 102
Virginia, 137, 138, 193, 203, 270

Wallace, Anthony F. C., 67–68
Wallace, Paul A. W., 108
wampum, 77–78, 80, 86, 94, 99, 101,
    103–4, 136, 168, 169, 225, 233,
    236, 245, 251, 262
"Wars of the Iroquois," 67, 225, 229–
    30
Wassenaer, Nicolaes van, 129–30, 134

Webster, Ephraim, 83
Weiser, Conrad, 83
White, Richard, 40
Wigglesworth, Reverend Michael, 15–17
wilderness, 15–17. *See also* landscape:
   European views of

Willard, Reverend Samuel, 33
Winthrop, John, Jr., 259
Wood, William, 30–31
Worster, Donald, 20

Library of Congress Cataloging-in-Publication Data

Dennis, Matthew.
    Cultivating a landscape of peace : Iroquois-European encounters in seventeenth-century America / Matthew Dennis.
        p. cm.
    Includes bibliographical references and index.
    ISBN 0–8014–2171–3
    1. Iroquois Indians—History—17th century.   2. Iroquois Indians—Government relations.   3. Iroquois Indians—Social conditions.   4. Europe—Colonies—America.   5. United States—History—Colonial period, ca. 1600–1775.   I. Title.
E99.I7D36 1993
974.7′004975—dc20   92–56771